The Construction Management Process

Kwaku A. Tenah, Ph.D., P.E.

Reston Publishing Company, Inc.
A Prentice-Hall Company
Reston, Virginia

Library of Congress Cataloging in Publication Data

Tenah, Kwaku A.
  The construction management process.

  1. Construction industry—Management.   I. Title.
HD9715.A2T45   1985   624'.068   84-26239
ISBN 0-8359-0955-7

© 1985 Reston Publishing Company, Inc.
   A Prentice-Hall Company
   Reston, Virginia 22090

10   9   8   7   6   5   4   3   2   1

PRINTED IN THE UNITED STATES OF AMERICA

Contents

Preface

Since the late 1970s there has developed an increasing awareness of the need to improve the management of engineering and construction projects. Management of engineering and construction projects has become more difficult and complex in recent years. These difficulties and complexities result from the technical aspects of the projects, increased government regulations, and the financial pressures the inflation-racked economy foster. Compounding these problems and complexities have been the inherent nature of the construction industry itself and the increased liability imposed upon all the members of the construction team. Costly time, budget overruns, and inadequate quality and safety performances have become more prevalent and of great concern for all members of the construction team. As a result, many management methods have emerged to deal with these difficulties and complexities.

This book deals with the existing and emerging management methods and focuses attention on successful management approaches. How to keep the construction projects within budget, on time, and within the specified quality and safety constraints is the underlying theme of this book, in addition to addressing the professional approach to management—its development, organization and applications in practice. Both broad and specific aspects of management techniques and actual case histories are addressed. Roadblocks to successful professional management goals are covered including restrictive relationship and liability aspects as well as overcoming restraints to changes in innovative project delivery systems.

In contrast to the many construction management books that have been written that address management techniques for a contractor or architect, this book devotes itself to the management processes. The processes covered include: the traditional design-bid-construct, the modified traditional process, the construction management (CM), project management, engineering management, and program management processes. The book also goes into some detail on basic management techniques including planning and control tools that apply in all of the processes mentioned.

The contents and organization of *The Construction Management Process* have been designed to provide students and practitioners with an in-depth introduction and orientation to construction management methods and to acquaint them with major engineering management techniques used in these processes. Ten case studies on the CM process alone are featured.

The first part of this book (the first nine chapters, excluding Chapter 4) describes the existing and emerging construction management processes—their concepts, characteristics, advantages, and disadvantages. Also described are planning, design, bidding, award, and construction phases of CM process as well as the legal aspects of CM. The second part of the book, Chapters 10 through 18 and also Chapter 4, describes some of the most important management techniques and tools that are part of any effective management process. These techniques and tools include: formation and organization for innovative delivery methods, management information systems and processing, value engineering, procurement, marketing, construction safety, productivity, quality assurance and quality control, management methods, and labor relations.

This book began with my Engineer's Degree thesis at Stanford University in 1975. Without the invaluable materials, support, constructive suggestions and advice from the following people and organizations it could scarcely have been written: Mr. Donald S. Barrie, Professor Boyd C. Paulson Jr., Professor Bob Tatum, American Society of Civil Engineers, Mr. Dale Kern, the authors of *Engineering and Construction Projects: the Emerging Management Roles*, Professors Keith C. Crandall and Ben C. Gerwick, Mr. A.T. McNeil of Turner Construction Co., New York, Mr. Edward Petersen of Bechtel Power Corporation, Mr. Jerry Kosro of HEW, San Francisco and Mr. William Linforth of Kaiser Engineers, and the numerous authors of the American Society of Engineer's *Journal of Construction Engineering and Management*. The author wishes to thank his family for their patience and prayers during the many hour of manuscript preparation.

1

Traditional
Design-Bid-Construct Process

1.1 INTRODUCTION

The whole process of facilities procurements, from decision to build to completion of a facility, has traditionally been a fragmented effort of (*a*) the owner, who is, or represents, the user of the facility; (*b*) the architect or engineer(s) in charge of designs; and (*c*) the contractor, who constructs the facility. The owner may consult a realtor, both for land purchase and project management, and financiers, initially, for short-term cash for the facility's construction as well as for long-term mortgage when the project is complete.

The architect designs the structure, usually in consultation with the structural and mechanical engineers, site planners, interior designers, governmental agencies in charge of zoning, codes, and city planning, and with manufacturers whose products he designs into the structure. The third key party, the contractor, has as his team subcontractors, labor from various crafts, and suppliers of equipment, materials, services, appliances,

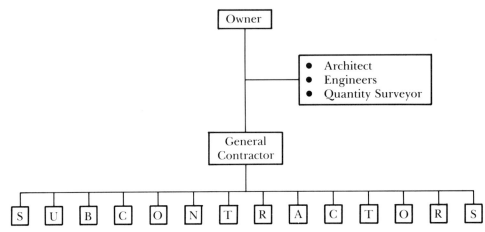

Figure 1.1.   The Traditional Contract Structure.

tools, and machines called for by the architect and required to complete the job. Figure 1.1 shows the structure of the traditional contract.

This chapter deals with the traditional process. It starts with major problems in the construction industry, then discusses four major phases of contracting, defines functions and responsibilities of members of the project team, and finally describes advantages and disadvantages of this process.

1.2   MAJOR PROBLEMS IN THE CONSTRUCTION INDUSTRY

Problems have been caused in the construction community by the conflict of increasing expectations and the constraints of diminishing resources.

Also thoroughly discussed and considered are the concerns that the traditional design-bid-construct process and procedures are unable to ameliorate many of the problems being evidenced. These problems include

1.   Economic difficulties resulting from inflation, energy shortages, high interest rates, recession or depression, life-cycle costing, and rising costs.

2.   Changing world patterns and new society standards.

3.   Shortages of resources, including materials, equipment, skilled workers, and technical and supervisory personnel.

4.   Increasing governmental, social, and legal obstacles as well as environmental involvement and demands.

5.   Challenges of time, quality, and quality-time-cost trade-offs.

6. Challenges of high-level coordination and controls, including scheduling, resource allocation, and resource leveling.

7. Challenges of labor, including jurisdictional disputes, strikes, productivity, and skills.

8. Challenges of project complexity, size, and sophistication.

9. Increasing technological complexity and more complex interdependencies and variations in relationships between organizations and institutions.

10. Increasing client involvement.

These problems have accelerated and probably will continue into the future. Figure 1.2 summarizes the elements that are involved in these problems.

1.3 CONTRACTING PHASES

The four phases common to all facility procurement methods and procedures, including the traditional ones, are (*a*) decision making, (*b*) design or engineering, (*c*) selection of a contractor, and (*d*) construction.

1.3.1 Decision Making

The first phase in the traditional construction process is decision making. This phase basically requires fact-finding, where the owner, be he a hospital board, university, corporation, or individual, establishes the need for a new facility and defines his requirements and budgetary constraints. He may perform these tasks with his own staff or employ outside consultants, depending on his sophistication. The owner selects and hires the architect, architect-engineer, or engineer at some point during the decision stage to prepare a plan of action that best fit his (the owner's) objectives.

1.3.2 Design or Engineering

The second phase is design or engineering. Here the architect, his engineers, and, in some cases, the professional quantity surveyor[1] (QS) develop a solution to the owner's requirements. This solution is reduced to a set of drawings and specifications to be included in the contract documents.

---

1. See Section 1.4.6 for the functions and responsibilities of a QS.

THE CHALLENGES OF CONSTRUCTION

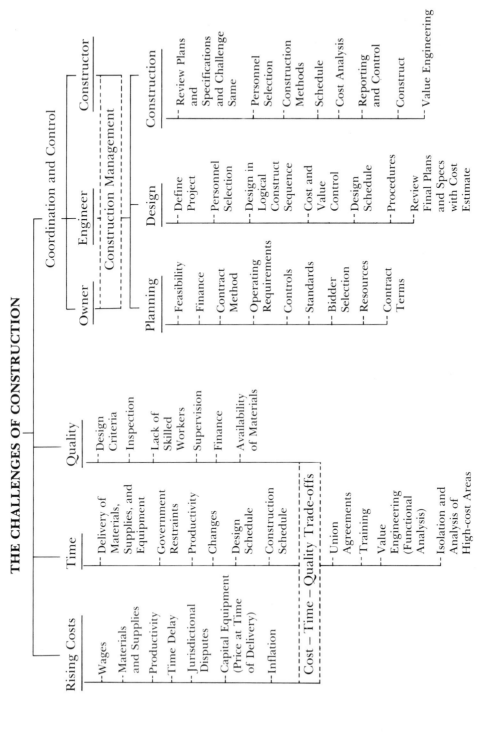

Figure 1.2. Challenges in Construction's Future. (From Boyd C. Paulson, Jr., *Goals for Basic Research in Construction*, Technical Report No. 202, Stanford University, Dept. of Civil Engineering. The Construction Institute, Stanford, CA, July 1975.)

1.3.3   Contractor Selection

Contractor selection is the third phase. There are two alternatives here: competitive bidding and negotiations. If the owner follows a competitive bid procedure, he or his agent issues copies of the contract document to general contractors interested in bidding on a project, and sets a specific time and place for opening the bids. Each bidding contractor then decides which elements of the construction he will subcontract, and he develops his cost estimates for the project on that basis. The owner generally awards the contract on the basis of the lowest estimate of cost, which is the practice in nearly all public works. If, on the other hand, the owner negotiates with a general contractor, the two parties ordinarily work out a contract that reimburses the contractor and pays him a fee on an agreed-upon basis.

1.3.4   Construction

The fourth and final phase is construction. The general contractor usually subcontracts most of the work. Thus his major effort goes to managing the flow of materials, his own men, and numerous subcontractors. The owner typically depends on his architect or engineer for inspection of the work performed by the general contractor and his subcontractors. The architect or engineer usually limits his inspection to a moderate level of on-site observation to assure himself and the owner that the intent of the plans and specifications have been carried out and that the contractor's request for payment represents work that has been done. On medium and large projects, the architect or engineer will appoint an inspector or clerk of works to oversee the day-to-day activities of the general contractor and his subcontractors. If the architect, engineer, or the owner decides during construction that a particular configuration, material, or method different from that described in the contract documents is desirable, then the architect or engineer enters into negotiations with the general contractor to define the scope and price of the desired changes. Finally, when the facility is completed, the architect or engineer conducts a last inspection, and, if approved, the facility is turned over to the owner for occupancy.

1.4   RESPONSIBILITIES OF MEMBERS OF THE PROJECT TEAM

This section examines the areas of responsibilities generally associated with the construction of medium- to large-scale projects. Responsibilities presented here include those of the owner, architect, developer and manager, professional quantity surveyor, contractor, subcontractor, attorney, municipal government, insurer, union, material suppliers, and equipment manufacturers.

1.4.1 The Problem of Responsibility

Five major causes of problems with responsibility in the construction industry are as follows:

1. All elements and functions necessary to create a project depend upon human beings to discharge various kinds and amounts of responsibility.

2. There are many types and degrees of responsible functions, attitudes, and physical products involved that must be coordinated, integrated, and accomplished.

3. Most facilities are tailor-made; only in certain cases is a design concept duplicated repetitively.

4. Rarely does the project and design team remain the same from project to project, either in the talents and disciplines required or in individuals on the team.

5. There are various laws, codes, local conditions, new projects, changing economic conditions, new labor relationships, and other factors of utmost significance to the successful discharge of responsibility in construction.

Projects have become increasingly complex, therefore requiring more specialists to prepare and execute drawings and specifications. Among the participants in facility construction today are not only the architect, mechanical, structural, electrical, and acoustical engineers, the general contractor and his myriad subcontractors, materials manufacturers, producers, and suppliers, but also consultants for urban planning, the construction of airports, schools, hospitals, power plants, industrial buildings, and housing, as well as environmentalists and other applications too numerous to mention here. Each participant has a responsibility to the owner, to the public, and to each other. Unfortunately, these people often do not have a direct contractual responsibility with one another in the process of construction.

To understand more thoroughly the responsibility in project construction, it is desirable to examine the relationships of the many different professions and trades engaged in constructing a facility and to evaluate their responsibility to the owner, to the public, and to each other. Construction intersects almost all fields of human endeavor, and this diversity is reflected in its projects.

1.4.2 Owner's Responsibilities

The owner has responsibilities in project construction in addition to the payment of bills. He must develop his own team to work all other participants in the project. His major functions and responsibilities may include the following:

1. He is responsible for selecting and hiring the architect or engineer to whom he may entrust responsibility for design and construction inspection.

2. He selects key people to make certain decisions, many of which may be in the field or on the spot. He must determine the latitude and limitations of such decisions and express them clearly to the architect or the engineer.

3. He ensures that the architect or engineer and the general contractor know their respective functions and responsibilities. He must make sure that the contractor understands the bid procedure to avoid misunderstandings at a later date.

4. He must carefully explain his cost accounting procedures to the general contractor so that the contractor can establish satisfactory billing procedures. He must specify the supporting papers (invoices, time sheets, and so forth) that the architect or engineer can examine and verify. He must always bear in mind that his own indecision and vacillations might contribute to the budget overruns.

5. He is responsible for providing the general public with such facilities as sidewalk bridges, barricades, protected pedestrian walkways, lighting, and truck entrances to the site, in addition to handling such public problems as site selection, site use, facility design, interior appointments, and environmental impact statement(s).

1.4.3   The Developer-Manager's Responsibilities

The developer may be an owner, but generally he is a real estate practitioner who assembles various segments of a deal that ultimately ends with a syndicated ownership of the property. His first major problem is the selection of a neighborhood and then a site in the specific area. This is the most important decision because the value of the facility in both the present and the future will depend upon location. He then decides with the architect or engineer and the contractor on the type of facility (i.e., composition, layout, size, and shape of units) to go on the site.

In general, the developer has the following responsibilities:

1. He ascertains what the land and site development costs will be.

2. He acquaints himself with the zoning requirements; this he shares with the architect or engineer.

3. He thoroughly studies the site and its neighborhood to provide sufficient in-depth material for deciding on the economic future of the facility in that area, the level of rents that can be obtained in the market, the probable stability of those rents, and the level of occupancy. This is the greatest responsibility of the developer.

4. He properly advises the architect or engineer regarding sizes, layout, and composition of the units in the facility.

5. He evaluates the economics of the facility (i.e., objective evaluation of income and expenditures). For this, he depends on the project cost estimates provided by the architect or engineer and the contractor for accuracy in his final figures.

6. He makes a definite contribution to the growth and development of the city or town in which he is building.

7. As a manager he has to run the facility on the same basis as any other business that deals with the public, and thus requires the approval of his product and his actions.

1.4.4   The Architect's or Engineer's Responsibilities

Included in the architect's or engineer's responsibilities are the following:

1. He interprets the owner's needs into drawings and specifications. He is responsible for providing drawings and specifications that do not contain conflicts, duplications, or omissions.

2. He approves all manufacturers' and suppliers' materials and samples, and deals with all questions of substitution.

3. He provides on-site monitoring services and reviews all inspection reports and change orders.

4. He is responsible for construction methods, costs, and schedules.

5. Through the contract requirements, he has indirect responsibility to the general contractor, as does the general contractor to him. He has no responsibility to the subcontractors.

1.4.5   The Contractor's Responsibilities

The general contractor's role has radically changed over the years. Actually, the name "general contractor" no longer strictly applies. He is a liaison person between the owner, architect, engineer, trade union, and subcontractors. His role usually begins in the bidding or contractor selection phase. Therefore, traditionally he plays very little or no part in the decision-making and design stages. Included in his major functions and responsibilities are the following:

1. He coordinates, supervises, and expedites work and job flows of the various subcontractors who actually undertake most of the construction.

He is responsible to them for providing good working arrangements and conditions, clear scope of work, and good scheduling of jobs.

2. He may be responsible for the procurement of major materials. He must make sure that he obtains the best dollar value for the owner.

3. He is responsible to the owner for the construction of the facility in accordance with plans and desires of the architect or engineer.

4. He has to see that all labor agreements are maintained and that all members in the project team—owner, architect, engineer, subcontractors, and unions—are content.

1.4.6 The Independent Professional Quantity Surveyor's (QS) Responsibilities

The professional quantity surveyor is normally found in the European, Australian, and other British Commonwealth of Nations' construction industries. His major functions and responsibilities are as follows:

1. He is the financial adviser to the owner or developer manager throughout the project.

2. He does cost analysis or cost planning.

3. He does value engineering management.

4. He is responsible for the preparation of an estimate during the preliminary design phase.

5. He prepares the detailed estimate (take-off, squaring, abstracting, and pricing).

6. As a design administrator, he prepares the contract specifications and administers them.

7. He prepares the bill of quantities (boq) from 2 through 6. With the architect or engineers, he gives out bid documents. He opens and evaluates bids with client and architect or engineer.

8. He modifies the bill of quantities for major change orders (as addendum).

9. He values change orders.

10. He measures and evaluates work in progress based on the bill of quantities for progressive payments (the architect or engineer has to certify the evaluations before the owner authorizes payments).

11. He reports to the owner and architect or engineer during the monthly or periodical site meetings concerning progress of work in terms of cost.

12. He prepares the final accounts when the project is completed.

13. He acts as an arbitrator in case there is a misunderstanding between any of the parties in the team.

1.4.7   The Subcontractor's Responsibilities

Subcontractors are generally specialty contractors who perform complex jobs that require highly skilled trades. They do most of the project construction work and therefore are important members of the team, along with the owner, architect-engineer, and the general contractor.

A subcontractor is primarily responsible to the general contractor for his position in the construction process. The major functions of the subcontractor are as follows:

1. He submits for approval a purchase schedule listing equipment and names of materials suppliers.

2. He thoroughly checks equipment details to be sure that the manufacturer is supplying the equipment specified.

3. He submits detailed delivery schedules to the contractor or to the owner in case the owner hires him directly.

4. He prepares a shop drawings schedule and uses it to help other trades.

5. He prepares a detailed work schedule indicating days or weeks required in each area of the project.

6. He assists the general contractor in the overall coordination of the various trades.

7. He is generally responsible for the completion of work entrusted to him according to plans, specifications, and terms of contract as well as within the agreed-upon time.

8. Finally, he is responsible for handling his own labor relations and complying with his own contract.

1.4.8   The Attorney's Responsibilities

The attorney's responsibility in the construction industry is no longer thought of as bringing suit or defending a client. His responsibilities extend to every facet of the construction industry depending on both the role of his client and the authority given him by his client. The attorney's major functions and responsibilities are as follows:

1. He succinctly and articulately defines, in written agreements in the early stages, the responsibilities and obligations of his client. He must define the terms, scope, and limits of the agreement of his client with the same precision and clarity that the architect or engineer uses in his designs.

2. He stands by his client and counsels him from commencement to completion.

1.4.9 The Municipal Government's Responsibilities

The municipal government must display the highest degree of responsibility in its administration of facility construction rules and regulations to protect and safeguard the community. Four major areas that require attention by the municipal government in the proper exercise of its responsibility to administer facility construction rules and regulations are as follows:

1. It must ensure the enactment of good building codes.

2. It must create codes that are readily amenable to technological advances. It must avoid a formal legislative amendment that is cumbersome, drawn out, and that submits highly complex and technical proposals to the political arena.

3. It must unify and consolidate the laws that affect facility construction and the multiple agencies administering these laws into a single, centrally administered body of law. This new body must be responsible for every aspect of facility construction from initial examination of plans to ultimate approval.

4. It should adequately enforce the code to be meaningful, for a code is merely a document containing construction ideas advantageous to the community.

1.4.10 The Insurer's Responsibilities

The insurer is an essential partner in the construction industry. The insurer, if used wisely and responsibly, provides necessary funds, protects the assets, and offers many other essential services. The principal forms of insurance coverage are as follows:

1. Public liability and property damage for injury or death to members of the public and damage to their property

2. Contractual completed operations coverage

3. Comprehensive automobile liability

4. Contingent liability

5. Workman's compensation and employer's liability for injury or death to employees

6. Umbrella excess liability

7. Contractor's equipment floater for loss or destruction to contractor's equipment

8. "Wrap-up" insurance program, wherein policies to cover the owner, engineer, general contractor, and all subcontractors are protected under a single insurance package

9. Builder's risk for loss or destruction to work in progress prior to owner's acceptance

10. Architect's, engineer's, and contractor's coverage for protecting valuable papers such as drawings, blueprints, and sketches subject to perils of fire damage

Insurance companies have a responsibility to provide protection, study, and service to the construction industry. This implies that they must also assist in meeting the normal and legal obligations of constructor to society for the design and construction of safe and efficient facilities.

1.4.11   The Unions' Responsibilities

The construction industry wants from its union a timely, uninterrupted, and sufficient supply of competent craftsmen when and where there is work to be done. By exploring the implications of these three words ("uninterrupted," "sufficient," and "competent"), some specific implications may be found of unions' responsibilities. These are as follows:

1. They are responsible for a continuous supply of craftsmen who are available to any employer at any time.

2. They are responsible for preventing or quickly settling all jurisdictional disputes and strikes, thereby enabling their members to work without interruption. Unions share these jurisdictional responsibilities with contractors, architects, engineers, and owners.

3. They are responsible for maintaining, developing, and improving apprenticeship programs with the cooperation of employers. This helps maintain a supply of the kinds of craftsmen that the construction industry needs now and will need in the future.

4. They see that their members work in areas that are safe, although it is the contractor's main responsibility to provide for that safety.

1.4.12   Material and Equipment Manufacturers' Responsibilities

To place responsibility where it can be effective for selling all kinds of construction materials or equipment, a manufacturer should assume the responsibility and control of the following:

1. He guarantees his equipment or materials for the qualities listed in his specifications. This implies that the material or equipment manufacturer must indicate in his literature the end-use performance characteristics of his products, spelling out limitations as well as benefits.

2. He must sell materials or equipment to users who understand his specifications, agree to apply the products accordingly, and maintain adequate supervision and trained employees.

3. He must demonstrate the physical performance of the specifications or systems as they are applied to actual practice.

4. He must advise the owner, architect, engineer, and general contractor on how to avoid trouble in the use of his products, stressing responsibility for designing and constructing the facility according to the manufacturer's criteria.

5. He should provide public liability insurance on his products that affords liability coverage to any person or organization concerned in the sale or distribution of the products in the event of any bodily injury.

6. Finally, he must evaluate his own policies regarding responsibilities to be assumed for the products he manufacturers.

In return, other members of the team—architect, engineer, owner, and contractor—must launch new product development programs through seminars and make their needs known to the manufacturers.

1.5 ADVANTAGES AND DISADVANTAGES OF THE TRADITIONAL PROCESS

1.5.1 Advantages of the Traditional Process

1. The traditional process, by nature, is sequential. It embodies a design in a set of substantially complete documents that are capable of transmitting all the owner's wishes to the general contractor. However, this advantage no longer exists in practice because facility designs have become more complex and construction processes or methods and materials have increased rapidly and become more specialized.

2. The contractual relations between general contractor and his subcontractors make it easy for the general contractor to fire, replace, or take over from subcontractor in case he defaults.

3. Owners are often guaranteed the maximum price for completing the entire project.

1.5.2 Disadvantages of the Traditional Process

The traditional approach to construction has the following disadvantages:

1. The process is sequential in nature; the result is that the escalation factor between the time a project is conceived and the time it is actually constructed can add significant costs to it. Furthermore, a delay in construction means that an owner is paying additional rent in his current facility or facilities, or that production in the new manufacturing facility is unhappily delayed.

2.   Throughout the process the owner has little or no direct control over what his facility will ultimately cost, but still pays the bills. During design or engineering, for example, he has no sure procedure for evaluating cost implications of the architect's or engineer's proposals. The proposed design or engineering may be a particularly impractical one for construction, or there may be far simpler and cheaper techniques available to provide the same result. Normally, alternative procedures become known only after the bid phase, at which time changes represent sweeping revisions and major expenditures of time and effort. Such changes would have been simple in the earlier stages. This implies that the owner is faced with the alternative of paying more than he had expected for the original design or engineering or waiting a longer time for a better process and receiving less for his (owner's) money because of spiraling costs.

3.   There are no real incentives for the general contractor to attempt to reduce the cost of the facility once it is under way; on the contrary, large incentives exist to increase costs. That is, subcontractors often quote a job low and then attempt to recover additional money during construction in negotiations for changes and extras. Since the general contractor will most likely work with these subcontractors in the future, he tends to side with them in these claims.

4.   Architects or engineers sometimes do not have enough knowledge or familiarity with the construction process to control it as closely as the owner desires. In addition, although the owner is called on to evaluate progress for payment (or the QS does this for the architect's certification), in practice he is seldom able to prevent the disproportionately high distribution of funds that tends to occur during the early stages of construction.

5.   The traditional process does not create a unified team in which experience, feedback, and new ideas are shared together. Thus advantages cannot be taken of a growing number of marketplace options in construction systems, fabrication, and materials.

6.   Within the project team of traditional process, (*a*) there is no overall management and coordination; (*b*) there is an artificial separation of design or engineering, and construction; and (*c*) manufacturers are remote from the process.

7.   With public procurement practices, there is an excessive time span for the whole process, a limited basis for bid evaluation, no incentive to reduce long-term costs, and no guarantee of cost and time.

8.   Within the owner's organization, there is inadequate economic analysis, a lack of long-term planning, and conflict over definitions of user requirements.

2

Construction Management: Concepts, Organization, and Role

2.1 INTRODUCTION

The basis of a good construction project is a proper balance of economy, speed, and quality. There has always been a demand for a team that can accomplish this.

The technology of today's construction is immensely complicated in the sophistication of materials and equipment in the facility itself as well as in the requirements of the occupancy. The owner must therefore know both his present and future needs. The architect's or engineer's responsibilities have expanded greatly since approximately 1945. This has led architects to use numerous consulting engineers and other specialists to assist in planning and designing major facilities. The constructor (i.e., general contractor) has been called upon to coordinate the delivery and installation of many more components than before, and to devise methods and details to accomplish a fit of the components. Consequently, this sophistication has led to more and more specialization, and to a need for teamwork starting often before the owner has crystallized his thoughts on the requirements of the project.

Until approximately 1945, a general contractor performed most of the work with his own labor force. Today, most work is performed by specialty contractors. The main role of the general contractor has become the coordination and control of trade contractors. The desire to take advantage of the constructor's planning and estimating skills at the outset, and of his management skill during construction, has produced the integrated design and construction or "construction management" type of contract. Construction management is one of the few project delivery systems that have gained wide usage and acceptance since early 1960s. The constructor is now included in the owner-architect-engineer team and works with them from project inception to completion. The common objective of this team is to serve the owner's interests.

This chapter describes in detail the evolution of the "construction management" method of planning, designing, and construction. It starts with the history of construction management—that is, its genesis and reasons for its instant fame—and then attempts to define "construction management" and "construction manager" (CM), the two controversial terms that mean different things to different people. Following the definitions are explanations of (1) who the CMs are; (2) how CMs are selected and paid; and (3) functions and responsibilities of members of the project team. The rest of the chapter focuses on case studies of construction management contracting versus the traditional process, and considers the future of construction management after discussing advantages and disadvantages of this approach.

2.2 HISTORY OF CONSTRUCTION MANAGEMENT

The concepts and practice of construction management as a project delivery system is not a recent development. Although practiced in various forms by the past "master builders," it has been performed somewhat as we know it today since the late 1950s and early 1960s. One of the early users and subsequent developers (development through periodic review and upgrading procedures) of construction management was the General Services Administration (GSA)—from the early 1960s to 1980. Though construction management is no longer used by GSA (due to various governmental regulations that made its use impractical), it is still judged to be a very successful delivery system.

Initially, the practice of construction management was deemed necessary by segments of the private and public sector to control, through team effort, the time, cost, and quality of a construction project due to the shortcomings of the traditional process in meeting the emerging changes and challenges in the industry, as well as satisfying the project owners' pressing needs. Project owners are utmostly concerned with the optimal control of the cost, time, and quality of the construction project. They desire to maximize the quality of the product while minimizing its total cost and time. Unlike time and cost, the quality of a project is predetermined at the design or engineering stage and constructor(s) should not deviate from the established quality specified in the contract documents. But the total cost and duration of the project cannot be predetermined accurately. Owners have to depend on the reliability of the designer's or engineer's estimate while making their budgets. Cost overruns often cause unanticipated financial and other problems. Likewise, delays in project completion will result in additional project costs, reduce the profitability of the project, and cause other problems to the owner. Thus construction management evolved primarily as a result of the failure of the traditional methods to meet the owners' objectives for the integrated control of cost, time, and quality of a procured product.

For many years progressive owners and developers of large and costly facilities in the private sector have taken the fastest and most economical means to obtain facilities of the quality they desire by creating a team of design professionals and contractors to work toward a common goal. Both design professionals and contractors recognized that (1) they were to work together to provide maximum benefit to the owners, (2) the owner was the ultimate leader and arbitrator of internal disputes, and (3) each member of the team had certain areas of expertise in which he was better qualified than others.

While the private sector was successfully completing many prominent facilities, many public agencies recognized that they were having great difficulty in accomplishing similar results. When compared, the major differences in approach to project delivery systems between the private and public sectors were in contracting methods. The public agencies were generally constrained by laws requiring publicly opened, lump-sum competitive bids from contractors. Often contracts for one facility had to be awarded to many prime contractors, with contract administration left to the design professional or the public agency. There was very little, if any, preconstruction input from contractors regarding costs, schedules, labor trends, market conditions, or practicality of details. It was impossible to start any activity until the entire design was completed. There could be no early assurance that the project could be constructed on time or within budget. Worst of all, there was never a team developed to work toward the goals of public contracts because the legally instituted systems created an adversary relationship between owner, designer, engineer, and contractor(s).

The four major reasons that have clearly called for the management approach in integrated planning, design, and construction of facilities are as follows:

1. A corresponding shift in contracting method toward the multiple contract system that still requires a single management to unify the process.

2. Inflationary costs that set a terrible price on delay and call for management to shorten the time from identification of need to handing-over of the completed project.

3. Increasing size and complexity of projects and the clients, public and private, who commission them.

4. Increasing complexity of management itself calls for special knowledge in the realms of network techniques, computer applications, and other techniques.

So professional construction management emerges as the unifying assembly of skills that keep the whole process in order and at highest efficiency. It must be a professional service because it participates in a role of agency toward the client rather than drawing on the profit margin in a construction contract. (Foxhall, 43:i)

2.2.1   Public Agencies Discovering Their Construction Problems

1. GSA'S STUDIES   The General Service Administration's (GSA) Public Buildings Service (PBS), disgusted with the fact that its construction projects were taking up to eight years from conception to completion, commissioned a study group to determine how similar projects in the private sector were being completed in two years or less. The study group's report, submitted to and endorsed by GSA Administrator Robert L. Kunzig in March 1970, summarized the results of three years' investigation of current construction practices, both public and private. The study group's purpose was to study "all reasonable alternative means of construction contracting" and to identify those which "would be most advantageous for the construction of public buildings" (GSA, 52:1-1). One result of the study was the commitment of PBS to "the use of construction managers in the planning, design and construction of new buildings over $5 million in cost" (GSA, 52:4-28).

2.   THE PORT OF NEW YORK AUTHORITY'S WORLD TRADE CENTER   The World Trade Center, "the largest office building project ever constructed" (Special Report, 129:14), was created by a quasi-public authority (operating with less freedom than enjoyed by commercial developers but more freedom than was available to GSA).

Required by law to award "at least four separate prime contracts on most public work," New York State awarding agencies, including the Port Authority, were prohibited by court decrees "from assigning the responsibility for coordinating and supervising the total work on a project to any one of the major prime contractors" (Special Report, 129:15). Finding the architect unwilling to assume such responsibility, the Port Authority was left with no choice but to hire 'someone' to provide this vital service of bridging the gap between the separate contractors and the owner. This 'someone' became known as the "construction manager." Therefore, it can be stated that for the Port Authority, construction management came into being out of necessity.

3. DEPARTMENT OF HEALTH, EDUCATION, AND WELFARE (HEW)

The employment of Construction Management Services during the design and construction phases of a project can provide the owner with necessary technical capability to overcome those problems associated with increasing construction costs, complex projects, and accelerated construction schedules, particularly those concerning higher education and medical facilities. (HEW, 58:3)

In other words, HEW had the same problems as GSA and the Port Authority, and therefore used the same method: the construction management approach. HEW, however, has two types of construction management contracts. These are Type I, where the CM does not give Guaranteed Maximum Price (GMP), and Type II, under which the CM provides a GMP for completing the entire project.

2.3   DEFINITIONS RELATED TO CONSTRUCTION MANAGEMENT

2.3.1   Definitions of Construction Management and Construction Manager

"Descriptions of construction management are a lot like descriptions of the elephant by the three blind men in the well-known fable. It all depends on which part of the animal you grasp," says Architect J. Karl Justin. "From the trunk end," he continues, "it seems pretty much like exploratory research. From any of the four corners, the legs give it the semblance of supporting function. And from the hindquarters, it is much like your favorite adversary" (Justin, 68:75). In other words, the term "construction management" as well as "construction manager," like many other catchwords, carry with them ambiguity and misunderstanding. The confusion arises because the terms mean different things depending upon who is using them and who is listening to them. Furthermore, there are many different ideas, some in conflict with others, as to what "construction management" and "construction managers" are.

More universal definitions of these two terms are being attempted by the members of the Construction Management Institute (CMI). CMI is a new organization whose members come from various backgrounds in construction. An effort will be made in this section to define these terms after first discussing what they mean to some of the organizations in the construction industry.

The Associated General Contractors of America (AGC) has a clear definition of construction management. The AGC defines construction management as

> One effective method of satisfying an owner's building needs. It treats the project planning, design, and construction phases as integrated tasks within a construction system. Tasks are assigned to a construction team consisting of the owner, the construction manager (CM) and the architect-engineer (A-E). The team works together from project inception to project completion, with the common objective of best serving the owner's interests. Interactions between construction cost, quality, and completion schedule are carefully examined by the team so that a project of maximum value to the owner is realized in the most economic time frame. The construction manager is the qualified general contracting organization which performs the construction management under a professional services contract with the owner. As the construction professional on the construction team, the CM works with the owner and the A-E from the beginning of design through completion of construction, providing leadership to the construction team on all matters relating to construction, keeping the construction team informed, and making recommendations on construction technology and construction economies. The CM proposes construction alternatives to be studied by the construction team during the planning phase and accurately predicts the effects of these alternatives on the project cost and schedule. Once the project budget and schedule have been established, he monitors subsequent development of the project to ensure that those targets are not exceeded without the knowledge and concurrence of the owner. The CM manages procurement of material and supplies, coordinates work of all trade contractors, assesses conformance to design requirements, provides current cost and progress information as the work proceeds, and performs other

construction-related services as required by the owner. (Special Report, 129:2)

The AGC's definition makes clear the following points about construction management and construction managers: (1) When the CM is selected; (2) What the CM's services are during the design and construction phases; (3) What the CM's responsibilities are; (4) How the CM is paid for his services. These points are discussed in detail in Sections 2.4 and 2.7.
  HEW defines construction management as

> a procedure by which an owner, desiring to construct a facility of unusual scope and complexity contracts for professional construction management services to provide technical consultation during the design stage of a project and also to provide for organizing and directing construction activities during the construction phase.

Construction manager is defined as

> operating as a member of an owner-architect-engineer team, and is normally responsible for cost estimates and cost control, review of design with a view toward value engineering, construction techniques, construction coordination and scheduling, and direction of all construction activities. (HEW, 58:2)

HEW, on the other hand, resorts to construction management techniques when it has projects of unusual "scope and complexity." The functions and services provided by the CM, however, appear to be the same as those provided by the AGC's CM. HEW does not specify "who" can perform the CM services.
  GSA's PBS, however, used "construction manager system" as a substitute for "construction management." PBS's definition for construction manager is as follows:

> A construction manager is a prime contractor (professional services) who will work with PBS and the architect to formulate the project budget, furnish the architect with information or construction technology and market conditions to insure that a building design stays within the budget, manage the procurement effort, supervise the construction of the building and provide, if desired, a wide range of other services. In order to discharge these responsibilities, he will be required to have a strong in-house capability which includes engineering, budgeting, cost estimating, scheduling, purchasing, inspection,

management and labor relations personnel. To be considered qualified as a construction manager, a concern must have a record of successful performance in both the management of construction and the furnishing of professional services during design. (GSA Report, 52:5-1, 5-2)

Here the construction manager functions as a member of PBS's project manager-architect team. His functions, responsibilities, and qualifications are clearly stated in the definition.

The AIA uses the term "Unified Team Action Program (UTAP)" instead of "construction management."

[UTAP] is management process that combines the knowledge of the architect, the engineer and the owner together with manufacturers, the suppliers and the contracting industries acting as a unified team to produce outstanding facilities within budget and schedule limitations.[1]

The emphasis is now shifted to the architect.

Architect George T. Heery, President of the Atlanta-based firm Heery & Heery, in his article, "Let's Define Construction Management," describes construction management as

that group of management activities over and above normal architectural and engineering services related to a construction program, carried out during the pre-design, design, and construction phases that contributes to the control of time, cost and quality in the construction of a new facility.

He considers the construction manager as "the individual or firm who ties himself to an owner in a professional arrangement and applies the proper combination of management activities to a construction project to achieve time and cost control" (Heery, 59:69).

Another definition is that "construction management is the composite of all modern project management methodologies having as their objective, the control of time, cost and quality in the design and construction of a new facility" (O'Brien, 104:1).

Approximately five years ago, a group of practitioners within the industry consisting of representatives of owners, architects, engineers, and contractors met over a period of time to discuss construction management practices. One of the first needs was to establish a framework of reference. This group in its deliberation developed the following definition:

---

1. Obtained from a slide prepared by AIA.

Construction management is a team effort of owner, architect/engineer and construction manager; it is a technical and business management service required for planning, implementation and control of the use of the resources necessary from the start of design to the completion of construction.

A careful examination of the various definitions of "construction management" and "construction manager" indicates that there are no standard and agreed-upon definitions for these terms. One thing, however, is evident: The concept centers around the introduction of a construction manager as the owner's agent and manager of the entire construction program. The following key elements are consistent in most definitions: team effort, control of time, cost, and quality and utilization of management technologies. Also, the CM's responsibilities may start from the inception of the project and continue until commissioning. He has two paramount characteristics, namely, construction know-how and management ability.

Synthesizing the foregoing definitions and analyses, the author also defines "construction management" as

a technical and business management service that integrates planning, design and construction processes of facilities under a project team. The objective of the combined and coordinated team efforts of the owner, A-E, and the construction manager is to satisfy the owner's construction needs and interests right from the beginning of the planning to the completion of the project. The team works together and carefully examines the interactions between cost, quality and completion schedule so that a facility of maximum value to the owner is realized in the most economic time frame.

Similarly, "construction manager" may be defined as

a specialized firm or organization which furnishes all the administrative and management services of a general contracting organization as well as all of the consulting services necessary and as required by the owner from planning through design and construction to commissioning. The CM has a professional services contract with the owner and provides consulting and managerial functions. The CM, as the construction professional on the project team, is responsible for design, liaison in the proper selection of materials and methods of construction, cost and scheduling information and control, as well as quality requirements. He is also responsible for managing the actual construction activities, including all construction operation normally associated with a contracting organization.

2.3.2   Construction Management Contracts and Formats

1. CONTRACTS   Alternative contractual approaches are being tried to gain better quality and project cost control and to save time. In each of the types described in this section, functions are rearranged so that some operations are undertaken concurrently and the relationships of the principles are altered to improve communications. Included in these alternative methods of contracting are the following:

A. **Construction Management** is basically a team approach to construction. The general contractor joins the owner along with architect-engineer to organize the construction phase of the project and to provide the experience of a contractor during planning and design. A construction manager supervises the entire process. The object is to leave the owner-architect relationship undisturbed, but to provide improved communications between the owner, designer, engineer, and constructor, so that there may be concurrent design and construction with the overall intent of providing the owner with the desired project in the shortest time and within the budget. Guaranteed Maximum Price (GMP) may or may not be provided depending upon the owner's desires.

B. **The Negotiated Contract** is a form of construction management. Here, the architect prepares a preliminary design and obtains approval from the owner on the basis of the sketch plan and preliminary cost estimates. A general contractor is then selected on the basis of a pre-tender bid. The general contractor teams up with the architect to provide working drawings and manages the construction within the terms of the pre-tender bid. This approach provides the owner with a figure for 'final cost' before detailed design and construction start, rather than a target estimate as in the case of construction management. The contractor in this case has more financial responsibility and much depends upon the close working relationship between him (contractor), the architect, and the engineer.

C. **The Design-Build Method** has been used in various forms such as Package Contracting, Developer Proposal Call Systems, or Turn-Key Contracts. This method, though not a construction management form of contract, has some characteristics similar to the construction management method, so far as coordination and supervision of design, planning, and construction are concerned.

The design-build method differs from the other types in that the owner deals with the prime contractor as the single administrative authority over all design and construction matters. The contractor agrees to provide the facility to the owner's specifications for the previously discussed price. Here, the contractor undertakes to provide the improved communications environment.

D. **The Project Management Method** is the culmination of the other types. In this method the owner accepts the financial responsibility normally assumed by the general contractor.

As his first step the owner usually appoints the project manager even before appointing the architect and other consultants. The project manager's function is to oversee the project from its conception through the selection of all consultants, determination of the contractual arrangement for construction, and on to the commissioning of the project.

The objectives of project management are to coordinate and control the design and cost of the project through the application of management techniques and to produce a well-designed and constructed facility to meet the functional requirements of the owner within his schedule and budget.

The major difference between project management and construction management is that the project manager joins the owner in the conceptual stage of the project and assists in all phases, whereas the construction manager's responsibilities relate only to liaison from the construction point of view as design proceeds and later, to management of the construction phase.

2. THE CONSTRUCTION MANAGEMENT FORMATS   Although there are a number of possible construction management structures for planning, design, and construction phases, most will fall into one of the five basic formats shown in Figures 2.1 (*a*) through 2.1 (*e*). Figures 2.1 (*a*) and 2.1 (*e*) show formats most commonly used on construction management contracts. Figure 2.1 (*b*) shows prime contracts that remain separate throughout the project for statutory of phasing reasons. The type of contract that uses this format is often referred to as "fast track." Figure 2.1 (*c*) shows a slightly modified form of the traditional process, often used on negotiated projects. Under this format the chances are that the A-E may have to approve the construction manager. Some contractors are advocating the reverse of this format so that CM is first to be selected and hired and then he helps to select the A-E. This, when done, more or less reverts to the project management type of contract. Figure 2.1 (*d*) shows a format similar to that shown in Figure 2.1 (*a*). The essential difference is that in Figure 2.1 (*d*), the CM is required to provide general conditions.

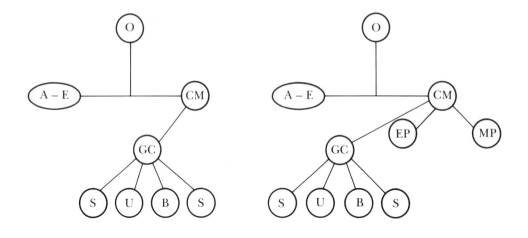

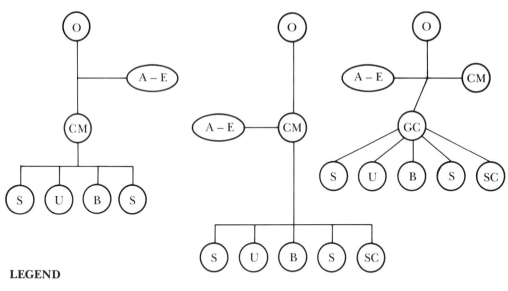

LEGEND

O = Owner   A – E = Architect – Engineer   CM = Construction Manager

GC = General Contractor   EP = Electrical Prime   MP = Mechanical Prime

SC = Support Conditions

Figure 2.1. Basic Construction Management Formats.

2.4   SELECTION AND PAYMENT OF A CM

2.4.1   Selection of CM

2.4.1.1   Problems Associated with CM Selection

The concept of a construction manager is relatively new and still poorly defined; hence selecting an organization or a firm to perform construction management services presents special problems for an owner. Some of these problems are enumerated as follows:

1. The need to match carefully the firm or organization providing the construction management services with the owner's organization. Only a few of the many individuals and firms that have recently moved into construction management from architecture, real estate, construction, and management are strong in every aspect that might be required of a CM.

2. The danger of over-skill—This often occurs especially on smaller or less complicated projects. Here, the CM's services may be redundant, unnecessary, and expensive.

3. Wide variety of CM's payment methods—There are no industry standards. Most of the time the CM works on a contract that reimburses him and pays him an agreed-upon fee.

4. Local knowledge—This is crucial because out-of-town CMs must secure such basic information as costs, availability of labor and materials, transportation, and community pressure.

5. Financial responsibility or liability—It is being questioned by opponents of construction management whether a CM has any liability in the event of a serious cost overrun. Such people argue that since CM has no entrepreneurial interest, there is less pressure on him to keep the project within budget. GMP contracts are exempted in this case. However, these critics often forget that the CM has his reputation at stake. Whatever the case, it will benefit the owner to spell out over-budget parameters right at the start.

6. When to hire the CM—The exact point at which to hire a CM depends on the owner's in-house capabilities and the characteristics of the project in question. However, the earlier he joins the team, the better things will be for the owner. That is, the overall capability of the construction manager influences the success of the project. The owner must carefully evaluate the potentialities of the CM prior to selection.

2.4.1.2   Basis for Selecting a CM

The key point in selecting the CM is not to look at his title, but to identify the skills and experience that he possesses. They should include (*a*) knowledge of design process; (*b*) knowledge of the construction process; and (*c*) fundamentals of general project management. The following parameters are the essential criteria for judging the capabilities of the CM firm:

1. The organization's financial strength, bonding capacity, insurability, and ability to assume a financial risk if the owner requires it.

2. The organization's in-house staff capability, technical performance, experience, as well as qualifications of the personnel who will manage the project. This must include the organization's capabilities in architecture, engineering, disciplines related to the construction, budgeting, cost estimating, scheduling (including CPM/PERT or precedence network analysis), purchasing, quality control, economics, cost accounting, management, value engineering, construction technology (methods, equipment, systems), and labor relations.

3. The organization's record of performance in completing projects on time, within budget, and satisfying the specified quality; the scope of CM services performed in past projects; familiarity or experience in the location or vicinity of the project location and references from previous owners, architects or engineers, and contractors.

4. The organization's demonstrated ability to work cooperatively with the owner and the architect or engineer throughout the project; display of leadership and initiative in performing its tasks as a member of the project team and resolution or avoidance of problems in previous projects.

5. The organization's success in performing the normal general contractor's functions on projects of comparable type, scope, and complexity.

6. Management capability evaluated in terms of availability of management information and control systems; availability of systematic procedures for performance and implementation of CM services; as well as depth of management skills in communication, administration, and systems orientation.

2.4.2 The CM's Compensation

The CM is generally paid a professional fee commensurate with the complexity of the project, time of construction, scope of services, and as otherwise negotiated with the owner.

In respect to payment, the AGC construction management contract takes a lump-sum approach that begins as a percentage and converts to a lump sum by the time the size and scope of the job are determined. The AIA construction management contract describes the various methods that can be used to describe a "professional fee" without recommending a specific preference. This implies that the owner will get whatever services he pays for, and the fee for construction services will have to be on a sliding scale with relation to job cost just as it is in other professional fees. To date, there has been no industry-wide standardization of either construction management payment or "fees" or the services a given fee might represent. Thus the payment structure of the construction manager is yet to be well defined as that of the architect, engineer, or other professionals. The CM's compensation should be commensurate with the professional services rendered, as well as comparable to that of the architects, engineers, or other professionals.

Construction management contracts have been successfully completed under different fee structures such as:

1. Cost reimbursement for home office and field costs plus a fixed fee for profit

2. Fixed fee for home office services, including profit plus cost reimbursement for all jobsite costs

3. Guaranteed maximum cost for CM services under a cost reimbursement plus fixed-fee type of contract

4. Lump sum

The total fee paid by the project owner varies widely according to the extent of professional services provided by the CM firm, the complexity of the project, and the duration of construction. However, the total fee paid to the CM in practice averages between 2% and 6% of the total project costs.

There is no universal standard form of contract for the CM process. Each CM contract is subject to negotiation between the project owner and the CM firm. The owner should have a detailed evaluation of the project and professional services to be performed by the CM firm before deciding on the type of contract and the payment structure. Selection of the CM should be based on qualifications and performance capability, and not on price. Some savings in fee may result in engaging an underqualified, inefficient, and job-hungry CM, rather than the best qualified professional who will deliver the best services to the owner.

2.5   FUNCTIONS AND RESPONSIBILITIES OF A CM

The function of the CM is to plan, administer, and control the overall construction program to suit the owner's project objectives. Objectives of the owner include minimum overall project cost, including the economic benefits of minimum design-construction time, compliance with recognized owner administrative and control requirements, and obtaining specified quality and utility in the finished product.

2.5.1   Responsibilities to Owner

The CM's functions and responsibilities to the owner include sincere and professional representation and advice free from economic conflict and conscientiously handled within the delegation of responsibilities that the owner elects to assign to him. The CM should keep the owner informed at all times regarding the current status of the project in comparison to the overall plan. While the CM's functions and responsibilities are oriented toward achieving the owner's objectives, he has a professional responsibility for basic fair and businesslike dealings with other participants in the project's team, including the architect, engineer, contractors, labor unions, and the industry as well as the general public.

2.5.2   Responsibilities to the Architect or Engineer

The CM's relationship with the architect or engineer must be thoroughly professional. If he is to be successful, he must achieve full cooperation of the architect or engineer who is designing the project. Only by working together can the full benefit of a design-phase value engineering program be achieved. Successful reduction of project cost while preserving value must be a joint effort, the credit for which must be shared equally between the architect and/or the engineer. Such savings must enhance the standing of the architect or engineer as well as the CM in the eyes of the owner if the relationship is to survive and prosper. The CM provides his economic knowledge of construction as a tool for the architect or engineer in furthering the objectives of the owner. The continuing responsibilities of the designer or engineer to the owner must be preserved and acknowledged by the CM. A truly successful CM will thus have a valuable partner in the architect or engineer. By working together, the economic interests of architect-engineer, owner, and CM will aid in achieving the owner's objectives.

2.5.3   Responsibilities to Contractors

The CM's relationship with the project contractors must be equally professional. He must faithfully interpret the plans and specifications. When plans and specifications are in error or are incomplete, he must assist in obtaining fair and additional compensation to the contractor who has bid upon the original documents. For many years the resident architect or engineer has been in charge of interpreting plans and specifications in an impartial manner, especially in deciding questions of fact and in resolving conflicts between the owner and contractor. Now the CM must discharge this responsibility to the contractors. The CM must insist upon compliance with the plans and specifications to ensure achieving the owner's objectives. He must equally insist upon compensation to the contractors for changes and modifications initiated by the owner, engineer, or architect, or for omissions or errors in the bidding documents.

2.5.4   Responsibilities to Others

The CM also has a duty toward labor. He must recognize the collective bargaining agreements under which the contractors and labor unions operate. He must have reasonable knowledge of craft jurisdiction as practiced in the area. Furthermore, the CM has a duty to the industry and to the general public. If qualified, he is aware of the many problems facing the industry. He should act as a knowledgeable professional in advising the owner and in conducting his own responsibilities in order to assist in solving underlying problems and economic conflict that are always present to some degree in a given project area.

2.5.5   CM's Services during Planning and Design Phases

A construction manager (CM) provides a wide range of professional services during both planning and design. These might include the following:

1.   He advises, assists, and makes recommendations to the owner and architect-engineer on all aspects of the project schedule requirements, completion priorities, and other scheduling information. He performs feasibility studies.

2.   He has the responsibility to the owner to identify the areas of the owner's responsibilities if the latter is not sophisticated or experienced enough to recognize them. He also develops a work plan that sets forth in detail the recommended approach to the project, including (a) overall approach; (b) home-office services; (c) field management services; (d) use of proposed work packages; (e) list of proposed contractors for further servicing; (f) preliminary design and procurement schedules; (g) value engineering program, and (h) life-cycle construction analysis program. He also designs the information flow channels.

3.   He reviews the architectural and engineering plans and specifications for the purpose of advising on such factors as construction feasibility, possible economies, availability of materials and labor, time requirements for procurement and construction, projected costs and life-cycle costs. He assists in the coordination of all sections of the drawings without assuming any of the A-E's normal responsibilities for design. He has the right to control design because it is his responsibility that the project be finished on time and within budget. He also conducts value engineering analysis, time-cost trade-offs of alternative designs, and assists in systems analysis.

4.   He prepares cost evaluations and budget estimates based on a quantity survey of the plans and specifications at the preliminary stage of development. These estimates are revised and refined as development of plans and specifications proceeds. The CM advises the owner and A-E if it appears that the budgeted target for the project cost or completion schedule will not be met. On many projects the CM will be required by the owner to provide a guaranteed maximum price (GMP) at the time in which the construction team has developed the drawings and specifications to a point where the scope of the project can be clearly defined.

5.   He recommends for early purchase and expedites the procurement of long-lead items to ensure their delivery by the required dates.

6.   He advises on the prepackaging of bidding documents for the awarding of separate construction contracts to the various systems and trades. Such advice includes the sequence of document preparation to facilitate phased construction work during completion of the design development.

7.   He analyzes and recommends to the owner and the A-E the type and scope of work represented by each bid package in relation to time required for performance, availability of labor and materials, community relations, overlapping trade jurisdictions, provisions for temporary facilities, and so forth, and participates in scheduling both design and construction procedures.

8.   He works some of the design operations into an overall CPM or other network scheduling operation when schedule criteria of design and construction emerge.

9.   He conducts prebid conferences among contractors, subcontractors, and manufacturers of systems and subsystems to ensure that each bidder understands the components of the bidding documents and the management techniques to be applied, including any computerized intercommunications network scheduling and cash-flow controls.

10.   He takes competitive bids for construction when working drawings and specifications are completed. He leads in the analysis of bids received and either awards the contracts or recommends to the owner that such contracts be awarded. CM's contract with the owner dictates the procedure for the contract awards.

11.   He prepares a progress schedule using CPM or other scheduling techniques for all project activities by the owner, A-E, trade contractors, and himself early in the project. Incorporated into this schedule are all aspects of the construction process, that is, design, bidding, procurement, and construction. He then monitors this master schedule during both the design and construction phases. He is responsible for providing all parties with periodic status reports on the work with respect to the project schedule. He also sees to it that the entire construction process is optimized in terms of cost and time.

2.5.6 CM's Services during Construction Phase

The CM assumes responsibility for managing the project during construction in much the same way as the general contractor has traditionally done. He provides the following services during the construction phase:

1. He maintains a competent full-time supervisory staff at the jobsite to coordinate and provide general direction of the work and progress of the trade contractors on the project.

2. On a day-to-day basis, he inspects the work being performed to ensure that the materials furnished and work performed are in accordance with the quality required by the working drawings and specifications. He also conducts factory inspections as required.

3. He works to facilitate on-site communication, defining lines of authority and procedures to assure coordination among the owner, A-E, contractors, and his own team.

4. He continuously gathers data on vendors and materials delivery dates to ensure that needed materials are available when and as required. He meshes the designs-drawing activity and the procurement-contracting activity.

5. In cooperation with the A-E, he establishes and implements procedures for expediting and processing all shop drawings, catalogs, and other project papers.

6. Acting as a "troubleshooter," the CM's functions are to maintain the information flow and compare results in terms of time and cost against projection so that bottlenecks and overruns can be anticipated and avoided. These functions require constant on-site vigilance.

7. He is responsible for the establishment of effective programs related to safety, jobsite records, labor relations, public relations, equal employment opportunities (EEO), and progress reports.

8. He reviews and processes all applications for payment by trade contractors and material suppliers concerned in accordance with the terms of the contract.

9. He negotiates change orders with contractors, maintains records of these change orders and their effects on schedules, and establishes back charges.

10. Either with his own forces or others, he furnishes all general condition items if required. If requested, he performs portions of the work with his own forces.

11. He schedules and conducts job meetings to ensure that the project is progressing in an orderly fashion.

12. He provides data processing services if requested by the owner.

13. He confers with architects and engineers when clarification or interpretation of documents becomes necessary.

14. Sometime before the completion of the project, he sets up a joint inspection to be made by contractors, project manager, owner, architect-engineer, and other interested parties. This inspection as well as the final inspection must be followed by decisions on the part of all concerned as to the most economical and expeditious ways of handling a "punch list" of incomplete items. He also coordinates start-up programs.

2.6   FUNCTIONS AND RESPONSIBILITIES OF THE OTHER MEMBERS OF THE PROJECT TEAM

2.6.1   Owner's Functions and Responsibilities

The advisability of constructing or altering a project involving a major investment is given careful thought by the owner. He considers such factors as the future use and the advantages to be derived before deciding to proceed. In addition to the payment of bills, his responsibilities might include the following:

1. He engages consultants (financial, A-E, CM, and so forth) to do the economic and technical feasibility studies when he recognizes the need for a new facility.

2. He participates in (*a*) the selection of the project team, and (*b*) decisions regarding phased construction and types of contracting.

3. He outlines the services, functions, and responsibilities of each member of the project team in their respective contract agreements. At times he may ask the individual members in the project team to outline their functions and responsibilities for his approval.

4. He sets his own priorities and establishes his goals, in many cases with the advice and guidance of the CM. The owner has the final say in all matters on the project including decisions on expenditure of project funds.

5. He furnishes legal, accounting, and insurance counseling services that are necessary for the project and also the required auditing services to ascertain how or for what purposes the contractors have used the money paid to them under the construction contracts.

6. He furnishes the CM with a sufficient quantity of construction documents such as the services, information, surveys, and reports mentioned in 3 and 4.

7. He establishes his representative (project director or PD) to direct the CM, provide the necessary responses, and participate in search for solutions. He invests in PD some authority and funds.

8. He gives prompt written notice to CM if he finds any fault or defect in the project or nonconformance with the contract documents.

2.6.2   Architect's or Engineer's Functions and Responsibilities

The appearance of a CM in the project team and services he provides have affected the normal architect's or engineer's roles and facilitated his functions. The architect or engineer has now been forced to adjust his communications network and his own responsiveness to accommodate the owner-CM situation. Included in his functions and responsibilities are the following:

1. He actually designs the project, interprets drawings and specifications, and approves all manufacturers, materials, and samples. This is done, in most cases, in conjunction with the CM.

2. He reviews inspection reports and deals with all questions of design and of substitution of materials. He does not provide continuous on-site reviewing services, but visits the sites from time to time to see to it that the aesthetic and technical plans of the contract documents are being carried out.

3. He may be required by code to furnish certain on-site inspections of structural, mechanical, and technical items. However, he is not responsible for construction means, methods, techniques, schedules, sequence, procedures, or for safety precautions and programs. These are the concerns of the CM.

4. He reviews change orders concerning matters of design and engineering, estimates their consequences, and returns them to the CM for the confirmation of cost and construction practicality so that they can be negotiated with the owner.

5. He reviews with the CM all written guarantees, instruction manuals, and similar data assembled from contractors.

2.7   WHO ARE THE CMs?

There has been proliferation in the number and types of organizations competing for the CM services market as the concept has become widely accepted in the industry. These organizations have been actively promoting their services as the best and most economical way to construct a project. CM services are offered by individuals or firms of various backgrounds, including owners, management consultants, architects, construction contractors, engineering design professionals, developers, CPM firms, the professional quantity surveyors, and self-appointed experts. At this point, these organizations will be analyzed and discussed in terms of their experience, capabilities, in-house staff, and other criteria.

2.7.1   The Owner

Most owner organizations perform some portion of the project manager functions with their in-house staff. Therefore, they retain limited CM functions. Some owner organizations have added A-E functions to their internal capability. Others have extended further to include some or all of the CM functions. Still others perform much of their own construction directly. The practicality of in-house capability for owner organizations depends on a number of factors, including general philosophy, volume of project activity, recurring nature of projects, uniformity of project activity (both as to type and amount), and availability of outside services. All these factors have economic implications.

The advantages to the owner in carrying out some or all of the management responsibilities are obvious: conflict of interest is eliminated, coordination is simplified, and trade-off studies involving long-term costs (i.e., life-cycle cost analysis) are encouraged. However, the work load problems may be such as to prohibit strong investment by the owner in the suitable staff. This tends to limit the in-house management option to large organizations.

2.7.2   The Architect

The architects have not really made up their collective minds as to their future in the management field. They are struggling with legal, ethical, and competitive problems. Few owners see the architect in the manager's role. The architects, with a few notable exceptions, face some hard selling to get back to the role of the master builder. It was largely the architect's weakness in providing cost information, value engineering, and estimates that created the need for a CM. Architects can lose management control, especially during the construction phase, because of their preoccupation with design. Unless the educational training of the architect is changed to include the fundamentals of general project management, construction process and controls, he might not be able to stand the tough competition from his opponents.

2.7.3   The Construction Contractor

The construction contractor organizations vary in capability. Some, primarily general contractors, have moved from their role as prime contractor to develop capabilities in some or all of the functions of the CM. This is preferred to a general contractor who has not developed the necessary capabilities but wants to perform the CM functions because they can supply the necessary input with the desired professional independence. The disciplines within the firm must include all the normal trades (especially mechanical and electrical ones) required on the proposed construction without dependence on subcontractors. Some have added design capability to their organizations resulting in a design-construct or turn-key company. Others enter the construction management field in joint venture with either design engineering or CPM firms.

The solid arguments in favor of the construction contractor are (a) his strong procurement and field operations background; (b) his ability to carry out the general conditions; (c) his ability to coordinate and supervise specialty contractors, and (d) his knowledge about the design process. Potential conflicts of interest and firmly established attitudes regarding the traditional owner-contractor relationship may be liabilities. Contractors, with a few notable exceptions, have limited organizations; their future, therefore, seems to lie in the joint venture concept.

2.7.4   CPM Engineering Firms

CPM engineering firms are strong in developing variations from the traditional approaches. They are experienced in CPM/PERT, management information systems, and are comfortable in the software and hardware world of the computer. Their fees are normally not linked directly to project costs, thus eliminating a possible conflict of interest. These firms, however, cannot carry out specialized construction or be responsible for the general conditions in the fields, nor do they have in-house capabilities to coordinate and supervise the various contractors.

2.7.5   Construction Management Consultants

Construction management consultants are usually organized by former executives of general construction contractors in association with such firms as CPM or engineering design professionals. These consulting firms are so organized that they combine the best features in the construction contractor with the best features of CPM firms or engineering design professionals. Thus they have the capabilities to provide all the CM functions from the inception of the project to its handing-over with the desired professional independence. In short, they are very competent at providing CM services that meet today's complex demands.

2.7.6   The Professional Quantity Surveyor

The professional quantity surveyor is also qualified to be a CM on the basis of the services he has been providing, as described in Section 1.4.6. Like the engineering design professional, the quantity surveyor has been associated with facility construction projects from inception to commission, and even thereafter, when preparing final accounts. He works with the architect for the owner to achieve responsibility in the real estate and financial areas. He is also associated with and competent in construction supervision, control, and observation. His main weakness is being unable to provide in-house resources (tradesmen, equipment, and plant) to perform the general conditions.

2.8   CASE STUDIES

This section describes how construction management has been used on some selected projects, some of which are highly complex and diversified. Project size/organization and cost/time comparisons are summarized, respectively, in Figures 2.2 and 2.3.

2.8.1   Comparative Studies of CM-Built Projects vs. Traditionally Built Projects

Comparison of traditionally built projects with CM-built projects is very difficult. To make such comparison easy and meaningful, one must have two identical projects going on side by side. Therefore, CM-built projects are converted to the traditional process using the sequential design-bid-construct approach before the necessary comparisons are made. Such conversions are easy to make in terms of time or schedule, but not in dollars. It is only assumed that since time is money, time saved or lost is money saved or lost. How much money saved or lost is very difficult to state.

2.8.2   Analysis of Case Studies

1.   WORLD TRADE CENTER   The World Trade Center is the largest office building ever constructed. It took many cooperating trades to finish the 110-story building in 28½ months, only 45 days behind schedule. The size of this project, the architects, CM, and the major role they played are summarized in Figure 2.2(1). Tishman's tight cost and schedule controls as well as its excellent general coordination and management contributed greatly. Tishman was paid a fixed fee of $3 million plus reimbursement of special costs such as CPM monitoring and purchasing assistance. Bids were not publicly opened on this project because

SIZE

PROJECT	No. of Stories	Sq. ft. of Floor Area (in million S.F.)	Site Area (Acres)	No. of Packages	Project Manager	Architect or A/E	CM(s)	CM's Major Role
1. World Trade Center Port Authority of NY, Lower Manhattan	110	10	16	170	The Port Authority	Minoru Yamasaki Assoc.; Emery Roth & Sons	Tishman Realty & Construction Co.	Coordination with architects, purchasing assistance, construction supervision, budget control, CPM monitor, change order administration, some inspection, detailed budget preparation, entire project phasing and coordination
2. Canadian Imperial Bank of Commerce (in Toronto)	56				Canadian Imperial Bank	I.M. Pei; Page & Steele	1. Mason-Kiewit (Gen. CM) 2. Sayers & Assoc. (Mech. system) 3. Standard Electric (Electric system)	Gen. CM functions and project administration Expediting, coordination, project programming, checking systems
3. University of Mass. campus in Boston—First phase		1.3	90		U. Mass. & Bureau of Bldg. Const. plus the CM	Pietro Belluschi & Sasaki; Dawson; De May Assoc. Inc. (all 3 master plan team; plus 1 arch. to each of the 6 buildings)	McKee-Berger Mansueto, Inc. joint venture	General coordination and supervision of design and construction in addition to maintaining cost and schedule control as well as project administration
4. Dallas–Fort Worth Airport			17,000	25 systems & 225 subsystems	Regional airport board retained a PM to analyze design & furnish estimates		1. Tippets-Abbett-McCarthy-Stratton (TAMS) 2. Parsons-McKee, Inc.	Coordination and management of overall project except terminal buildings and spine road In charge of terminal buildings and spine road

Figure 2.2. Project Size and Organization[1]

39

PROJECT	SIZE				Project Manager	Architect or A/E	CM(s)	CM's Major Role
	No. of Stories	Sq. ft. of Floor Area (in million S.F.)	Site Area (Acres)	No. of Packages				
5. University of Pennsylvania Student Housing Program in Philadelphia	25	1.7			H. E. Manly, a U. official acted as U. agent to provide skills nec. to carry out program	W.G. Kling Arch'l advsr. A. Clauss; R.J. Heubre; W.W. Eshback and H. Perkins	Meridian Engineering, Inc.	Feasibility studies, coordination and supervision of design and construction
6. Opelika High School in Alabama		.13		3	The school superintendent, Dr. Zeanah, acted as PM	Candill Rowlett Scott (CRS)	CM Assoc.—a sister co. of CRS	Cost and schedule controls of design and construction, coordination architects and contractors, coordination of the various building systems
7. The Renovation/Addition of St. Luke's Hospital Medical Center in Phoenix, AZ	7 for the highest building	.341[2]	N/A	29	Kitchell Contractors of Phoenix, AZ	Varney, Sexton, Lunsford & Aye	Kitchell Contractors of Phoenix, AZ	Budget and schedule controls of design and construction, responsible for coordinating and controlling team effort through its management information system, provision of construction expertise during pre-design and design phases and performed construction work as CM/General contractor during construction phase
8. Saint Mary's Hospital at Rochester, Minnesota	9 total (4-story base and 5-story tower)	.53	N/A	13	The Builders Barton-Marlow of Minneapolis, MN	Joint Venture between Naramore Bain Brady and Johanson of Seattle and Hammel Green & Abrahamson of St. Paul (NBBJ/HGA)	The Builders/Barton-Marlow of Minneapolis, MN—also Joint Venture	Cost and schedule controls of design, construction and occupancy conforming to PBS' CMCS program; developing and maintaining management plan for design, design/construction overlap and construction; administering, coordinating and inspecting all contracts; other functions and responsibilities included drawing and specification review, procurement of contractors and materials, value management, job safety and performing all necessary General Condition items.

1. The information for this figure was obtained from the following references: Special Report (129:14–16), Freedman (44:AF1–AF38), Foxhall (43:49–52), Thomsen (139), 1 Kaiser Engineers (69), AGC (5:9–39, 119–162).
2. Made up of 240, 390 SF new and 100,854 SF remodel.

Figure 2.2. Project Size and Organization[1] (Continued)

PROJECT	Original Schedule (months)	Months Completed ahead of (or behind) Schedule	Percentage ahead of (or behind) schedule	Original estimate (million dollars)	Amount ahead (or below) estimate (million dollars)	Percentage above (or below) estimate
1. World Trade Center, NY's Port Authority in Lower Manhattan	27	(1–1/2)	(5.6)	550	(30)	(5.5)
2. Canadian Imperial Bank of Commerce in Toronto	—	over 24	—	—	—	—
3. University of Mass. Campus in Boston, First phase	33	18[2]	54.5[2]	150	(20)	(13.3)
4. Dallas–Ft. Worth Airport Phase one	—	18[2]	—	296	(20)	(6.8)
5. Food Distribution Center, Tulsa, Oklahoma	10	(1)	(10.0)	3.6	(.1)	(2.8)
6. University of Pennsylvania Student Housing Program in Philadelphia	60	(18)	(30)	66.1	(9.5)[3]	(14.4)
7. Opelika High School, in Alabama	24–36	12–24	50.0	3.5	(.37)[4]	(3.5)[4]
8. The Renovation/Addition of St. Luke's Hospital Medical Center in Phoenix, AZ	46[5]	(3/4)	(1.6)	30.0[6]	(.25)	(.83)
9. St. Mary's Hospital at Rochester, Minnesota	36[5]	(16)	(44.4)	53.1[7]	(.121)	(2.27)

1. The information for this figure was obtained from the following references: Special Report (129:14–16), Freedman (44:AF1–AF38), Foxhall (43:49–52), Thomsen (139), Kaiser Engineers (69), AGC (5:9–39, 119–162).
2. Construction time savings.
3. Includes $4.5 million incremental income resulting from early occupancy.
4. Savings from escalation.
5. Including both design and construction phases.
6. Construction cost only.
7. Total project cost including A/E fees, CM fees, special installed equipment, construction cost and other owner costs (e.g. legal fees, insurance, land acquisition, special consultants, testing and inspection).

Figure 2.3. Cost and Time Comparisons[1]

it was strongly felt that public opening of bids never produced the most favorable prices. All the contractors submitted competitive bids, and prices were disclosed after the award. For time and money saved on this project, see Figure 2.3 (1).

2. CANADIAN IMPERIAL BANK OF COMMERCE   The bank maintained an active supervisory role with its own staff that was built up during a previous project. Construction management was divided into three parts: general construction (including structure), mechanical systems, and electrical systems. The CMs coordinated and supervised the activities of the contractors. Imperial Bank retained its own mechanical and electrical consultants. Freer working relationships between the management contractors and the consulting engineers resulted in quality and performance improvement in certain components as well as a savings of over twenty-four months in design and construction time. See Figure 2.2(2) for further information.

3. UNIVERSITY OF MASSACHUSETTS CAMPUS IN BOSTON—PHASE ONE   The project had a highly complex organizational structure. The master plan for the project was commissioned to three architectural firms, as mentioned in Figure 2.2(3). In addition, each of the six buildings had its own architect. Site work for the entire project was done by still another firm. It was a big task to bring all seven parts together and organize the work of some twenty firms toward a completion schedule of thirty-three months. The project began with problems such as unresolved planning and designs, no clearly defined role from the project management team, and site preparation problems (e.g., underground fires, noxious gases, rat colonies). A kind of management triumvirate consisting of the university, the Bureau of Building Construction, and the construction management firm was created to solve these problems in order to complete the project within time and budget estimates. The CM on this project played the roles of both CM and project administrator. The whole project management team was divided into four teams: design management, design specialists, construction management, and project administration. Each firm selected representatives to serve on these teams, whose purpose was to see that the design and construction processes were managed as a single effort. The project size, the people, the firms involved, as well as cost and time performances are shown in Figures 2.2(3) and 2.3(3).

4. DALLAS–FORT WORTH AIRPORT—PHASE ONE   The world's second largest airport complex was managed by two CMs: one managing everything except the spine road and the terminal buildings (i.e., only the airfield), and the other managing the terminal buildings and spine road. The airfield contract involved coordinating, organizing, and supervising thirty-five prime contractors and $158 million worth of work. The terminal area CM managed twelve prime contractors and $138 million worth of work. The whole project was broken up into 25 primary systems and 225 subsystems. In all, eighteen months of construction time and some $20 million were saved, as seen in Figures 2.2(4) and 2.3(4).

5. UNIVERSITY OF PENNSYLVANIA STUDENT HOUSING PROGRAM   This project was completed within forty-two months (eighteen months ahead of schedule) from authorization through start of design to total occupancy, at a cost of $56.6 million. See Figures 2.3(6) and 2.2(5). Out of the $9.5 million net savings, $5 million represented cost savings due to concurrent design and construction, and the rest resulted from incremental income from early occupancy. The CM's (also called "consultant") fee was based on an extended contract that described the broad scope, with negotiations each year to establish a cost not to be exceeded during that fiscal year. Tasks added to the scope were negotiated independently.

6. FOOD DISTRIBUTION CENTER IN TULSA   As Figure 2.3(5) shows, this project was completed one month behind schedule. The same project, when converted to the traditional process, made a savings of about 4½ months over the traditional sequence design-bid-construct process. See Figure 2.4. Again, about $.1 million or 2.8% of the budget was saved. See Figure 2.3(5). The saving resulted from the concurrent design and construction concept. The bidding time was unusually long under the CM contract and that might have contributed to the one-month delay.

7. OPELIKA HIGH SCHOOL (ALABAMA)   This school was constructed within 12½ months, that is, 12 to 24 months ahead of the norm, about 50% more building time than the budget traditionally would have bought. It was also built within budget. There was an urgency to have the school completed as quickly as possible, but the school superintendent did not want a "rush job." At the same time, much of the allocated $3.5 million was required to be spent on the inside, where the children would be. Combining the efforts of construction management, fast-track, and system building, CM Associates was able to achieve the goals of the school superintendent. See Figures 2.2(6) and 2.3(7).

8. THE RENOVATION/ADDITION OF ST. LUKE'S HOSPITAL MEDICAL CENTER, PHOENIX, ARIZONA   Despite the extensive changes in scope, this project was completed practically on time and within budget—that is, only three weeks behind original schedule and about quarter of million dollars below budget. See Figures 2.2(7) and 2.3(8). As felt by the project team (AGC, 5:25-33) and agreed with by the author, owner's needs and objectives were effectively satisfied because (1) CM was

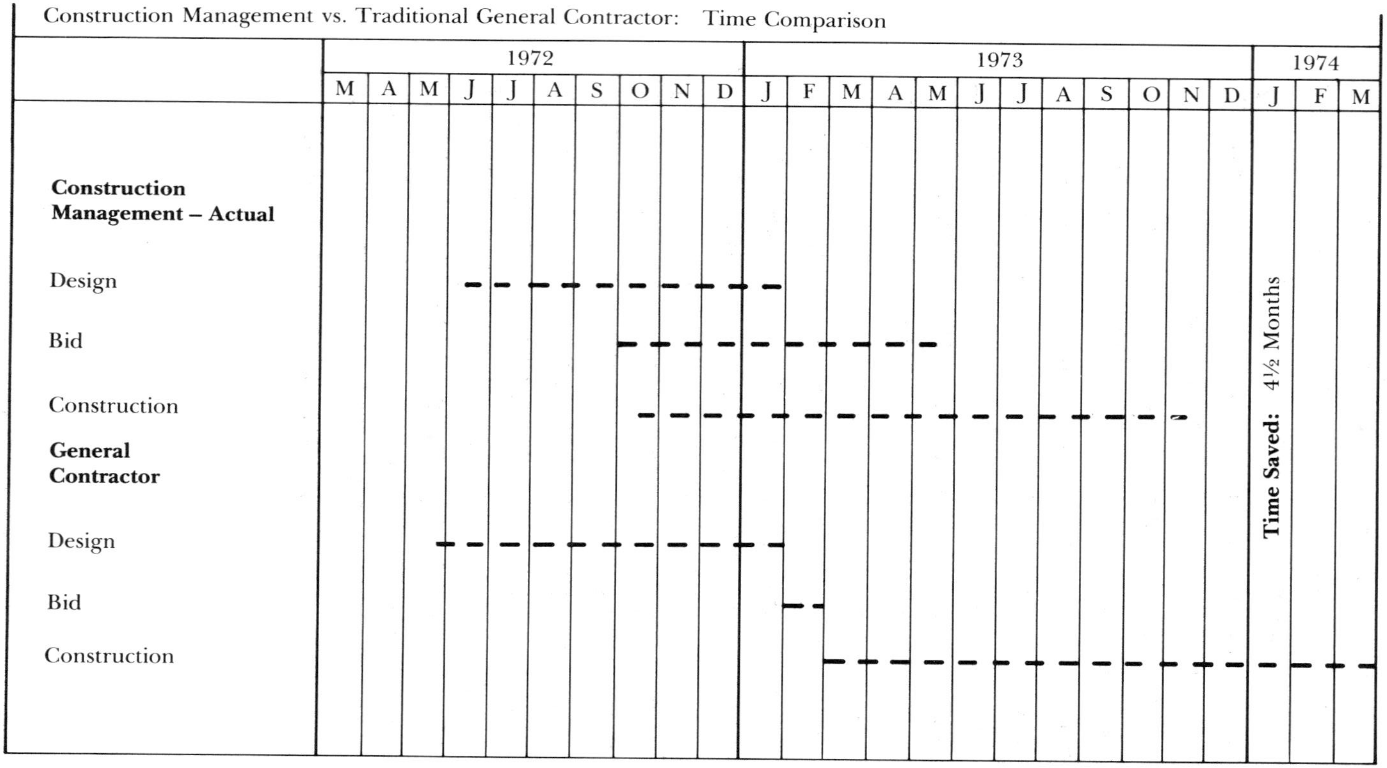

Construction Management vs. Traditional General Contractor: Time Comparison

	1972										1973											1974		
	M	A	M	J	J	A	S	O	N	D	J	F	M	A	M	J	J	A	S	O	N	D	J	F	M

**Construction
Management – Actual**

Design

Bid

Construction

**General
Contractor**

Design

Bid

Construction

Time Saved: 4½ Months

Figure 2.4.   Food Distribution Center.

able to control cost and time effectively as a result of his dual role as CM/ General Contractor; (2) use of GMP had a positive impact on project; (3) involvement of the CM from the very beginning (i.e. the component planning phase) brought the needed strengths of construction expertise, cost estimating, value management, and project management to the project team; (4) there was mutual trust and confidence between team members, and (5) each project team member concentrated on what it was most capable of doing and these strengths were properly coordinated and used to the utmost.

9. ST. MARY'S HOSPITAL AT ROCHESTER, MINNESOTA

As seen from Figure 2.3(9) this project was completed 16 months behind original schedule. The 16-month delay can be attributed to geological problems, late design changes, and complicating factors such as material shortages, labor shortages and severe weather. This case study shows that, through the application CM methods and techniques, the delays were minimized and the project was kept within its original budget of $53.1 million. See Figure 2.3(9). For the project size and organization information, see Figure 2.2(8). One weakness of this project is that the CM was brought in at the end of the schematic design phase. For this reason, the closer coordination of design concepts and construction planning as well as earlier development of consistent systems for tracking cost and schedules were missing.

2.9   AVOIDABLE PITFALLS AND DESIRABLE OBJECTIVES OF CONSTRUCTION MANAGEMENT

2.9.1   Avoidable Pitfalls of Construction Management

The following are the potential pitfalls of the CM process. Some of these pitfalls are avoidable shortcomings of the CM format used and the personal attributes or incapabilities of the CM firm personnel involved in the project.

1. The CM is an addition to the traditional three-party team of owner, A-E, and the contractor(s). The owner therefore incurs additional fees over and above that paid to the A-E, and the contractor(s), for the services of the CM firm. However, considering the potential benefits of the CM to the owner, the additional fees paid may be a worthwhile investment.

2. Because each contractor has a prime contract with the owner, any bonding requirement is the responsibility of the individual contractor. Since many specialty contractors have weak finances, it may be difficult for some of them to procure surety bonds if required by the owner. Thus some competent contractors may not be able to bid on the project, and less contractor competition may result in less competitive prices for bid packages.

3. The construction manager's lack of direct contract relationship with the separate prime contractors reduces his potential authority in making the contractors perform to the owner's best advantage.

4. It is difficult to organize, coordinate, and control multi-prime contractors on "phase" or "fast-track" contracts. Some of the problems associated with these contracts are (a) the difficulty of clearly defining who is responsible for what in overlapping trades, (b) the difficulty of the specialty contractors assuming the more demanding role or responsibility attendant to prime contracting, and (c) the difficulty of going through the tedious, expensive, and time-consuming process of negotiating with a bonding company to obtain relief for a defaulted contractor.

5. The CM firm has limited liability as to the project cost and time; unless the firm is financially involved or there is a guaranteed maximum price contract, it is not liable to any delays or cost overruns.

6. The leadership and management capabilities of the CM personnel will influence the relationship among participants and also the effectiveness and efficiency of the CM process. An authoritarian individual may not benefit the teamwork concept of the system, but neither will a weak, democratic person be effective in the long run.

7. Selection of the CM on the basis of price. This is dangerous because an unqualified and job-hungry CM can offer a price too good for an owner to pass up and then fail to perform efficiently.

2.9.2   Desirable Objectives of Construction Management

The main benefits of the CM process are only realized by the project owner if the project is completed on schedule and at minimum costs. The growth in the use of CM contracts validates the efficacy of the system. Other benefits of the CM process are as follows:

1. The CM process allows a system approach to project management. By being involved in the project from inception to completion, the CM firm is in a position to interrelate and control all the relevant variables that influence cost, time, and quality of the project.

2. The CM process enables the construction manager to contribute his construction knowledge early in the design phase. He performs value analysis and life-cycle cost analysis to ensure optimal design of the project regarding cost, time, and quality.

3. The construction manager by his everyday involvement in the construction industry has better access to cost information than most A-Es. He is, therefore, in a better position to make dependable preconstruction estimates. This will improve project designs, prevent delays as a result of duplications and project letting iterations as a result of bid overruns.

4. The CM firm offers the owner an independent, objective manager working on his behalf to provide a single integrated management for the entire project. The CM's management skills complement both the A-E's design skills and the contractor's construction skills to procure optimal design and construction. This also assures the owner that he will receive an information base for decision making that is truly multi-disciplined and objective in outlook.

5. The CM process has the potential to minimize the project owner's time commitment and need for an in-house staff necessary to make some decisions pertaining to the project. When adequate trust exists, the construction manager should be able to make most decisions for the owner once the scope and the budget of the project are established. The CM firm can handle functions such as project planning, change orders, the selection of contractors, financing, and monitoring owner's cash. The CM can be structured to enable the owner just as much involvement as he prefers or needs because construction management contracts allow this flexibility.

6. The CM firm's knowledge of the construction industry enables a better execution of owner-purchased materials than in the non-CM process. This offsets the consequences of material shortages, lengthy project delays, or escalating material costs resulting in escalated project costs. The CM is expected to know and forecast the availability and cost of materials before the contract to install them is awarded. Thus long-lead items can be purchased early and expedited so that they get to the site when required.

7. The CM approach enables project team members to concentrate on functions and responsibilities that they could perform most. The reduction of the A-E's involvement in project estimating and contract administration offers potential reduction of A-E fees.

8. The CM contract offers potential reduction in the contractor's overhead through the elimination of the general contractor. This also increases fairness in competitive bidding by specialty contractors because they can bid directly as prime contractors, thus eliminating bid shopping, auctioning, and other unethical practices some general contractors adopt in selecting subcontractors.

9. Competitive bidding on all systems by contractors in the CM contract gives the project owner the opportunity to oversee bidding processes and select the best bidder. He will also accrue the potential savings from competitive bidding.

10. The direct prime relationship in the CM contracts enhances the contractor's early receipt of progress payment and owner-held retainer.

11. The CM process has the potential to reduce or eliminate adversary relationships that characterize the non-CM process. By emphasizing teamwork the CM process encourages the project participants to work with, rather than against, each other, thus creating a harmonious team.

12. The use of separate owner-contractor contracts in the CM process facilitates the phasing of design and construction. It is feasible for the project owner to receive bids and performance from some of the early phase contractors, for example, excavation, foundations, before later types of construction are designed. This overlapping of design, bid, and construction often results in considerable reduction in total project time, thus reducing the impact of inflation on total project costs.

2.10   FUTURE OF CONSTRUCTION MANAGEMENT

The future of construction management appears to be one of growth and determined direction. An analysis of the firms providing CM services during the 1971–1976 period by Parviz Rad and Marvin Miller (Rad, 116:515-524) concluded that the use of CM services is growing throughout the construction industry. Their analysis showed that the number of firms providing CM services is greater among all design firms, 50% of the firms surveyed then, than among all contractor firms, 28% of the firms. This trend will continue. Considering the number of management courses and programs that have been introduced in both architectural and engineering schools in recent years, it is obvious that design professionals are aware of the shortcomings in their predominantly technical education in coping with the emerging situations in the industry. Likewise, there has been proliferation in the degree programs, as well as continuing education in construction engineering and management all over the country. The potential constructors are receiving more management training, and the contractors are also learning and adopting modern management techniques to maintain their leadership role in the industry.

Construction management evolved primarily to provide the type of management necessary to unify the design and construction phases of the project, and to coordinate and communicate the entire project. The CM process emerged at the right time to stimulate the awareness of the design professionals and the contractors to the pressing concern of the project owners for better control of cost and time. The CM process allows the owner to be more participative in the construction process through his agent, the construction manager.

With the present increase in construction management education for both design professionals and the contractors, it is probable that the services now being offered by the CM firms may eventually be incorporated partly into design services and partly into construction contract functions. However, the project owners may still require the services of a CM to coordinate the entire process.

The recently formed organization of construction management firms—Construction Management Association of America (CMAA)—has a great potential of becoming the regulatory body for construction management practice in the country. This may build construction management services into a formidable professional service, as well as resolve some of the ambiguities plaguing the system. It is likely that the CMAA will be successful in establishing itself as a legitimate body and that eventually most states will follow the paths of Indiana and South Carolina. With this growth, perhaps, will come the control of licensing by the individual state boards.

2.11   SUMMARY

Construction management has been highly praised and widely accepted as a breakthrough in the history of construction, but it is really not a new discovery. It is a mixture of techniques and procedures, dating back to antiquity (its earliest ancestor being the "master builder" of ancient Egypt, or later, in the Middle Ages, cathedral builders), that have been fused together under the pressure of the present construction crisis. What is new about construction management is the speed with which it is taking hold in many areas where it was not thought possible in the past. The catalyst for this rapid change or fusion is the owner's determination to force the construction industry to regard its highly fragmented series of decisions and events as a single process. Such government agencies as GSA and HEW, on finding that the traditional design-bid-construct system was becoming impractical in the rapidly escalating, highly complex, and costly construction market, led the "attack" for a new and better system of construction.

A major problem with construction management seems to be in defining the term itself, which means different things to different people. However, it is agreed by almost everybody that the concept centers on involving a construction manager as the owner's agent and manager of the entire planning-design-construction process of the project. It is also accepted that the raison d'être of the CM process is to minimize the cost and time of a construction project while maximizing or maintaining its quality.

The construction manager should be selected on the basis of his experience and qualifications, not his price, to provide technical and business services and judgment. He must be paid a professional fee commensurate with the project's complexity, time of construction, and scope of services.

The construction manager's role is demanding and all-encompassing. His functions can begin with a feasibility study to determine whether a job should ever be started, continue through complex design and construction phases, and end with the keys of the facility being handed over to the owner. Along the route he administers salaries and copes with financial, legal, and procurement problems, as well as labor relations. He coordinates engineering and design, works with the architect, and helps choose contractors. Above all, he has to control time, quality, and cost. He carries out these assignments as the owner's representative, concerned with the owner's interests at all times.

Creation and development of the project team are the responsibilities of the owner. His full-time involvement in the management of the project is a must since he has the only and the final say in all matters on the job. Under the construction management system, the owner has to set his priorities and establish his goals as early as possible.

The appearance of the CM into the project team has affected the normal A-E roles and facilitated his functions. The A-E is still in charge of all matters concerning actual design and engineering, but he has been relieved of his on-site reviewing and supervision services by the CM.

There are many organizations now entering the construction management field. He who develops the necessary skills to meet the challenge of today's costly and complex projects wins. He can be the architect, the construction contractor, the professional quantity surveyor, CPM firm, or the design engineering professional. He must have (a) construction process knowledge, (b) knowledge of the design process, and (c) knowledge of general project management.

The construction management system, now enjoying expanded publicity, has been with us for many years and is here to stay. It will encroach upon but not eliminate the domain of the general contractor. It does provide an alternative method of contracting that can be more effective on large and complex projects. It has many benefits that are not normally available in the traditional design-bid-construct process.

It seems likely that the future of construction management will be characterized by diversity of experimental application, which will lend it to more acceptance. Some notable success will be achieved, and many owners will be encouraged to expand and intensify the applications of the concept.

3

Other Emerging Management Approaches to Project Design and Construction

3.1 INTRODUCTION

Since the early 1970s there has been development and an increased awareness of the need to improve the management of design, engineering, and construction of projects. Costly time, budget overruns, and inadequate quality control have become prevalent and major concerns for the construction industry. The special nature of the industry itself contributes to the inherent management complexities associated with project planning, design or engineering, and construction. As a result, many varied management roles have emerged to deal with these complexities.

This chapter deals with these emerging management roles and focuses attention on successful management approaches. How to keep construction projects within budget and on time is the underlying theme of these emerging management approaches, in addition to addressing the professional approach to management—its development and application in practice. Although there are many types of contracts and organizational arrangements, these techniques and approaches can be roughly classified, into six main processes: traditional, construction management, modified traditional, project management, engineering management, and program management. Since the first two processes have already been discussed in the previous chapters, only the last four will be discussed here. Each process has advantages and disadvantages, and it is important to understand under what circumstances each process should be used.

3.2 MODIFIED TRADITIONAL PROCESS

3.2.1 Concepts

As mentioned in Chapter 1, the traditional process of project delivery suffers from a number of deficiencies. These include vague divisions of responsibility, no overall management and coordination, artificial separation of design and construction, manufacturers remote from the facility procurement process, and so forth. To overcome these obvious deficiencies of the traditional process, a variety of modified versions of the traditional process have been developed (see Fig. 3.1). With all these approaches, the owner still secures the "design" through a contract with a professional design consultant and the "construction" through a contract with a general contractor. However, the modified approach differs from the traditional approach in the following areas:

1. PROJECT DEFINITION   With the modified process, the design documentation need not have been completed and the contract can be awarded on the basis of the schematic drawings and general specifications.

2. OPEN COMPETITION   With the modified process, there is not necessarily open competition and the number of contractors allowed to bid on a project can be limited by prequalification or by invitation. If necessary, a contract is simply negotiated between the owner and the selected contractor.

3. FIXED PRICE   With the modified approach, there is not normally a fixed price and the final contract sum can vary either within agreed limits or according to an agreed set of conditions.

It should be noted that the modified traditional process can include the "cost-reimbursable contracts" such as "cost plus" contracts tied to a fixed or sliding scale of fees, and a target price contract with penalty and bonus clauses designed to encourage the completion of the facility within budget, quality, and time restraints. It is these forms of the modified traditional process that have been further developed and have evolved into the construction management process.

Contract Form, Project Definition (PD)	Primary Advantages	Primary Disadvantages	Typical Applications	Comments
LUMP SUM BASED ON DEFINITIVE SPECIFICATIONS PD: General specifications, design, drawings, and layout—all complete.	1. Usually results in maximum construction efficiency. 2. Detailed project definition assures client of desired quality.	1. Separate design and construction contracts increase overall project schedule. 2. Noncompetitive design may result in use of over-conservative design basis. 3. Responsibility is divided between designer and constructor.	Where client solicits construction bids on a distinctive building designed by an architectural firm, or where a federal government bureau solicits construction bids on project designed by an outside firm.	Clients are cautioned against use of this type of contract if project is not well defined.
LUMP SUM, BASED ON PRELIMINARY SPECIFICATIONS PD: Complete general specifications, preliminary layout, and well-defined design.	1. Competitive engineering design often results in cost-reducing features. 2. Reduces overall project time by overlapping design and construction. 3. Single-party responsibility leads to efficient project execution. 4. Allows contractor to increase profit by superior performance.	1. Contractor's proposal cost is high. 2. Fixed price is based on preliminary drawings. 3. Contract and proposal require careful and lengthy client review.	1. Turn-key contract to design and construct fertilizer plant. 2. Turn-key contract to design and construct foreign power-generation plant.	1. Bids should be solicited only from contractors experienced in a particular field. 2. Client should review project team proposed by contractor.

Figure 3.1. Chart Showing Modified Forms of the Traditional Process.

Contract Form, Project Definition (PD)	Primary Advantages	Primary Disadvantages	Typical Applications	Comments
UNIT-PRICE CONTRACTS, FLAT RATE PD: Scope of work well defined qualitatively, with approximate quantity known.	1. Construction work can commence without knowing exact quantities involved. 2. Reimbursement terms are clearly defined.	1. Large quantity-estimate errors may result in client's paying unnecessarily high unit costs or contract extra. 2. Extensive client field supervision is required to measure installed quantities.	1. Gas-transmission piping project. 2. Highway building. 3. Insulation work in process plants.	Contractor should define the methods of field measurement before the contract is awarded.
UNIT-PRICE CONTRACTS, SLIDING RATE PD: Scope of work well defined qualitatively.	1. Construction work can commence without knowing quantity requirements. 2. Reimbursement terms are clearly defined.	Extensive client field supervision is required to measure installed quantities.	1. Gas transmission piping project. 2. Highway building. 3. Insulation work in process plants.	Contractor should clearly define the methods of field measurement before the contract is awarded.
CONVERTIBLE CONTRACTS PD: Variable; depends on type of contract conversion.	1. Design work can commence without delay of soliciting competitive bids. 2. Construction price is fixed at time of contract conversion, when project is reasonably well defined. 3. Overall design and construction schedule is minimum, with reasonable cost.	1. Design may not be optimum. 2. Difficult to obtain competitive bids, since other contractors are reluctant to bid against contractor who performed design work.	1. Where client has confidential project requiring a balance of minimum project-time with reasonable cost. 2. Where client selects particular contractor based on superior past performance.	Contractors selected on this basis should be well known to client.

54

TIME AND MATERIALS PD: General scope of project.	1. Client may exercise close control over contractor's execution methods. 2. Contractor is assured reasonable profit. 3. Reimbursement terms are clearly defined.	1. Project cost may not be minimized. 2. Extensive client supervision is required.	Management engineering services supplied by consulting engineering firm.	Eliminates lengthy scope-definition and proposal-preparation time.
BONUS/PENALTY OPERATION AND PERFORMANCE PD: Variable, depending on other aspects of contract.	Directs contractor's peak performance toward area of particular importance to client.	1. Application of penalty under certain conditions may result in considerable loss to contractor. 2. Difficult to obtain exact operating conditions needed to verify performance guarantee.	Where client desires maximum production of a particular by-product in a new process plant, to meet market requirements.	Power to apply penalties should not be used lightly.
BONUS/PENALTY, TIME AND COMPLETION PD: Variable, depending on other aspects of contract.	1. Extreme pressure is exerted on contractor to complete project ahead of schedule. 2. Under carefully controlled conditions, will result in minimum design and construction time.	1. Defining the cause for delays during project execution may involve considerable discussion and disagreement between client and contractor. 2. Application of penalty under certain conditions may result in considerable loss to contractor. 3. Pressure for early completion may result in lower quality of work.	Usually applied to lump-sum contracts where completion of project is absolute necessity to client in order to fulfill customer commitments.	1. Project execution should be carefully documented to minimize disagreements on reasons for delay. 2. The power to apply penalties should not be used lightly; maximum penalty should not exceed total expected contractor profit.

Figure 3.1. (*continued*)

55

Contract Form, Project Definition (PD)	Primary Advantages	Primary Disadvantages	Typical Applications	Comments
COST-PLUS WITH GUARANTEED MAXIMUM AND PROVISION FOR ESCALATION PD: General specifications and preliminary layout drawings.	1. Maximum price is established without preparation of detailed design drawings. 2. Client retains option to approve all major project decisions. 3. Protects contractor against inflationary periods.	1. Contractor has little incentive to reduce cost. 2. Contractor's fee and contingency is relatively higher than other fixed-price contracts, because price is fixed on preliminary design data. 3. Client must exercise tight cost control over project expenditures.	1. Project involving financing in semi-industrialized countries. 2. Projects requiring long time schedules.	1. Escalation cost-reimbursement terms should be based on recognized industrial index. 2. Escalation clause should be negotiated prior to contract signing.
COST-PLUS WITH GUARANTEED MAXIMUM AND INCENTIVE PD: General specifications and preliminary layout drawings.	1. Maximum price is established without preparation of detailed design drawings. 2. Client retains option to approve all major project decisions. 3. Contractor has incentive to improve performance since he shares in savings.	Contractor's fee and contingency is relatively higher than other fixed-price contracts, because price is fixed on preliminary design data.	Where client desires fast time schedule with a guaranteed limit on maximum cost, and assurance that the contractor will be motivated to try for cost savings.	Incentive may be provided to optimize features other than capital cost—e.g., operating cost.

| COST-PLUS WITH GUARANTEED MAXIMUM
PD: General specifications and preliminary layout drawings. | 1. Maximum price is established without preparation of detailed design drawings.
2. Client retains option to approve all major project decisions.
3. All savings under maximum price remain with client. | 1. Contractor has little incentive to reduce cost.
2. Contractor's fee and contingency is relatively higher than for other fixed-price contracts, because price is fixed on preliminary design data.
3. Client must exercise tight cost control over project expenditures. | Where client desires fast time schedule with a guaranteed limit on maximum project cost. |
| COST-PLUS
PD: Minimal. (Scope of work does not have to be clearly defined.) | 1. Eliminates detailed scope-definition and proposal-preparation time.
2. Eliminates costly extra negotiations if many changes are contemplated.
3. Allows client complete flexibility to supervise design and construction. | 1. Client must exercise tight cost control over project expenditures.
2. Project cost is usually not optimized. | 1. Major revamping of existing facilities.
2. Development projects where technology is not well defined.
3. Confidential projects where minimum industry exposure is desired.
4. Projects where minimum time schedule is critical.

Cost-plus contracts should be used only where client has sufficient engineering staff to supervise work. |

(SOURCE: Project Management Seminar, Department of Public Works, Canada.)

Figure 3.1. (*continued*)

The modified traditional process encompasses many different options (see Fig. 3.1). Depending on the needs of the owner, the traditional process can be modified to stress the priorities of the owner concerning cost, time, quality, and risk. Thus the modified traditional process examines how to overcome some of the drawbacks of the traditional process without making any major organizational modifications and, in particular, without doing away with the role of the independent designer. The key identifiable issues are:

1. Information and communication
2. Quality assurance and responsibility and
3. Standardization of components in the facility

3.2.2   Information and Communication

With the traditional process, there is no overall management and coordination of the planning-design-construction process; therefore, communication between the independent organizations involved becomes all-important. While much effort has been expended in rationalizing the production of specific items of information (e.g., computer-based specifications), communications overall in the construction industry are very inefficient. Usually, the same item of information has to be generated several times by different organizations during the planning-design-construction process. This is particularly true of information required for the estimating and ordering of material and products. In order to develop a more rational flow of information, a more detailed knowledge of the information needs of the different project participants is required. Perhaps the computer is the key to improved communications. If a system of data coordination were introduced on an industry-wide scale, it would be possible to set up a data file for each project, with the various participants contributing and drawing information and instruction as and when required. The computer can be used to integrate the independent organizations of the facility planning, design, and construction processes.

Because the construction industry is made up of a large number of small organizations that cannot afford to develop extensive libraries or data banks, a number of centralized information services can be developed. These should include data banks concerning life-cycle costs, construction costs, labor productivity, man and environment factors, product information, and so forth. Although the setting up of centralized data banks is probably a good idea, and in the long run these services may save money, there is the problem of who is initially going to fund the setting up of the information services. The funding question has two aspects: (1) Who is going to pay to set up the operations? and (2) Who is going to pay for the service (e.g., production, distribution, receipt, storage, and "dissemination of information") once the system is operational? There is no solution to the funding question, and some formal government assistance will probably be required.

3.2.3 Quality Assurance and Responsibility

With craft construction, the independent design professional, usually the architect or engineer, has been responsible for quality assurance. Quality assurance means that the independent design professional is responsible for both guaranteeing that the quality specified is adequate and for ensuring that the final facility will be produced according to the stated specifications. The present trend toward industrialization is putting severe strains on the century-old routines of quality assurance. Because of the nature of industrialized facilities (e.g., buildings), the architect or engineer simply selects products produced by the various manufacturers, instead of specifying the quality standards required. The architect or engineer is still, however, responsible for guaranteeing that the quality of those products is adequate. With more and more complex products coming on the market, this task is becoming increasingly difficult, and in many cases, the architect or engineer simply does not have the expertise or the necessary information to make these judgments.

The independent design professional's role of quality assurance is duplicated in part by the public sector's role of facility and product approval. The public's interest in health and safety is protected by means of a set of regulations and codes that prescribe acceptable methods of facility construction. Legally, however, the public sector is not reliable if the quality of the facility or project proves in practice to be inadequate.

In carrying out its role of facility approval, the public sector faces the same problem as the design professionals. With craft construction, it is the responsibility of the local facility inspector to inspect the work on site. However, where a large proportion of a facility is produced in a factory, the situation is much more complex. It is impossible for the local facility inspector to inspect all the industrialized products being manufactured, in many cases hundreds of miles away from his area of local jurisdiction. In these cases, the quality of the product is either guaranteed through the use of industry-wide standards or, for more unconventional products, through certification by an independent testing agency. The certification agency both tests the quality of a typical product and inspects the quality control procedures set up in the factory to make sure that the manufacturing firm is capable of producing quality products on a continuing basis.

The second aspect of quality assurance, ensuring that the facility is produced according to specifications (i.e., quality control), has traditionally been the architect's or engineer's responsibility. The architect or engineer was responsible, and in some states still is, for supervising construction on site. Once the architect or engineer has accepted that the facility is built according to the plans and specifications, he accepts total liability.

3.2.4   Standardization of Components

One facet of the industrialization of the construction process is the increasing use of factory-made components. This is seen as a way of reducing the incidence of manual site "work" operations, replacing them with easy site "assembly" operations. As long as some of the components are designed specifically for each project, the responsibility for ensuring that they will fit together rests with the individual project designer, who is able to make the appropriate decisions. However, only the largest projects are able to command a sufficient number of these special components to allow efficient industrial production methods to be used for their manufacture, and only the largest projects, therefore, allow for the special developments of effective labor-saving assembly routines. Consequently, an increasing emphasis is being placed on the use of standard components, which, it is hoped, can be produced industrially without being limited to the requirement of any one project or being dependent upon one project for their market. However, because they are not designed for any specific project, particular arrangements must be made to ensure that they are technically compatible, that is, that they will fit together.

In order to create a situation where factory-finished, standard components designed and manufactured by separate manufacturers are selected by independent designers for individual projects, there is a need to introduce some degree of standardization. These standard conventions, if widely accepted, would mean that it would be possible for project components that are chosen ex-catalog from different manufacturers to be compatible and thus able to be fitted together next to each other. The rules of compatibility would cover such aspects as coordination of dimensions and tolerances, joints and jointing, and on-site assembly prerequisites.

3.3   PROJECT MANAGEMENT[1]

3.3.1   Definition and Background

Project management is generally defined as an organization form, using the dual reporting relationship of a matrix structure. It is used on finite duration projects where dual focal points of equal importance are required. On engineering and construction projects, this dual focus results from

---

1. This section was based on the reference by Scarola (121:318–325).

concurrent emphasis on project cost and schedule along with such technical requirements as engineering, design, procurement, and construction. Personnel assigned or matrixed to the project report to the project manager regarding work priorities and to a functional manager in the firm regarding technical adequacy of the work.

The project management system was initially applied to the aerospace industry where the dual emphasis of successful project completion and technical excellence was intense. On these multi-billion dollar projects, strong overall leadership is essential for successful project completion. Because of the extreme technical complexity of the tasks being performed, strong engineering leadership in each of the specific technical activities is also necessary. The matrix structure therefore evolved to satisfy these dual needs.

The project management approach has been utilized on various types of projects. These have included such fields as defense, aerospace, pharmaceuticals, and engineering-construction. In each of these areas the matrix structure has been necessary because of the simultaneous technical and management challenges implicit in the major project task. The diversity of successful application, to complete both large and small projects, illustrates the ability of this structure to produce results when properly implemented.

With the increased number and types of large engineering and construction projects that are being planned, it is anticipated that the project management form will find further application in the future. Previously, large construction projects were concentrated in the industrial segment. Current requirements for a strengthened national defense, expanded mass transportation, urban renewal, reindustrialization, and expanded energy supply all create demands for large projects. Although individual firms vary, the functional structures from which project personnel are matrixed, organizational forms for specific projects have remained relatively constant. Because of the unique and complex requirements of these projects, and despite the difficulties of the matrix structure, no acceptable alternate form of organization is currently apparent. The need to manage interfaces is a prerequisite to schedule and cost adherence, and matrix structure satisfies this need.

The Project Management Institute (PMI) was formed in 1968 to serve as a forum for transfer of experience in the use of this organization structure. Its membership, which represents several segments of industrial activity, reflects the diverse applications of this process. At PMI's annual meetings, papers are presented concerning both project management organization theory as well as its practical application. Through an expanding system of local chapters, PMI has conducted frequent meetings on project management topics and has sponsored specialty conferences. Consequently, a large body of literature has been developed by PMI to transfer experience regarding project management. INTERNET, a European counterpart to PMI, was developed in response to an interest in the use of this organization structure in the Common Market countries. In the United States several of the technical societies have also pursued the study of various management processes including project management.

3.3.2   Implementation of Project Management Process

Prior to the development of the project management form, engineering, construction, or engineer-constructor firms were organized on a functional basis. With the increasing scope and complexity of large projects it became apparent that alternate organization forms were needed. The difficulty of communication between the functional departments and the greater involvement of client and external organizations were two key factors forcing this change.

The actions required for implementing a project management system and its likely consequences are (1) Responsibility Assignment, (2) Organizational Transition, (3) Functional Department Acceptance, (4) Project Personnel, (5) Project Manager's Functions and Qualifications, and (6) Necessity and Benefits.

1. RESPONSIBILITY ASSIGNMENT   Under the project management system, the project team is assigned responsibility for project execution within the confines of scope, schedule, budget, and contractual requirements. To assess financial performance, each project is generally established as a profit center with all contributing departments operating as cost centers. To achieve successful project completion, the project manager is assigned the dual responsibility of acting as the client's representative and the engineer-constructor management's representative. This requires fulfilling the contractual obligations on schedule, within budget, and to the satisfaction of the client, while ensuring that the engineer-constructor's interests are fully protected.

The duties and responsibilities normally assigned to the project management department under this structure are

(a) Participation in the early stages of the proposal, contract, and estimate preparation and the subsequent negotiation for contract finalization

(b) Provision of centralized company leadership for execution of all project activities on a continuing basis

(c) Administration of the project contract to ensure performance in accordance with the terms and conditions stated therein

(d) Provision of guidance and leadership to engineering, construction, and control personnel in the development of the project plan

(e) Preparation and updating of the project budget and overall schedule

(f) Development of a system of accounts appropriate for the project and authorization of charges to these accounts by the functional department

(g) Monitoring project cash requirements and cash flow

(h) Maintenance of cost and schedule control for the project by reviewing actual costs and accomplishments compared to the budget and project plan as well as instituting remedial measures when required.

2. ORGANIZATIONAL TRANSITION   The implementation of a project management system in a large engineer-constructor firm is a major change. To realize the benefits of this approach, and to make this transition with the minimum possible disruption, several management actions are essential.

Role definition is critical. This begins with assignment of responsibility and delegation of authority, but it also requires discussion of roles. The project manager's role as leader of the project team must be clearly defined and communicated to both matrixed personnel and their functional department superiors. Similarly, the functional manager's role in providing technical direction within that discipline must also be clearly understood. One means of assisting project and corporate managers in understanding these roles is a thorough discussion of reporting relationships. In general terms, project personnel report to the project manager for work priority, cost, schedule, and client matters, and to the functional departments for technical, administrative, and professional development matters. However, discussion and further definition is necessary for application and complete understanding of these guidelines on each project. It is important to understand that project management must clear interface obstacles so that functional departments can implement their expertise in the most effective manner.

3. FUNCTIONAL DEPARTMENT ACCEPTANCE   The project management system creates difficulties for functional departments because of shifts in responsibility. Selected functions previously assigned to departmental managers during a specific phase of work are shifted to project management. These difficulties can be lessened by the role definition steps described previously, along with monitoring and insisting on resolution of problem areas by management personnel.

Project schedules, budgets, and insufficient project definition can frequently cause conflicts. Individual functional departments may be accustomed to greater flexibility in these areas than is allowed under the project management system. With the responsibility for total costs and schedule, the project manager will have to resolve differences with individual departments to attain proper interfacing and to meet project goals. Also, the departments may have previously operated by direct client contact to report progress and to resolve problem areas. In order to coordinate all discipline activities, overall responsibility in these areas must rest with the project management. Where these differences cannot be resolved at the project level, an established conflict resolution procedure should be utilized. The steps in this process generally include involvement of higher levels of management until resolution is reached. Problem resolution must be timely and should be aimed toward establishing a policy framework that provides guidance concerning project management responsibility to all personnel. For the project team to be effective and build confidence in themselves as well as upper management, involvement of higher levels of management for resolution of problems should be the exception.

4. PROJECT PERSONNEL   Personnel matrixed from the functional departments experience difficulty in compliance with the dual direction. The resultant confusion impedes performance of specific work tasks on the project. There is a tendency toward intense competition for scarce resources between the individual projects within a corporate structure. Project requirements, in all likelihood, will suffer and be subservient to functional priorities. These factors place severe demands on personnel seeking to satisfy both a project manager and a functional supervisor. Project managers also experience difficulty in the setting up of priorities and direction of work activities by personnel from functional departments. With limited participation in performance appraisal and professional development of the technical personnel, the project manager must rely on persuasion and leadership to obtain necessary performance by matrixed personnel.

5. PROJECT MANAGER'S FUNCTIONS AND QUALIFICATIONS   The project manager is the key person in the project team. As the leader of the project team, the project manager represents both the client and the engineer-constructor management. He must meet project cost and schedule objectives while clearing the obstacles for the experts to complete their specialized taks. The project manager interfaces between engineering, construction, and project management. To be effective and successful in these interfaces, he must provide unbiased project leadership. The project manager must also set priorities and make decisions on a project basis. He must recognize the necessity for effective and timely completion of the pieces for successful completion of the whole. In order to make decisions predicated on input from a number of informed sources, he must be open to alternatives. He ensures that the needs of the marketplace are met. At the same time, he must constantly balance day-to-day pressures for production with a complex schedule and with cost considerations. He must be cognizant of the political and social events of his time because they will have an impact on his organization and the project. These functions and responsibilities result in strong managerial challenges and the need for a balanced business and technical capability. A manager, in order to deal with his multiple constituents, must have a well-rounded background. The changing attitudes of society now demand that a manager exhibit an ability to get along with people. Interpersonal skill is a must when a matrix is involved. A project manager must be a listener. A project manager must have business sense.

6. NECESSITY AND BENEFITS   The dual reporting requirements and the need for a precise definition of responsibility make the project management structure a difficult process to implement. However, the complexity and scope of current engineering and construction projects require the use of specialized organization structures for adequate performance.

The technical scope of engineering and construction projects, particularly in the industrial sector, increased substantially during the 1970s. This increased complexity resulted from both the development of technology and the implementation of regulations for environmental protection. Certain types of industrial projects, such as power plants, now require an engineering services effort that is several times greater than for similar size units designed during the late 1960s. In addition to this expanded scope, the technical complexity of certain tasks, such as dynamic analysis of structures or piping systems, has increased significantly. Consequently, technical specialists are required to complete this extremely sophisticated work. Project management plays a vital role by clearing the obstacles for these specialists and by providing the coordination necessary for their work.

Many of the demands created by this process result from the necessity for dual forces and emphasis. Project completion, in accordance with cost, schedule, and other goals, is a key focus of the team's activity. However, satisfaction of increasingly complex requirements in each of the technical disciplines, to assure technical adequacy of the completed product, is of equal importance. Through the matrix structure, the project management system emphasizes these dual focal points. Despite the organization complexity and difficulty of implementation described previously, this approach has met specific needs and has found increased application in managing large engineering and construction projects.

3.3.3   Project Management Relationships

Successful projects require the establishment and maintenance of effective interfaces between design (engineering), construction, and project management.

1. ENGINEERING MANAGEMENT   The relationship between project management and engineering management varies during the major project phases of conceptual engineering, detailed engineering, construction, and start-up. In each of these phases, there is a strong need for a team approach to satisfy both project and technical requirements.

During the conceptual engineering and licensing, the project team must translate the owner's facility requirements into criteria for conceptual definition of the project. This frequently requires extensive client interface to obtain agreement on the basic project or facility parameters. Cost and schedule evaluation of numerous basic alternatives for facility plans is frequently required. Development of the necessary inputs for project licensing also requires extensive efforts by the project team. In many of these early activities, the project manager must represent an unbiased viewpoint to assure that conceptual engineering decisions and licensing commitments are made from an overall project standpoint. Determination of the engineering services scope is another area of active project management or engineering management interface during the early project phases. On heavy industrial projects, examples of the key scope decisions include the extent of rebar detailing, conduit routing, two-inch and under pipes routing and pipe support design, HVAC duct detailing, and instrument tubing routing. In each of these areas, the project manager must determine the optimal scope with respect to overall project cost and schedule, rather than to a specific functional department.

During the detail engineering and procurement phase, the project management interface with the engineering management is concentrated on meeting schedules. This includes procurement of equipment and materials, as well as completion of drawing and specifications. Many problem areas develop, such as delays in the supply of vendor information, which require project management involvement for resolution.

As the project enters the major construction phase, both project management and engineering management emphases must shift to completion of a detailed design and the delivery of materials and equipment in support of the construction schedule. In addition, a priority must be established and resources committed to timely resolution of field problems. These can result from omissions or errors in the detailed design, change in design, or installation errors that require engineering evaluation or redesign.

In the testing, turnover, and start-up phase, project management must assure engineering and construction responsiveness to systems problems and other support requirements. This includes all necessary actions to closeout systems and to incorporate as-built data.

2. CONSTRUCTION MANAGEMENT   The key initial interface between project management and engineering management occurs during preconstruction planning activities. Significant project benefits can result if detailed preconstruction planning is initiated during the conceptual engineering, for it is at this phase that construction input can result in the greatest cost and schedule savings. Project management should insist on this construction involvement and should assure that this input is fully evaluated. At times the project manager will be required to resolve conflicts between engineering and construction regarding this input. A key note is assurance that important decisions in the conceptual engineering are made on a project priority basis and, as necessary, have client input on a timely basis.

During construction, project management should maintain an active interface with this phase of work. This involves monitoring overall progress and assuring the adequacy of all parties' support for the project needs. It is also necessary for project management to support construction programs with the owner.

3.4   ENGINEERING MANAGEMENT[2]

3.4.1   Definition and Background

Engineering management involves all phases of engineering and design activities, from establishing the concept, planning and packaging the work to be done, determining the schedule, developing the budget, to controlling the project. Engineering management's role includes the overall responsibility for the management of engineering and design activities on specific projects, the identification and development of management skills that are most beneficial for direction of engineering activities, and the development of management capability by individuals with an engineering background. The major element in the engineering management approach is the application of management principles and skills to the completion of large-scale engineering and design activities.

The American Society of Civil Engineers (ASCE) formed an engineering management division in 1978. The division's charge is "increasing the civil engineer's awareness of, and expertise in, applying modern techniques in the effective utilization of engineering personnel and other resources." These tasks are being worked at three levels of technical committee activity, with the following specific charges:

1.   Organizational Level: "investigate and disseminate information which stimulates the development and application of sound management techniques at the organization level."

---

2. This section was based on reference by Yates (146:1–18).

2. Project Level: "application of sound management techniques at the project level."

3. Individual Level: "good practice in matters relating to management at the individual level."

These tasks have been performed by the respective committees through the sponsorship of technical sessions, which include papers on several engineering management subjects. Examples of the topics previously studied include effective management of engineering design, performance appraisal and professional development, engineering organizations, organizing and managing joint ventures and prime or sub ventures, organizational change, and project communications.

These activities by ASCE, along with the work of other professional organizations, from a basis for defining the scope of engineering management. The ASCE Engineering Management Division conducted a specialty conference on the effective management of engineering design in April 1981. Topics covered included managing design activities, communication, conceptual planning, work packages, scheduling and budgeting design activities, control of consulting services to architects, and information systems.

3.4.2   Organization of Engineering Management

Engineering management on a project is concerned with producing high quality engineering output on schedule, within budget, and in accordance with contract obligations. The output consists of studies, specifications for equipment, specifications for construction use, drawings, equipment delivered to the site, regulatory documents, and direct engineering support to construction. The functions that are considered part of engineering management are those needed to lead, direct, coordinate, and control the output as well as to interface with construction, project management, and the client. The personnel involved in engineering management during the peak activity period of a large industrial project, when the technical staffing may number between five hundred and six hundred, is approximately twenty-five. The engineering effort may require three to five years on such projects.

The major steps in organizing the engineering activities on a large project include development of the basic organization structure, definition of scope, preparation of schedules and budgets, assignment of personnel, and preparation of project procedures.

1.   ENGINEERING ORGANIZATION   Figure 3.2 shows a typical project organization chart for a large project. The key management personnel are shown on this figure and include

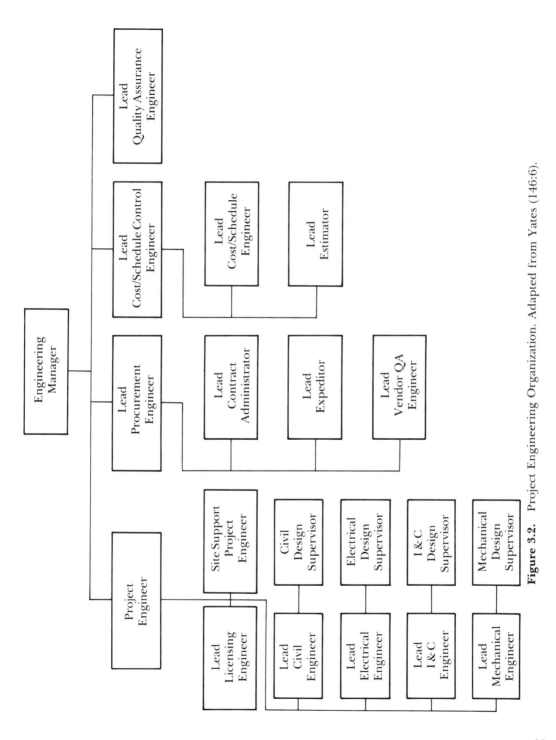

Figure 3.2. Project Engineering Organization. Adapted from Yates (146:6).

69

(a) *Engineering Manager*—Responsible for all aspects of engineering services on the project and interfacing with construction, project management, and the client on engineering matters.

(b) *Project Engineer (PE)*—Responsible for technical leadership, including the scope definition, interdiscipline coordination, and problem resolution.

(c) *Site Support Project Engineer*—Responsible for leading the site engineering group set up to handle routine construction requests for drawing clarification, field changes, and approval of nonconforming conditions. This group operates with authority delegated from home office engineering.

(d) *Lead Discipline Engineers*—Responsible for seeing that their discipline's work is produced on schedule and within budget.

(e) *Lead Procurement Engineer*—Responsible for placement of purchase orders, execution of necessary contract modifications, contract administration, expediting equipment, and coordinating vendor quality assurance activities.

(f) *Lead Cost and Schedule Control Engineer*—Responsible for the engineering schedule and budget development and monitoring as well as the interface with the construction schedule.

(g) *Lead Quality Assurance Engineer*—Responsible for ensuring that QA procedures are followed, review of vendor QA plans, and interface with client QA personnel.

Figure 3.3 illustrates a typical organization structure and defines the relationships between individuals matrixed to a specific project and the remainder of the Architect-Engineer firm. Many such firms utilize a matrix organization in which each functional department is responsible for the technical performance of its personnel, training or personnel development, and providing the proper mix and number of staff to the project. For example, in the engineering disciplines the final specification and drawing approvals are the responsibility of the chief engineers, and the ultimate technical responsibility rests with the vice-president of engineering. This type of organization structure ensures that company standards and reference designs are used and allows good communications between various projects' engineers. The full-time personnel on the project are collected in a project grouping.

2. SCOPE   The first task of engineering management is to define the scope for all services. The contract and preselected major plant components form the basis for this scope definition. In almost all cases, a detailed document is required. It usually takes the form of a project specification, which might consist of one or two three-inch thick volumes

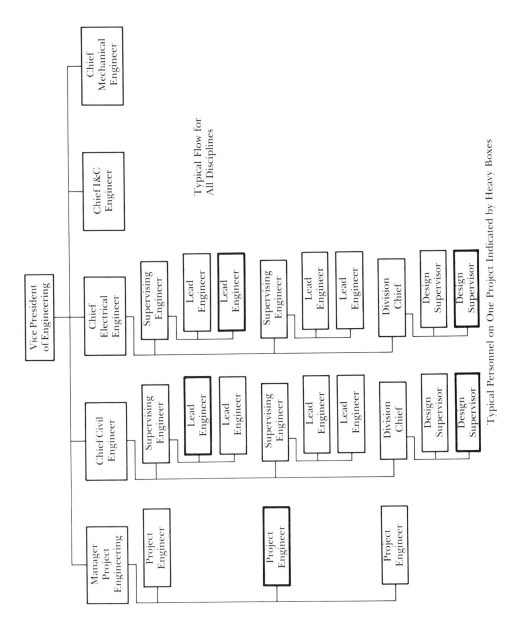

Typical Flow for
All Disciplines

Typical Personnel on One Project Indicated by Heavy Boxes

Figure 3.3. Functional Engineering Organization. Adapted from Yates (146:8).

that outline the scope in considerable detail. This project specification defines the extent of the services, gives key design criteria such as the site conditions and other major assumptions, and discusses the reference plant design and necessary adaptations of it for the project. It also includes the preliminary site and plot plans and general arrangement drawings. The project engineer leads the effort to develop this document, coordinates the input from the lead personnel in each discipline, and approves the final product.

The interface with construction and definition of what will be included in engineering's scope as opposed to construction's or the construction contractor's scope is an important part of this effort. Once construction, project, and client approvals of this document are obtained, the schedule, budget, and staffing levels can be set.

3. PROJECT PLAN   The key schedule dates and budget are usually given in the proposal or contract. The lead cost and schedule control engineer heads the effort to develop the detailed engineering schedule and budget for the project. All other key personnel in engineering participate in this development. The starting point is a generic set of logic diagrams, schedule data, and budget requirements. These are adapted to the project by adjusting them to agree with the scope given in the project specification and with the key schedule dates given in the contract. The initial output is a Level 1 schedule that is developed in conjunction with construction. A typical Level 1 schedule is given in Figure 3.4.

The Level 1 schedule is then broken down to lower schedule levels until it reaches the level of individual studies, drawings, and specifications prepared by the various technical disciplines. Resource loading is applied at this lowest level. Interdiscipline interfaces and vendor data inputs are also added to the schedule. The PE and lead procurement engineer play key roles in ensuring that all disciplines' requirements are included in the schedule and that realistic time periods for procurement and vendor data inputs have been assumed. Also, agreement must be reached with the client on which items require his approval, and the lead times allowed to obtain these approvals must also be set.

The resultant resource loaded schedules are then run on a computer system to identify critical paths and schedule problems. Discipline personnel requirements are also printed out and manpower levelizing is factored in. Once the engineering schedule is debugged, it is again run in conjunction with the construction and start-up schedules and problems resolved. Once this is completed, the engineering schedule is handled as a separate network with a defined envelope in which it can operate, an envelope set by constraints from construction. The schedules are routinely rechecked against each other during the course of the project to flag problems and schedule opportunities.

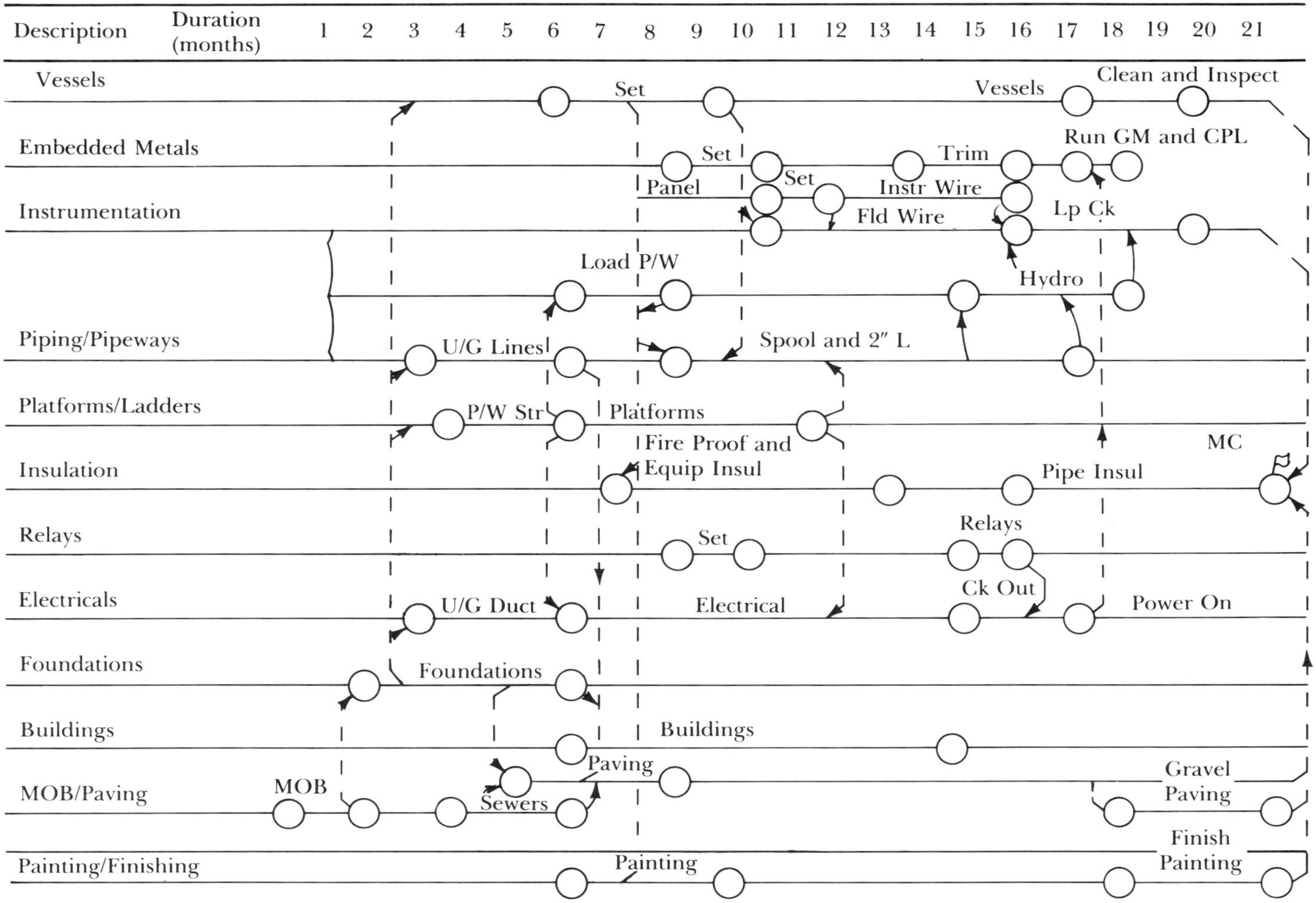

Figure 3.4. Typical Level 1 Refinery Plant Schedule.

73

The schedule that is developed will have different levels of detail at each phase of the project. In the conceptual design stage it will contain a relatively small number of activities compared to those included during the main production phase of the project. It is important that the schedule system used have the flexibility to handle changes in scope and schedule and also be applicable in the closeout phase of the project, when only punch list activities are left for many tasks. Given the complexities available in current computer programs, a prime task of engineering management is to maintain the number of activities so that the schedule is manageable and the transitions between phases of the project are made smoothly, without changeover of systems and the retraining of personnel to use new schedule tools. It is important to keep in mind that the desired output of the engineering effort is not a perfect computerized network including every task on the project, but rather the drawings, specifications, and equipment.

The final schedule and resources loading form the basis for the earned value system used for monitoring as well as for the budget, to which only out-of-pocket expenses, overheads, and other costs must be added. Also, the staffing levels required of each discipline are specified throughout the life of a project by the resource loaded schedule. The functional departments are responsible to staff these levels with the proper mix of experienced personnel. Engineering management must review and agree with the experience levels and mix and approve the appointment of the lead personnel.

Also, engineering management is responsible for the layout of the project grouping to assure that disciplines who work closely together are seated together. This grouping is a dynamic arrangement that changes throughout the life of the project as the staffing levels grow and shrink. One common problem on engineering jobs of the magnitude discussed here is the turnover of personnel. This will occur due to promotions, transfers, and resignations. A well-run project and closely knit team are the best defenses against voluntary turnovers. The best means to ensure that turnovers do not disrupt the job is a well-planned project with scope, schedule, budget, and procedures completely defined.

4. PROJECT PROCEDURES   The key procedures that are required for engineering are those covering calculations, specification and drawing preparation, review and sign-off, and configuration control. Those required for procurement are ones covering request for proposal preparation, bid evaluations, the handling of vendor data, and contract modifications. Finally, overall procedures on scope and schedule changes, as well as engineering cost accounting, are necessary.

The procedures to be used on a project are the company procedures adapted to fit the project. In order to keep operations across projects uniform, it is desirable to do as little adaptation as possible, and management must resist its own and the client's impulses to rewrite them continually. Also, care must be taken not to develop procedures to control lower and lower levels of detail, thus make operation of the project and completion of the design difficult. However, a good set of procedures is essential to maintain the consistency and high quality of the engineering product, serve as training aids for new engineers, and regulate commercial matters between the engineers and vendors. These procedures also set up the guidelines that are used to control the project.

3.4.3   Direction of Engineering Operations

Engineering management's role in the direction of the project consists of leading the engineering and design effort, coordinating the discipline and vendor interfaces within engineering and external coordination with construction, project management, the client, and regulatory agencies.

1. PROJECT LEADERSHIP   Project leadership requires fostering good communications on the project, motivating the engineering and management personnel, and building rapport among the project staff. Good communications among all parties are essential for the project to be successful. These can be fostered by such things as a good physical layout of the engineering project group, well-defined meetings, and good examples set by management. The project personnel must know what is expected of them, when it is due, and what form it is to take. They, too, must be able to express their needs and problems and get results. Open discussion of problems and alternatives is important, and all must understand the rationale for the direction chosen. Face-to-face discussions are preferred to handle problems and their resolution. The tendency to write memoranda should be resisted by engineering management, for this form of communication frequently solves nothing, but simply leads to more correspondence. Also, in large groups, interdisciplinary memoranda writing tends to develop but should be discouraged except for items that need to be documented, such as design criteria or the results of studies.

Project personnel can be motivated by giving high visibility to the progress made on the project, above all, highlighting effective discipline efforts and treating them as professionals. Another important aspect is developing the attitude among the engineering management personnel that their task is to remove obstacles in the way of disciplines. As a result, they can get their work done, additional restraints and requirements are not imposed on them, nor is their work monitored at too fine a level of detail. The disciplines have the responsibility to do the work, and they must be motivated to do a complete job without leaving loose ends or unresolved issues.

There must be a professional rapport between the engineers and managers so that decisions are accepted and implemented. On a large project, the size of the organization creates inertia, and therefore the attitudes of personnel are important to effect changes in direction. One way to build rapport is to seek recommended solutions to a problem from the affected groups and lead the groups to a consensus. One test of a good manager is his ability to lead the group to a decision that is accepted by all. He must be able to bring out alternatives so that the best solution for the project has been found. Given finite time and dollar resources, the timing of such decision making is crucial, and the focus must be kept on the problem and converge on the solution. Another way to build rapport on the project is through team-building sessions, usually held off the business premises, where key team personnel discuss the operation of the project, areas that are working well, as well as those that are not working well. The staff of the personnel department lead these sessions, and the open discussions and interchange they bring about often lead to better communications and ways of operating on the project. These sessions are also useful in broadening the often narrow approach of individual disciplines and developing in them an appreciation of the other discipline needs and method of operations.

2. COORDINATING DISCIPLINE AND VENDOR INTERFACES   Coordination of the interfaces involves both written material and the physical plant design. The key written items, such as design criteria or calculations required between disciplines and interface requirements from vendors, are included in the schedule network. These items are highly visible and are usually taken care of in the course of business with not much more than oversight required from engineering management. However, there are always items required that are not spelled out in the schedule, and there is the potential of misunderstanding the items that are scheduled. Normal communications between disciplines such as routine specification reviews will take care of most of the items. An effective way for engineering management to ensure that communication is open and proceeding is to hold periodic reviews on a system or design where open items are discussed and discipline needs and commitments reaffirmed. The working tool for this type of meeting is the list of open items from the schedule system plus other applicable punch lists. Once construction has started, these meetings involve construction personnel also. In addition to regular interface meetings, the project engineer and other lead project personnel, by staying in touch with what is happening on the project, are able to recognize problems as they develop and call people together to resolve them. They are charged with getting timely decisions to allow work to proceed.

Physical interfaces are coordinated through interdiscipline drawing distribution and review along with the use of an engineering model. The schedule plays a crucial role in physical interfaces both in ensuring that vendor drawings are available when needed and in phasing all discipline's work in an area that allows the design to develop in an orderly manner. As with written material, normal interaction between disciplines is relied upon for the development of the design, and periodic interface meetings are used to discuss open items and resolve problems.

A model is an essential element of complex industrial plant design. The most important areas to be modeled include those with a high degree of congestion and a large number of mandatory criteria. These models must include all discipline's equipment and supports, particularly electrical tray and conduit, piping, HVAC, and plumbing. A scale of ½ inch to 1 foot or larger is required to do adequate interference checking. Given the complexity of the design, it is virtually impossible to produce an interference-free design without a model for these key areas of the plant. The model is also useful for construction planning and work sequencing.

3. CONSTRUCTION MANAGEMENT INTERFACE   The engineering manager has an extremely important interface with the construction manager. In implementing project priorities, the professional engineering manager will at times need to alter normal work sequences or specific design details to support construction requirements. Key elements of communication at this interface include status of work as compared to both the engineering and the construction schedule, impending changes, and problem areas. Early warning of possible impacts can frequently allow mitigation by alternate design approaches or construction work-arounds. Provision for and response to construction input to the design is another important element of this interface. If construction management personnel are assigned to the project at an early date, valuable input to the design can be developed early enough to allow its incorporation. This information concerns construction methods, techniques, sequences, and schedules. Therefore, this input can have a significant impact on the design process.

These key interfaces and responsibilities establish the environment and basic performance requirements for the engineering manager. A good initial schedule is a prime requirement for coordination with construction. Once construction is under way, interface meetings are necessary to discuss the current schedule, potential work-around or changes, the status of the design, and key design or vendor problems. Engineering management should encourage direct contact at the lead engineer level and above, as well as routine visits of engineers to the site and construction personnel to the home office. Also, it is important that site needs' lists be set up that emphasize requirements among the scheduled items or delineate items that are levels of detail below those on the schedule. Weekly critical item conference calls are also an important part of management of the interface between the groups.

Given the costs incurred through delay of construction activities, a sense of urgency must be developed in the home office for handling construction requests. Also, there must be an attitude change in engineering once construction starts. Prior to this time engineering controls most project activities, and the project outputs are drawings completed and equipment delivered. Once the construction phase begins, the project focus shifts and all efforts are aimed at placing concrete or installing pipe or other commodities. The contacts discussed previously are important in bringing about the change in engineering attitude.

4. PROJECT MANAGEMENT INTERFACES   Under the matrix structure frequently used on engineering and construction projects, the engineering manager reports to the project manager. The project direction he receives concerns overall schedules, budgets, and work priorities. The engineering manager, in turn, provides this direction to project engineering, cost and schedule, and procurement personnel. Important communication topics at this interface include project impacts of technical activities or changes, engineering schedule problems and proposed solutions, and work priority definitions.

A key aspect of the project management interface with engineering management is assurance that decisions regarding design activities are made on a project priority basis. The engineering manager should be prepared to expend additional services effort if this investment is cost effective for the project. Providing direction regarding the engineering work scope and schedules that are necessary to support project goals is a critical element of project management responsibility in this interface.

5. COORDINATION WITH THE CLIENT AND REGULATORY AGENCIES   Engineering management is the primary interface with the client, that is, the primary contact, and they must be cognizant of client attitudes, concerns, and desires. One aspect is their ability to obtain timely client decisions where required. Communication will be by telephone, letter, progress report, and meetings. As with construction, lead engineer level contacts and above with the client should be encouraged, subject to the controls discussed in the following section.

The level of reporting is developed in conjunction with client wishes. Management should work to keep the reporting levels high enough so that large amounts of time are not spent writing reports, since it is much more important to keep key engineers working on completing the design. Occasionally, client requests result in the addition of people to the project whose only function is reporting in order to free the engineers to do design work. As with a client, interfaces with regulatory agencies are very important and must begin as soon as a client's desires are known. These interfaces must be cognizant of the regulatory agencies' attitudes, concerns, and requirements. Both informal and formal communications with regulatory agenices are encouraged and are to be documented.

3.4.4   Engineering Control

Engineering management is responsible for control of the engineering scope of work, configuration, budget, and schedule. Also included are control of capital cost and client communications on engineering matters. Major elements necessary for control on a project are well-defined scope and criteria, a detailed schedule and budget, and a system for monitoring and status reporting. A control procedure giving the types of controls in different phases of the project, levels at which controls will be applied, and required approval level is essential.

1.   SCOPE   Controlling the scope of the job is primarily involved with being cognizant of the interactions between engineering, construction, the client, and regulatory agencies. Open communications are encouraged, but engineering personnel must be instructed that scope changes are to be handled per the established procedures. This is essential to ensure that proposed changes are thoroughly evaluated and approved prior to implementation and that the necessary schedule, budget, and capital cost adjustments are made. The same requirements for evaluation and approval exist for state-of-the-art changes developed within the company and company procedure changes. Furthermore, establishing a means of timely response for necessary changes is an important element of scope control procedures.

2.   CONFIGURATION   Configuration control starts at the early stages of a project. The basis for control is a combination of the proposal, the contract, and the applicable reference plant system descriptions, criteria, and arrangements. As designs are developed they are checked against these basic criteria. Significant changes in system descriptions, process-flow diagrams, electrical one-line diagrams, and general arrangement drawings must be reviewed and approved by the appropriate groups. The control requirements become more restrictive as the design progresses until, finally, all physical design changes are controlled after the release of drawings for construction. At this point, construction concurrence is required prior to implementation of a change. However, as most changes are mandatory, the only option usually open to construction is incorporation at this point in time or later, sometimes after start-up.

This type of progressive configuration control allows incorporation of the multitude of minor changes required to accommodate vendor and other discipline data early in the design but severely restricts nonmandatory changes late in the design process. The key engineering management tasks are to see that evaluations are completed and that timely decisions are made. These two conditions are difficult to satisfy simultaneously.

3. BUDGET AND SCHEDULE   In order to control the schedule and budget, they must be monitored. The tools for this monitoring are inherent parts of the scheduling system. These tools focus on deliverable product status, negative and positive slack in the CPM network, and parameters derived from earned value calculations such as schedule and cost performance indices. These latter parameters provide trend analysis that compares workdays spent to complete a particular task to those scheduled to be spent and to those earned for the work done. Nevertheless, there is so much data available that a prime management responsibility is to see that the data is collected and summarized so that the various levels of the organization get the information required and do not get overwhelmed with detailed reports to digest and update.

Details within a discipline are generally left to the lead discipline engineer to monitor. Engineering management personnel should review activities that should have started during a period, interdisciplinary and vendor data input and output, and completion of deliverables. The main emphasis should be on early recognition of problem areas so that action plans can be set up to resolve them. The lead cost and schedule control engineers' personnel look at the status of individual drawings and specifications while the engineering manager monitors overall performance and key problem areas. Good visibility of all aspects of work on the project with open discussion of status, problem areas, and proposed resolution is necessary. It is also important to keep senior management informed of problem areas on the project.

The actual controls to be applied to budget and schedule will depend on the significance of the change or deviation and agreements made with the client. Generally, schedule dates for deliverables, for example, drawings and specifications, as well as interface points with construction are tightly controlled, whereas events under the control of one discipline are not. Budget control points would depend on the magnitude of the proposed change. The types of formal controls generally used concern requests to change the budget or schedule, which are submitted to the engineering management for formal approval, or sign-on/sign-off and transmittal, which are submitted to the project manager/client for approval, if the change is outside the authority level of the engineering manager.

4. CLIENT COMMUNICATION   Informal client communications are encouraged as discussed previously and are expected to be documented through telecon notes or meeting minutes. Formal correspondence is controlled by requiring approvals of the engineering management and the project manager prior to submittal to the client.

3.5 PROGRAM MANAGEMENT[3]

3.5.1 Definition and Concepts

Program management is a proven approach to the implementation of major capital improvements programs (CIPs). Program management is utilized where separate projects are active simultaneously. This approach centralizes the responsibility of design and construction coordination. There are two major benefits to program management: (1) in the long term, it can significantly reduce the overall costs of a CIP; while (2) in the short term, it can relieve a public agency/owner of the burdens of performing a majority of program and project management activities. Generally, private industry maintains the diverse management talent necessary to implement major CIPs, while the public sector does not. This is especially true in the utility and industrial construction industry, where public agencies are not usually staffed to the extent where they can implement and manage major capital improvements programs of the magnitude that may occur only once or twice every twenty years. To provide both the manpower and expertise necessary to cost control a multi-year, multi-million-dollar CIP, many public agencies have turned to and retained experienced engineering consultants to serve as their program managers or program management assistants.

The control of time and money—critical to the success of a major CIP—depends on the availability of accurate and up-to-date information on which management decisions may be based. The public agency/owner launching a major CIP requires the management tools that can provide this information, as well as the expertise with which to use them. The intent of program management is to reduce the implementation time and costs of a capital improvements program by centralizing the responsibility for design and construction coordination with a manager or management team experienced in planning, design, design review, value analysis, construction, contract administration, financial control, and facility start-up and acceptance.

3.5.2 Program Management Forms

There are three alternative forms of program management from which a public agency/owner may choose. First, the public agency/owner may choose to manage its CIP on its own by utilizing in-house staff or expertise to manage the program on its own. This may be referred to as internal program management. Second, an engineering consultant can serve as

---

3. This section is based on reference by Wong (145:29–42).

program manager when the public agency/owner does not have the sufficient in-house staff or expertise to manage the program on its own. Under this approach, design engineers for individual program projects contract directly with the engineering consultant serving as the program manager. With this system, a public agency/owner delegates the authority for coordinating design contracts to an engineering consultant. This approach may be referred to as external program management. Third, the public agency/owner may possess a substantial in-house staff offering certain necessary expertise, but chooses to contract with an engineering consultant to perform the majority of the program and project management duties to complement, rather than overextend, this staff. This approach is referred to as program management assistance.

Figure 3.5 provides a comparison of these three approaches. Figure 3.6 also shows how program management is developed, monitored, coordinated, and implemented. The major advantages shared by external program management and program management assistance may be summarized as follows:

1. Both provide the public agency/owner with proven expertise in managing major CIPs. The engineering consultant is able to anticipate problems common to the implementation of major CIPs before they become insurmountable—and to recommend creative solutions.

2. Both utilize management tools that have been developed and tested and that can be tailored for specific needs with only minor modifications. One tool is a well-designed scheduling system indicating which projects are critical to meeting the overall goals of the program, and which projects do not have to be initiated immediately. Other tools provide strong measures for program cost control. By establishing budgets for the major project elements and tracking these budgets monthly or quarterly, costs on a project can be controlled over time.

3. Both provide close control and coordination of all design and construction firms, including prime engineers, specialty subconsultants, prime construction contractors, and trade subcontractors involved in the various program projects.

4. Both minimize permanent staff requirements on the part of the public agency/owner. Both approaches utilize the expertise of an outside firm's resources, reducing the owner's staffing requirements. An in-house staff can instead be assigned to key areas to provide the owner with the desired degree of control and involvement.

3.5.3 Program Management Tools

As mentioned previously, the program management approaches utilize a variety of management tools to achieve successful program planning and

Figure 3.5. Comparison of Program Management Approaches. Adapted from Wong (145:31).

Roles	Program Management By Owner (Internal)	Program Management Assistance	Program Management (External)
Organizational Form	Owner/Program Manager → Architect-Engineers, Design Contracts, Construction Contractors, Construction Contracts	Owner/Program Manager (Program Assistance) → Architect-Engineers, Design Contracts, Construction Contractors, Construction Contracts	Owner → Program Manager → Architect-Engineers, Construction Contractors
Description	• Individual Firms Contract Directly with Owner • Owner Provides Technical and Administrative Direction Coordination, and Control on a Project-Specific and Program-wide Basis	• Individual Firms Contract Directly with Owner • Program Manager Assists the Owner in Providing Technical and Administrative Direction, Coordination, and Control on a Program-wide Basis • Program Manager Does Not Direct the Activities of the Individual Firms • Owner Provides Overview of Design and Construction Firms and of Program Manager Activities	• Individual Design Firms Contract Directly with Program Manager • Individual Construction Firms Contract Directly with Construction Manager or with Owner • Program Manager Provides Technical and Administrative Direction, Coordination, and Control on a Program-wide Basis • Program Manager Directs Activities of the Individual Design Firms • Owner Provides Overview of Program Manager Activities
Technical Quality	Variable	• Good – Excellent Project-Specific • Excellent Program-wide	• Good – Excellent Project-Specific • Excellent Program-wide
Management Costs	Lowest	Average	Highest
Schedule Performance	Variable	Excellent	Excellent
Owner's Staff Required	Largest	Small	Smallest
Flexibility	Good	Excellent	Excellent
Creativity	Good	Excellent	Excellent
Consistency	Variable	Excellent	Excellent
Comments	• Lowest Management Cost • Cost and Schedule Control Variable, Depending on Experience and Qualifications of Owner's Staff	Provides Strong Cost Control Ability for Modest Additional Costs, Since Owner's Staff Plays a Significant Role	Provides Strong Cost Control Ability for High Additional Costs, Since Owner's Staff Plays Minimum Role

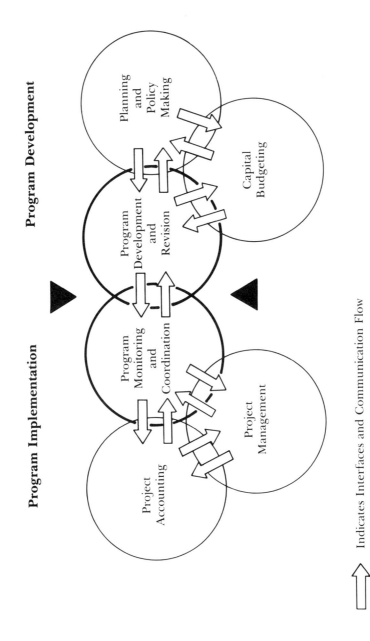

Figure 3.6. Program Management System. Adapted from Wong (145:37).

Table 3.1. Program Variables vs. Management Tools

Program Variables	Management Tools
Time	Project CPM schedules
	Computerized CPM schedule updates
	Program schedules
Program organization	Program "trees"
Cost	CIP expenditure schedule
	Expenditure tracking system
	Revenue tracking system
	Cash-flow reports
Quality	Value analysis review
	Technical Review Committee
Information flow	Document control system
	Action tracking system
	Public information program

Adapted from Wong (145:32).

implementation. The program variables that require control and the tools used to manage these variables are listed in Table 3.1. These program management tools are generally defined as follows:

1. TIME

(a) *Project Critical Path Method (CPM) Schedules*—Schedules charting the flow of and essential relationships between project activities. Each activity has an associated time duration for completion. The "critical path" is the longest series of activities in terms of time duration from project start to project completion.

(b) *Computerized CPM Schedule Updates*—Computerized reports regularly providing the program manager with status updates of each program project. Exception reports, payment estimates, and cash-flow curves for each project can be produced each time program progress is updated on the CPM diagram.

(c) *Program Schedules*—Simplified CPM schedules that identify milestone activities (such as preparation of requests for proposals, bid review, and contract award) that are necessary as a project progresses through the predesign, design, preconstruction, construction, and start-up phases.

2. PROGRAM ORGANIZATION

(a) *Program "Trees"*—Hierarchical organization of projects by programs essential for planning purposes, as well as for monitoring progress. The project groupings allow the program manager to foresee both the constraints between projects, as well as those projects that may influence seriously the successful completion of the program.

3. COST

(a) *CIP Expenditure Schedule*—A schedule that displays the remaining costs required to complete ongoing projects, plus the costs for new project starts by quarter over a selected time period (normally five-year intervals). The CIP expenditure schedule is essential to represent the planned financing of projects.

(b) *Expenditure Schedule*—A system used for monitoring specific design and construction contracts, including the work assigned to the public agency/owner's staff (force account work). For projects funded by federal grants, an expenditure tracking system is essential since cost will be audited as separate line items in the total grant. The tracking system must also accommodate the modifications to the original contract amounts due to change orders and contract amendments. Effective tracking systems require that expenditure information be recorded quickly so that cost-to-date information is current—and budget variance data meaningful—allowing sufficient time for corrective action to be taken.

(c) *Revenue Tracking System*—A system that tracks the receipt of revenues from budgeted funding sources.

(d) *Cash-Flow Reports*—Reports providing the public agency/owner with information necessary to make program adjustments due to cash flow, such as delaying the start of certain noncritical projects or accelerating the work on certain ongoing contracts.

4. QUALITY

(a) *Value Analysis Review*—A technique used when reviewing plans and specifications that permits the identification of areas where potential cost savings could be realized. Savings could result from prepurchasing long-lead-time equipment, standardizing purchasing specifications, and reviewing the use of alternate materials for cost effectiveness. Value analysis also ensures uniform and biddable contract documents, which usually attract more favorable bids.

(b) *Technical Review Committee*—Committee of technical experts drawn from the program manager that utilizes engineering, construction, and management expertise to review program plans and specifications.

The committee is composed of specialists brought in only on as-needed basis.

5. INFORMATION FLOW

(a) *Document Control System*—A system providing document organization and computer-assisted retrieval to support a major capital improvements program spanning several years and involving numerous prime contracts. When federal funding is involved, program records will be subject to audit. The proper management of project documentation also assists with the resolution of construction claims.

(b) *Action Tracking System*—A computerized system for tracking and reporting all program or project correspondence requiring action. The system facilitates timely management decisions and staff actions, and also can be made compatible with the document control system.

(c) *Public Information Program*—A concerted effort by program management staff to inform the public regularly and respond to their comments on project activities. Timely news releases, audiovisual presentations, and planned public forums can aid in creating a positive impression of the program and the public agency/owner. Public information programs are critical when capital improvement funds or operating revenues must be raised through local bonds or utility rate increases; these programs may be required when federal funds are involved.

3.5.4   Program Management in Practice

A $500-million capital improvements program at the Detroit Wastewater Treatment Plant (DWWTP) provides an excellent case study for the application of program management and its tools.

The Detroit Water and Sewerage Department (DWSD) provides water and waste-water service to more than three million people in over seventy southeastern Michigan communities, including Detroit. In the mid-1960s the DWSD began the planning and design work necessary to upgrade the DWWTP to provide secondary treatment. Land acquisition was complete and a portion of the construction under way when, in 1972, amendments to the Water Pollution Control Act mandated secondary treatment for all municipal waste-water treatment discharges by June 1977. Despite the massive effort undertaken by the DWSD, the DWWTP—processing between 805 and 1,000 million gallons of waste water per day—was not able to meet the effluent criteria required by law. Consequently, the U.S. Environmental Protection Agency filed a civil complaint against the city of Detroit, the state of Michigan, and the DWSD's contracted communities resulting in a Consent Judgment in which the DWSD agreed to meet a schedule of specific technical and administrative objectives. The DWSD found itself with an extraordinary management problem. At that time, there were fifteen separate construction contracts under way at the plant, in various stages of completion, totaling $115 million. In addition, seventeen consultant services (A-E firm) contracts, with a total value of over $70 million, were in various stages of design development. This design work represented more than $500 million worth of future construction.

To address its critical management needs, the city established a program management team headed by the DWWTP administrator, the assistant administrator, and the director of the DWSD. The Office of Program Management Assistance (OPMA) was formed to serve as program management staff. The OPMA consisted of professional staff from both the DWSD and Camp Dresser & McKee (CDM), an environmental engineering consultant agency that was selected to serve as lead consultant in a program management assistance capacity. One of CDM's primary assignments was to develop a program management system providing for the following: (1) the establishment of a framework that would allow the DWSD to gain—as quickly as possible—complete control over the managerial, budgetary, technical, legal, administrative, and contractual aspects of the capital improvements program; and (2) the development and utilization of program management tools necessary to bring the DWWTP effluence under compliance by June 1981.

To implement this system, CDM structured the OPMA (as presented in Fig. 3.7). CDM also defined the roles and responsibilities of each of these management positions. Under the program management system, four key but previously unlinked management groups within the DWSD were joined into two new functional areas: program development, as well as program monitoring and coordination (as illustrated in Fig. 3.6).

1. PROGRAM DEVELOPMENT   The program management system developed for the DWSD was designed to facilitate the evaluation and reporting of information at several program levels (as illustrated in Fig. 3.8). The most detailed is the project level, where reports based on CPM schedules were prepared on a routine basis as part of the project monitoring and control function. Groups of related projects required to accomplish an objective or set of objectives were organized into programs. These, in turn, were grouped into primary programs, each concerned with a major waste-water treatment subsystem. The Detroit Wastewater Management Program, a statement of DWSD policies and priorities concerning improvement and expansion of the waste-water treatment system, maintains the highest level. (An example of a primary program grouping or "tree" is shown in Fig. 3.9.)

2. PROGRAM MONITORING   Once the program development process was completed, a system for monitoring the schedule, scope, and budget for each project on a program-by-program basis was designed.

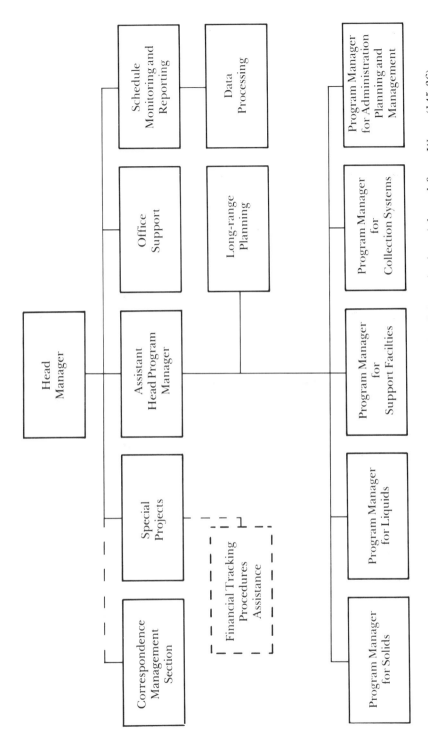

Figure 3.7. Office of Program Management Assistance Table of Organization. Adapted from Wong (145:36).

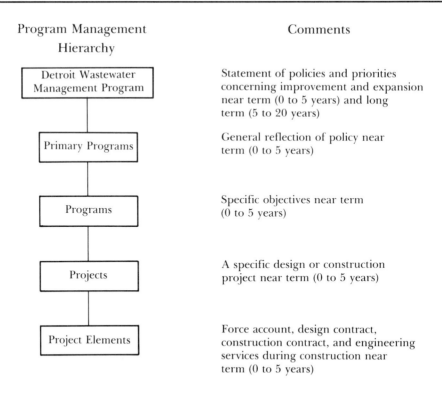

| Program Management Hierarchy | Comments |

Detroit Wastewater Management Program — Statement of policies and priorities concerning improvement and expansion near term (0 to 5 years) and long term (5 to 20 years)

Primary Programs — General reflection of policy near term (0 to 5 years)

Programs — Specific objectives near term (0 to 5 years)

Projects — A specific design or construction project near term (0 to 5 years)

Project Elements — Force account, design contract, construction contract, and engineering services during construction near term (0 to 5 years)

Figure 3.8.   Program Management Levels. Adapted from Wong (145:38).

(a)   *Schedule*—Projects were monitored by developing CPM schedules for each project in the capital improvements program. These schedules were prepared by the program management assistance staff in the "activity on-arrow" form. Construction schedules were cost-loaded and design schedules manpower-loaded. CPM scheduling specifications were developed by the OPMA staff for incorporation into the DWSD's contract documents. Project/2, a proprietary computer software package, was selected to revise schedules and produce project update and payment reports. More than 140 project schedules were developed over a two-year period. Progress meetings were held monthly to update project schedules with each of the prime contractors and design consultants as well as with project managers from the DWSD field engineering section, the DWSD design section, and the OPMA scheduling and program management staff.

(b)   *Expenditure Budgets*—To control project expenditure, a manual financial tracking system was developed by the OPMA staff and maintained by the DWSD's engineering division and accounting section. Accrued

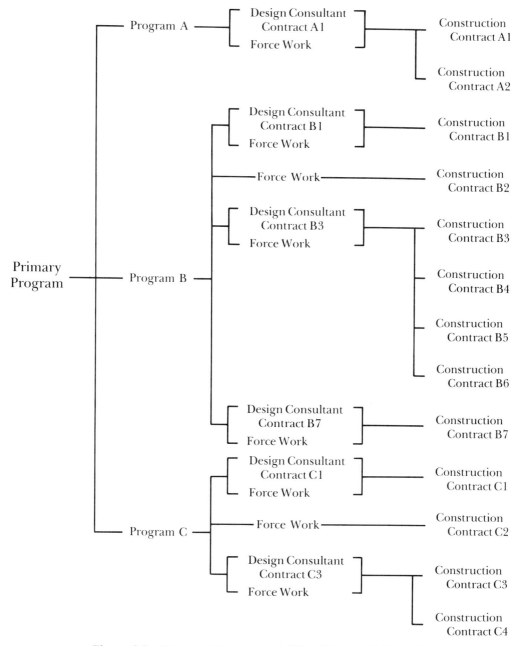

Figure 3.9. Program Management "Tree." Adapted from Wong (145:39).

expenditure could be tracked against project budget by force account, the consulting engineer's contract, and the construction contractor's contract. Budget adjustments based on change orders, contract amendments, or revised estimates to complete force account work were monitored monthly, along with expenditures.

(c) *Revenue Budgets*—With most of the design and construction contracts partially funded by the state of Michigan (5 percent) and the EPA (75 percent), revenue budgets were established, by funding source, for each project. A manual tracking system was developed to monitor monthly cash received from the EPA, the Michigan Department of Natural Resources, local bond revenues, and operations-and-maintenance fund transfers from operating revenues against revenue budgets established for force account work, engineering contracts, and construction contracts.

(d) *Capital Improvements Program and Cash-Flow Monitoring*—With the latest financial information available on project expenditures and revenues, the OPMA staff was able to assist the DWSD with a timely updating of the capital improvements projects and a monitoring of program/project cash flow. For example, the cash-flow monitoring process projected shortfalls in available local funds. To compensate, low-priority projects not yet started were delayed, and in other cases, ongoing design work was completed but construction deferred to a later fiscal year in the CIP.

(e) *Document Control*—The document control system developed and implemented by the OPMA staff consisted of two computerized systems using the same software. A document retrieval system was developed for use on the larger engineering projects. This system provided a computerized index to most of the documents associated with the project, such as incoming and outgoing correspondence, third-party correspondence, contracts, shop drawings, design reports, bulletins, change proposals, change orders, payment reports, schedule status reports, and test logs. The system allowed immediate retrieval of all coded documents that satisfied certain criteria. A typical retrieval order might state: "Find all documents received between the dates 7/15 and 9/1/81 which refer to specs sections 11R and 16C and which were originated by the contractor." The system would then respond with a list of document numbers and a brief description of each document. The document control engineer would then seek, in the conventional files, the original of that paper work, which he wished to review in detail.

(f) *Action Tracking System*—A computerized action tracking system was established using all incoming and outgoing mail related to the capital improvements program. The system was designated the correspondence management system. This system produced weekly "tickler" reports that listed, by date, the type of action required for each document. These reports were automatically sorted, then sent to the DWSD manager scheduled to act on the documents. Summary computer reports listing documents on which action was expected but not yet received were produced by the OPMA staff. A document remained on the report until action was taken or until it was determined by the OPMA staff that no further action was required. An action that resulted in the production of a new document caused the new document to be entered into the system linked to the old document. The resultant "chains" (leading from one document to another) were maintained by the system and were available to allow the production of reports that displayed these relationships between documents.

3.6 SUMMARY

Traditionally, the tasks of predesign were carried out effectively by the client on an ad hoc basis. With the emergence of the institutional owner and the increasing complexity of projects, project size, and delivery systems, the tasks of predesign have to be managed effectively and given deliberate attention. The key emerging processes discussed in this chapter include the modified traditional form, project management, engineering management, and program management. Each of these delivery systems is appropriate in specific circumstances. The common element in these varied approaches is the application of management principles and skills to the completion of large-scale activities of a specific project.

4

New Mechanism: Formation and Organization for Innovative Procurement Methods

4.1 INTRODUCTION

The need for a closer relationship between owners, manufacturers, architects, engineers, contractors, and unions has been developed over the years. As project costs have escalated and construction time has been extended, owners have come to realize that they are the only agency equipped to institute the necessary changes for improvement. Owners, as facility buyers, have experimented with different procurement methods and processes and have installed professionals in new roles as project team members. Owners are beginning to understand that a stronger and more direct relationship between themselves as buyers, and manufacturers, architects, engineers, contractors, and unions as sellers, could have important ramifications. The sellers provide the products, technology, know-how, and manpower of design, construction, and maintenance. If improvements of the procurement processes and methods require research or technology, these sellers provide the products, technology, know-how, and manpower of design, construction, and maintenance. If improvements of the procurement processes and methods require research or technology, these sellers have the capital and the management.

The Construction Industry Cost Effectiveness Project, undertaken by the Business Roundtable (owners and users), has identified problem areas for research. In a sense these owners are looking forward to the seller to get more involved in the construction industry problems by taking over and providing the necessary resources to finish the research and implementation of these problem areas.

Some form of action is needed if innovative procurement procedures are to be introduced and implemented successfully. Much success will be achieved if a new mechanism or organization is set up with the objective of encouraging the introduction and implementation of innovative procurement methods.

This chapter first discusses the restraints to change. It then goes on to describe the formation of a new organization, as well as the advantages of open system organization. It finally addresses the whole question of communications.

4.2   THE RESTRAINTS TO CHANGE

Chapter 1 briefly identified the main problems to be resolved in the organization and management of the traditional procurement process. Chapters 2 and 3 described a number of solutions to some of these procurement problems, which have proved to be successful. These 'success' stories showed that it is possible—by introducing certain organizational changes—to provide facilities of better quality at less cost and in a shorter period of time.

Exact cost comparisons between the various new processes of construction on the one hand, and traditional practice on the other, are very difficult to make because there are so many variables involved. Generally, it is thought that a 10% to 15% reduction in cost is feasible.

The following question is then raised: "If there are literally millions of dollars to be saved by introducing these organizational concepts, why aren't these new forms of organization and new processes of construction utilized more often?" The answer is that there are many restraints to change. Reorganization of the construction process is actively resisted by certain sectors of the construction industry. In particular, change is resisted by those who have the most to lose: the architects, the engineers, the contractors, the manufacturers, and the unions. Progress is also prevented by certain legislative and judicial restraints and also by obsolete bureaucratic procedures. In many cases, these restrictive procedures are retained as a result of political pressure applied from interest groups within the industry.

There is a difference of opinion as to why these interest groups obstruct the introduction of innovative organizational concepts. There are those who believe that it is simply a question of people within the industry protecting their self-interest; there are others who have a more generous attitude and claim that change is resisted because people are afraid of progress. Some of the arguments made by Toffler in *Future Shock* are put forward, and it is argued that

> With the traditional approach, each player knows his role and the role of others. He understands the status quo and his territorial rights and he also has a healthy regard for the other guy's territorial rights. With the systems approach, the roles overlap; some take on new responsibilities, team work is essential and the required changes can be the source of hidden fears. These hidden fears result in frustration and insecurity and the desire on the part of some to fight "reason" or what is called "the systematic approach." Those who have a career of implementing the systems approach, find it very difficult to relate to the traditionalist[s] and cannot empathize with their concerns and cannot help them over the hurdle. The public sector like the private sector is faced with the problem of soaring costs. This problem is complicated by the demands of users for better amenities and a better overall environment. Thus the need for change is obvious to everybody. The systems approach is being implemented, despite opposition and despite the concerns associated with the systems approach. The result is polarization. I think that there are a lot of traditionalists that are fighting new approaches just because they are new, and there are a lot of systems people who are fighting traditionalists primarily because they don't understand their side of the problem.

At a more theoretical level, the motivation of those who resist innovation is explained thus:

> If you have an investment in current technology your cost analysis is different from one you would make if you did not have an investment in current technology. There is a problem of capital obsolescence, both in software and hardware. If you are adversely affected by an innovation, you first attempt to kill it, then you attempt to ignore it, then you attempt to absorb it and finally you accept and live with it.

There are many viewpoints on the best way to overcome opposition to organization reform. The differing viewpoints can be roughly classified into two approaches: confrontation or negotiation—the course of action depending primarily on the motivation of the opponents.

If the opposition to new organizational concepts is purely from a selfish point of view, direct confrontation is unavoidable. On some occasions it is necessary to polarize things, to get attitudes out in the open. It is even necessary to classify people, for example,

- who an owner is and what his needs are;
- who an architect or engineer is and what he does for a living;
- who a contractor is and what he does for a living;
- who a manufacturer is and what he does for a living;
- and so forth.

However, if the opposition results from a fear of the consequences of change, this resistance has to be overcome by means of persuasion, education, and compromise.

In the case of the construction industry, there were two key factors preventing organizational reform: (*a*) direct political opposition from interest groups adversely affected by the proposed changes in the industry and who have considerable political influence in the legislature; and (*b*) inertia, both in government and in industry. The restraints to change and ways of overcoming these restraints fall under the following headings:

1. legislative and judicial restraints;
2. procedural and bureaucratic restraints;
3. resistance to change: architects, contractors, and unions.

4.2.1   Legislative and Judicial Restraints

1. LEGISLATIVE RESTRAINTS   The laws may not be as bad as people perceive them to be. The government tends to retreat behind the laws and says, "This is the regulation and the regulation is responsive to the law." However, if you were to go back to the original legislation, you would find something quite different. Very often the laws are written broadly, but the regulations are written for a particular moment in time. The regulations, which were written ten or fifteen years ago, may be out of date, but the law itself may still be appropriate. Thus studies can be made to identify the regulations that are giving the industry the most trouble. Then one can go back to the legislature to propose legislation to remove these restraints. The statutes are not the major problem. All major innovations the GSA is doing in the core of the systems procurement are within the federal statutes. What is needed, therefore, is to educate the legislature to start respecting what the construction industry is doing.

2. JUDICIAL RESTRAINTS   The contractors say, "You cannot do that, it is illegal." The professions say, "You cannot do that, it is unethical." Frequently, the industry is forced into accepting a standard contract format that may, or may not, be valid for a given project. These restraints can be challenged. Some owners and users in the construction industry have rewritten contracts; they are writing a contract for architects that is quite different from the standard AIA contract, but architects are finding they can be happy with it. Some have gone to cost contracting, which is a completely different mode of payment for professional services; yet because cost contracting for professional services was seen as a threat, it was initially challenged. Now that architects have accepted it, it has improved owners relationships with the architects; there are less arguments and debates because owners spell out what services they are buying.

With a typical government contract, there is half a page stating what government is going to buy, half a page stating what government is going to pay for, and twenty-five pages stating what government is going to do when it gets into trouble! This is a mistake. The contract should state what you are buying in clear and precise terms, what the compensation is going to be, and also include, of course, the legal provisions that protect the owner. The contracts should be balanced to give protection in a legal sense and also to discourage claims. You should use preventive medicine instead of corrective surgery.

A research study into existing practices showed that in *legal terms*, existing restrictive practices in the industry may already be attacked judicially as an unconstitutional burden on interstate commerce. The problem is not one of law so much as one of organization; even though in theory the law could be on the side of the owners, in comparison with other interest groups, the owners are disorganized. For example, the architectural profession carefully briefs its counsels on the implications of past ruling and, if necessary, assists in the appeal of any precedent-making case to the highest levels. Perhaps the owners should unite to fight certain cases, to set legal precedents more in their favor. The standards of structural collapse, for example, are imposing excessive requirements on high-rise buildings. It is known that the standards employed in England came about as a result of Ronan Point, but an exaggerated requirement with respect to structural safety is now required by HUD. The New York City Building Authority picked up HUD's interim standard and published it as the standard to be observed, without almost any review. They copied it exactly and even included the typographical errors that were in the HUD preliminary standards!

4.2.2   Procedural and Bureaucratic Restraints

The barriers the industry faces are mainly institutional and related to the perceptions, customs, and attitudes of the people involved. Professional obsolescence is one of the worst fears the industry has to deal with inside the bureaucracy, where any changes are resisted. For example, there is a tradition that the government is difficult to deal with because of an excessive amount of involvement in bureaucracy, extraordinary technical review of the documentation, six inspectors for every laborer or craftsman on the jobsite, and antiquated design criteria. How can we erase this image? The best way is to educate the legislature.

4.2.3   Resistance to Change: Architects, Contractors, and Unions

1. ARCHITECTS   Some owners are bitter toward the professional societies because they, above everyone else, should be taking the lead, rather than looking after their own business interests. The architect has the responsibility to improve things, but he not only fails to do this, in many instances he has actually worked against the introduction of technological innovation. For example, when the design-build process was introduced, certain groups felt threatened. The architects, for example, said, "You're trying to take our professional role away from us. You're trying to bring in the contractor and make him the architect; he decides what is going to be built, what it is going to look like, and what materials are going to be used." From their point of view, if design-build becomes the accepted way of procuring facilities, it is really going to deprive the architects of income and will change their role. One must deal with this fear as a realistic threat because it *is* a threat. In this situation the name of the game is communication. One doesn't say, "We are going to do it," and take no notice of the architects. Instead, one sits down and hears their side of the story and makes compromises. Eventually, you get them around to the point where they are beginning to contribute to the 'process' itself. They may even agree that in a certain set of circumstances, design-build is the only way to do business.

The problem is that the national organization and the state organizations that theoretically look after the independent professions are not doing their jobs. Because the senior members of the profession are also running the profession—and they are interested in keeping everything exactly as it is—they are not interested in a systems route that implies changes of professional roles. To overcome resistance from architects, and for that matter from contractors and unions, an owners' organization should be formed to act as a pressure group.

2. CONTRACTORS   Like any national or state organizations, the contractors initially will fight any restriction that does not look after their interests. But after much education or legislative bills, they will give in and go along with it.

3. UNIONS   The unions have a tremendous grasp on legislative lobbies. They have so much power in the legislatures that they can get almost anything accepted; that is too bad. Unions have their place in our society, but they have more power than they should have. Some owners literally cannot build hospitals because the costs are so high that it is not possible to generate revenue to pay for the facility over the required period of time. Furthermore, high wages and restrictive practices are some of the reasons why construction costs are so high.

Everybody is talking about codes and unions preventing industrialized building; it is not so. It depends upon how you make the arrangements. Granted, there are accommodations that have to be made, but they can be made. Traditionally, the plumbers in New York City would not allow a contractor to assemble pipes in his own plant; all the pipes had to be assembled on the site; they even had to be brought up to each floor and assembled there. It was arranged with the local plumbing union, with the help of the international office, to try out a new approach—a prefabricated plumbing wall. It was not easy. It took a year to negotiate, but finally the unions decided that if the owner would accept some things, the union would go along on others. The owner had to accept that the plumbing would be fabricated in the city of New York by the same union membership that was being replaced. At that point, the plumbing subcontractor started to resist with all his might. He kept saying, "It won't save us any money." The owner had to make a detailed analysis in terms of the number of man-hours required to assemble the plumbing wall. Because the owner had picked a project that is highly repetitive, he was able to demonstrate that, instead of the thirty-two man-hours normally required, the plumbing wall could be put together on site in six man-hours. That fact alone told everyone that the owner was going to save a lot of money.

The union leader is in a difficult position because he knows that he must go back to the membership periodically to get reelected. There is always some young member who is going to get up at a meeting and say, "Down with the President. I want to be President. Look at what he gave away." Even though the union leader may agree with you, he often cannot come out openly and say so. One advantage of a large-scale program is that it is easier for the union leadership to go back to the members and say, "Look here, you're going to have a lot of work. We're not giving anything away because if you don't accept this, it kills the whole program."

If management meets ahead of time with the union leadership and says, "This is what we intend to do. What kinds of accommodations and what kinds of arrangements do we have to make?," the leadership will come around and tell you how the program can be made to work. With the unions, it is not the wages that you pay them, it is the environment that they create. For example, an owner built a building in Buffalo, New York, and charged between $40 and $42 a square foot and lost money on it. Two hundred miles away, an owner can build the same building for $32 and come out with a profit. In each case, the buildings were shipped from Madison. There is a difference in cost, not because the owner paid the men any more—he paid them about the same—but because of the working environment; it is just the "unknowns." The foreman on the job cannot talk to the carpenters, he has to talk to an interpreter who tells the carpenters what to do. Just imagine what it costs; it breaks down the whole system of communication.

The craftsmen do have a problem. These men do have a trade and they know that their work is going to be cut out. It is the same kind of resistance that was faced when the plasterers' union fought to keep out dry-wall construction. It was the government who insisted that they were going to use dry-wall. There was picketing by the plasterers' union, but they had to lose; today the plasterers' prices have gone down and are competitive with dry-wall; plasterers are fighting for survival.

4.3   OVERCOMING THE RESTRAINTS

4.3.1   Direct or Indirect Government Action

Unlike governments in Europe, in the United States the government does not tackle a problem directly. If there is a housing crisis, the government does not step in and organize the market, but operates indirectly, for example, by encouraging research and development. This indirect non-participatory response to government is a political reality that has to be faced in proposing any future course of action.

In proposing future courses of action, what is needed is some form of government assistance. In some cases, government intervention is not necessary. For example, the development of industrialized building methods is dictated primarily by economic factors and occurs regardless of intervention by government or by professional societies.

4.3.2   Political Leadership or Grass Roots Movements

Two schools of thought emerge on how best to bring about organizational reform, namely, (a) a call for high-level political leadership to bring about changes in the construction industry, and (b) a claim that it is not necessary to wait for political leadership because procurement decisions pertain to middle management and changes can be instigated by persons within an organization.

One therefore asks, "How can you build the different approaches into the construction industry as a way of life that everybody accepts—and that will survive the comings and goings of any particular individual?"

At the present time, to bring about a change of attitude at an institutional level requires an enormous amount of political momentum and this does not exist. Therefore, a realistic course of action is the formation of a new mechanism.

4.3.3   The Formation of a New Mechanism

There is a need to form a new mechanism or institute in the construction industry to encourage the introduction of innovative procurement procedures. The structure and function of such an organization should be carefully considered. Some of the issues to be examined include the following:

(a)   Should the new mechanism be

- a small group of experts?

- a national organization representing all sectors of industry and government?

- a joint organization representing owners' representatives and producers?

- an organization made up of only owners' representatives?

- a network of regionally based action groups?

- a number of organizations each concentrating on one construction type?

- a formal or an informal organization?

(b)   Should the objective of the new mechanism be

- to educate owners on the advantages of the new procurement methods?

- to act as a pressure group countering the influence of the existing, more conservative pressure groups within the industry?

- to coordinate the preparation and definition of user needs?

- to assess whether there is any advantage in introducing common procurement procedures?

- to develop alternative innovative procurement methods?

- to exchange information on new procurement methods?

- to exchange information about legal and statutory constraints on procurement?

- to survey innovative procurement procedures used in other countries?

- to investigate mechanisms set up in other contexts in order to achieve cooperation?

The following should be considered when deciding what the objectives and structure of the organization will be:

1. A NUCLEUS OF EXPERTISE   That the best way to encourage the adoption of new procurement techniques in the construction industry is by educating the owners about the advantages of the new techniques. However, before this educational process can begin, it is necessary to define the procurement techniques that are available to the owner groups and the circumstances under which these techniques should be used to yield advantages. This task could be carried out effectively by a nucleus of expertise that would be formed specifically for that purpose.

2. A NATIONAL INSTITUTION   What is needed is a new mechanism or institution representing all sectors of industry and government concerned with technological innovations. A national organization such as Building Research Advisory Board (BRAB) already exists, but these consensus organizations are not very effective in bringing about change.

3. AN OWNERS' GROUP   Rather than form a 'consensus' organization, the owners' representatives should get together and set up an owners' group. In fact, it is easy for owners to get together and figure out how, from their viewpoint, they can get the best hardware, the best construction techniques, and the best management techniques made available to them. The goal is to reach the decision makers and to get them to unify and clarify their requirements. These decision makers do not think in terms of a national construction scene. While groups like BRAB serve a very useful function, the decision makers generally do not know it exists. They do not think about the construction industry in such broad terms. They are more likely to be reached in regard to their specific problems, which are generally in regard to their specific construction types. For example, decisions are made by decision makers in local school boards, and they are concerned with local school problems. How can you reach these people and talk about 'system' building? These people consult the National School Boards Association, the American Association of School Administrators, or similar groups. Thus owners will be persuaded primarily by their own peer group and not by an external organization.

Therefore, there is a need to form an owners' organization that will organize user needs and the corresponding effective demand in such a way that the producers can respond to them and thus produce the needed products within time, cost, and quality limits. The owner is the only viable agent who can force significant improvements in the construction process. With the present fragmented group of participants in construction, the owner is the only one concerned with the facility; he pays the bill. Efforts to organize owners so that their needs can be consolidated and easily interpreted by industry would probably effect the necessary changes more quickly than any other conceivable activity.

The owners' representatives should get together because it is the representatives who dictate in essentially technical terms what the producers are going to produce. If they can agree on a set of criteria, then industry will respond to them if there is a big enough market. The technical criteria for the different construction types are the same or are only marginally different; there would be advantages to all owners if existing work in defining user requirements were to be consolidated.

4.4   THE ADVANTAGES OF OPEN SYSTEM OF ORGANIZATION

While the traditional organization has its deficiencies, it has also several implicit advantages. In the past, simplistic solutions to the problems of the traditional process have been put forward, and they have turned out to be worse than the original symptoms. In proposing solutions, one has to understand the advantages of the existing organization of the construction process. This section describes, from a theoretical viewpoint, the advantages of the traditional or 'open' organization of the construction process.

4.4.1   Integration and Differentiation

The classical organizational theory does little to explain how the construction industry operates. The classical organizational theory concentrates on principles of the internal organizational functioning of firms that are, to all intents and purposes, closed systems. It assumes that the task of the manager is 'universal' and that the manager is concerned with the best way to divide the tasks of the organization as well as to obtain an integration of the parts of the organization itself. Implicit in these assumptions are the beliefs that the function of management should be separated from tasks of production and that organizations should be broken down into departments, sections, or work groups that are functionally independent. In short, this classical organizational theory applies to closed, large, permanent organizations.

However, recent developments in modern organizational theory are at last recognizing that the closed system is not the only form of organization and that other forms of organization are equally valid in particular circumstances.

The "Contingency Theory of Organizations" proposed by Lorsch and Lawrence (Lorsch, 87:280) is an example of this new approach. Here a continuum of organization types is suggested, ranging from authoritarian, apersonal organizations in a stable environment to work groups bound together only by a degree of commonality of objectives in a rapidly changing environment. Lorsch and Lawrence claim that the more different the pattern of thought and behavior of the individuals who are required to work together, the more difficult it is for them to achieve an integrated effort.

In order to resolve the tension, formal differentiation between the individual activities and organizations is a requirement for high performance, provided that—thus differentiated—their actions are properly integrated.

In short, as far as Lorsch and Lawrence are concerned, the appropriate organizational structure depends on the environmental conditions and requirements of the task, and that there is a continuum of organizational types with closed system-stable environment—defined task—at one extreme, and open system-unstable environment—undefined task—at the other.

Applying Lawrence and Lorsch's work to the construction industry, it can be argued that for the typical one-off, large-scale project, an open system of organization is appropriate. For small-scale, but ongoing projects, such as housing, schools, and clinics for which there is a more continuous demand, a more closed system of organization is appropriate.

Two other modern organizational theorists, Miller and Rice (Miller, 94), argue that the reasons for the present poor performance of the construction project organization are, first, the lack of integration between the individual organizations and, second, the considerable differentiation between the individual members of the design-construction process, but its impact is reduced because the boundaries are both ill-defined and wrongly situated. Social and technological changes have invalidated the traditional organizational boundaries, and the informal practices that have grown up in response to the demands of reality have blurred the formal boundaries. As a result, there is a situation of uncertainty. Rice and Miller claim that unless a boundary is adequately located and clearly defined as to its nature and its location, different people will draw it in different places and hence there will be confusion between 'inside' and 'outside.' In the individual, this confusion leads to anxiety; in the enterprise, to inefficiency and failure. The authors suggest that there is a need to redraw the organizational boundaries of the construction process so that the formal boundaries coincide with the changes that have occurred; the technical and social interfaces should coincide with the administrative interfaces.

The boundaries between the different organizations in the construction process are defined formally by the contractual arrangements; consequently, by changing the contractual arrangements one can effectively alter the position of the organizational boundaries, which, in turn, alters the 'mechanism' known as the construction process. The contractual arrangements are the principal integrating device of the construction process and formally link together the different organizations of the project organization. By introducing changes in the contractual arrangements (i.e., in procurement methods), it should be possible to increase integration and therefore improve the performance of the planning-design-construction process.

4.4.2   The Sentient Group

In connection with temporary project organizations, Miller and Rice stress the importance of the sentient group: an organization that provides emotional support to the individual in a changing situation and controls, by means of a code of professional ethics, the individual's conduct in a temporary organization.

One example of a sentient group is the set of professional institutes that control the activities of architects and engineers in the project team. Another example is the building trade unions. Both types of organizations play a key role in the construction industry; thus both organizations could be dominant forces in bringing about organizational change in the industry.

4.4.3   A Systems Analysis of the Building Industry

In his study, P. W. G. Morris (Morris, 97) applied both systems analysis and organizational theory to the building industry. Morris described the systems approach as follows:

> The primary concern of the systems approach is that any system should be treated as a whole. It is recognized, however, that individual interests should not go unrecognized. Obviously the initial step—and one of the hardest—is to define what is being meant by the particular system under consideration. This is done by first defining the objective of the system and then by identifying the parts bearing on the objective. These parts may then be grouped around subgoals to form subsystems. The idea is that the subsystems' boundaries should be so defined that the initially complex situation becomes clarified into relatively simple arrangements of subsystems. Having these boundaries clearly defined means that the places where attention is required can be identified more readily. For this reason "boundary management" is a key systems concept: management is centered on the system's most critical areas.

Morris claimed that organizational theory has been influenced by developments in systems analysis. For example, one of the major concerns of organizational theory over the last decade has been establishing general criteria upon which the boundaries of an organization's subsystem can be founded. Another concern has been to see how changes in the organization or its environment affect the definition of those boundaries.

These two developments are the key to Morris's work. He showed that by splitting a complex construction project into a series of project subsystems, the various key groups and their interactions could be identified more readily and thus their management could be made easier.

4.5 COMMUNICATIONS

This section concerns the whole question of communications. A distinction will be drawn between the need to disseminate detailed information on procurement methods to the technical decision maker in the construction industry and the need to sell the new procurement methods to key decision makers both in the private and public sector. As far as the dissemination of technical information is concerned, there is no real problem. Many publications already exist and are carrying out this function effectively. However, as for communicating with the key decision makers, there is a problem and there is a need to develop some new form of communications vehicle. Several options are available. The key ones are described in the following subsections.

4.5.1 Case Studies

One effective way of persuading owners of the advantages of the new procurement techniques is by publishing a series of case studies. These cases studies would evaluate a number of projects where innovative procurement methods were used, describing both the successes and failures, and in each case, reasons for the project's failure or success would be given. Obviously, these case studies would have to convince the owners that if they were to follow through these recommendations on a new organizational concept, they could get certain benefits. The benefits are savings in time, savings in cost, and possibly improved quality. This substantiating data has not been put together. No reputable organization has shown that these savings will definitely result.

4.5.2 Conferences and Regional Meetings

Another way of getting the message across to the key decision makers in industry would be to hold a follow-up national conference or a series of regional meetings and to invite top level representatives from industry and commerce. However, it is difficult to get these key people to attend such meetings. People in industry and finance had been invited to these workshops, but nobody showed the interest to attend. The basic problem is that a more efficient construction industry is not a high priority as far as people in business and industry are concerned. They are not interested in talking about how to reduce the cost of buildings by 10% when there is a general inflation rate of 15% or more, or talking about how to reduce maintenance and running costs when these costs can be written off against tax. Nevertheless, these attitudes can be changed eventually by (*a*) involving these decision makers in the conferences and meetings and (*b*) identifying and addressing their real needs at such conferences and meetings.

4.5.3   Publications

There is a need for a new publication whose primary aim would be to sell the new procurement options to the decision makers in industry and government. The stance of the publication would be activist, and it would act as the mouthpiece of a new pressure group within the construction industry.

4.6   SUMMARY

The introduction of innovative procurement procedures is actively resisted by certain sectors of the construction industry. In particular, change is resisted by those who have the most to lose: the architects, the engineers, the contractors, the manufacturers, and the unions. Progress is also prevented by certain legislative and judicial restraints; in many cases, these restrictive practices are retained as a result of political pressures applied from interest groups within the industry. Another cause of the slow rate of change is inertia, both in government and in industry. Courses of action were suggested to overcome this opposition to organizational reform in the construction industry.

It was suggested, in this chapter, that a mechanism or organization be set up with the objective of encouraging the introduction of innovative procurement methods. Some guidelines were provided on what the structure and function of this proposed new mechanism should be. Another course of action proposed is that an "open" system of organization is appropriate for one-off, large-scale projects, whereas a "closed" organization is more appropriate for small-scale, ongoing projects. In order to communicate to the key decision makers the need for new procurement methods, new forms of communication vehicles such as the publication of case studies, follow-up national conferences or regional meetings, and new publications concerning new procurement options are needed.

5

Planning Phase

5.1 INTRODUCTION

The planning phase may last from weeks to years. It begins with a definition of the project as a possible consideration and is completed with its authorization in the form of a budget backed by fund appropriation. Projects may continue an existing program, such as a college, or may be developed to solve a specific requirement, such as a manufacturing facility. Decisions made as a result of mere conceptual planning are almost always based on insufficient information and represent a beginning stage in the evolution of the project. Value analysis during the stage of conceptual planning should result in emphasis of the positive factors of the project and identification of those that are of obviously poor value or worth. Following the conceptual planning are scope and definition, programming and site selection. Figure 5.1 illustrates the characteristic phases of a project. Some activities in private industry may have more of an overlap, particularly in the funding phase.

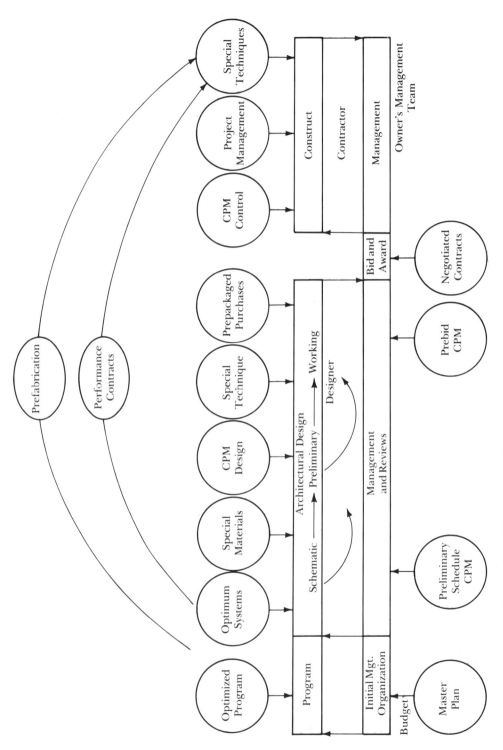

Figure 5.1. Plan–Design–Construct Project Cycle Showing Systems Inputs. Adapted from O'Brien (145:24).

Success or failure of construction management is founded in planning. A sound plan for implementing the project is essential if the owner's goals are to be fulfilled. The plan forms the standard upon which the project control system is based and by which future performance is to be judged. For best results, the construction manager should be appointed prior to the beginning of detailed design. Sufficient preliminary planning by the owner and his designer should be available so that the general scope of the project is apparent to the manager. Depending upon the owner's method of selecting the construction manager, some preliminary planning may have been accomplished in a proposal submitted by the prospective manager. This technique can be used to evaluate the kind of program each prospective manager proposes to implement if awarded the contract. The construction manager's initial planning is divided into several stages, including conceptual planning, project scope and definition, feasibility studies, budget planning, value engineering, and program planning.

5.2   NEEDS, OBJECTIVES, AND FACT-FINDING

5.2.1   Needs

Prior to implementation of any planning in the construction management process, there has to be an establishment or identification of a "need." The basic process of decision starts with the recognition that there is a need for a capital improvement or for a new development. This can cover the gamut from the simple desire of a private individual wishing to enlarge his or her quarters to the more complex decision-making process within a governmental department or segment of industry implementing a long-range master plan for development, including the growth and need for expansion and additional facilities. This need may be identified later in the planning process as having been improperly established, overvalued, or false in its basic concept; nevertheless, the process is commenced, and the role of the construction manager is born and already exists at this time. The construction manager may have immediate input at the project's inception. The CM's knowledge of the project requirements, limitations, and options can influence the results of the decision process. Indeed, such input should be sought from a project team member at this early time of development, not only to provide the continuity of having the CM firm involved from the beginning of the project development, but to draw upon the CM's specific construction and planning knowledge.

5.2.2   Objectives and Fact-Finding

These steps are often neglected but represent major keys to unlocking facts and information necessary to construct a successful project. Each construction project is unique, both in terms of the structure being built and the geographic and economic factors prevalent at the work site. If the manager is thoroughly familiar with the project area and the local economic considerations by virtue of long-time associations, fact-finding for a particular project can be confined to visiting the work site and familiarizing himself with the planned structure as well as the objectives, needs, and requirements of his client, the owner, and those of the designer. Fact-finding will include the following considerations.

1. CLIENT OBJECTIVES AND REQUIREMENTS   Meet with the owner's representatives to understand his objectives and requirements, including

(a) Project schedule requirements, completion priorities, and other scheduling information.

(b) Obtain cost estimates, cost criteria, appropriations, and other budget considerations.

(c) Obtain owner drawings, specifications, and preferred construction techniques.

(d) Obtain owner operating procedures, including contractual requirements, bidder qualification requirements, bonding requirements, and other internal procedures required or preferred by the owner.

(e) Define responsibilities of owner, designer, and construction manager as well as the extent of delegation to each.

(f) Determine the specific functions the owner intends to perform for himself and the extent that supplementary assistance may be required.

(g) Define responsibilities of key individuals on both the owner's staff and that of the construction manager.

2. DESIGNER OBJECTIVES AND REQUIREMENTS   Meet with designer representatives in order to understand his objectives and requirements and to establish ground rules for a mutually rewarding professional relationship, including

(a) Review design criteria, conceptual planning, and detail design to date.

(b) Review or develop a preliminary design schedule that will aid development of a phased construction program.

(c) Develop basic understandings necessary to commence a partnership value engineering program utilizing manager, designer, and owner.

(d) Determine designer experience in the area and his understanding of jobsite economic factors relating to construction work.

(e)   Review overall completion requirements and preliminary scheduling.

(f)   Establish a meeting of the minds with the designer on construction responsibilities to both owner and manager and responsibilities of the manager to the designer.

(g)   Review the delegation of authority to each party by the owner.

(h)   Define responsibilities of key individuals in both organizations.

5.3   SITE SELECTION

Traditionally, the most common practice in the development of a project is for the owner or ultimate user to establish the site for a new facility. The designer may provide some input by having the option to prepare plans or schematics for alternate sites. But such sites would have been predetermined through the owner's selection process. Although the owner may have utilized the services of a specialist or real estate consultant, the decision making would be essentially complete prior to the implementation of design. Usually, the designer's mandate is to design and plan a facility on a preselected or predetermined site. The expert or real estate analyst's selection would have been made on sound financial feasibility and valid engineering grounds, but site selection per se would have been treated as a separate function or task; the owner would be the only member of the project team being involved in the total project development process.

The need for experts to analyze and evaluate specific sites exists even more today than in earlier times. Because of urban growth, corporate relocations between urban centers (e.g., the movement of various corporate company headquarters from New York City to Houston, Texas in the 1960s) as well as the legislation of new zoning limitations and building restrictions, together with growing environmental considerations and increasing local, state, and federal regulations, the evaluation of the appropriate real estate has become a more crucial aspect of the project development process than ever before. As the need for the utilization of experts has grown and becomes evident, the need for a coordinator and manager has also grown at this phase of project development. The function, often performed by the owner, is a proper coordination and management task of a construction manager. During the real estate phase of the development project, the CM has a specific task to perform.

The CM process, concerned as it is with the life cycle and life-cycle costs, must consider land use and land values. Land as a commodity is generally classified as urban and rural. Although the construction manager would not usually be an expert in these areas, the need for a single management and coordination role becomes more significant with the need for proper coordination and control of all the factors that can influence or determine the direction and development of a project.

In the project coordination role, in order to evaluate land use and function, the following long-range facets must be considered since they will have an influence not only at the time of site selection but during various stages of development, or even permanently. These facets are land characteristics, value, and zoning.

(a) *Land Characteristics*—Not that land is unique and not that parcels with similar characteristics cannot be found, but each project site will presumably have different features and physical attributes. Although the main consideration of a "site" will be in how it is used, the ultimate use may be controlled or at least affected by its natural condition.

To identify physical characteristics, one need only consider the following physical features:

- Location: urban or rural
- Size and topography
- Elevation in relation to surrounding areas
- Growth or fertility of soil
- Subsoil conditions or mineral deposits
- Water supply and natural water table
- Climatic conditions
- Drainage

Also, the availability of utility services must be an early consideration in a site analysis. Such services will include

- Electricity (power)
- Gas
- Sanitary and storm drainage systems
- Public safety: fire and ambulance; police protection

As is patently evident, each of the aforementioned "characteristics" and "services" has to be considered and evaluated during the design-construction process. To ensure proper evaluation at the appropriate time, the construction manager, as part of his involvement in project concept development and planning, should play a key role in site selection.

(b) *Land Value*—The immediate consideration of value is property cost. This naturally is the market value that is represented and established in the free marketplace. More readily defined, value is the price a prospective buyer is willing to pay and a seller is willing to accept.

The purchase price is only the beginning of the value analysis of a real estate parcel. Every parcel of property is subject to property tax, which, although levied by the local governmental body having jurisdiction over the property, may include—in addition to the local municipal tax—county, state, and regional-authority taxes and levies. Local taxes are levied to finance services, such as the usual housekeeping and public safety. The larger governmental unit tax is levied on property to support functions such as county welfare and institutional costs (educational, health, correctional) as well as such regional services as sewer construction or cost of transportation facilities.

Property is assessed to establish the value for purposes of raising revenue. In addition to assessment and tax impacts on value, the methods and availability of financing may influence value. Because real estate normally represents a sizable investment, financing through mortgaging the property is the most common method of raising funds to purchase the property.

(c) *Zoning*—The purpose of zoning is to control the orderly growth of property development. Zoning establishes purposes for which property within a governmental boundary may be utilized. Although a tool for regulating urban growth in accordance with a preestablished master plan, it is only based upon the states' power to regulate health, safety, and general welfare. As a consequence, there are legal boundaries concerning the use of zoning to achieve "orderly growth." For every locality depending upon the social and economic values dominant within the community or political entity will interpret such powers differently. The CM and the owner must therefore study the scope and the extent of the zoning laws and their implications on the proposed project.

(d) *Site Visit*—Whether the CM was selected before, during, or after site selection, the CM must visit the jobsite during the planning phase. The CM must spend sufficient time at the jobsite and surrounding area to develop local factors and requirements, including

- Visit jobsite location noting key factors.
- Review local work practice and jurisdiction.
- Ascertain local craft productivity and availability.
- Obtain collective bargaining agreements.
- Determine locally favored methods and materials.
- Ascertain key local prices for standard items.
- Obtain climate information for use in developing weather constraints.
- Screen local contractor capabilities, work load, and interest.
- Visit with key local contractors, trade associations, labor union representatives, and other knowledgeable industry representatives.

- Determine building permit requirements and local agency jurisdiction and permit requirements.

5.4   FEASIBILITY STUDIES

As the project takes definite form, feasibility or economic studies of the project and its proposed results should be conducted. This stage is often performed informally, or even omitted. Value-analysis techniques can be utilized to perform a significant portion of the feasibility study. External factors, such as the prime lending rate, are often an important consideration in the economic study. Feasibility can simply amount to an individual's evaluating his financial resources and looking into the marketplace to determine whether there is a facility that he can construct or purchase that will satisfy his needs. This is how many basic decisions are made and various alternatives are considered to gain the ultimate objective. Even this analysis of the existing marketplace can be complex.

The feasibility of the project and evaluation of its practicality, which naturally are dependent upon the extent and scope of the particular project, will identify the comprehensive nature of the feasibility studies that are undertaken. In the basic construction industry, most feasibility projects are considered and classified as either engineering or economic feasibility studies. The feasibility study of a project should consider and evaluate the following aspects:

1. *Alternate courses of action*: What are the alternative solutions to satisfying or meeting the need?

2. *Engineering evaluation or analysis of such alternate solutions*: Practical design solutions, cost estimates, and basic engineering analysis.

3. *Economic evaluation of such alternatives*: What is the probable or possible manner of financing? What are the basic revenues? What economic impact will the project have?

4. *Social analysis of project*: What is the impact upon society or the community of the project under consideration?

5. *Political considerations*: The political factor may be considered one of the realities or practicalities of implementation, depending upon different and opposing political points of view that may change over the period of time and within the area in which the project is being planned and analyzed.

5.5   BUDGETING AND FUNDING

5.5.1   Budgeting

Each organization has its own procedures for budgetary approval. Generally, the complexity of the procedures is proportional to the size of the organization, whether corporate or governmental. The budgeting process in these more formalized situations may require many months and may also be tied to specific calendar dates, such as the federal fiscal budget. In terms of the project timetable, the budgeting process is one that should be defined and understood.

The budget is the formal document within which the project is identified, and the point in time at which it is authorized in terms of the ever-important funding phase. The budget must accommodate many types of programs, including

- Continuing programs from prior years
- Debt service on existing capital structure
- Administration funds for existing departments
- Replacement of existing structures
- Meeting of obvious needs (fires, riots, natural disasters)

After the budget structure has addressed itself to the aforementioned list, and perhaps others, the amount of resources that can be programmed for new projects is considered. Strong, well-defined programs have a much better opportunity for selection. Marginal or poorly expressed programs usually receive little consideration. The budget selection process is one that can be continued over years. Until a project has been approved, it has sponsors—but no managers. In most cases, the CM/PM team cannot be selected until the budget for at least the initial planning phase has been approved.

5.5.2   Funding

Funding may require separate authorization, such as governmental appropriations, or may be contingent upon the sale of corporate or government bonds. Most organizations have guidelines concerning how much design work can be accomplished before the appropriation has been assured. Again, this has an important impact upon the project timetable.

5.6   PROGRAMMING

Programming is an important phase of the project. Unfortunately, it is one that is often omitted. Development of the program is based upon information developed during the needs, objectives, and fact-finding and budgeting stages. It converts the broad generic goals expressed in the budget into specific requirements. It provides the natural basis for design. When omitted, it imposes upon the design team the role of selecting a specific approach. Some owners deliberately omit programming, anticipating that they are getting something for nothing by having their design team perform this very important stage.

5.6.1 Preliminary Program

After determination of owner and designer objectives and requirements, coupled with a thorough knowledge of the jobsite and surrounding area, as well as budgeting and funding, a "Preliminary Program" for the project can be developed. This program will include some or all of the following items, depending upon information available:

1. Criteria and conclusions developed from the site and surrounding area investigation.

2. Develop a proposed "Work Plan" setting forth in detail the recommended approach to the project, including (*a*) overall approach; (*b*) home office services; (*c*) field management services; (*d*) list of proposed work packages; (*e*) list of proposed contractors for further screening; (*f*) preliminary design schedule and package procurement schedule; (*g*) value engineering program; (*h*) preliminary CPM precedence diagram; and (*i*) bar chart schedule.

3. Submit preliminary magnitude estimate of project cost for preliminary control purposes and for prequalifying selective bidders.

4. Submit a detailed estimate of construction management costs if not previously presented as a part of the proposal.

5. Assign key personnel and submit schedules for future personnel to be assigned.

5.6.2 Final Agreed Program

After preliminary plans have been reviewed with the owner and designer, the project plan is finalized and issued to all three partners for use in controlling actual progress. Final planning will include the following items and instructions: (1) design schedule broken down by contemplated construction contract packages; (2) list of proposed contract packages, including detailed scope of each; (3) finalize and issue overall project CPM schedule; (4) establish project control systems; (5) begin value engineering program; and (6) issue procedures manual for project in which key duties and responsibilities are set forth.

5.7 CM'S TASKS

The functional construction management tasks during the planning phase can be divided broadly into two major stages or subphases typical of most construction projects: (1) conceptual and (2) programming.

5.7.1   CM's Tasks during Conceptual Phase

1. DEVELOP CONCEPTUAL ESTIMATES

(a) From schematic drawings develop budgets within agreed-upon range.

(b) Provide cost trade-off analysis for alternative concepts.

(c) Know available system and component alternatives.

(d) Understand the cost trade-off consequences among the basic labor crafts for alternative designs.

(e) Understand cost and time trade-offs for alternative designs.

2. DEVELOP CONCEPTUAL SCHEDULES

(a) Be able to list all project requirements, including long-lead-time procurement, design durations by component or system, and construction activity durations.

(b) Prepare network analysis schedule of all project activities.

(c) Have insight into time constraints imposed by local social and economic conditions.

(d) Know the owner's time requirements and other limiting constraints.

(e) Be able to superimpose resource requirements on conceptual schedule activities.

(f) Be able to simulate total project time under varying conditions.

(g) Have computer-based scheduling capability.

3. PROVIDE INPUT TO PROGRAM RISK ANALYSIS

(a) Provide project sensitivity analysis.

(b) Have knowledge of experience gained in similar projects—problems and solutions.

(c) Prepare shopping list of solutions to identified problems.

(d) Estimate impact of identified problems on project time, cost, and quality parameters, and be able to simulate them.

5.7.2   CM's Tasks during Programming Phase

1. PROVIDE CONSTRUCTABILITY ANALYSIS

(a) Study various design configurations to optimize owner needs.

(b) Know the various project systems and their interface requirements with other project components.

(c) Know area trade practices—construction methods, materials, labor, subs, and equipment.

(d)   Local climatic conditions.

(e)   Know site conditions—both above and below ground—and their impact on structure.

(f)   Know site availability and access routes.

2.   IDENTIFY POTENTIAL MAJOR CONSTRUCTION PROBLEMS

(a)   Identify potential high-risk activities.

(b)   Provide in-depth analyses of all untried or new systems and designs.

(c)   Understand local labor conditions, practices, and contract durations.

(d)   Study availability of material.

(e)   Analyze quality of local material supply.

(f)   Analyze capability of potential contractors.

(g)   Understand local weather constraints.

(h)   Analyze equipment availability.

(i)   Provide construction sensitivity analysis.

(j)   Prepare shopping list of identified construction problem solutions.

(k)   Estimate impact of identified problems on construction time, cost, and quality.

(l)   Identify transportation systems.

(m) Establish delivery times.

(n)   Identify favored haul routes.

(o)   Identify potential transportation bottlenecks.

3.   DEVELOP PROJECT RESOURCE REQUIREMENTS

(a)   Utilize resource loading from conceptual schedule.

(b)   Check availability of all major resource requirements (subs, labor, material, and equipment).

(c)   Prepare schedule of resource requirements.

(d)   List and verify alternative sources for key resources.

(e)   Check supply for labor.

(f)   Verify supply of funds.

(g)   Study funding requirements and constraints.

(h)   Analyze and detail equipment requirements.

4. INVENTORY AVAILABLE AREA RESOURCES

(a)   Early in the project acquire or provide a genuine understanding of the construction methodology used in the area.

(b)   Provide an understanding of other ongoing work in the area. Determine interest level of local suppliers and subcontractors or work package primes.

(c)   Determine local trade practices: (i) union, nonunion, or mix; (ii) also inquire about subs, find out if they normally provide bonds; and (iii) determine size, habits, and prejudices of contractors who will price and compete for the work packages.

(d)   Labor market: (i) general availability; (ii) peculiar work rules; (iii) interest in project; and (iv) level of cooperation available.

(e)   Provide a conclusion as to how project should be planned and marketed as a result of these findings.

5. ASSIST IN DEVELOPMENT OF CAPITAL BUDGETS

(a)   Provide a budget checklist for capital costs to be sure all requirements are included: (i) land costs; (ii) road-transportation costs—permanent improvements; (iii) utility costs; (iv) site development costs; (v) building costs; (vi) construction finance costs; and (vii) design and other "soft" building costs.

(b)   Review and comment on capital budget in lieu of specific area knowledge.

(c)   Measure planned costs versus end dates sought.

6. ASSIST IN DEVELOPMENT OF CASH-FLOW PROJECTIONS

(a)   Provide time-oriented progress or projected spending.

(b)   Provide time-oriented progress of cash availability.

(c)   Equate spending and availability into periods of surplus and need to permit acquisition and investment planning of fund use during construction.

7. DEVELOP PARAMETRIC ESTIMATES AND COST BUDGETS

(a)   Break conceptual package into basic program of work packages using Uniform Construction Index (UCI) trade categories to start. Breakdown is to be based on typical percentage of cost per trade category found in similar projects.

(b)   Define item (*a*) to fit area restraints.

(c)   Define item (*a*) to fit project restraints.

(d)   Apply to dollar availability and comment on seeming practicality.

(e) Set parameters and work descriptions included in each line item, refining and revising periodically.

(f) Set cost budget for each line item.

8. UPDATE PRELIMINARY SCHEDULE

(a) Develop time-oriented bar chart for entire endeavor.

(b) Detail and adjust bar chart to show known general restraints from each bar to others.

(c) Seek accord and set rules for schedule revisions and time extensions.

(d) Break each activity into detailed network analysis. Degree of detail should suit conditions prevailing. Seek accord and constantly monitor and issue written comments on progress versus schedule.

(e) At appropriate times detail via CPM network analysis the project's design and construction packages into gross and working detail.

9. DEVELOP PRELIMINARY PROJECT CONTROL SYSTEM

Capabilities required for performance and measurement criteria for evaluating performance:

(a) Working knowledge of available scheduling systems to be potentially utilized on the project.

(b) Knowledge of construction and engineering cost control systems.

(c) Background of successfully implementing project control systems on similar size projects.

(d) Proven performance in use of project control systems to identify problem size projects.

(e) Working knowledge of project control systems that evaluate resource availability and requirement for maintenance of schedule milestones.

(f) Estimating capability to prepare timely conceptual estimates for the impact of proposed project changes.

(g) A realistic approach to control system implementation, especially the level of detail of systems required for effective control.

(h) Display a capability and experience in effective project planning.

(i) A flexible control system implementation approach that indicates high potential for compatibility with architecture-engineer (A/E) and contractor system and for provision of all information required by owner.

10. DEVELOP PRELIMINARY PROJECT MANAGEMENT INFORMATION SYSTEM

(a) Possess a successful system of project status reporting, addressing all phases of project activity at various levels.

(b) Know various reporting systems software available.

(c) Be able to provide information necessary for owner, MIS updating, in a form compatible with existing owner information and decision-making systems.

(d) Display a flexibility of MIS implementation approach that indicates high potential for compatibility with A-E and contractor systems.

(e) Understand specialized systems for (i) procurement and delivery status reporting; (ii) drawing and specification status reporting; (iii) construction progress measurement by reporting installed quantities of major construction materials; (iv) turnover and acceptance status reporting; and (v) accounting and record keeping.

(f) Present examples of proven services cost information systems that produce management level and detail reports giving budget, actual, and forecast man-day expenditures by various departments of the construction management (CM) organization.

11. DEVELOP PROJECT SAFETY PROGRAM

(a) Display a familiarity with the Occupational Safety and Health Act (OSHA) state implementation of this legislation (if applicable) and any specific local health and safety programs.

(b) Present a record of safety program implementation and successful performance on past construction management projects.

(c) Possess a working knowledge of safety program experience in the project area, including hazards, frequent problems, and contractor safety performance.

(d) Present a comprehensive, up-to-date safety manual that provides for implementation and enforcement of an effective safety program.

(e) Present adequate plans for safety facilities for the project, including (i) first-aid facilities; (ii) ambulance; (iii) building ventilation; and (iv) air-quality monitoring.

(f) Possess a proven program of safety training for safety engineers, supervisors, and craftsmen.

(g) Display an accident rate (frequency and severity) considerably below the national average for that type of construction project.

(h) Present a working knowledge of the various types of insurance programs available for the project, and a satisfactory rating from a carrier of the appropriate insurance.

(i) Have a working knowledge of fire protection methods and requirements applicable to the project.

(j) Display familiarity with various types of contract provisions that define contractor responsibility for safety program implementation.

12. DEVELOP PROJECT LABOR RELATIONS PROGRAM

(a) Possess a working knowledge of labor relations in the project area.

(b) Be familiar with all agreements that will be in force on the project.

(c) Have experience in conducting prejob conferences on similar size projects in the area.

(d) Present a comprehensive labor relations manual addressing both overall approach and implementation guidelines.

(e) Have a working knowledge of local contractor approaches, capability, and performance in labor relations.

(f) Present organizational experience in resolution of labor problems at the local, district, and international levels.

(g) Have a detailed knowledge of jurisdictional assignments and area practices in the project vicinity.

(h) Present a record of assistance in contractor resolution of work stoppages, and of low time loss due to work stoppage.

(i) Visit site to interview labor leaders, Associated General Contractors (AGC) personnel, local contractors, local designers, local subcontractors, determine area practices, obtain local labor agreements, obtain climatic records, determine favored materials and methods, obtain key local prices, analyze labor availability, and determine local contractor skills and interests.

(j) Analyze and interpret results of the fact-finding.

13. ASSIST IN DEVELOPMENT OF INSURANCE PROGRAM

(a) Provide owner with the economic and objective analysis of alternative insurance programs.

(b) Determine if the size of the project warrants a wrap-up insurance program.

(c) Prepare standard adherence requirements for contractors and establish disciplinary procedures for nonadherence.

14. ADMINISTER ELECTRONIC DATA PROCESSING (EDP) SERVICES

(a) Select appropriate data processing equipment and format.

(b) Build data base.

(c) Make sure EDP reports are appropriate for various management reporting levels served.

(d) Prepare circulation list.

(e) Follow up to make sure EDP reports are useful to all who receive them.

(f) Verify accuracy and timeliness of reports.

(g) Administer all necessary changes to project control systems (PCS) and management information systems (MIS).

(h) Provide statistical analysis of data.

5.8 SUMMARY

The planning phase is an evolutionary process. The time expended is often unaccounted for, since the exact sounding of the "starting gun" may not be until the budget has been completed. It is clear that CM input in this very important phase can be significant. It is also, unfortunately, clear that the selection of the CM may not be made until this phase has been completed. In both government and the private sector, a significant compromise approach has been utilized. As soon as the project is defined, a project manager is assigned. Later, as the project develops, the organization retains its project manager in a top-level liaison role, assigning a construction manager to handle the actual CM duties and functions.

The CM interfaces with the professionals and consultants, and they, in turn, are responsible for solving design problems involving many separate functional areas. Each major member of the design team accumulates his or her own information and formulates his or her own solution. The results, in turn, should be coordinated with the other primary disciplines.

In the planning phase a project becomes identified as a concept, then project scope, definition, budget, funding, and programming are evolved. The construction manager performs a wide range of tasks in this phase. These tasks range from development of conceptual estimates, schedules, and project resource requirements through providing constructability analysis to development of safety programs, labor relations programs, and project management information systems.

6

Design Phase

6.1 INTRODUCTION

The design phase is a separate function in the CM process. Over the years this has been formalized and structured by the design professionals, both architects and engineers, through various professional groups. The design phase of a project is usually in three phases or stages. These stages are schematic, preliminary, and final. Each sequence more specifically defines the concept, culminating in the final set of plans and specifications to be utilized for construction purposes. The American Institute of Architects has formalized the appropriate definitions and scope both as professional functions and in contract terms. The functions are categorized as (*a*) schematic design, (*b*) preliminary design, and (*c*) final design. This chapter will discuss these three phases of design after discussing the design budget and its significance. Finally, the chapter discusses the CM's tasks during this phase.

6.2   DESIGN BUDGET AND ITS SIGNIFICANCE

There are two basic methods for establishing construction budgets. The most popular is to determine the cost per square foot of a similar facility and apply an escalation factor based on historical information. The second and more favorable is to develop a master-plan action program that researches the various subsystems of the proposed facility. This program progresses concurrently with the development design stages.

6.2.1   Schematic Design Costs

During the initial (schematic) design phase, the cost estimate would consider the following factors:

1. *Basic scope*—Study and evaluate basic provisions of the budget relative to the program scope.

2. *Equipment*—Set aside equipment budget allowance.

3. *Site work*—Identify special requirements of master-plan action program that may influence site costs.

4. *Basement and special foundations*—Study and identify probable effect of master plan, soil, and site conditions on foundation or basement design.

5. *Impact of master plan*—Study and identify the probable effect of the master plan on siting, geometry, acoustics, and links to other parts of the master plan, present and future.

6. *Market abnormality*—Initiate study of market conditions.

7. *Research*—Study program and identify areas of design and cost where research is required. Study program and identify unknowns. Initiate research for future phases of development.

8. *Time*—Initiate study of projected market conditions.

9. *Local market*—Identify influence of local labor and material costs on choice of materials and systems. Identify market deviations from normal.

10. *Physical design development*—Develop with the design team layouts of typical spaces to determine if the program function or activity can be accommodated in the area programmed.

11. *Basis for cost evaluation*—Analysis, research, and experience.

12. *Content of estimate*—Restatement of program budget.

13. *Detail of estimate*—Confirm adequacy of the budget for project and site.

6.2.2   Preliminary Design Cost

The preliminary design (or design development) phase formalizes the adopted scheme and concept into basic plans for all major components of the facility. The plans now include more detailed presentations of architectural, structural, mechanical, and electrical components of the facility. Materials are selected and systems are established. Although this phase is described as "preliminary," certain final determinations as to structure, systems, materials, and architectural treatment are actually made. As a rule of thumb, in the A-E profession the preliminary phase of design is considered to constitute a work effort of 25% of the total design. This yardstick is carried over to the determination of value, and the 25% factor is used to establish the cost of the fee of the designer's work at completion of this phase. This can be misleading because of the need to develop, or at least initiate, many of the final designs and systems during the preliminary phase of design development.

The basic stages in this design phase include

1. Unit studies of plan elements to determine feasibility of concept.

2. Modular analysis of typical spaces to determine constructibility and cost practicality.

3. Preparation of architectural plan at a scale proper for accurate layout of basic spatial solutions.

4. Development of tentative scheme of mechanical and electrical systems.

5. Development of personnel and equipment layouts for functional areas.

6. Development of exterior design of the structure.

7. Preparation of outline of materials and finishes (skeleton specification).

8. Preparation of a cost estimate.

This stage is, in a sense, a reiteration of the initial stage. However, the entire operation is based upon the spatial solution that was selected at the end of schematic design. Design development first validates that spatial soultion, then expands the level of detail. Construction management in this stage should be oriented toward the constructability and feasibility aspects. Alternate approaches within the parameters (if possible, of the initial spatial solution) should be posed and studied.

During design development, the design team seeks previous modular solutions for incorporation into their overall scheme. Generally, these proven modules are materials or equipment that have been previously utilized and tested, and are available commercially.

In monitoring the design of a structural steel system, the construction manager would attempt to impose practical guidelines such as the use of standard structural sizes, limitation on the use of special shapes, and the use of standard column sizes where appropriate.

Life-cycle costing is an important consideration during design development. The energy flow and dynamic balance for the facility can be evaluated at this stage. The result will affect the roofing and exterior skin, as well as the size of the heating, ventilating, and air-conditioning equipment. This, in turn, has direct impact upon the electrical requirements.

During the preliminary phase, outline specifications are prepared and the design progresses in sufficient detail to make it possible to define costs. Such costs are also "preliminary"; however, they are based on sufficient detail to make it possible to evaluate initial budgets, to make basic changes or decisions within the initial guidelines for the facility, and to hold budgets or seek budgetary revisions, as may be necessary.

6.2.3   Final Design Cost

The final design (or contract document) phase of effort formalizes and details all aspects of the facility. All components, systems, and materials are selected and defined. The basic and inherent details for not only a functional facility but for one of aesthetic value and any special requirements of a specific owner are documented and translated into plans and specifications. Such plans and specifications are the basic part of the contract documents issued to implement the project.

The detailed design phase takes the design concept that has been defined in the design development stage and adds a level of detail that is required for the contractors to construct the facility. This is the development of the documents that will be the basis of the construction contract and that will also instruct the contractor on the quality and quantity of the materials he is to provide and install. Major components of the design include

1. Layouts of partitions and interior fixtures
2. Engineering design and structural elements
3. Architectural design of construction detail
4. Layout and design of mechanical systems
5. Location of fixtures and utility outlets
6. Chart of materials and finishes
7. Specifications of materials and equipment
8. Layout and design of electrical systems

The CM activity in this stage should emphasize the selection of better values within the spatial solution and modular decisions made in the previous two stages. If a different HVAC system should have been selected or another structural system would have been more appropriate, these decisions should have been made as part of the value analysis at the beginning of the design development stage. Value analysis in the design document stage should be of the type where one material can be substituted directly for another. In a masonry wall, for instance, a larger block might be selected. (Analysis would have to include an evaluation of the labor practice in the area to determine how many of the larger-size blocks can be laid up under present working conditions.) A different roofing scheme might be selected within the dimensions of the roof, as defined in the previous design phase. Details such as flashing for roofing systems should be studied. Analysis might also indicate that more expensive approaches should be utilized to ensure the integrity of the entire building. Similarly, studies might determine that the life-cycle aspects of maintenance would indicate a better value solution in the use of epoxy-based finishes rather than low-cost acrylic paint in hallways.

6.2.4   Significance of Design Phase to Project Costs

Well over 90% of the project's costs are determined or committed by the time the preliminary design is over. This is so because certain final determinations on the project are made during this phase. It is important that a cost control program be established during the planning phase and be continuous throughout the design. CM must review preliminary plans as they develop and offer suggestions and cautions about particular systems, standardized components, and construction methods. He also contributes to the development process; he must supply up-to-date and local information on cost and the availability of labor and materials and provide preliminary estimates. A series of "hard-nosed" value analyses are necessary to identify unnecessarily high cost areas and alternatives suggested. The CM must possess a high degree of competence in evaluating costs and in the employ of costs as elements in a dynamic planning process. In this regard, he must be sensitive to the cost relationships in the design process. The potentials for individual value-analysis evaluations and life-cycle costing are obviously greatest at the beginning of the design, when there is sufficient time for these analyses. Such analyses and evaluations followed by suggestions and acceptance of alternatives not only help the design team stay within the budget but also help to avoid "surprises" during bid openings. Therefore, the significance of cost control during design cannot be overemphasized.

6.3   SCHEMATIC DESIGN PHASE

The function of construction management during schematic design is best identified by discussing some tasks that may be included in the CM service.

The CM may assist the owner in the selection of the A-E designer for the contemplated project. Governmental authorities, especially federal, state, and major municipalities, have established procedures for A-E selection, but this procedure is not applicable to all owners, public as well as private. Depending upon the capabilities required, the construction manager is qualified to recommend to the owner the type of design firm that the latter should consider for an assignment. For instance, should the owner seek a primary architect or an engineer? The answer may not be self-evident to an owner if his needs are other than standard categories of building (architects) or heavy construction (engineers); the project may be a building in which aesthetics is secondary to function (warehouse— movement of goods); or other factors, such as site conditions (seismic or soils consideration), may outweigh others. In this instance, it may be advantageous to the owner to seek engineering-architectural service as differentiated from A-E services. The construction manager can further advise the owner on the capabilities of individual firms for the owner's consideration. While the CM can play a significant role in advising, it is almost always the owner who makes the final selection of the A-E designer.

The construction manager should obtain all data relating to the site and surrounding area to enable the designer to implement the design. Such data may include aerial photographs, topographic surveys, property deeds and maps, and subsurface information, including borings. If such data are not available, the CM may obtain them by subcontracting or by purchase, if available, from other sources. This in itself may require the taking of competitive bids, as, for instance, for extensive soil borings or testing. Although such data are usually obtained during the design process, the construction manager will have recognized the need for the data in the early stages of project development, and such data will have been obtained in a timely manner when required by the designer to develop design details.

The CM, together with the A-E, should document the owner's objectives. This aspect may be only an amplification of prior activity on the part of the owner and the CM. Again, depending upon the time when the CM is brought into the project development, the scope and extent of such documentation would be appropriately defined. This may only involve documentation for the benefit of the A-E, with its purpose limited to obtaining input from the design team to define properly such goals and objectives in light of the functional aspects of the project. The construction manager will assist or collaborate with the A-E in a program of evaluation of the owner's requirements, but this program review should be made to assess the scope of program within the budget and schedules previously prepared. Although this is often a basic-design function, its significance in the CM process is for a strict definition and evaluation in light of budgetary and time constraints, whose significance is not as readily apparent during the formative stage as at later stages, when detailed estimates are being prepared.

The construction manager should analyze the program in conjunction with the A-E to assess the costs and benefits of alternative architectural, structural, and mechanical systems both at the initiation of and during the schematic stage. He should report these recommendations to the owner. The construction manager and architect-engineer should jointly develop a schedule for all A-E work during preconstruction phases. The CM should identify all tasks, milestones, and reviews to be incorporated in the A-E's schedule, as well as identify sequencing and time required to perform during each phase. The contruction manager should prepare cost analyses of systems proposed by the A-E and identify other feasible systems, including cost analyses of these alternatives. The CM should prepare narrative reports for all systems being considered, describing the advantages and disadvantages of each system. (These reports are in addition to the cost analyses.) They can include

- Area: net to gross ratios
- Structure: tons/cost per square foot
- Lighting and power: watts/cost per square foot/watts per square foot
- Heating: Btu/cost per square foot/Btu per square foot
- Air conditioning: tons/cost per square foot/tons per square foot
- Plumbing: cost per square foot
- Total cost per square foot
- Furniture and fixtures: cost per square foot/total cost

The construction manager should prepare cost analyses of all materials, equipment, fixtures, and methods proposed; identify feasible materials, equipment, fixtures, and methods that have not been suggested; and prepare cost analyses of these alternatives. The CM may prepare narrative reports for materials being considered, in order to describe the advantages of each material.

6.4   PRELIMINARY DESIGN PHASE

During design development the CM should independently investigate costs and availability of systems proposed by the designer. The construction manager should advise the designer or the architect-engineer as to the availability of proposed systems, his evaluation of such systems costs, and the availability and costs of possible alternate systems. Independently, the

CM should monitor budget and time schedules for the design phase of the project development. This schedule should be reviewed at regular intervals with the A-E's specific project objectives and design requirements.

Depending upon time schedules and needs of the owner established in the prior and early stages of project development, the construction manager should assess the design together with the A-E to develop appropriate design packages for construction implementation. Such input will be necessary in the early stages of design to assist the A-E in preparing the appropriate documents for phasing construction if such phasing is deemed appropriate. Depending upon the project criteria and needs, such phasing—also called fast tracking—may consist of issuing complete documents for certain elements prior to total design completion. In early stages it is possible not only to issue contract documents for construction implementation but also to identify long-lead material items for early purchases. Such purchasing would be initiated and implemented by the CM on behalf of the owner, with the product purchased in this manner turned over to the contractor for installation.

During design development the construction manager performs necessary periodic reviews of the proposed design in order to monitor preestablished budgets and cost limitations. If during such review the CM evaluates the design aspects, he should review them with the A-E to formulate appropriate recommendations to the owner. The importance of a review and check of estimates becomes more obvious after a look at the uncertainties of the price structure, evidenced not only by the steep inflationary spiral of the 1970s but by the dislocation of the supply market in 1974. Such dislocation, which is not limited to petroleum products, has made it impossible to estimate costs with certainty over extended time frames.

The construction manager should review preliminary specifications prepared by the architect-engineer, including quality control standards and criteria for site development, architectural, structural, plumbing, electric, and site utilities. The preliminary specifications should describe the total design to date, including economic justification reports where required by the owner. In accordance with the review of the total design, which may include design aspects such as the architectural, civil, mechanical, electrical, and structural plans, the construction manager should consider both construction feasibility and possible economy that may be affected by different choices of proposed materials and construction methods. It is assumed that the architect-engineer, in the development of a design and performing his assignment in a professional manner, will make the most economical, functional, and efficient selections of materials and construction methods. The CM, however, serves as a third party to give the benefit of an objective and professional review and to develop possible recommendations for consideration.

At the conclusion of the preliminary design phase, the CM makes a very important estimate. This is the first point at which major structural, mechanical, and electrical systems have been defined. This information, combined with the spatial solution of the schematic design, can be cost-estimated with a high degree of accuracy. The cost for each component and system can then be compared with the budget and with standards for the type of construction. Budget variances must be adjusted. This cost information should also be used as the basis for a value-analysis cycle by the construction manager.

6.5   FINAL DESIGN PHASE

The CM should review the drawings and specifications and make recommendations throughout the design stage concerning the following:

1. Availability of materials and labor.

2. Conflicts and overlapping jurisdictions among contractors and subcontractors.

3. Coordination among the drawings and between the drawings and specifications.

4. Construction detailing, to ensure that the methods, details of wall sections, and other sections, shown are buildable and adequate to ensure a reliable, permanent, trouble-free installation.

5. Quality control standards and criteria.

6. A detailed review of the completed working drawings and specifications.

7. On-site temporary facilities to enable the construction manager, architect, and owner to perform their duties.

8. Items of a temporary nature necessary for the performance of the contractors.

9. Availability of a storing area for each contractor and subcontractor.

Prior to completion of the final design plans, the construction manager together with the architect-engineer should analyze the total design effort and establish the appropriate division of work for the final contract documents and plans and specifications. This is required for the taking of bids or for negotiation of separate contracts. In establishing such bid packages, appropriate consideration will have to be given to time of performance, availability of labor, overlapping trade jurisdictions, and related work items. Such review will also ensure that when the plans and specifications are issued to bid and become part of the final contract documents, all overlapping functions will have been eliminated. Such review will also ensure that there is no omission of a function or specification for the total implementation of the project.

The construction manager prepares a detailed cost estimate of the proposed construction during various stages of planned development. Such work can possibly be limited to an analysis and review of estimates prepared by the architect-engineer, who will have prepared such estimates in the normal course of design development. Because of the complexities of the construction marketplace and with the ever-increasing price pressures, an independent, detailed take-off based upon a quantity survey of the plans and specifications, together with a detailed unit-price estimate, fills a useful purpose during the design phase and is performed by the CM. Such cost estimates can be utilized for comparisons with the preestablished budgets prior to the taking of competitive bids, or utilized as a guide during the negotiation of prices with preselected contractors, or may even serve, as they do in some instances, as a guaranteed outside price if a contracting entity takes on the implementation and construction of the work on such a basis.

In conjunction with the detailed estimate, the CM should review and comment on contract documents prepared by the A-E. These documents are composed of copies of all drawings, specifications, including quality control standards and criteria, necessary for the construction as described by the approved preliminary documents, fully coordinated for bidding by the various contractors and subcontractors. This includes all engineering drawings, plot plans, floor plans, sections, elevations, details, soil exploration data, key construction milestones, and other data required to obtain complete bids.

Near the end of the working-drawing preparation, prebid CPM construction networks should be prepared. These networks establish the time of construction, including key milestones, which are very useful for control by the CM during the construction phase.

The construction manager may recommend the purchase of long-lead items. In this case, the CM, upon the placement of the early purchase order, should assume the function of monitoring the purchase contract. Such monitoring may consist solely of ensuring that all requirements previously established for the specified materials, for example, preselected pump or generator requiring lengthy fabrication, are met. It may also include expediting such prepurchased items. In the traditional construction process, expediting becomes the responsibility of the contractor who is furnishing a specified and purchased piece of equipment.

Often, however, construction is delayed because a critical item is delayed during the fabrication process. Such a delay can be the result of numerous factors beyond the control of a contractor and often becomes known to him only at the time he is seeking its delivery to the jobsite. The expediting role of the CM may require monitoring the fabrication process of critical fabricated items. The extent of such monitoring will be dependent upon many factors, including the financial solvency of the manufacturer, and pressures on the fabricator to meet other deliveries or commitments.

6.6   CM'S TASKS DURING THE DESIGN PHASE

Specifically, the CM performs the following tasks during the design phase:

1.   OVERALL PROJECT PLANNING

(a)   Make an early identification of the owner's real needs.

(b)   Assist the owner in site selection; make recommendations concerning probable soil conditions, traffic patterns, access to the site; advise on availability, location, and capacity of existing utilities; and be able to estimate cost trade-offs between alternative sites.

(c)   Know local zoning requirements, codes, the permit process, and environmental impact requirements.

(d)   Understand project financing alternatives.

(e)   Advise owner on alternative project configuration schemes, for example, high rise versus low rise, steel versus concrete, or underground versus above-ground construction.

(f)   Assist the owner in selection of the A-E, if requested.

(g)   Help organize and develop "the project team."

(h)   Possess local, regional, and nationwide forecasting capabilities. This capability should include social and economic considerations as well as resource allocation requirements.

(i)   Be familiar with similar projects under construction or previously completed.

(j)   Advise the owner on alternative construction administration methods, such as phase construction.

2.   ASSIST IN DEVELOPMENT OF PROJECT LIFE-CYCLE COSTS

(a)   Determine systems to be evaluated on a life-cycle basis.

(b)   Determine who will assemble and how they will assemble life-cycle input.

(c)   Review and react to work product provided previously.

(d) Determine when life-cycle evaluations are to be made.

(e) Assign and follow through for final decisions on system selection by owner. Get written decisions on written cost alternates.

3. EVALUATE COST TRADE-OFFS

(a) Establish a system of disclosure or discovery of cost-trade-off potentials.

(b) Designate time and a person to make decisions for these. Establish a backup man for decisions if not made in time.

(c) Establish dollar consideration to make cost decision on trade-off necessary.

4. PROVIDE VALUE ENGINEERING FUNCTION

(a) Present an experienced record in the successful implementation of value engineering programs on equivalent projects.

(b) Have a working knowledge of current engineering approaches and techniques.

(c) Present a complete program for value analysis, including the following: (i) orientation; (ii) information; (iii) speculation; (iv) functional analysis; (v) program planning; (vi) program execution; and (vii) summary and conclusions.

(d) Demonstrate methods of functional analysis of design details and resultant simplification and cost savings.

(e) Have a data base regarding historical unit performance at a detailed level on all types of construction activities.

5. PROCURE LONG-LEAD-TIME ITEMS

(a) Identify special market factors that influence procurement lead times, and estimate the actual lead times for major construction materials and equipment.

(b) Develop construction schedules in detail to allow definition of required at-site date for all potentially prepurchased materials. Special construction schedule logic constraints, such as access limitations and potential for use of permanent equipment during construction, should be considered.

(c) Based on lead time and construction schedule logic assessment, define those construction materials that should be prepurchased and supplied to the construction contractors.

(d) Review each material procurement specification and purchase order to assure that the following items are defined: (i) milestone delivery dates (to be put in by construction manager from the project construction schedule); (ii) shipping configurations; (iii) requirements for special handling attachments or devices; (iv) maximum size constraints; (v) packaging requirements; (vi) requirements for supplier definition of special storage conditions; and (vii) documentation submittal requirements.

(e) As a part of the scheduling activities, schedule the required dates for the various procurement activities on long-lead-time items. This includes the date of bidding, bid opening, recommendation for award to owner, owner award, and release of shop drawings for fabrication, if required.

(f) Utilizing the schedule dates, monitor the status of equipment procurement and delivery operations, and expedite deliveries, if required, and if included in the CM scope.

(g) Receive, inspect, and place into storage all prepurchased material delivered prior to installation contractor mobilization. Perform periodic inspections and maintenance of equipment in storage, if required.

(h) Following acceptable delivery or operation, provide recommendations for authorization of vendor payment.

6.   FINALIZE PROJECT SCHEDULES

(a) Finalize conceptual network analysis simultaneously with completion of conceptual drawings and the conceptual cost estimates, including determination of major milestones.

(b) Finalize detailed network analysis simultaneously with completion of detailed estimates from detailed drawings.

(c) Issue complete project schedule in bar-chart form for information of all concerned.

(d) Develop reporting and monitoring procedures so that actual progress can be compared to planned progress at all times.

7. FINALIZE PHYSICAL LAYOUT OF CONSTRUCTION AREAS

(a) Identify all required construction buildings and facilities. This includes facilities required by the construction manager and those anticipated for all construction contractors.

(b) Identify all necessary access paths to permanent structures and remove these areas from consideration as construction facility locations.

(c) Define areas necessary for material laydown, subassembly, and staging. Laydown areas should include adequate space for both the prepurchased and contractor furnished materials. Anticipated contractor requirements for yard subassembly and fabrication should also be addressed. Areas in close proximity to structures and also to rail spurs should be reserved for material off-loading and staging.

(d) Establish the preliminary location of all required construction facilities.

(e) Define grading and drainage requirements necessary to support the construction facility locations defined previously. This includes balance of earthwork quantities for projects requiring site grading, and definition of all drainage requirements to assure provision of acceptable working conditions.

(f) Establish locations of all general condition facilities to be shared by the various construction contractors. This also includes defining the location of corridors for utility services to be provided to all construction facilities.

(g) Prepare sketches and contract document provisions that define the limitations on contractor facility locations, as well as requirements for contractor conformance to the overall construction area layout.

8. FINALIZE PROJECT CONTROL SYSTEMS (PCS) AND MANAGEMENT INFORMATION SYSTEMS (MIS)

(a) Quantify time, cost, and quality objectives where possible.

(b) Include the quantitative date on objectives to the project control system.

(c) Test the management information systems to verify that they produce data compatible with that required by the PCS.

(d) Prepare general sample reports and get approval from all participating management levels.

9. ASSIST IN OBTAINING ALL REQUIRED PERMITS AND LICENSES

(a) Define the requirements for all federal, state, and local permits required for project construction.

(b) Provide input for regulatory agency submittals to obtain these permits. These submittals should establish only realistic commitments that can be satisfied by the individual construction contractors during performance of their work.

(c) Establish a schedule of permit receipt dates that are required to support the project construction schedule. These dates must assure that the permits are received that do not restrain the performance of various construction activities at the most efficient time.

(d) Include provisions in all construction contracts to obligate contractors to perform the work in accordance with all permits and other commitments.

(e) Plan and implement a program for assuring compliance with all permits and owner commitments.

10. PROVIDE INPUT AND REVIEW OF CONTRACT DOCUMENTS

(a) Provide the ability to review plans and specifications for scope of work, contract forms, general and special conditions and define owner, architectural, construction manager, and contractor relationships.

(b) Examine each set of plans and specifications for contract package to assure a clear definition of scope of work and contract limitations. Also assure logical grouping of construction activities in a single contract.

(c) Advise the owner which field services will be provided by the construction manager, acting for the owner to provide the most economical solutions, and avoid separate contractors providing duplicate services. Items such as this could be sanitary facilities, welding facilities, fire protection facilities, first aid, and medical programs.

(d) Prepare contract special conditions to reflect field conditions schedule and contracting interfaces.

6.7   SUMMARY

The design phase of a project is usually in three phases or stages. It involves a complex interplay between the design disciplines. These stages are the schematic (or sketch design or conceptual), design development (or preliminary), and final design (or working drawings). Each stage becomes more complex, requiring more time and increasing the potential for error. Accordingly, construction-management input should be tailored to the inflexibility of the design as it evolves.

These three phases or sequences of design (schematic, preliminary, and final) are enumerated to identify the evolvement of design, whether or not such phases are structured or formalized in the design process. On complex and major design efforts, each of these phases is defined and normally followed by a review and approval process.

The previous definition has presented design as a theoretical and total process for an individual facility or project. It does not, however, have to be implemented or to progress from beginning to end, from concept to bidding document. Depending upon need, the nature of the facility, budgetary and time restraints, and total design can be "phased."

The CM performs the following major tasks during the design phase:

(a) Development of overall project planning

(b) Development of project life-cycle costs

(c) Evaluations of cost trade-offs

(d) Provision of value engineering functions

(e) Procurement of long-lead-time items

(f) Finalization of project schedules, physical layout of construction areas, and project control systems and management information systems

(g) Procurement of all permits and licenses

(h) Provision of input and review of contract documents

7

Bidding and Award Phase

7.1 INTRODUCTION

The execution of the planning and design phases is divided into two equally important objectives. These objectives are the following: (1) the job must be "bought out" at a price within the budget and (2) the project must be completed as designed and on schedule. In a phased construction program, the first packages must be developed shortly after commencement of detail design and will proceed simultaneously with detail design work. Items to be considered during the bidding and award phase will include the following: (1) finalize preliminary contractor bid lists by contract package; (2) prequalify selected contractors based upon qualifications criteria; (3) issue final invited bidder list by contract package; (4) prepare bid packages; (5) review bid packages; (6) issue "Requests for Quotation"; (7) prepare detailed fair-cost estimate for each bid package; (8) review and analyze bids; (9) recommend contract awards; and (10) issue "Notices to Proceed with Fieldwork."

This chapter will discuss the bidding and award phase. Specifically, it discusses (1) phasing and packaging work, (2) qualifications, (3) preparing bidding documents, (4) bidding and award, (5) the role of planning in this phase, and (6) the CM's tasks during this phase.

7.2   PHASING AND PACKAGING WORK

7.2.1   Phasing

It is economically advantageous in an escalating market to start construction quickly. But doing so requires a design and construction approach that is normally incompatible with the standard practice of bidding on a specific set of plans and specifications. Starting a job early, while the rest of the project is being developed, means "phase design and construction," "phasing," or "fast tracking." By either name, phasing means breaking design into phases or components in such a manner that certain design elements can be deferred sufficiently to permit construction of the facility to commence before final design is completed (see Fig. 7.1). Thus various parts of design and construction phases of a project will overlap. The main objective of phasing is to condense the overall project time schedule. Since time is money to a potential project owner, phasing or fast tracking has the objective of decreasing the cost of a project.

It is during the planning phase that the CM has to have an eye toward phased construction. The project is then planned so that major segments of the work can be designed and released for construction in logical order throughout the job. The subsystems of the facility or project must be selected in the beginning so that the succeeding design phase can proceed without delay. In other words, while one phase of the project is being constructed, the following phase is being designed.

7.2.2   Work Packaging

One of the first steps to any project is preparing contract bid documents. Before these contract documents can be drawn by the designer, the owner, through his CM, must be consulted to identify the schedule and the order of the phases to be collected for separate contracts.

The two different and distinct methods of preparing construction contract packages are the following:

1. Prepare individual contract packages from relatively standard specifications and drawings similar to those prepared for a single general-contract project. Here the design firm updates or modifies standard specifications it has developed over many years to fit the requirements of the project under consideration.

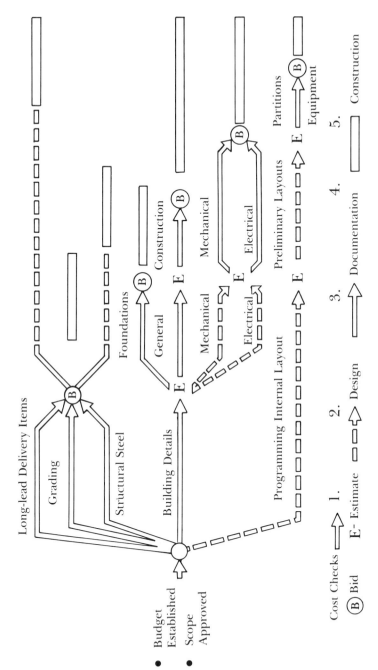

Figure 7.1. Phased Design and Construction. Adapted from Special Report (129:11).

2. Prepare individual contract packages from individual specifications and drawings prepared with the overall scope of the desired contract packages in mind.

7.2.3 Advantages and Disadvantages of Phasing and Work Packaging

Although phasing and work packaging have many advantages, they are not without potential disadvantages.

1. ADVANTAGES The phasing and packaging of several individual construction contracts provides several benefits, including the following:

(a) Gives project owner more control over the individual contractors.

(b) Gives the project owner and his CM more flexibility and control in the selection of the individual contractors.

(c) Allows for a reduction in the amount of overhead related to one contractor marking up his subcontractor's work.

(d) Provides for a means of awarding contractor work packages that are of a scope and size compatible with procuring competitive contractor bids.

(e) Provides a means of structuring work that accommodates various governmental or external agency requirements, including minority set-aside programs.

(f) Enables a control system that pinpoints individual contractor performance or nonperformance with the potential for improved control of the construction phase.

(g) Accommodates the phasing of construction work in that individual construction packages can be awarded as a design evolves.

2. DISADVANTAGES Phasing and packaging of design and construction work are not without their potential disadvantages. These must be weighed when evaluating the use of phasing and packaging and the number of phases and packages to be awarded. Included in the disadvantages of phasing and work packaging are the following:

(a) The potential of omissions in covering all work to be performed because of the division of the total construction phase into pieces.

(b) The potential for overlaps in contractor responsibilities because of several construction packages.

(c) Loss of contractor coordination and control because of the lack of a single contractor.

(d) Less bidding competition among specialty contractors because of the need for the individual contractors to bond their own portion of the construction.

(e) Potential increased contractor costs associated with managing individual contracts.

Although each of these disadvantages should be recognized, it is also true that an effective CM can reduce or eliminate these negative considerations.

7.3 QUALIFICATIONS

There are statutes that many states have enacted that require a general contracting firm wishing to do public work to be judged qualified before it can be issued bidding documents or before it can submit a proposal. This is called prequalification. Other states require that the contractor's qualifications be judged after he has submitted a proposal. This method is called postqualification. Many other public bodies, including agencies of the federal government, require some form of qualification for contractors bidding on their construction projects. The merits and drawbacks of the process have been debated for many years, but qualification in some form has become almost standard practice in the field of public construction. The main purpose observed by qualification is to eliminate from consideration the incompetent, overextended, underfinanced, and inexperienced contractors.

In those states in which licenses are required, contractors must be licensed before applying for prequalification. To prequalify, contractors must submit detailed information concerning their equipment, experience, finances, current jobs in progress, references, and personnel. Evaluation of these data results in a determination of whether the contractor will be allowed to submit a proposal. In jurisdictions having postqualification, the contractor is called on to furnish certain information along with his bid. The information is much the same as that required for prequalification, but it serves the qualification purpose only for the particular project being bid.

The description so far has been based entirely on publicly financed projects. The same procedures can be utilized on private jobs. A somewhat different procedure often used in closed biddings is for the contractor to submit an individualized qualification summary with his bid. This is essentially a sales document and contains information designed to enhance the contractor's qualifications in the eyes of the owner. During the bidding and award phase, the CM first qualifies potential bidders and then prepares a prequalified contractor list. He usually rates these contractors on their experiences, especially on equivalent projects in the site area, their financial strengths, their previous commitments, their personnel, and their performance records on similar jobs.

7.4   PREPARING BIDDING DOCUMENTS

Bidding documents for a construction management project must be developed as a joint effort of the designer, owner, and CM. Bid package makeups will vary depending on owner requirements and on designer and CM procedures. A typical bid package might consist of the following items:

1. INVITATION TO BID   The invitation to bid is sometimes called the Advertisement. It can be a telephone call, a written letter, or a paid advertisement placed in a newspaper telling contractors that plans and specifications are ready for bidding. The law requires that public projects be advertised in the press when they are ready for bidding. The purpose is to let all interesteed parties know about the work and prevent favoritism. In private work the owner has the right to limit the bidding, yet may choose to publish an advertisement. In any case, the more common type of invitation is by letter or telephone. The invitation is simply a request that a contractor submit a bid on a project. It may or may not be included in the book specification.

2. INSTRUCTIONS TO BIDDERS   When there is no advertisement, the Instructions to Bidders is the first section in the specifications. It informs those interested in bidding when the bids are due, how to fill out the proposal form, and where to deliver it when it is completed.

3. PROPOSAL OR BID FORM   The architect or engineer prepares the proposal or bid form. This form is sent to the various bidders, who fill in the blank spaces giving their prices for doing the specified work and sign the same. Legally, the proposal is an offer. If the owner accepts the offer, a contract is made. The purpose of having the architect or engineer prepare the proposal or bid form is to ensure uniformity. Thus the price each bidder submits will be easy to compare with those of others, and the low bidders can be determinated easily. Thus one can understand that if each bidder were permitted to prepare the bid or proposal submitted, no two bids would be made on the same basis.

4. BID BREAKDOWN   The bid breakdown is filled in by the bidder, and it gives the individual price components that sum to the total contract price. This breakdown may later guide progress payments.

5. CONSTRUCTION CONTRACT   A sample contract is included to inform prospective bidders of the type of contract each will be expected to sign if his executed proposal form is accepted by the owner.

6.   GENERAL CONDITIONS   The General Conditions, more correctly called the General Conditions of the Contract, describe conditions required on every construction project. They cover such items as insurance, ownership of drawings, royalties and patents, protection of the work, claims for extra cost, termination of the contract, and payments. Because the General Conditions are always the same, they are usually printed. The American Institude of Architects sells a very excellent set of printed sheets, and these are used in most construction projects. The federal government and various state and local governments print their own documents for their use. Many large companies also prefer to print their own documents for their use. Furthermore, many large companies prefer to print their own general conditions, each adapted to their own use.

7.   SPECIAL CONDITIONS   The Special Conditions are sometimes called the Special Conditions of the Contract or the Supplementary General Conditions. They are similar to the General Conditions in that they deal with conditions of work. However, Special Conditions deal with specific items that apply only to groups of contracts or to the particular contract under consideration. For example, a contractor estimating the costs for constructing a water treatment plant must know how to get the material to the jobsite. Either there is or there is not a railroad siding on the property where work is to be performed. The contractor should know whether there is a railroad and under what conditions it may be used for delivery of the material. This would affect the price. Such an item would normally appear in the Special Conditions, since each job and each building site would have different conditions. If, however, a single company had a single plant and an established policy for handling a contractor's freight, this information could appear in the company's printed General Conditions. The same information should be given about who will furnish water or electrical power. The contractor must know the working conditions in order to submit an intelligent quotation.

8.   CONTRACTOR'S WORK   A (general) contractor who has a contract with an owner has duties and obligations that he alone can perform. These can be placed in a separate section of the specifications. It is more common, however, to include the general contractor's work as a subsection in the Special Conditions.

9.   WORK INCLUDED IN CONTRACT (OPTIONAL)   This section may designate provisions of a standard specification applicable to the particular contract to be awarded.

10.   WORK NOT INCLUDED IN CONTRACT (OPTIONAL) This section may exclude provisions of a standard specification not applicable to the particular contract to be awarded.

11. SPECIFICATIONS, ADDENDA, AND DRAWINGS   These items provide technical requirements of the contract; taken together, they define the scope, extent, and quality of the work.

12. SUPPLEMENTAL PROVISIONS   Supplemental provisions may include items not suited for inclusion in the Special Conditions, such as definition of the status of the construction manager, and prevailing wage rates, if applicable.

13. ALTERNATES   An "alternate" is a request for a price for making a specific change in the contract documents. Not all specifications have alternates, and if none are required, the section can be omitted. If one or more alternates are requested, these alternates should be specified in a separate section. Alternates can be simple or intricate.

14. CONSTRUCTION SCHEDULE   This section shows schedule milestones and overall completion requirements for the particular contract being bid. It also provides an overall schedule showing general relationships between work packages and design activities.

15. OWNER-FURNISHED ITEMS   This section describes all items to be furnished to the contractor by the owner and others. It may include such items as materials, equipment, temporary utilities, storage areas, water, sanitation facilities and survey controls.

7.5 BIDDING AND AWARD

7.5.1 Analysis of Bids

Once all proposals have been received, the construction manager first prepares a spread sheet tabulating all quotations and notes other pertinent factors such as qualifications, omissions, unit prices, and completion times. He then reviews alternates requested or proposed by the bidder.

If they are encouraged prior to bidding and are dealt with fairly in the bid valuation, alternates proposed by the bidders themselves form an excellent value engineering opportunity. Proposed alternates, either volunteered or requested, should always be reviewed jointly with the designer, and ideally, a joint recommendation should be made to the owner. In some cases, only the owner can evaluate the desirability of a savings resulting from a proposed modification.

One method of assuring that bidders are treated fairly in the evaluation of volunteered alternates provides the following guidelines:

1. When a bidder who is not low under the basic bid volunteers an alternate judged by the designer to be equal to the specified requirements, and thus becomes the new low bidder, the award will be made to that bidder; both the bidder and the owner gain from the bidder's ingenuity.

2. When, under similar conditions, a bidder submits an alternate that represents a sizable monetary savings, but is not equal to the specified product, and if in this event the proposed substitution is acceptable to the owner because of the magnitude of the cost savings, all bidders in contention should be given an opportunity to quote on the acceptable but lower-quality alternate, and the award should be made to the subsequent low bidder.

3. When an alternate is volunteered by a high bidder who would not be low even after taking the alternate into account, and if the alternate is acceptable to the designer and the owner, the low bidder may be contacted and requested to quote on the proposed modification.

In all these proceedings, the construction manager must apply fairness and good judgment to avoid any practices bordering on unethical "bid shopping." Where alternates will be accepted, guidelines of the type given here must be stated in the bidding document.

7.5.2 Recommendation for Award

After evaluation of the bids, including alternates, a recommendation for award is made to the owner. After approval by the owner, actual award can be made either by the manager or directly by the owner.

In the event that the award is recommended to other than the low bidder, a full explanation of the reasons for such a recommendation should be made to the owner, and his approval should be obtained. Under an invited, prequalified bid list, the award should normally go to the low initial bidder unless schedule demands or other equally significant considerations indicate that the award should go to a bidder whose volunteered alternates or other qualifications make him a more cost effective choice.

Some companies follow a policy of opening all bids in the presence of the bidders. Others will advise all bidders of the bid results for the base bid. Where the owner is in the continuing-work-load classification, such policies can benefit the owner as well as the bidders.

7.5.3 Negotiating Contracts

Occasionally, it is necessary to contact bidders to obtain clarification in order to evaluate the bids properly. At other times, drawings revisions approved shortly after the receipt of bids may require price changes. The manager must be aware of the practices within the industry. When further discussions or negotiations are required, the manager must pay particular attention to conducting such discussions in an ethical manner. The manager is responsible to the industry and the owner to avoid any taint of "bid shopping," as pointed out earlier. No rules can be laid down to cover all situations, but a qualified construction manager must know what is right.

7.6   CM'S TASKS DURING THE BIDDING AND AWARD PHASE

The construction manager performs the following tasks during the bidding and award phase:

1. QUALIFY POTENTIALS BIDDERS

(a) Present experience regarding the successful qualifications of potential bidders on equivalent projects in the site area.

(b) Possess a data base regarding the capability and performance of all local area contractors.

(c) Have a fully implemented program of bidder qualifications, including (i) questionnaire; (ii) analysis; (iii) experience; and (iv) recommendation.

(d) Understand the owner's special requirements for contractor performance on the project.

(e) Present an organizational structure that includes the capability to analyze all aspects of potential bidder qualifications, including (i) financial stability; (ii) legal constraints; (iii) experience; (iv) quality assurance programs; and (vii) past performance.

2. FINALIZE BID WORK PACKAGES

(a) Prepare a logical program of contracting based upon results of site visits and overall estimated economy, including number of contracts and preliminary scope of each.

(b) Review design requirements to support the program with the architect or engineer.

(c) Modify program to meet designer capabilities and overall owner schedule requirements.

(d) Publish design schedule by contract package with sufficient scope so that all parties (owner, designer, and construction manager) understand the plan.

(e) Review preliminary work packages developed by the designer.

(f) Finalize biding documents.

3. FINALIZE PREQUALIFIED CONTRACTOR LISTS

(a) Finalize bonding requirements, if applicable.

(b) Develop preliminary contract lists from site visit.

(c) Develop prequalification requirements.

(d) Meet with potential bidders and review and obtain prequalification information. Obtain bidder suggestions for inclusion in the program.

(e) Analyze information submitted by prospective bidders, check reference, financial strength, and so forth.

(f) Recommend a reasonable number of qualified contractors for competitive bidding for each package.

4. RECEIVE AND EVALUATE BIDS AND AWARD PRIME CONTRACTS

(a) Maintain qualified bidder's lists.

(b) Screen prospective bidders for financial stability, adequacy of management controls, and past performance.

(c) Establish bid packages recognizing unique aspects of project and area.

(d) Evaluate technical and commercial aspects of proposals, such as: (i) escalation; (ii) terms and conditions of payment; and (iii) exceptions.

(e) Conduct preaward meetings.

(f) Negotiate special conditions or bid exceptions.

(g) Administer insurance and bonding programs.

7.7 SUMMARY

The bidding and award phase establishes the framework for project construction. The use of CM in this phase offers a major opportunity for project time reduction and, consequently, cost savings. Participation of the owner and the designer with the construction manager is important for review and decision making.

The use of phasing and work packaging during this phase is very much encouraged, for they have good merits. The complete set of plans and specifications must be subdivided and categorized in such a way that no items are omitted, none are duplicated, and all contractors bidding on a given package are indeed bidding on the same scope of work. The construction manager's contractor-type knowledge of area and trade work practices is essential to this step. Development of work packages is followed by preparation of bidding documents, which is again a joint effort of the designer, owner, and manager. Items typically included are the invitation to bid; bid form; bid breakdown; construction contract; general conditions; special conditions; specifications, addenda, and drawings; supplemental provisions; owner-furnished items, and construction schedules.

The selection of the best contractors will be aided by prequalification and by keeping the number of contractors small enough so that the best contractors will know they have a reasonable chance of obtaining the work to make bidding worthwhile. The construction manager should also prepare his own fair-cost estimates; these will help him evaluate bids more knowledgeably and find previously undiscovered errors in the contract documents. By specifying fair and reasonable procedures for evaluation, the construction manager can also encourage bidders to submit worthwhile value engineering proposals and volunteered alternates.

The CM performs such major tasks as qualification of potential bidders, finalization of bid work packages, evaluation, and award of contracts.

8

Construction Phase

8.1 INTRODUCTION

Once the contracts have been awarded, the construction manager works to facilitate on-site communication, defining lines of authority and procedures to assure coordination among the owner, architect-engineer, contractors, and his own team.

As early as possible the construction manager works with individual contractors so that he can expand the preliminary schedule and modify it into a workable overall plan that adequately describes both construction activity and resource utilization. This plan can then be used as a benchmark against which to compare progress. Similarly, he continually gathers data on vendors' and materials' delivery dates to ensure that needed materials will be available when required. Here he must mesh the drawing-designing activity and the procurement-contracting activity. Throughout construction, he has full-time representation at the jobsite. While part of his job is to act as a "troubleshooter," his major functions are to maintain the information flow and compare results in terms of time and cost against projection, so that bottlenecks and overruns can be anticipated and avoided. These functions require constant on-site vigilance. On a day-to-day basis, he inspects for quality and progress, he approves requisitions for payment, he negotiates change orders with contractors, and he establishes back charges. He may be required to establish safety programs, or consult on labor issues, or head a public relations effort.

This chapter discusses home office and field operations, project relations and organization types, contract administration and coordination, quality control and inspection, claims, occupancy, and commissioning, as well as CM's tasks during the construction phase.

8.2   HOME OFFICE AND FIELD OPERATIONS CONTROL

8.2.1   Home Office Involvement

The basic requirement for home office organization throughout construction is control. Field offices can be staffed to provide all, or a major part of, the necessary services during construction, and the home office must depend upon the field construction manager to oversee the project in accordance with the predetermined plan. However, the overall responsibility and accountability to the owner for developing and monitoring a proper control system are at the top; they cannot be delegated entirely to the field construction manager.

Once the construction manager has chosen a sound, qualified, on-site construction team and has developed a plan for achieving the objectives of the owner, his remaining duty is to know at all times whether the project is proceeding according to plans so that he can react quickly, when necessary, to modify, assist, and correct prior planning. Apart from control responsibilities and accountability to the owner, most or all construction phase management tasks can be delegated to the field construction manager and his assistants. On small- and medium-sized jobs, the minimum home office staff will thus consist of a part-time project manager or construction executive qualified to oversee project accomplishment, accept control responsibilities, and retain overall accountability to the owner. The home office staff can, in addition, provide the field construction manager with part-time services that cannot economically be staffed at the jobsite. On the other hand, on certain large projects located in remote areas, many of the responsibilities for the preplanning, planning and design, and bidding and award phase outlined in preceding chapters can be handled best from the field construction site.

The extent of detailed work performed in the home office during construction will dictate organization requirements. Each project is unique, and for optimum results each will require different planning and assignment of responsibilities between the home office and the field construction office. The location of the owner, designer, and sources of supply will affect the balance for an individual project, as will the extent of delegation by the owner to the manager and the designer. For a project requiring full-time personnel, it is probably more economical and satisfactory to staff the project site than it is to perform the functions in the home office.

A home office may perform, in part or in whole, the following tasks:

1. Provide management-level reporting to the owner through a straightforward quantitative description of project status.

2. Keep the owner informed of current and anticipated problems and their proposed or planned solutions.

3. Provide general supervision to assist, counsel, and direct field activity when necessary.

4. Monitor or administer project control systems; initiate remedial action when warranted.

5. Provide assistance to the field construction manager where desirable. Such assistance may include preparation of schedules, estimates at completion, fair-cost estimates for extra work, claims negotiations, and expediting critical materials or equipment.

8.2.2   Field Office Involvement

At first, the construction manager will probably be represented by a limited staff because he will not yet have provided his full complement of field forces. The CM and his senior representatives are, however, on the jobsite immediately to staff the project. The CM will have to operate within a budget based on his fee or cost quotation for services. As has been previously stressed, each project's needs are unique (e.g., constructing a hospital or an institution). The scope of services can be different and can vary greatly depending upon location (urban versus rural; a new site or expansion of an existing facility) and even upon the timing of the retention of the CM, which can be as late as the start of construction. The field office normally performs the following tasks:

1. Establishes field office, including provisions for general conditions items, such as sanitary services, water supply and temporary electrical items to be furnished to the contractors by the owner.

2. Hires the testing laboratory and surveyor jointly with, or with the approval of, the designer. Services needed include soils engineering, concrete inspection and testing, and other specialized requirements. On major projects, surveying and inspection normally are provided by the construction manager. On medium-sized and smaller projects it is often more economical to contract for such services on a part-time basis.

3. Obtains necessary permits on behalf of the owner. Depending on project conditions, the designer or owner can share some or all of this responsibility.

4. Manages, coordinates, and inspects the work of contractors to help achieve project cost, schedule, and quality objectives. Conducts weekly contractor meetings, in which minutes taken, are worthwhile.

5. Performs schedule, progress, and cost control functions as needed for a particular project. Requests home-office assistance for specialty items where indicated.

6. Maintains job diaries, drawing registers, and other records to document the development of the project and promote a businesslike relationship with all contractors. These records will further assist in evaluating change-order requests and claims.

7. Initiates notice to proceed for individual contracts, prepares or approves progress-payment requests, and develops final contract closeout in accordance with owner and local requirements.

8. Maintains progress-and-record photographs not only as part of progress and schedule controls, but also to document potential claims, accidents, or similar occurrences.

9. Prepares input for the project control system by evaluating progress of each contract.

10. Maintains job safety in accordance with contract and legal requirements. While safety is primarily the responsibility of each contractor, the manager has the duty to assist and to insist upon compliance with contract provisions. Recent legislative and judicial decisions have given the construction manager greater responsibilities in this area.

11. Maintains liaison with the designer, requests his assistance to interpret plans and specifications, and keeps him informed of the status of the project.

12. Obtains or develops information for "as-built" drawings, including maintenance of a current set of working drawings at the jobsite, which are available for all contractors and show all current revisions and field changes.

13. Prepares field reports, including weekly progress reports, force reports, delay (or force majeure) reports, contract status reports, evaluation of claims, evaluation of requests for change orders, and reports covering other significant and periodic requirements.

8.3   PROJECT RELATIONS AND ORGANIZATION TYPES

8.3.1   Organization and Procedure

The CM has to establish his own on-site organization with the responsibility of providing the coordination, inspection, and total services enumerated herein. The on-site organization may be structured as an autonomous staff from the CM's project staff, but if the construction manager has been involved in earlier construction stages and broader aspects of the project, the field or on-site organization will be an operating arm of the complete construction management organization. A simple table of organization may be structured, as shown in Figure 8.1. The CM will define and require on-site procedures affecting all parties. It is therefore the construction manager's obligation to document such procedures properly and to identify the responsibility of his own organization. This is only identified as a separate task under the CM's services to identify its importance. This, naturally, would be a task accomplished in the very earliest stages of construction at which time the procedures to be followed during the construction process would have been defined. Any of these procedures would have already been reviewed at the preconstruction, and possibly at the preawards, meetings. The responsibility herein, however, is a total documentation of such procedures for all parties who would initially be involved or who would become involved in the construction of the project.

8.3.2 Organization Types

Each project is physically different, has different objectives, and is constructed under different local conditions. Depending upon project size, location, and other factors, certain functions can be performed in either the home office or the field project location. Also, there are several different ways that a CM contract may be arranged. A few examples are shown in Figures 8.2 through 8.4. A CM may have several general contractors working under him who, in turn, subcontract portions of their work. If the owner does not want the CM to do any work with his (CM's) own forces, the contract may be arranged so that the CM hires five or more prime contractors, including a general trades contractor who both sublets and does some of the work himself. In this case, all the contracts flow to the owner. In another form of contract, usually a very large one, the CM may subcontract directly and perhaps do portions of the work with his own forces. The CM must provide home-office supporting services to job personnel for many specialties such as EEO, safety, and labor relations. Sometimes on CM jobs, there is a very heavy EEO component and the CM has people on the job designated specifically for community relations.

In another arrangement, the CM may hire or select a few separate prime contractors for the project, and designate one as a general contractor to handle some of the paper work. Here, the CM acts as a monitor. For example, he may not check the shop drawings himself, but he makes sure that they flow by monitoring his general contractor's activities. With this type of arrangement, the CM's in-house staff is quite small. This does not

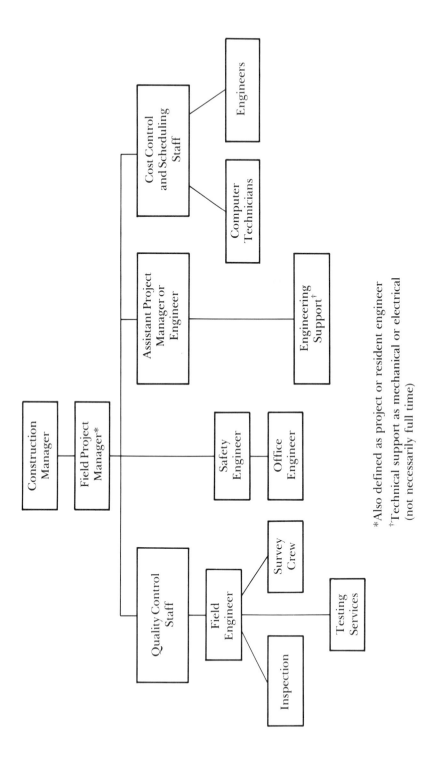

*Also defined as project or resident engineer
†Technical support as mechanical or electrical (not necessarily full time)

Figure 8.1. CM Table of Organization.

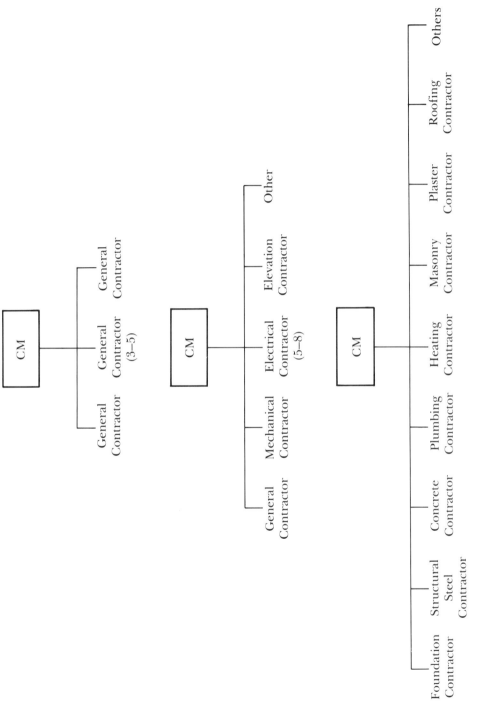

Figure 8.2. Alternate Formats of Construction Management. Adapted from Post (114:96).

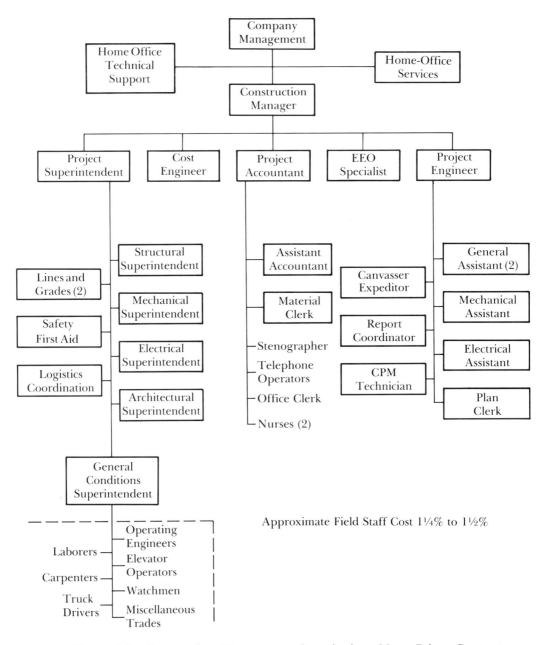

Figure 8.3. Construction Management Organization: Many Prime Contracts (Adapted from Post (114:97).

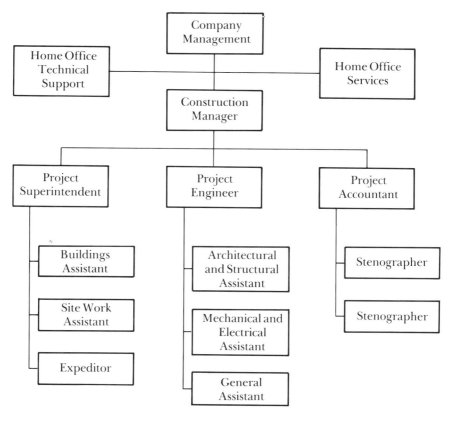

Note:
- All Technical Inspection By Others
- No General Condition Work
- Purchasing Support through Home Office
- Approximate Field Staff Cost ¾% to 1¼%

Figure 8.4. Construction Management Organization: Few Prime Contracts (Adapted from Post (114:98).

mean, however, that the owner pays less money; the general contractor and other trade contractors pick up part of the CM fee in provisions they have made in their bids for providing these services.

8.4 CONTRACT ADMINISTRATION AND COORDINATION

8.4.1 Contract Administration

Administration of construction contracts requires thorough and timely documentation. Such documentation facilitates performance of work, assists in closeout and acceptance, and helps reduce the possibility of claims. Typical reports and records that have been helpful so far as documentation requirements are concerned are as follows:

1. NOTICE TO PROCEED   The "Notice to Proceed," usually issued by the CM or his representative, is a document that refers to the provisions of the contract, the type of work to be performed, and the date or dates that the work is to commence. It is to be issued in advance of the required starting date in order to provide the contractor adequate lead time.

2. CHANGE ORDERS   It is not uncommon that projects have changed during the course of construction. Most changes are incurred for the benefit of all parties. They may be due to an unforeseen field condition or because of a change in the original scope of the contract, or for setting forth other modifications. Change orders are written on a standard form and include a complete description of the change and its effect on the contract price and schedule.

It is the CM's responsibility to ensure that all extra work items requested by the contractor are properly analyzed and reviewed. The first review, however, is made by the designer, who will analyze such an extra-work or change-order request in light of the specific design or contract requirements. The CM will then review and evaluate the request considering the actual field conditions and the value of work that he believes has been accomplished. The change order is then recommended or not recommended, as the case may be. If recommended, a change-order authorization is issued and the contract amount is revised by the change-order amount. The same procedure is followed, whether it is for additional (extra) work or a reduction (credit).

It is also the CM's responsibility to initiate change orders, if he deems that a change to the basic contract criteria is warranted during the course of construction. Such initiation takes the same course and procedure as an extra-work order requested by the contractor, with the sole exception that the CM requests the contractor to submit a quotation for an extra or anticipated credit for the proposed change or variation in the course of the work.

3. PROGRESS-PAYMENT REPORTS   The construction manager is responsible for verifying and approving periodic requisitions for payment. In the normal course of business, these requisitions are submitted on a monthly basis by individual prime contractors. It is essential that an orderly procedure for payment to the contractor be established to ensure the contractor's receipt of payment for work accomplished without any delay. The first step in the sequence of payment is approval by the owner's on-site representative, who is the construction manager. It is his responsibility to verify that all the work for which requisition is being made has been accomplished properly. Based upon such approval, the owner can make payment for the previously approved amount to the contractor.

4. FINAL INSPECTION AND ACCEPTANCE OF WORK   As part of the quality control and inspection function, the construction manager will ensure that prior to the contractor's leaving the jobsite and prior to final payment all work will be completed, all previously observed deficiencies will be corrected, and no outstanding work items will remain. Jointly with the architect-engineer, the CM will make a full inspection of the site and prepare a detailed report, commonly described as the "punch list." It is thereafter utilized as the final checklist of outstanding items. Upon completion of all items on the punch list, the contract construction work is considered complete.

There are many stages of completion, however. Although a project is not actually complete until the punch-list items and all contract matters are taken care of, it may have already passed through other stages of completion, which can include:

(a) Substantial completion target date for essential completion of work making facility usable.

(b) Beneficial occupancy completion—date at which owner occupies the facility or assumes operating responsibility.

(c) Partial occupancy completion—date at which owner occupies a portion of the facility, such as certain classrooms or a wing of a hospital.

The aforementioned dates and definitions have significance because dates have to be established to define completion of the work, which can amount to substantial completion, because of liquidated-damage provisions in the contract or time at which the guaranteed period for a piece of equipment starts. The dates for acceptance, occupancy, and takeover of a facility can therefore be different, and again depending upon the nature of the facility, the duration of time between these dates can vary greatly.

Prior to final acceptance, the CM must determine not only that the work is complete but that all outstanding contract matters are settled. These include

(a) Certification of payment subject to receipt of final payment to all subcontractors, vendors, and material suppliers by the prime contractors.

(b) Waiver of liens by all contractors and subcontractors.

(c) Filing of all required guarantees for the specified guarantee periods, usually for one year, except for mechanical equipment.

(d) Submission of all required operating and maintenance manuals, equipment manuals, parts lists, and so forth.

(e) Completion of as-built record drawings, showing details of the project as actually built; this can be a joint effort for contractors, A-E, and CM.

(f) Summary of claims, if any, that remain for resolution by negotiation or through legal or arbitration processes.

5. OTHER RECORD KEEPING The CM becomes the prime record keeper on the jobsite. His records will include not only those relating to the specific items that he is required to accomplish and pursue under his CM tasks, but records that relate to the total project and the activities during construction. As basic as this may seem, it is interesting to draw up a list of all records and files that should be maintained during the construction process. This list includes:

(a) Daily log—record diary maintained by resident project manager.

(b) Listing of all contractors, subcontractors, and suppliers.

(c) Emergency—first-aid notices.

(d) Applicable regulations and codes.

(e) Technical handbooks as references.

(f) Activity and progress reports—daily, weekly, or monthly (as applicable).

(g) Photograph—(progress) records.

(h) Shop-drawing log.

(i) Minutes of all meetings, including required periodic meetings.

(j) Correspondence files: (i) among contractors, (ii) with owner, (iii) with architect-engineer, (iv) with others.

(k) Construction schedules—original and revised.

(l) Cost accounting records—for work accomplished by change-order or time and materials basis.

(m) Change-order logs and records.

(n) Payment estimates—including contractor's requisitions, projected estimates of owner's cash requirements.

(o) Insurance certificates.

(p) Progress reports.

8.4.2 Contract Coordination

If there is any one word that best describes the role of the CM during construction it is that of coordinator. Although this term is as misused as the term "construction manager," coordination of the total activities of a construction project is the prime function of the CM. By proper coordination of the various groups that are involved in the construction implementation of a project, the CM performs his task most efficiently and expeditiously. The construction manager has the reponsibility to have not only a sufficient, but competent staff on the jobsite at all times to provide the necessary direction, control, and coordination.

In the traditional construction process, the general contractor has been the coordinator for all the forces on the jobsite. The general contractor has the responsibility to coordinate the work of his subcontractors, and the A-E also has a coordination role concerning design conformance. In the CM process the coordination role for all activities of contractors, A-E designers, separate consultants, specialty contractors, owner, or operating agencies is clearly defined. The CM has this responsibility. Coordination requires not only the efforts of the various contractors, both prime subcontractors and the general contractor on the jobsite, but also the efforts of the other parties who are involved in the construction process. The tools utilized by the CM to perform this function may include schedule monitoring, job and organizational meetings, administrative procedures of record keeping, progress reports, implementation of management information systems, or any combination thereof to effect a team effort on the construction site.

8.5   QUALITY CONTROL

8.5.1   Inspection

This can be a traditional engineering or architectural function. Traditionally, this responsibility has been performed by others than the design A-E; certain major corporations and some public agencies, because of their continuing capital expansion and construction programs, maintain staffs who perform on-site inspection service, with the A-E role limited to field consultation. Traditionally, it has also not been uncommon for an A-E other than the designer to assume the inspection role. In the CM process, however, it is logical for this function and task to be undertaken by the professional serving as the CM. As with the engineering or architectural function, the inspection of work requires review and supervision to ensure its conformance with the contract plans and specifications. This, as a professional task, does not require, nor is it intended to require, the direction of the contractor's labor forces. Such inspection, therefore, will require on-site staff and qualified inspection personnel to ensure that these criteria are met. Again, depending upon the nature of the total construction, the extent of the necessary quality control will depend upon the specific work. It may require inspection of (1) concrete in place and at the batch plant, (2) pile driving (under the New York City Building Code, pile inspection must be conducted by a registered professional engineer), (3) paving operations, or (4) structural steel operations. Separate tasks may require detailed reports, as provided in the specifications prepared by the A-E. The CM, through an inspection staff, will ensure that there is compliance with these specifications.

8.5.2   Testing: On- and Off-Site

As part of the inspection process, the CM includes all required testing and inspection procedures. The contract specifications and local building regulations will identify the required laboratory testing to be performed during construction. Certification of construction methods and procedures is coordinated and accomplished through the construction manager. This may, and usually does, require the retaining of services of testing laboratories that are structured to provide the specialized needs for such inspections. These services may include concrete testing (taking of concrete cylinders and concrete strength reports), soil compaction tests, fill analyses, welding inspection, and so forth. In addition, these requirements may include off-site inspection. They may also provide the necessary inspection at a concrete or asphalt batch plant, or possibly inspection of a precast or steel fabrication process at a supplier's mill or factory. Necessary inspection would be provided through the CM. This more often than not requires separate contracts, which may be placed directly by an owner or as part of the CM contract and reimbursed through payment to the construction manager.

8.6   SETTLEMENT OF CLAIMS

There are potential claims and back charges in every construction project. In any contractual relationship, situations can develop whereby any or all parties to contract may believe that they have legitimate claims. If any disputes or claims for additional compensation are not resolved, the construction manager has an added responsibility. In certain instances, a contractor may feel that he should be paid for additional work, but the recommendation by the designer or CM has perhaps been contrary to such a request. The contractor may have been directed to accomplish work, and he may have filed a notice that he is accomplishing the work under protest, for which he will submit an added claim. The responsibility in this task is not intended to infer that the CM has a legal position or posture; he does, however, have an active and specific role in the analysis of claims if they have been submitted by a contractor. This role will precede any action upon the claims, which may be limited to negotiation and resolution between the parties but can also, if there is no agreement, require the CM's detailed analysis or even expert testimony if the claim ends in litigation.

All claims are not necessarily resolved by litigation. A not uncommon CM role is that of auditor—not in the strict accounting definition, but a construction manager may be called upon to audit costs. Although a CM routinely certifies work for purposes of payment, he may well be required, or find it necessary in performing his CM function, to review and audit books and records of a contractor to confirm costs and cost allocations. This may be similar in substance to performing an audit for verification of costs incurred, but the essential purpose of the cost review is to identify costs as allocable to specific work functions. This audit or payment certification task is often utilized in the claim process to arrive at negotiated settlements between an owner and a contractor.

8.7   CM'S TASKS

8.7.1   CM's Tasks during Construction Phase

The major tasks performed by the CM during this phase include

1. DEVELOP AND ADMINISTER AREA TRANSPORTATION SYSTEM

(a) Study the project access and hauling requirements, and define critical loads, sizes, and traffic flows.

(b) Perform a survey of the local transportation system to identify availability of access roads, railroads, and barge shipment facilities. This assessment should include identification of load limitations, traffic-flow constraints, usage permit requirements, tolls and usage fees, and any other conditions or restrictions that might influence project transportation.

(c) Based on the results of transportation requirements, definitions, and the study of transportation facility availability, prepare a comprehensive program describing requirements for transportation facility development. This program should include a detailed definition of the scope of work, schedules for work performance, suggested methods for both design and contracting, and requirements for obtaining the necessary permits.

(d) Following owner approval of the transportation development plan, contract for and manage construction of any additional facilities required.

(e) Assist the owner in obtaining permits necessary for utilization of transportation facilities.

(f) Prepare a standard contract provision giving information and restrictions regarding utilization of the area transportation system. If necessary, prepare traffic plans and provide flagmen or other traffic control means as required to assure access to the site for the anticipated volume of traffic.

(g) Coordinate with local port, railroad, state highway department, and county engineer personnel to advise them of anticipated transportation requirements, as well as planned utilization of existing facilities or plans to develop new facilities.

(h) Manage the contractor flow of traffic to and from the project site to assure that access is provided at all times.

2. ADMINISTRATION PROJECT EEO PROGRAM

(a) Contact the federal and state Equal Employment Opportunity Commission offices in the local area.

(b) Obtain the federal and state poster applicable to equal employment opportunity in English and in any required foreign languages, and post at project site.

(c) Contact the local state unemployment office and establish a relationship for hiring people who are available through this local governmental agency.

(d) Maintain a log of all applicants interviewed. This log should consist of the following information: (i) the source of the applicant and application; (ii) the name, sex, and race of the applicant; and (iii) the disposition of the application: hired, offer extended and whether it was accepted or rejected, or no offer extended and justification for this position.

(e) Notify local unions that the work will be conducted in accordance with Executive Order 11246.

(f) Notify all potential contractors that the work will be conducted in accordance with Executive Order 11246.

(g) State on all purchase orders that the provisions of the equal opportunity employment policy should be followed.

(h) Contact schools and notify them that you are an equal opportunity employer, that is, you will hire people without regard to race, creed, color, sex, or national origin.

3. ENFORCE PROJECT SAFETY PROGRAM

(a) Develop and include in all contract documents standard wording for contractor compliance with all applicable safety regulations and for contractor implementation of an acceptable safety program.

(b) Develop a construction manager safety program for the project, which includes the following items: (i) reporting requirements and format; (ii) safety inspection plans; (iii) means of providing construction ventilation and other special construction facilities to create a safe working environment; (iv) first-aid and ambulance facilities to be provided; (v) fire protection requirements to be enforced; and (vi) identification of local medical and emergency contracts.

(c) Through the construction manager's safety representative, perform periodic inspections of the project site to identify any unsafe working conditions.

(d) Conduct periodic safety meetings with both contractor manual and nonmanual personnel to promote a safety awareness and to assure that all requirements and regulations are satisfied.

(e) Assure that all required accident and safety program implementation reports are submitted by the contractor to the local authorities, the construction manager, the owner, and the owner's insurance carrier.

(f) Take necessary corrective action for enforcement of safety requirements during the performance of work on all portions of the project.

(g) Present awards to contractors for safe work performance and accident frequency and severity less than national averages.

4. COORDINATE LABOR RELATIONS

(a) Become acquainted with local labor leaders and their objectives.

(b) Become acquainted with local AGC or other contractor representatives and their objectives.

(c) Recognize extent of open-shop work.

(d) Frame work packages to avoid local problems.

(e) Keep abreast of potential labor problems, including expiration of agreements and jurisdictional disputes.

(f) Require contractors to handle their own direct relationships with labor unions.

5. MANAGE AND PERFORM GENERAL CONDITIONS TASKS   Example responsibilities include the following:

(a)   Construction warehouse.

(b)   Construction office.

(c)   Civil test laboratory.

(d)   Welder qualification facility.

(e)   Non-Destructive Examination (NDE) laboratory.

(f)   Construction roads.

(g)   Construction parking.

(h)   Construction grading and drainage.

(i)   Construction fencing.

(j)   Construction security facilities.

(k)   First-aid facilities.

(l)   Shop and maintenance areas.

(m)   Construction trash facilities, including refuse containers, incinerators, and landfill areas.

(n)   Erosion control and other environmental protection facilities, and related testing and laboratory facilities.

(o)   Oil-spill prevention and countermeasure facilities, including oil-spill cleanup kits.

(p)   Construction sanitary facilities, including toilet trailers, sewage treatment plants, and portable toilets.

(q)   Construction ventilation facilities and work-area, air-quality-monitoring instrumentation.

(r)   Construction heating system for building areas.

(s)   Construction fire protection facilities, including fire-water-storage tanks, fire pumps, fire headers and hydrants, hose station, sprinkler systems, and fire extinguishers.

(t)   Construction water system, including potable water, water coolers, concrete curing water, general usage construction water, and flushing and hydrotest water.

(u)   Construction-compressed air systems, including compressors, receivers, distribution headers, and manifolds.

(v)   Welding-gas systems (oxygen, argon, propane, acetylene), including cryogenic storage facilities, distribution headers, and manifolds.

(w)   Construction building dewatering and drainage systems.

(x)   Construction power and Ground Fault Interruption (GFI) systems for general usage.

(y)   Construction welding-machine power grid.

(z)   Construction grounding system for welding machine and miscellaneous equipment grounding.

(aa)   Construction lighting for provision of a safe working environment in both building and yard areas.

(bb) Special process transportation facilities, such as improved roads, railroad spurs, and barge unloading facilities.

(cc) Building access facilities, such as special openings, elevators, ramps, material handling platforms, and bridges.

(dd) Shared time-keeping facilities such as brass alleys and access turnstiles.

(ee) Construction communication facilities, including radio systems, telephones, and paging systems.

(ff) Construction records—retention and document-control facilities such as reproducton equipment and document vaults.

6. IMPLEMENT TIME- AND COST-CONTROL SYSTEMS

(a) Establish jobsite time and cost staff. The number of personnel in the staff will be determined by the size of the project as well as whether the information is gathered in the field and compiled in the field or whether the information is transmitted to the central accounting office.

(b) Investigate the method that the client uses for accounting and develop a system to accommodate his accounting procedures.

(c) Estimate cash-flow expenditures. This can be in the form of an S curve.

(d) Establish schedule for project with start dates for subcontractors and duration of period for work to be performed. Monitor scheduled performance.

(e) Establish a code of accounts for the various components of the project. Monitor estimated versus actual costs.

(f) Establish purchasing system for field and central office.

(g) Establish a method for reviewing and processing change orders.

7. MANAGE DAILY CONSTRUCTION ACTIVITIES

(a) Coordinate field-office activities.

(b) Document significant activities.

(c) Monitor contractor's construction schedule.

(d) Record inspection and test data.

(e) Maintain job files and records.

(f) Record as-built data on record drawing set.

(g) Prepare progress reports.

(h) Maintain log of contractor submittals.

(i)   Review monthly payment requests.

(j)   Make field measurements for pay quantities.

(k)   Review change-order proposals.

(l)   Review and recommend on merits contractor claims.

(m)   Issue field directives.

(n)   Attend management and coordination meetings.

(o)   Require conformance with safety provisions.

(p)   Anticipate and assist in solution of field problems.

(q)   Manage and supervise Quality Assurance (QA) inspections program.

(r)   Conduct final punch-list inspection.

(s)   Prepare notice of substantial completion.

(t)   Review and recommend on final payment request.

(u)   Certify completion of project.

8.   ADMINISTER PRIME CONTRACTS

(a)   Conduct project meetings as necessary to maintain schedule.

(b)   Coordinate overall project schedule (CPM or other), including activities of contractor, designer, and owner.

(c)   Obtain determination of design documentation clarification (in writing).

(d)   Formalize management procedure for project coordination and decision making.

(e)   Secure permits and approvals.

(f)   Obtain services of special consultants.

(g)   Coordinate all shop drawings and samples.

(h)   Manage project EEO program.

(i)   Coordinate job safety program.

(j)   Coordinate environmental and social (community) efforts dictated by construction operations.

(k)   Manage project cost control program; monitor cash flow and contract commitments.

(l)   Prepare list of incomplete items for determination of substantial completion.

(m)   Coordinate project management information system.

(n)   Evaluate, document, and process claims.

(o) Maintain effective labor relations program.

9. RECEIVE, REVIEW, AND APPROVE CONTRACTOR'S REQUESTS FOR PROGRESS PAYMENTS

(a) Establish procedure for processing payments.

(b) Validate percentage of work completed and quality of work in place.

(c) Review payment requisitions for duplication, invalid charges, and so forth.

(d) Recommend approval to designer or owner.

10. ADMINISTER CONTRACT CHANGES AND CLAIMS

(a) Establish procedure for processing changes and formalizing change orders.

(b) Validate change estimates through comparative check estimates.

(c) Monitor progress of changes performed on a "cost" basis.

(d) Review and evaluate contractor's claims.

(e) Provide claim documentation.

(f) Recommend approval of changes and claims.

(g) Assist the owner in negotiating changes.

11. QUALITY ASSURANCE AND INSPECTION

(a) Develop quality assurance and surveillance plan.

(b) Supervise materials testing.

(c) Conduct sampling and on-site testing.

(d) Review and recommend action on test report data.

(e) Review requests for materials substitutions.

(f) Inspect materials delivered to the site.

(g) Make plant inspections of off-site fabricated materials.

(h) Inspect to assure conformance with plans and specifications.

(i) Assure protection of materials stored at the site.

(j) Reject faulty materials and workmanship.

(k) Provide specialty inspections as required.

(l) Evaluate manufacturers' product data.

(m) Confirm conformance of materials delivered to specification requirements.

(n)   Participate in final punch-list inspections.

(o)   Document all significant activities.

(p)   Submit reports of daily construction activities.

(q)   Prepare test reports and summary data.

12. INTERPRET CONTRACT DOCUMENTS

(a)   Clear up all ambiguities in the contract documents.

(b)   If possible, resolve all disputes as they arise; if not, make sure adequate documentation is maintained.

(c)   Prepare equitable contract adjustments where they are in order.

(d)   Clarify all technical questions with design engineers or architect.

8.7.2   CM's Tasks during Closeout and Start-Up Phase

1. PROJECT CLOSEOUT

(a)   Conduct frequent inspections during finishing stages of the work.

(b)   Request contractor notification of readiness for prefinal inspection.

(c)   Establish dates for equipment testing, acceptance periods, warranty dates, and instructional requirements.

(d)   Conduct prefinal inspection (include operational check of all working parties).

(e)   Prepare preliminary punch list indicating all deficient items remaining.

(f)   Meet with contractor to determine final requirements for acceptance.

(g)   Begin partial reduction of field-office staff.

(h)   Take inventory of construction manager's and owner's property at field office.

(i)   Check contractor's record-drawing status.

(j)   Obtain the following from the contractor: (i) guarantees; (ii) operating manuals and instructions; (iii) keying schedule; (iv) maintenance stock items, spare parts, special tools; (v) completed-record drawings; (vi) bonds, roofing, maintenance, guarantees; (vii) certificates of inspection and acceptance by local government agencies; and (viii) release of all liens.

(k)   Transfer construction manager's and owner's field-office property to an off-site location.

(l)   Move field-office operations to off-site location.

(m)   Obtain contractor's advice when punch-list items have been accomplished.

(n)   Conduct final punch-list inspection.

(o)   Execute "Certificate of Substantial Completion" if minor items remain (list all items).

(p)   Record document at recorder's office.

(q)   Receive contractor request for final payment.

(r)   Check quantity and value of work completed.

(s)   Retain funds to cover remaining punch-list items.

(t)   Recommend payment by owner.

(u)   Notify owner of availability of premises for occupancy or beneficial use.

(v)   Monitor completion of pick-up work on punch-list items.

(w)   Check for lien claims at end of holding period for retention money.

(x)   Release retention and make final payment of pick-up items, if there are no outstanding liens.

(y)   Certify to owner of completion.

(z)   Record acceptance of the work by the owner.

(aa)   Record final completion document if not previously done.

(bb)   Prepare final project report.

(cc)   Prepare final project accounting.

2. SYSTEMS VALIDATION, TESTING, AND START-UP

(a)   Prepare start-up program to test, start up, and bring to an operational level the total plant facility.

(b)   Witness construction testing of a component or system in accordance with applicable codes, plans, and specifications until ready for initial operation.

(c)   Upon completion of construction testing of a system or component, turn system or component over to start-up program.

(d)   Prepare detailed plan and schedule for unit and station start-up in connection with construction and owner operations personnel. Include procedures for clearing and tagging system, cleanups, oil flush, and so forth.

(e)   Coordinate all efforts of construction mechanical and electrical personnel, the owner's operations personnel, and manufacturers' representatives.

(f)   The start-up program is carried out by start-up personnel and manufacturers' representatives working with owner's plant operating staff and contractor's construction forces.

(g)   Owner's operating staff will obtain training during this operation.

(h)   Initial operations under control of start-up engineer until formal acceptance of system is made by owner.

8.8   SUMMARY

The field construction phase will begin prior to the award of the first contract. Home-office management and control will parallel the field effort. On certain large projects, the two may be combined in the field location through choice of proper personnel.

The construction manager's tasks during the construction phase will be to (1) establish a field office; (2) hire testing laboratory and surveyor; (3) obtain necessary permits; (4) manage, coordinate, and inspect the work of individual contractors; (5) maintain job diaries, drawing register, and other records and photographs; (8) prepare input for project control system; (9) prepare field reports and schedules; and (10) prepare contract closeout and acceptance documents.

9

Legal Aspects
of Construction Management

9.1 PROFESSIONAL LIABILITY CONSIDERATIONS

Once the market for professional construction management (PCM or CM) services became readily apparent in the early 1970s, many firms responded to this challenge in an attempt to fill the "leadership vacuum" created by the increased liability imposed upon all members of the building team, which, in turn, has caused them to limit their duties in order to avoid their liability exposure. However, what was not widely understood by CM practitioners was the tremendous liability exposure they assumed under this project delivery system. As the wheels of justice turn slowly, case law did not begin to keep pace with the rapid deployment of the CM concept. Literally hundreds of firms were providing services for which there was

This chapter is based on references by Lee [83:43–55], Nielson [102:56–76], and Smith [128:107–120].

no legal precedent and little appreciation for potential areas of liability. Only recently has this issue been addressed substantially in writings, and only recently have significant disputes concerning CM liability reached the courts for judicial decisions. Finally, in the rush to implement CM services, very little attention was given to the preparation of contract documents in light of this new delivery system. Consequently, standard contract forms developed for other contractual relationships were routinely "cut and pasted" for use on CM projects.

Current thinking with regard to the legal profile of the construction manager is still evolving, but it is generally acknowledged that the CM concept embodies substantial liabilities for the practitioner. Potential areas of exposure include liability factors. The CM is most involved with the complex relationships between project team members and where the construction manager must exert his leadership role to the fullest.

The two most significant and innovative management techniques available to the construction manager in fulfilling his leadership role are the judicious use of multiple prime contracts and fast-tracking techniques. The combination of these two concepts allows a construction manager to shorten project durations and minimize costs as well. These schedule and cost benefits are widely recognized in the industry, and although their extensive use has been criticized by many, inflation and high-interest rates dictate that these techniques will continue to be used extensively in the future. In an attempt to maximize the benefits of these techniques, some CM practitioners may have gone too far by utilizing an abundance of prime contracts. When this is done the potential for delays and claims is unlimited, as the coordination task becomes infinitely more complex. Each prime contractor will rely on the construction manager's ability to mesh his work into the overall project plan. Even if this task is performed competently, it is still relatively easy for a prime contractor to blame another member of the project team for his delays. In the traditional single contract, fixed-priced approach, the general contractor took on the burden of adjudicating conflicts of this nature involving his subcontractors. However, this was often accomplished through the economic leverage of "might makes right" rather than an analytical approach and resolution to such problems. The construction manager has a higher duty than a general contractor to adjudicate such disputes impartially. In addition, his economic leverage to resolve such disputes is severely limited under the CM approach.

9.2   CONTRACT RELATIONSHIPS AND LIABILITY

9.2.1   The Traditional Construction Triangle

The traditional roles in legal relationships of the owner, engineer, and contractor are widely known and accepted by the industry. These relationships provide a basic foundation upon which to make decisions and conduct business. The scope of authority and the duties allocated to each party have been defined through years of experience and have become a matter of custom and standard practice in the construction industry. Liability for harm to one of the parties in the traditional construction triangle is based upon breach of a duty, either expressed as a provision of the contract or implied by the courts as a custom of the industry.

Because these duties are well defined and universally understood, exacting a damage judgment from a breaching party to compensate the aggrieved party agrees with accepted notions of justice and fair play. The breaching party understood, or should have understood, his duty and thus accepted any risk of harm associated with the breach as part of a business decision.

For example, when an engineer rushes plan and specification preparation, in order to meet a demanding schedule imposed by a client, he assumes a risk, however slight, that normal quality control measures may be inadvertently compromised. This engineer thus assumes the risk that the rush could result in an error or omission that could subject him to liability. The engineer is aware of these risks and cognizant of the standard of performance required by his profession. He is thus able to weigh those risks against the advantages of acquiring a new contract, satisfying an old account, or appeasing a client whose project was rescheduled or delayed. He is also able to reduce the risk by assigning his most competent employees to the project, adding an extra review prior to construction, increasing his construction involvement, or utilizing a combination of these risk management tools. The decision to assume the risk related to an expedited schedule is a management decision that is frequently made in a business environment. Most of the time, if errors result from an expedited schedule, they are minimal and are corrected before injury occurs. But in the unusual case, when the errors are not minor and are not corrected, the engineer will risk substantial liability. However, imposition of liability in that situation is considered equitable and not detrimental to the stability of the traditional system because (1) the risks were known and assumed, and (2) the engineer had an adequate opportunity to ameliorate the risk.

9.2.2 Modification of the Traditional Structure

Although the relationships formulated by the traditional structure are well defined and universally known, the rigidity of the structure tends to stifle more innovative construction techniques (such as design-build contracting, construction management, phased design and construction, two-step formal advertising, and life-cycle costing procurement). These innovative techniques can reduce construction costs substantially by

1. In design-build, permitting the contractor to maintain control of the design process, thus enabling him to use the construction methods and products that he is familiar with.

2. In construction management, increasing the communication and cooperation between the A-E and the contractor during both the design and construction phases of the project, without the adversary relationship inherent in the traditional structure.

3. In phased construction, reducing the time by replacing the traditional sequential construction with time-saving phased construction.

4. In life-cycle costing procurement, allowing procurement based on the design concept that has the lowest life-cycle cost.

Frequently, the advantages of these approaches are combined to utilize more fully the capabilities of the local construction industry and to meet the requirements of the procurement entities. To accommodate these innovative approaches, the relationship of the traditional structure has been revised, modified, or, in some cases, completely restructured.

The role of the construction manager has emerged from the traditional structure as the key to the successful utilization of these innovative concepts. The construction manager's (CM's) role has been formulated as a composite from each of the traditional roles, combining the scheduling and coordination responsibilities associated with the general contractor, the cost analysis and budget management of the owner, and the project management functions traditionally performed by the A-E. Specific responsibilities and authority are tailored to meet the project objectives of each procurement entity. Thus the construction manager has been introduced in several models, each having a different name, with different duties, authority, and contractual relationships with the other participants in the construction industry. Under the construction management approach alone, the construction manager's role varies to the extent that he may or may not be in construction privity with trade contractors, and may or may not be responsible for approving change orders, withholding partial payments, terminating trade contractors, or guaranteeing a maximum price.

9.2.3 Defining the Relationships

The structure of the new relationships is defined primarily by the various contracts between the parties of the construction team. Liability is imposed upon the construction manager according to the structure of these relationships. Often, the construction manager's duties and responsibilities are not properly expressed in his contract, and are therefore implied by the courts to correspond to his expressed or assumed authority.

Because there is no uniformity in trade practices regarding the construction manager's role, and very little case history upon which the courts can rely, the duties impressed on the construction manager may vary and depend upon implications of his authority or conduct. Further, the "professional" status of a construction manager is still not defined. Therefore, in a negligence action, there is no definitive authority establishing the level or standard of care required by his profession. Liability may be thus imposed on a construction manager who is unaware of the potential risk assumption or of the standard of care imposed by his professional status. The construction manager who is unaware of these potential problems cannot take adequate precautions to manage the risks. Nor does he bargain for adequate contract consideration to compensate for the potential liability thus assumed.

The construction manager's duties should therefore be expressed carefully in all contractual relationships. His duties should be defined to reflect

1. HIS QUALIFICATIONS AND TECHNICAL CAPABILITIES Although the standard of care required by the professional status of the manager has not been defined, courts will imply an agreement in his contractual relationships that (*a*) he possesses the degree of skill that is ordinarily possessed by others engaged in the same profession or trade, and (*b*) he and his employees will perform their services with that degree of prudence and care ordinarily possessed and observed by others engaged in the same or like employment. Further, as a practical matter, the construction manager's normal compensation does not justify the substantial risk incurred by the assumption of duties outside the scope of his technical training and experience.

2. HIS INSURANCE COVERAGE OR HIS FINANCIAL CAPABILITIES As an example, professional liability insurance coverage does not include damages arising out of a guaranteed maximum price. Also, most policies for construction managers do not include coverage for design errors and omissions. The construction manager who assumes such duties should therefore be in a financial position to cover these risks.

3. HIS AUTHORITY GRANTED UNDER THE CONTRACT If the construction manager's expressed duties exceed his authority, he will be ineffective and unable to accomplish his duties; but if his authority exceeds his expressed duties, the court may imply duties and thus potential liability commensurate with his authority.

Obviously, then, prior to assuming contractual responsibility for services, construction managers should examine and evaluate the sources of potential liability for the particular project.

9.3   SOURCES OF POTENTIAL LIABILITY

The scope of a construction manager's liability for failure to perform his duties is still largely unsettled. The following discussion of potential liabilities is primarily based on analogies to liabilities that have been imposed upon the traditional parties in the construction industry. The liability for a particular project must be examined at the time of litigation in light of the applicable state laws and the pertinent contract provisions.

9.3.1   Design Deficiencies

The extent of the construction manager's liability for design errors is primarily dependent upon his responsibilities and duties during the design process. These duties are generally defined in the contract with the owner. If the construction manager's contract includes expressed responsibility for design review, he will probably share liability for errors and omissions with the A-E. In most contract documents formulated for construction management, such as AIA B801 or AGC Document No. 8, the level of design control is limited to an advisory role and the A-E retains responsibility for the sufficiency of the design.

Despite the inclusion of broad exculpatory provisions for design deficiencies in the construction manager's contract, the court may impose liability on the construction manager when his contractual relationship with the owner places the owner in reliance of him for final checking, coordinating, and inspecting the work. His liability exposure for design deficiencies is increased as the A-E's construction involvement is decreased.

9.3.2   Construction Operations

The construction manager will be held liable to the owner for negligently performing or failing to perform a service during construction, within the expressed scope of his contractual duties. Of course, his failure to perform an expressed duty properly must first cause injury or damage. Thus if damages for defective work can be linked to his negligent conduct, liability may be imposed for obligations to review shop drawings, inspect construction, or reject work performed by the trade contractors. Furthermore, despite expressed contractual obligations to the contrary, the construction manager may be liable to the owner for duties implied from his authority, either expressed or assumed, during construction.

Liability may also be imposed upon the construction manager for personal injuries to workmen and economic injuries to trade contractors resulting from his negligent performance of contract obligations. The construction manager's potential exposure to liability for the personal injuries to workmen is exemplified by *Simon* v. *Omaha Public Power District*.[1] The plaintiff, Simon, was an employee of a subcontractor to Omaha Public Power District (OPPD), which owned the premises and acted as its own

---

1. 189 Neb. 183, 202 N. W. 2d 157 (1972).

general contractor. While working at the site, Simon fell through a duct opening in the floor, which had been left unguarded for three months prior to the accident. He was impaled on vertical reinforcing rods set in concrete, which were intended to form part of the machine foundation. Simon bought a negligence action against OPPD and the construction manager, as well as the consulting A-E firm.

The Nebraska court held OPPD liable to Simon for failure to exercise reasonable care in maintaining its premises in a safe condition. Turning to the liability of the construction manager, the court found that the consulting firm had contracted "to protect the District's interests in safety" and had attempted to perform this duty. The court, rejecting the argument that the construction manager had no authority to stop the work or commandeer the forces necessary to build covers for the duct opening, affirmed the jury verdict against both OPPD and the construction manager.

9.3.3   Cost Overruns

The construction manager guaranteeing a maximum price is, of course, liable for all cost overruns. As previously stated, guarantees of maximum price are specifically excluded under professional liability insurance policies. The construction manager who makes such a guarantee should be in the financial position to cover any overruns and should obtain a fee commensurate with the risks. The allocation of risks for cost overruns is generally considered to be the primary difference between a construction manager and a general contractor. The construction manager who assumes responsibilities for a cost guarantee should therefore be capable of functioning as a general contractor in many aspects of the work.

Even when the construction manager does not assume the risk of a maximum price, he may be liable for cost overruns to the extent of his professional fee. If his contract states that there is a limited budget available for the project, then adherence to the budget may be considered a contractual "condition precedent" to recovery of his fee. Particularly when the construction manager has a role in the design process, adherence to his estimate may be implied as a condition precedent to payment of the fee, even when the contract makes no reference to a budget limitation. To the extent the cost exceeds his estimate, the construction manager may forfeit his fee.

In an effort to circumvent this problem, the AIA Standard Agreement between Owner and Construction Manager states that the construction manager's judgment as a professional is not intended to establish a fixed limit as a condition of the agreement. Similar disclaimers in the AIA Standard Agreement between Owner and Architect, however, have not always protected architects from forfeiture of their fees when the low bid exceeded the budget.

9.3.4   Delays

Claims for damages from delays, disruptions, and interferences are probably the construction manager's greatest liability risk. Moreover, a recent investigation found no commercial insurance policies available to construction managers that would cover liability resulting from delay or improper scheduling.

Although the responsibilities of a construction manager vary according to the terms of each contract, the duty to schedule and coordinate the construction operations is a prime feature of virtually all construction management relationships. Even on absent specific contractural provisions to schedule and coordinate the work, the courts have implied a duty of the construction manager to coordinate, direct, and supervise the construction operations. If the owner incurs damages for delays attributable to the construction manager's negligent performance of his scheduling or supervisory duties, the owner may therefore seek recovery in tort for negligence or for breach of contract.

If the construction manager contracts directly with the trade contractors, as provided in the AGC documents, he is in a position analogous to a general contractor. As yet, no cases have been reported in which trade contractors have sought to recover delay damages from a construction manager who contracts directly with them. If the construction manager is in contractual privity with the trade contractors, however, his liability should be similar to that of a general contractor. Even on absent expressed contractual obligations, the courts will probably imply duties similar to a general contractor: to cooperate with the trade contractors, and to schedule and coordinate their work with other trade contractors. The construction manager would thus be potentially liable to trade contractors for failing to perform his implied duties.

Assuming the duties implied to the construction manager are similar to those implied to a general contractor, liability will be imposed for delays resulting from (1) a failure to supply necessary materials, (2) a failure to have the construction site ready, (3) a failure to have required utilities available at the site, (4) a failure to coordinate operations and remove hindrances, (5) a failure to protect against delays or interferences by other trade contractors, and (6) a failure to keep the work in such a state of forwardness that a trade contractor can perform his work within a limited time.

9.3.5   Indemnification

Most contracts between construction managers and owners contain an expressed indemnification provision for claims arising from the negligent performance of the manager's duties. Indemnification clauses typically seek to shift or transfer the owner's potential liability from third parties to the construction manager. Indemnifying the owner would thus expose the construction manager to liability that might otherwise be barred. Even on absent expressed indemnification provisions, an agreement to indemnify may sometimes be implied or an indemnification rule may be applied under equity principles.

The construction manager should avoid, to the extent possible, broad indemnification provisions such as the following:

> The construction manager agrees to idemnify and hold harmless the owner, its officers and trustees, from any and all loss, damage or expense of any nature as to all liens, claims, demands, suits, actions, and causes of action or liabilities resulting from accidents, negligence, failure to act, errors or omissions, or from any other cause whatsoever on the part of the construction manager or the contractors during the performance of the work in respect to the project.[2]

Such a provision would likely be construed to encompass any conceivable claim for economic injury that could arise from alleged negligent project administration.

The AGC's standard agreement between construction manager and owner, Article 12.1.1, contains a limited indemnification clause holding the owner harmless "from all claims arising for bodily injury and property damage ... that may arise from the construction manager's operation under this Agreement." Generally, the courts have strictly construed indemnification provisions, and a limited provision such as the AGC clause will probably be held inapplicable to claims for economic injury caused by the construction manager's negligent scheduling and coordination.

9.4   AVAILABLE DEFENSES

9.4.1   Privity of Contract and Third-Party Beneficiary Theory

Under the traditional common law doctrine of privity of contract, a plaintiff seeking recovery for breach of a contractual duty is barred unless he is a party to the contract. The privity doctrine was originally construed to bar third-party suits arising from negligence as well as third-party suits arising from a breach of contract.

This privity bar to most negligence actions brought by third parties has long been rejected in a majority of jurisdictions. The erosion of the

---

2. Smith (128:113).

privity bar in negligence actions for construction litigation, however, has taken longer. In construction litigation today, the privity doctrine is seldom applied to determine liability to third parties for negligence actions. Rather, the court determines whether the defendant's scope of duty includes third parties based primarily on the foreseeability of the injury and the closeness of the injury to the breach of duty. Considering the level of control during construction normally associated with the duties of a construction manager, the courts will probably extend the scope of his duties to include most third-party damages arising from negligent contract administration.

Third-party suits arising from breaches of contract may, in some cases, escape the privity bar by application of the "third-party beneficiary" concept. This exception to a requirement of privity is utilized by the courts where the contract was actually, or by implication, made for the benefit of a third party. A third party who is only incidentally benefited, however, may not enforce the contract against one of the contracting parties. A clear intent to benefit the third party must exist at the time of contract before a third party will be allowed to enforce the terms of the contract.

Whether the terms of an owner-construction manager contract is intended to benefit a trade contractor, and is therefore enforceable against the construction manager, has not been established conclusively. The decisions will vary according to the contractual relationships established by the contract documents for the construction project. Where the construction manager agrees to perform portions of the construction work himself, the terms of the owner-construction manager contract are more likely to be enforceable by the trade contractor as a third-party beneficiary. In such a situation, the construction manager will probably be under a mutual obligation to coordinate and cooperate with all other contractors.

In situations where the construction manager is not performing construction work, third-party liability for breach of contract can probably be avoided by including a specific provision in the owner-construction manager's contract. The provision should simply state that the parties do not intend to confer any benefit on third parties. Such clear expressions of intent are usually enforced by the courts.

9.4.2 "No Damage for Delay" Clauses

To limit liability for a trade contractor's damages for delay, disruption, and interference, construction managers should utilize so-called no damage for delay clauses in the trade contractor's contracts. No damage for delay clauses have been extensively used by general contractors in agreements with subcontractors with varying degrees of protection, depending upon the language of the clauses and the specific facts of each case. Generally, the courts have enforced no damage for delay clauses as valid. These clauses are usually strictly construed, however, to mitigate their harsh results. They have thus been limited to allow recovery of damages for delays: (1) not specifically enumerated in the clause, (2) incurred regardless of postponement of completion date, (3) not reasonably foreseeable by the parties at the time of contract, (4) for an unreasonable time, and (5) resulting from "active interference" of the protected party.

The term "active interference" has also been broadly extended by the courts to reduce the impact of a no damage for delay clause. Although active interference has been held to require more than mere negligence, past decisions have included within its scope (1) failure to act in an essential manner necessary for prosecution of the contract, (2) a failure to schedule removal of utility poles, (3) a failure to provide heat for the construction site, and (4) failure to furnish master construction schedules, to coordinate the work of contractors, and to permit the work to proceed in an orderly fashion. As can be seen from these examples, no damage for delay clauses are strictly construed to prevent a party from willfully causing delays or unreasonably disregarding the rights of other parties.

A no damage for delay clause should be carefully drafted to be specific, and yet to encompass as many circumstances as possible. The following clause represents an attempt to meet this criterion, and is recommended for most circumstances:

> The contractor acknowledges that the contract price is based on the fact that the construction manager [owner should be substituted for construction manager if trade contractors contract with the owner] is not liable to the contractor, absent any actual fraud or intentional and active tortuous act, for any damages or costs due to delays, accelerations, nonperformance, interferences with performance or sequence of the contractor's work. Should the contractor's performance, in whole or in part, be interfered with or delayed, or be suspended in the commencement, prosecution or completion, for reasons beyond the contractor's control and without its fault or negligence, the contractor shall have notified in writing, the construction manager of the cause of the delay within two (2) days of the occurring event, and shall be provided a similar extension of time, if needed, as is allotted to the construction manager by the owner. The construction manager owes no damage, duty, obligation or liability to the contractor as a result of any delay, interference, suspension, or other event, except for seeking an extension of time from the owner.[3]

3. Quoted from R. Cushman, M. Simon and M. Strokes, *Construction Industry Form Book*, 1979 p. 166.

9.5   SUMMARY

The traditional legal relationships between the owner, designer or engineer, and contractor have been modified to accommodate innovative construction approaches using a construction manager. Because the construction manager's role has emerged as a combination of certain facets of the traditional roles of the owner, the engineer, and the contractor, his legal duties and liabilities are unsettled. The construction manager should therefore carefully define his contractual duties to reflect

(1)   his qualifications and capabilities,

(2)   his insurance coverage and financial capabilities, and

(3)   his contractual authority.

Although the limits of the construction manager's liability are unsettled, his liabilities will be analogous to liabilities imposed on the traditional parties in the construction industry. The scope of the construction manager's liability may be extended to include

(1)   design deficiencies,

(2)   construction operations,

(3)   cost overruns,

(4)   delays, disruptions, and interferences, and

(5)   indemnification.

The best protection against liability is the careful and prudent administration of a contract. To minimize the construction manager's exposure to liability, a contract with the owner should be negotiated and drafted in such a form so as to

(1)   define the construction manager's duties and authority;

(2)   avoid broad indemnification clauses;

(3)   expressly provide that third parties are not intended to be benefited by the contract with the owner;

(4)   include a specific, and yet broad, no damage for delay clause.

Each state's laws and requirements of each procurement entity will be different. Therefore, the potential liabilities, both expressed and implied by the controlling jurisdiction, should be reviewed by the construction manager's attorney and insurance company in each instance.

10

Management Information Systems (MIS) and Processing

10.1 INTRODUCTION

A management information system (MIS) can be anything that owner and manager wish it to be, since both parties realize that it cannot think or make decisions. In the simplest mode, it may consist of letter and reporting writing. Most commonly, today, it involves the use of a data processor and is integrated with a CPM, Precedence, or PERT network. A construction or facilities MIS is now utilized where only CPM data is not considered sufficient to present the required picture. The most common approach is development of a Time-MIS and Cost-MIS system, which presents information at four levels of detail for corresponding levels of project management. A well-conceived and well-executed system is a planning, monitoring, control, and reporting tool. It can be designed to achieve the following objectives:

1. Provide an organized and efficient means of measuring, collecting, verifying, and quantifying data reflecting the progress and status of the operations on the project, as well as the total project with respect to schedules and cost.

2. Provide standards against which to measure or compare progress and status. Examples of standards include CPM schedules, control budgets, and procurement schedules.

3. Provide an organized and efficient means of converting the data from the operations into information. The information control system should recognize (*a*) the means of processing the information (e.g., manual or computer), (*b*) the skills available, and (*c*) the value of the information compared to the cost of obtaining it.

4. Report the correct and necessary information in a form that can best be interpreted by management and at a level of detail appropriate for the managers or supervisors who will be using the information.

5. Get this information to the correct manager or supervisors, that is, to those in position to make use of it.

6. The information must be received on time so that, if necessary, corrective action may be taken on those operations that generated the data in the first place.

In keeping with the principles of management by exception, the following two objectives should be added:

7. Identify and isolate the most important information for a given situation.

8. Give it to the right person as quickly as possible for his consideration, decision, and action.

This chapter begins by outlining the structure, objectives, and general principles underlying management information systems (MIS) and their modules. It next describes how management information should be organized and routed. The remainder of the chapter focuses on project management information systems and information processing.

10.2   STRUCTURE OF MIS

10.2.1   Basic Objective of MIS

The major objective of MIS is to provide managers and supervisors (i.e., the decision makers) with superior engineering, construction, and other operational information that will help (1) reduce project durations, (2) make better use of resources, (3) increase labor productivity, and (4) decrease cost/price.

10.2.2 MIS' Basic Principle

The basic principle underlying MIS and its modules is that in order to manage, one should be able first to quantify, then to define, then to measure, and finally to control. This concept implies a hierarchy of detail that needs to be considered when decomposing and managing engineering and construction projects. Halpin[1] defines this hierarchy as

PROJECT→PROJECT PHASES→COMPONENTS→SUBCOMPO-NENTS→ELEMENTS→WORK ITEMS OR ACTIVITIES
(Cost Accounts)

This means that a project should be broken down into project phases, project phases into components, components into subcomponents, subcomponents into elements, and elements into work items or activities. The lowest level is obtained when a unit or subdivision has a small duration and a constant expenditure rate suitable for planning and control purposes. The required labor, equipment, other resources, and the unit rates are established at this lowest level.

The framework for decomposing a project into elements or activities is as follows: (1) defining the work to be accomplished; (2) constructing a network plan; (3) summarizing the cost and schedule status for progressively higher levels of management; (4) breaking down the company's organization along the functional lines, with the performing department (of an activity, or aggregate activities) constituting the lowest level; (5) establishing a chart of accounts and charge numbers (accounting codes) that are compatible with the structure of relevant budgets and estimates, against which the actuals are recorded; (6) establishing a rate table that contains the unit rates, the overhead, burden rates, and any adjustment factors to be used for manpower, material, or equipment classifications; and (7) constructing an accounting calendar to reflect the accounting system used. For reporting purposes, the accounting calendar has to be the same as that used for the planning and scheduling.

A project that is broken into such hierarchical elements or activities requires a feedback control system for its effective planning, measurement, control, and management. Figure 10.1 models the operations, flow of information, and decision-making processes typical of the feedback control

---

1. Adapted from Halpin (54:338–340).

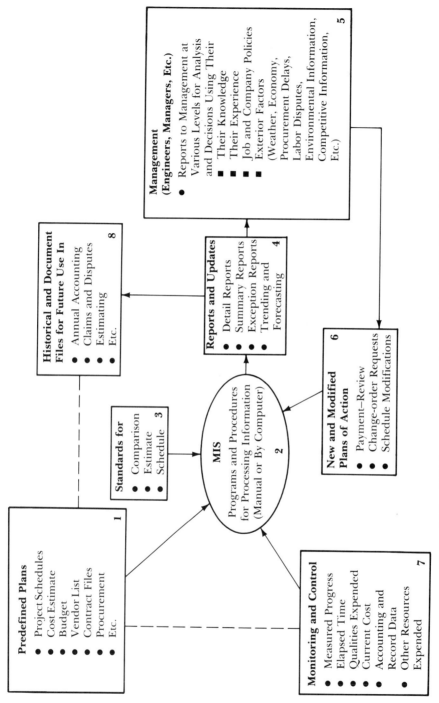

Figure 10.1. MIS Structure. Adapted from Paulson (109:71) and Post (104:66).

system suitable for managing construction organizations and medium to large engineering and construction projects. This model can be used or applied in any form of contract, be it the traditional form (where design and the construction phases are often separated), or the construction management form (where there is a strong interplay between design, procurement, and construction). A typical project begins with predefined plans, for example, schedules, estimates, budget, and value engineering (box 1). Information from the reports on similar projects found in the historical and document files (box 8) is used in establishing these plans, which become reference standards for control purposes (box 3). As the operations get under way, work in place, time, money, and resources expended (box 7) are fed as data into MIS (box 2) to produce reports and updates (box 4) for the management (box 5) or for future reference (box 8). Reference is made to the plans (box 1) in the information processing to show deviations and variances so that trends and forecasts can be made. The managers analyze these reports in the light of their own knowledge, experience, the company policies, external factors (e.g., the weather, economy, labor disputes, procurement delays), and other information and judgment. The new or modified plans of action (box 6) arrived at by the managers' decisions are used for controlling and managing the project operations. This is a feedback control system that operates throughout the project's life. If the time associated with the feedback through boxes 2, 4, 5, 6, and 7 is cut to the minimum, then managers can receive accurate, up-to-date, and timely information to make decisions and formulate plans of action. Thus a major need in project planning and control is to improve and expedite operations in boxes 1, 2, 4, 5, 6, and 7.

Automatic data processing methods are a must in processing the volumes of information in order to monitor and control the progress of the project operations under way. MIS consists of programs, algorithms, and procedures to process information. It allows application of modern data processing methods as well as manual processing methods. It is adapted to the peculiarities of the construction environment. It provides superior financial and operational information to the management. MIS supports such functions as planning, organizing, coordinating, scheduling, and budgeting; reports progress, costs, and accounting documentation; and identifies deviations and problems. The synthesis of MIS modules to a total system is shown in schematic format in Figure 10.2. Figure 10.2 shows the five modules of MIS. Each module operates both as integral and independent parts of the system.

10.3   MIS MODULES

MIS consists of five fundamental modules or groups of reports that are basically derived from the five groups of reports (except summary and

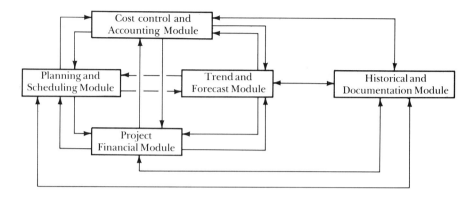

Figure 10.2. MIS Configuration.

narrative reports) that managers at the five management levels receive. These modules are structured both horizontally (by type of information) and vertically (by management level of the person receiving reports). These modules are as follows: (1) planning and scheduling; (2) cost control and accounting; (3) project financial; (4) trend and forecast; and (5) historical and documentation. The first four modules provide the reports listed in Tables 10.1 through 10.4, respectively. The fifth module serves as a source of documentation for all the project changes. The synthesis of the MIS modules to a total system is shown in Figure 10.2. They all have the basic principles and hierarchy of detail as shown in the previous section.

10.3.1   The Planning and Scheduling Module

This module fulfills two major objectives. First, it provides the project management with information on project duration and identifies the

Table 10.1.   Planning and Scheduling Listing

DESIGNATION	TITLE OF REPORT
T1 and T2	The master schedule and master network, respectively
T3 and T4	The engineering summary and detail schedules
T5	The procurement schedule report
T6 and T7	The construction summary schedule and construction summary schedule by responsibility
T8 and T9	The construction 90- or 180-day schedule report and the 90- or 180-day schedule by responsibility
T10	The construction weekly work plans
T11	The schedule report by start float

critical engineering-procurement-construction-start-up sequence. This information is also used by the estimator to arrive at better estimates of the project's direct and indirect costs. Second, it enables managers and supervisors to identify and control project execution problems.

The areas that the planning and scheduling module cover include the owners (clients), engineering, procurement, construction or start-up. Each agent of these areas develops plans of operation and delineates all activities to be performed in a network format. These become the basis for the project planning, control, and start-up. The planning and scheduling module coordinates the plans between the agents or areas involved in the project accomplishment. The planning may start as soon as contact is established between the owner, the designer, and the constructor, and continue until the project's completion or start-up.

The input for the planning module is the sequence of the project activities, their precedences, and durations. These are processed by means of computer or manual method to produce the outputs. Specifically, output gives (1) total project duration; (2) early and late starts and finishes of the activities; (3) free and total floats of the activities; and (4) project critical paths. The outputs generated by the planning and scheduling module are organized into the reports listed in Table 10.1. Note that these reports do not differ significantly in information provided or in format from those provided by many commercially available CPM/precedence programs.

The planning module is also capable of handling the following types of tasks: (1) job scheduling and updating at the project level; (2) quarterly or semiannual scheduling of all projects at the district/division or company level; and (3) generation of progress reports and documentation.

10.3.2 The Cost Control and Accounting Module

This module accomplishes the following three functions: (1) compares actual and predicted (forecast) costs of ongoing projects against the estimated (budget) cost; (2) obtains production rates for estimating new work and creating historical files; and (3) forecasts the project's final cost.

The cost control and accounting module's coverage may include engineering, procurement, construction, or start-up depending on the type of contract and scope of the work. Labor, equipment resources, material resources, unit rates, and production rates are established and applied at the cost accounts level. The main characteristics of this module are that (1) it measures and controls costs at the project, division/district, and company levels; (2) it gives the site management-expenditure limits proportional to its responsibilities; (3) it periodically detects all variances regarding cost at the activity, element, component, phase(s) and project levels; and (4) it does not necessarily replace existing accounting systems

Table 10.2.   Cost Control and Accounting Reports Listing

DESIGNATION	TITLE OF REPORT
C1	The project summary cost status report
C2	The detailed cost estimate report
C3 and C4	The original/current project budget report, and original/current project budget report by responsibility
C5 and C6	Cost and commitments by control code and by the purchase order number reports
C7	The direct material cost and commitments by the purchase order number by responsibility

based on organizational structure for costs to be identified with proper degree of detail.

The cost control and accounting module measures and controls costs in terms of the same entities of the project as those used for planning and scheduling the activity. The module is based on the cost estimates developed at the inception of the project. The inputs for this module are the budgets, actuals, estimates, commitments, and obligations involving labor, materials, and equipment. These inputs are processed and organized into several reports that provide the project participants with the project's current cost/estimates status versus the budget. The reports produced by the cost control and accounting module are found in Table 10.2. Note that the cost summary reports are organized in a format compatible with the average contractor's estimates.

10.3.3   The Project Financial Module

The primary objective of the project financial module is to provide management with the flow of funds and their accumulation with time for the total project as well as for the materials, labor, equipment and subcontracts. It also provides the budget differences resulting from scheduling on the basis of early or late times.

The information provided by the project financial module helps the project management and supervisors in areas such as (1) contract commitments; (2) cost, change orders, and claims; (3) contractor payment approval; (4) current comparisons of funds available, funds committed, and funds required to complete the project; and (5) accounting tool and audit trail. The project financial module covers such areas as engineering, procurement, construction or start-up.

The inputs for the project financial module include the unrestricted planning/scheduling data that have been augmented by cost and account-

Table 10.3.   Financial Reports Listing

DESIGNATION	TITLE OF REPORT
F1	The multi-phase financial status report
F2 and F3	The programmed and actual contract cost reports
F4	The project file report
F5	The project payment report
F6	The contractor payment approval report
F7	The fund requirement projection report
F8	The projects accounts report
F9	The vendor, contract, invoice, allotment of funds, reimbursable expenses, and composite project costs files
F10	The change-order files report
F11	The job progress report on uncompleted work

ing data, period of payments, initial project funds, retention (by owner for security purposes), project duration, and early or late start and finish times of the activities. The output provides (1) the cumulative cost distributions for materials, labor, equipment, and total project costs on the basis of activity start times anywhere between the early and late starts; (2) contractor's payment approval; (3) multi-phase financial status; (4) vendor files; (5) claims and change-order files; and (6) the flow of funds for the total project. The outputs generated by the project financial module are organized into the reports shown in Table 10.3. Note that at this point the separation of payments into parts identifying the portion of direct and indirect costs is only for project control purposes and does not imply that the project owner has knowledge of the relative magnitudes of these parts. The fundamental principle remains that the contractor and the design firm(s) are paid periodically in amounts proportional to the work accomplished between payment periods.

10.3.4   The Trend and Forecast Module

The major objectives of the trend and forecast module are (1) to accumulate man-hours and quantities for comparison with the budget and to evaluate and control labor performance; (2) to assess the effects of construction labor performance on a planned schedule; (3) to provide analyses of the effects of major variables that affect the forecasted manpower and schedule; (4) to supply the current manual man-hours and material quantities, budgets, and forecast so that an audit trail can be kept on these changes; (5) to provide more detailed analyses of individual labor accounts or categories of accounts than are available in the other three modules;

Table 10.4.   Forecast and Trend Reports Listing

DESIGNATION	TITLE OF REPORT
A1 and A2	The summary and detail man-hour overrun reports
A3 through A5	The project performance, the responsibility performance, and performance summary reports, respectively
A6	The quantity and unit-rate report
A7	The detailed analysis report
A8	The man-hours summary report
A9	The percent complete and man-hour percentage report
A10 and A11	The manpower equivalency and block summary reports
A12	The current budget and trend forecast report
A13	The quantity forecast report
A14 and A15	The detailed labor forecast review report and labor forecast review report by responsibility

(6) to provide a convenient and efficient method of maintaining information used to monitor, forecast, and control manpower, unit rates, and physical percent complete, and (7) to provide man-hour performance and progress data in a format that quickly allows management to develop a forecast of manual labor man-hours.

The trend and forecast module basically deals with engineering, procurement, and construction. The inputs for the trend and forecast module are (1) project activities, their sequence and duration; (2) the budgets, costs, estimates, and commitments involving materials, equipment, labor, and subcontracts; and (3) weekly man-hours expended and quantities installed. These inputs are then processed to produce the outputs. Specifically, output gives (1) material and man-hour budgets, forecasts, and overruns; (2) labor performance, productivities, and unit rates; and (3) manpower equivalency. The outputs generated by the trend and forecast module are organized into the reports shown in Table 10.4.

10.3.5   The Historical and Documentation Module

This module provides (1) documentation of all changes made in the approved schedule, budget, and quantities so that complete traceability is maintained between the original plans (schedule, budget, and quantities) and the latest approved plans; (2) a complete record on each construction activity in the plan showing how much time the activity takes to accomplish and how much it actually costs to complete. The information provided by this module is for future use in annual accounting, claims, and disputes, and for estimating similar jobs. It has the same inputs, outputs, principles, and hierarchy of details as the four modules described earlier.

10.4   MANAGEMENT INFORMATION ORGANIZATION AND ROUTING

There is a constant stream of information flow within the construction organization. This information covers many aspects, from the objectives through the strategies, planning, and control, to detailed operations of the organization as well as the projects the organization is involved in. For the individual managers at the various management levels, this information proves to be significant. For the proper decision making that leads to optimal utilization of resources and for keeping all managers informed of each other's activities and problems, usable information is particularly necessary. Good flow of information facilitates access to information. At the present time, useful and good information organization and flow can be worthwhile attributes, especially when one looks in the general context of the information explosion that is occurring in the construction industry. Also, information flow leads to greater involvement so that managers at the various levels, too, have a better understanding of what is happening and can make a better contribution. These managers can then appreciate the depth of their responsibilities and their relationships with other members of the organization on similar or related subjects.

This section presents the techniques and step-by-step procedure for good management information organization and flow or routing.

10.4.1   Information Type

Information is defined as "the behavior-initiating stimuli between sender and receiver and in the form of signs that are coded representations of data."[2] Data differ from information in that data are considered signs, usually recorded observations. Data do not affect the behavior of people or machines. However, data may become information if behavior becomes affected. For example, the data base for computer systems consists of masses of such signs that are not affecting behavior. Until the data are actually viewed, and properly organized for a manager so that he/she reacts to them, they are not information. Thus management information is not just the forms and reports produced. It includes all the data and intelligence—cost, financial, schedule, trend, forecast, productivity, duration—that are needed to plan, operate and control a particular project or the organization as a whole.

---

2. Murdick, Robert G., et al., *Information Systems for Modern Management*, 2nd ed., Prentice-Hall, Inc., Englewood Cliffs, N.J., 1975, p. 438.

Full and free information to everyone is an appealing idea, but the result can be so much information that the organization can fail to function effectively. Under such circumstances, construction personnel may be flooded with information they do not need, to the point that they cannot concentrate on the information they need. Furthermore, sorting and selecting among the myriad reports may be so time consuming that there is little opportunity to do anything else. The information thus loses its reliability, accuracy, and value when the manager receives too much or scanty information. In the interest of economy, only information that is necessary is provided and that which is supplied to others is simplified as far as possible. The crucial requirement is to determine what is really important and requires immediate or quick action.

Construction personnel require simple and concise information in an inexpensive form. Therefore, it is possible to optimize the effectiveness and efficient working of the organization and to make the maximum use of resources. The information needs of the project and functional managers include detailed and formalized project costs, schedules, and financial information. The managers in the director, president, and construction management levels require the summary format of the cost, schedule, and financial information. Thus the information required by the managers at these five levels fall into five basic groups. These are the summary and narrative, schedule, costs, financial, and trend and forecast information. Therefore, the reports issued to these managers to satisfy their needs are of five basic types, namely, summary and narrative (designated S) reports (see Table 10.5), schedule (or T) reports, cost (or C) reports, financial (or F), and trend and forecast (or A) reports. These reports are issued monthly or weekly.

The summary and narrative reports are basically going to the board, the president, and the construction management levels. Each of these reports covers at least one of the following areas: schedule, cost, finance, and forecast and trend. They are prepared manually. The summary and narrative reports and their designations are listed in Table 10.5. The individual detail reports coming from each of the five groups of reports are listed in Tables 10.1 through 10.5.

10.4.2   Management Reports

The reports listed in Tables 10.1 through 10.5 are, at this point, properly organized into good and useful information so that they satisfy the information needs of the managers receiving them. To do this, the recipient(s), the preparing party or parties, the purpose(s), the frequency, and the contents for each report are determined. Samples of the management reports (taking the first ones for each of the reports from the five groups) are presented in Tables 10.6 through 10.10. The contents of these

Table 10.5.   Summary and Narrative Reports Listing

DESIGNATION	TITLE OF REPORT
S1	The board's summary report
S2	The president's narrative report
S3 through S6	The vice-presidents' (finance, engineering, operations, and administration) narrative reports, respectively
S7	The procurement director's narrative report
S8	The chief engineer's narrative report
S9	The chief accountant's narrative report
S10	The public relations director's narrative report
S11	The operations manager's narrative report
S12	The district/division engineer's narrative report
S13	The procurement manager's narrative report
S14	The construction manager's narrative report
S15	The labor relations manager's narrative report
S16	The project manager's narrative report

General Comments: The S1 report goes to the director's level, S2 through S10 go to the president's level, S11 through S15 go to the construction management level, and the only one going to the project management level is S16.

reports illustrate how reports are organized into good and usable information.

10.4.3   Reports Organization by Information Type and Management Level

The cost, planning and scheduling, financial, and trend and forecast reports described previously provide the horizontal information. However, they are interrelated and are structured by management levels. Each level of management receives only the reports and level of detail it needs. There are five management levels that will receive these reports: the board of directors, the president, the construction management, the project management, and the functional management. Most of the information provided by these reports is familiar to all experienced owners and engineers. What is different is the manner in which it is produced and presented. As shown in Table 10.11, each management report is prepared by qualified personnel (designated by letter "P") and sent to the manager directly responsible for the report (designated by letter "A"), with copies (designated by letter "C") to managers above, below, and at the same level or sublevel as the responsible recipients for their information, comments, and review. This method of producing and transmitting reports is different from the present practice in the construction industry. Most management reports are sent directly to their responsible recipients and they, in turn,

Table 10.6.   The Board's Summary Report

MANAGEMENT LEVEL:	DIRECTOR REPORT #S1
RECIPIENT(S):	The board of directors and its chairman
PREPARED BY:	The president
PURPOSE:	To provide the directors and the shareholders with a current awareness of the financial status (i.e., profitability, dividends), progress, and problems of the company.
FREQUENCY:	Once or twice a year and as required
CONTENTS:	(*a*) Current jobs' time and cost status
	(*b*) Jobs completed during the reporting period
	(*c*) Latest environmental and competitive information and effects
	(*d*) The company's financial report
	(*e*) Market and planning development
	(*f*) General comments

Table 10.7.   The Master Schedule and Master Network

MANAGEMENT LEVEL:	PROJECT MANAGEMENT REPORTS #T1 AND T2
RECIPIENT(S):	The construction manager, the project manager, the chief engineer, the vice-presidents, the resident project engineer, and the client
PREPARED BY:	The chief planning/scheduling engineer or the project planning/scheduling engineer
PURPOSE:	To provide a summary schedule of the project activities, to assist in project planning, and to provide a framework for the development of detailed schedules for each phase or area of responsibility
FREQUENCY:	The T1 and T2 reports are prepared after the project award and issued monthly. Rescheduling occurs only when absolutely required and with proper approval
CONTENTS:	(*a*) Major engineering-design activities
	(*b*) Major procurement activities
	(*c*) Major construction activities
	(*d*) Major start-up activities

General Comments: The master schedule and master network are intended to give a complete picture of the project without excessive detail and in a simplified manner. They list approximately fifty work items with each item further divided into its engineering, procurement, construction, and start-up activities.

Table 10.8.   The Project Summary Cost Status Report

MANAGEMENT LEVEL:	CONSTRUCTION MANAGEMENT REPORT #C1
RECIPIENT(S):	The construction manager, division/district manager, the project manager, and the client. Copies are sent to the project accountant and the resident project engineer
PREPARED BY:	The project cost engineer
PURPOSE:	To provide an overview of the project's total cost and budget status, and to forecast and control the total cost of the project based on current information.
FREQUENCY:	Monthly and as required
CONTENTS:	(a) Each major cost code (broken down into labor, material, equipment, and total for the code) (b) Original and current estimates (c) Cost commitments and expenditures (d) Projections to project completion (total amount, variance in both dollars and percentage)

Table 10.9.   The Multi-Phase Financial Status Report

MANAGEMENT LEVEL:	CONSTRUCTION MANAGEMENT REPORT #F1
RECIPIENT(S):	The construction manager and the division/ district manager. Copies are sent to the project manager, the resident engineer, and the client.
PREPARED BY:	The project cost engineer
PURPOSE:	To provide a current awareness of the cost and financial status of each major project element; to alert management to potential cost overrun areas or fund shortages; and to highlight trends in the cost and financial status of the project.
FREQUENCY:	Monthly and as required.
CONTENTS:	(a) The description of the phase and phase number (b) The budget, estimated costs, and contract amount for the phase (c) Allotment of funds, approved outlays, and balance (d) Unpaid commitments, and commitments to complete

Table 10.10.   Summary Man-Hour Overrun Report

	FUNCTIONAL
MANAGEMENT LEVEL:	MANAGEMENT REPORT #A1
RECIPIENT(S):	The general superintendent, the area superintendent, and field-office engineers. Copies are sent to project manager, the planning scheduling engineer, and the resident project engineer.
PREPARED BY:	The project cost engineer
PURPOSE:	To highlight the significant potential man-hour overruns for the top twenty to twenty-five man-hour overruns.
FREQUENCY:	Weekly
CONTENTS:	(a) Account number, account description, and percent complete
	(b) Current budget man-hours and forecast man-hours
	(c) Overrun man-hours for account and total project man-hours overrun

General Comments: Account is considered overrun when it is two hundred or more hours over the forecast and is below 75 or 80% complete.

circulate these reports laterally, above and below them. The method presented in Table 10.11 allows managers to simultaneously receive information so that uniform action can be taken. Together the horizontal and vertical organization of the information provides the report structure that organizes and presents most of the information necessary for the management team to carry out its management role effectively. Table 10.11 shows the report(s) each manager or supervisor receives to perform his/her role.

10.4.4   The Flow of Management Information

The flow of information is necessary to help construction personnel carry out their duties more efficiently. It has already been stated that benefits accrue when it is possible to ensure the provision of the facts at the right time. When more people are added to the organization and the volume of work increases, the drive for growth then concerns the proper utilization of data. The information that is provided links the internal and external affairs so that work can be continued and monitored.

For the organization to function properly, it is essential to encourage information to flow in all directions, that is, upward, downward, and laterally. This allows the managers to learn simultaneously about the organization, its projects, and its problems so that decisions and instructions can be made and received uniformly, with opportunities for clarification and adjustments to be made as quickly and as efficiently as possible. Thus timing, reliability, scope, means, accuracy, value, and feedback are achieved. This information that flows in all directions carries the concerns of many aspects of the company—from the company objectives and strategies, through the planning and control, to the detailed operation of the company and the projects in which it is involved. Figure 10.3 is a typical organization chart that shows the direction information flows. The information paths or communication lines are indicated by both solid and broken lines.

10.5   PROJECT MANAGEMENT INFORMATION SYSTEMS (PMIS)

10.5.1   Developing PMIS

An information system is as essential to the effective control of projects as it is to meeting external reporting requirements, to reporting project progress to top management, and to performing effective project planning.

Often, construction managers develop ad hoc project information systems that suit their individual needs. Some construction managers are able to develop information systems that permit them to foresee potential problem areas and to act in time to alleviate them. Other construction managers may have systems that allow them to monitor the progress of their projects but that are not truly effective in indicating areas of future trouble within the project.

The development of a project information system involves the gathering and coalescing of data from the functional units supporting the project. An information system should be designed to serve two purposes: first, visibility for the functional manager, in terms of his input to the PMIS; and second, visibility for the construction manager, in terms of cost, time, and performance. Many construction managers rely on historical information, which depicts the past and present rather clearly but which does not allow them to foresee the future in a manner that would permit control actions to be taken before minor project problems become major ones. In any case, whether the information systems developed by individual construction managers are good or bad, the systems are often not well integrated. Thus, while each information system may provide the individual construction manager with the information he desires, the output of the various systems may not provide the information that is adequate for decision making and planning at the overall project or organizational level.

Table 10.11.   The Reporting Structure

KEY

P: Manager preparing report

A: Addressee - directly responsible

C: Copy - for review, comments or information

SUMMARY REPORTS (S)

- S1: Board's Summary Report
- S2: President's Narrative
- S3: Vice-President - Finance Narrative
- S4: Vice-President - Engineering Narrative
- S5: Vice-President - Operations Narrative
- S6: Vice-President - Administrative Narrative
- S7: Procurement Director's Narrative Report
- S8: Chief Engineer's Narrative Report
- S9: Chief Accountant's Narrative Report
- S10: Public Relations Director's Report
- S11: Operations Manager's Narrative Report
- S12: District/Division Engineer's Narrative
- S13: Procurement Manager's Narrative Report
- S14: Construction Manager Narrative Report
- S15: Labor Relations Manager Narrative Report
- S16: Project Manager Narrative Report

SCHEDULE REPORTS (T)

- T1: Master Schedule
- T2: Master Network
- T3: Engineering Summary Schedule
- T4: Engineering Detail Schedule
- T5: Procurement Schedule
- T6: Construction Summary Schedule
- T7: Construction Summary Schedule by Responsibility
- T8: Construction 90/180 Day Schedule
- T9: Construction 90/180 Day Schedule by Responsibility
- T10: Construction Weekly Work Plans
- T11: Schedule Report by Start Flow

MANAGEMENT RECIPIENTS	S	S1	S2	S3	S4	S5	S6	S7	S8	S9	S10	S11	S12	S13	S14	S15	S16	T	T1	T2	T3	T4	T5	T6	T7	T8	T9	T10	T11
1. BOARD OF DIRECTOR'S LEVEL																													
Board of Directors		A																											
Chairman of the Board of Directors		A																											
2. THE PRESIDENT'S LEVEL																													
The President		P	A	C	C	C	C																						
Vice-President Finance				A	C	C	C		C	C	C	C							A	A									
Vice-President Engineering				C	A	C	C		C	C	C	C							A	A									
Vice-President Operations				C	C	A	C		C	C	C	C							A	A									
Vice-President Administration			P	C	C	C	A		C	C	C	C							A	A									
Client Agency															C				A	A									
Director of Procurement								A		C			C																
Chief Engineer					P			C	A	C	C	C																	
Chief Accountant				P				C	C	A	C	C																	
Public Relations Director							P	C			A																			
3. CONSTRUCTION MANAGEMENT LEVEL																													
Operations Manager						P		C	C	C	C	A	C	C	C														
Assistant/Deputy Chief Engineer									A	C	C	C																	
Chief Estimator									C			C	C	C			C												
District/Division Engineer									P				A	C	C	C	C				A								
Procurement Manager								P						A		C				A				A	A		A		
Construction Manager												P	C	C	A	C	C		A	A	A			A	A		A		
Labor Relations Manager																A													
Public Relations Officer											P					C													
4. PROJECT MANAGEMENT LEVEL																													
Project Manager												C			P	C	A		A	A	A			A	A		A	C	A
Assistant/Deputy Chief Estimator									C			C	C	C			C												
Planning/Scheduling Engineer																			P	P	P	P	P	P	P	P	P	C	P
Cost Engineer																													C
Estimator																													
Purchasing Agent														P															
Accountant										P																			
Saftey Engineer															P														
Field Office Engineer																								A		A	A	A	A
Project Engineer												P					P		A	A	A	A	A	A		A			A
5. FUNCTIONAL MANAGEMENT LEVEL																													
General Superintendent																											A		A
Superintendent(s)																											A	P	A
General Foremen/Foremen																												A	
Field Engineers																							A		A	A	A	A	C
Subcontractors																									A		A		A

Code	COST REPORTS
C	COST REPORTS
C1	Project Summary Cost Status Report
C2	Detailed Cost Estimates
C3	Original/Current Project Budget
C4	Original/Current Project Budget by Responsibility
C5	Cost and Commitments by Control Code
C6	Cost and Commitments by Purchase Order Number
C7	Direct Material Cost and Commitments by Purchase Order Number by Responsibility
F	FINANCIAL REPORTS
F1	Multi-Phase Financial Status Report
F2	Program Contract Costs Report
F3	Actual Contract Cost Report
F4	Project File Report
F5	Project Payment Report
F6	Contractor Payment Approved Report
F7	Fund Requirement Projection Report
F8	Project Accounts Reports
F9	Vendor, Contract, Invoice, Allotment of Funds, Reimbursable Expenses, and Composite Project Cost Files Reports
F10	Change Order Files
F11	Job Progress Report on Uncompleted Work
A	FORCAST AND TREND REPORTS
A1	Summary Overrun Report
A2	Detail Overrun Report by Responsibility
A3	Project Performance Report
A4	Responsibility Performance Report
A5	Performance Summary Report
A6	Quantity and Units Rate Report
A7	Detailed Analysis Report
A8	Manhour Summary Report
A9	Percent Completed and Manhour Percentage
A10	Manpower Equivalency Report
A11	Block Summary Report
A12	Current Budget and Trend Forcast Report
A13	Quantity Forecast Report
A14	Detailed Labor Forecast Review Report
A15	Labor Forcast Review Report by Responsibility

211

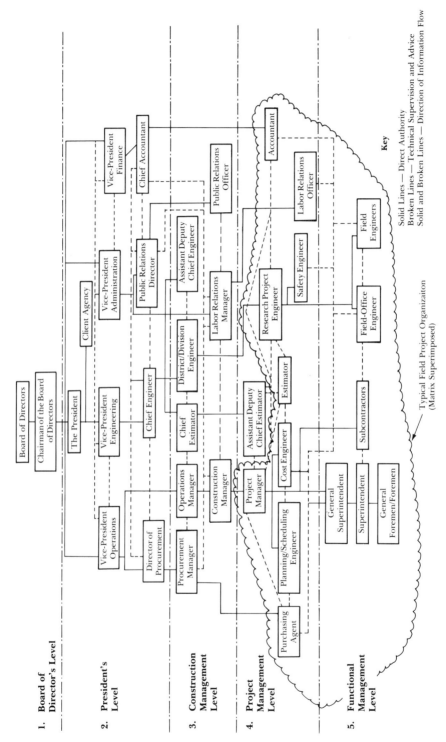

Figure 10.3. Typical Construction Organization Chart.

1. Board of Director's Level
2. President's Level
3. Construction Management Level
4. Project Management Level
5. Functional Management Level

Board of Directors

Chairman of the Board of Directors

The President

Vice-President Operations

Vice-President Engineering

Client Agency

Vice-President Administration

Vice-President Finance

Director of Procurement

Operations Manager

Chief Engineer

Public Relations Director

Chief Accountant

Procurement Manager

Construction Manager

Chief Estimator

District/Division Engineer

Assistant Deputy Chief Engineer

Public Relations Officer

Purchasing Agent

Planning/Scheduling Engineer

Project Manager

Assistant Deputy Chief Estimator

Cost Engineer

Estimator

Labor Relations Manager

Research Project Engineer

Accountant

General Superintendent

Superintendent

General Foremen/Foremen

Subcontractors

Field-Office Engineer

Safety Engineer

Field Engineers

Labor Relations Officer

Typical Field Project Organization (Matrix Superimposed)

Key

Solid Lines — Direct Authority
Broken Lines — Technical Supervision and Advice
Solid and Broken Lines — Direction of Information Flow

212

10.5.2   Basic Objective of a PMIS

A project management information system (PMIS) may be developed within an organization to serve as a model information system for all projects. The term "model" is used here in the sense of a basic information system structure that will provide essential information to the construction manager and to top management; at the same time, it will be

1. Sufficiently flexible so that it can be modified to suit the needs of the individual construction manager

2. Adaptable to many different projects

3. Adaptable to differing customer information requirements

Such a PMIS model will provide a basic information source to meet the requirements of functional manager, contract manager, construction manager, top management, and customer information. It can serve as a point of departure for the construction manager who desires to implement his own systems. By virtue of this flexibility, it should provide all levels of management with the required information and, at the same time, provide standardized information that is integrated into an overall planning and control system.

10.5.3   PMIS Criteria

In addition to the requirements for flexibility and adaptability, which are inherent in the concept of a model PMIS, a number of criteria for the design of such a system can be readily stated. PMIS must

1. Provide essential information on the cost-time-performance parameters of a project and on the interrelationships of these parameters.

2. Provide information in standardized form to enhance its usefulness to top management for multi-project control and long-range planning.

3. Be decision-oriented, in that information reported should be focused toward the decisions required of the construction manager and top management.

4. Provide for customer-reporting requirements such as those outlined in current government specifications.

5. Be exception-oriented, in that it will focus the manager's attention on those critical areas requiring attention rather than simply reporting on all areas and requiring the manager to devote attention to each.

6. Fit into the overall organization information system and strategic planning system.

7. Be prospective in nature rather than retrospective, in that it should give special attention to potential problem areas within the project; it should, in effect, be an "early warning" system for the construction manager.

8. Incorporate both external and internal data to provide a capability for keeping track of evolving projects in the customer's organization. In this fashion, the PMIS can interface with an organizational strategic information system.

9. Be consistent with existing construction management guides and procedures.

10. Be consistent with policy documentation developed earlier by the organization.

11. Provide a capability for routine reporting, exception reporting, and special analyses (such as statistical analyses), which may be desired by the construction manager or top management.

12. Provide for measurement at the critical project-functional interface, so that the construction manager and functional manager will have data on which to base those decisions for which authority and responsibility are shared.

13. Provide a basic data requirement for functional managers to furnish to the project office and to facilitate in-house functional visibility.

14. Provide for project visibility during the phases of a project's life cycle.

The best of information systems will not keep the construction manager out of trouble, but it will keep him from being surprised when trouble comes. The information system is only as good as its input. A standardized reporting system can be set up that will give "visibility" to the project. Such a reporting system will make the delegation of authority easier, because everyone will be able to ascertain quickly who is in charge of each part of the project and where to reach him. Without an adequate information system, it can be difficult to tell who is responsible for a particular aspect of the project and how that individual is doing in his work.

Reports should be specified for each project and reviewed frequently for applicability and need. The use of existing information should be encouraged; only where a new problem exists, or a new approach is being tried, should new techniques be employed. The tendency to apply all currently popular administrative and control techniques indiscriminately should be resisted.

10.6 MANAGEMENT INFORMATION PROCESSING

Information processing, simply put, means taking raw data or input and converting it into the desired reports, files, or answers input and converting it into the desired reports, files, or answers to inquiries. It involves organization, storage, searching, and retrieval of information. Information processing may be done manually, by computer, or both. The entire subject has received an increased amount of attention in recent years, not only because simpler information processing systems are needed, but also because the planning, designing, and controlling of information and information systems rely on an extensive data base of high quality to be a useful tool in solving the complex problems of today and of the future.

The summary and narrative, cost, schedule, and financial reports discussed earlier are so simple in format and content that they can be processed manually. This makes their use easy and suitable for small, medium, as well as large-sized construction and design or engineering organizations. Cost, schedule, and financial reports can be produced entirely by computer or partially by computer and partially by manual means. The summary and narrative reports should always be produced manually. Because of the turnaround time (i.e., the frequency of production) and the contents, the trend and forecast reports do not lend themselves to easy and quick manual processing.

The extensive use of a computer has now become very common. Procedures, too, have become more standardized and there has been a considerable interflow of information. With computer service, speed, accuracy, and economy are the notable characteristics. It is certainly more difficult to function in a medium or large organization without any formal computerized information processing system. However, the cost of the service by computer should always be checked to see if it is justified, because, in some respects, economic forces can cause changes from computer to manual or vice versa.

10.7 SUMMARY

A useful MIS accumulates, processes, stores, and transmits information relevant to people in management. The system informs and must serve a worthwhile purpose. Cost is a major consideration, and the MIS must have a reasonable cost compared to its worth. The economics of information systems requires constant balance between the value of the information carried in the system and the cost of designing and operating it. Both the owner and construction manager must be constantly aware of the project cost factors and treat the MIS as a working tool whose continuation must be justified.

Development and implementation of a comprehensive project control system is essential if the full potential of a construction management program is to be realized. The controls must be based upon realistic goals developed during planning and design. The control system by itself will not manage the project, but it will measure current status against programmed goals so that the competitive management action when warranted can be applied.

11

Value Engineering (VE)

11.1 INTRODUCTION

The concept of value engineering or value analysis began during World War II when shortages of materials and labor necessitated changes in methods, materials, and traditional designs. Many of these changes resulted in superior performance at a lower cost. After the war the General Electric Company pioneered in the development and implementation of an organized value-analysis program. This technique was adopted by a number of industrial companies and government agencies, and in 1962, value engineering was included as a requirement in the Armed Services Procurement Regulations (ASPR). This change in ASPR introduced value engineering to two of the largest construction agencies in the country, the U.S. Army Corps of Engineers and the U.S. Navy Bureau of Yards and Docks. During the 1970s a large number of other governmental agencies and jurisdictions adopted value engineering, and notable progress was made in furthering the use of value engineering in the construction field by the Public Building Service, General Services Administration (GSA).

Growth of construction applications of value engineering in the public sector was fostered by legislation and regulation. However, there has been no sign of an equally impressive growth of value engineering utilization in the private sector.

The chapter first defines value engineering. It next discusses the fundamentals of value engineering and areas of opportunity for its applications. The rest of the chapter focuses on value engineering methodology and life-cycle costing.

11.2   DEFINITION OF VALUE ENGINEERING

The first question to ask is usually, "What is value engineering, anyway?" "Value engineering" is a systematic evaluation of a project design to obtain the most value for every dollar of cost. By carefully investigating costs, availability of materials, construction methods, shipping costs or physical limitations, planning and organizing, cost/benefit values, and similar cost-influencing items, an improvement in the overall cost of a project can be realized.

The entire value engineering effort is aimed at a careful analysis of each function, as well as the elimination or modification of anything that adds to the project cost without adding to its functional capabilities. Not only are first costs to be considered, but even the later in-place costs of operation, maintenance, life, replacement, and similar characteristics must be considered. Thus, although the name is new, value engineering is simply a systematic application of engineering economy, which was taught in every engineering course long before anyone ever thought of a catchy name for it.

The principal difficulty of applying value engineering principles to construction is the problem of having a third party, who may not possess the same degree of expertise in the subject area as the architect or engineer, cause changes in design that simply substitute the value engineer's judgment for that of the designer—a risky process at best. Theoretically, the value engineer does not "cause" a design change, but by placing the architect or engineer in the position of having to defend the original design, the entire production schedule is threatened.

In the construction phase, however, things are different. Now the value engineer is the contractor, whose experience is in construction methods, techniques, and costs. The contractor's input can often offer the benefit of construction experience and a knowledge of the marketplace and labor force that the designer did not possess. It is here that the greatest cost benefit can result with a minimum of conflict with the designer. Often, in federally funded construction contracts, a value engineering incentive clause may be provided, in which the government will allow the contractor to retain up to 50% of the cost savings realized in any value engineering proposal submitted by the contractor that is accepted and implemented.

11.3   FUNDAMENTALS OF VALUE ENGINEERING

11.3.1   Function

In value engineering, the "function" is defined as the specific purpose or use intended for something. It describes what must be achieved. For value engineering studies, this function is usually described in the simplest form possible, usually in only two words: "Support weight," "prevent corrosion," and "conduct current" are typical expressions of function.

11.3.2   Worth

"Worth" refers to the least cost required to provide the functions that are required by the user of the finished project. Worth is established by comparison, such as comparing it with the cost of its functional equivalent. The worth of an item is not affected by the possibility of failure under the value engineering concept embraced by the federal government. Thus, if a bolt supporting a key joint in a large roof truss fails, the entire roof of the structure may be caused to fail. Nevertheless, the worth of the bolt is the lowest cost necessary to provide a reliable fastening.

11.3.3   Cost

"Cost" is the total amount of money required to obtain and use the functions that have been specified. For the seller, this is the total cost in connection with the product. For the owner, the total cost of ownership includes not only the purchase price of the product, but the cost of including it in the inventory for its total usable life. The cost of ownership may also include a proportional share of expenditures for development, engineering, testing, spare parts, and various items of overhead expense.

11.3.4   Value

"Value" is the relationship of worth to cost as realized by the owner, based upon his needs and resources in any given situation. the ratio of worth to cost is the principal measure of "value." Thus a "value equation" may be used to arrive at a Value Index as follows:

$$\text{Value Index} = \frac{\text{Worth}}{\text{Cost}} = \frac{\text{Utility}}{\text{Cost}}$$

The value may be increased by doing any of the following:

1. Improve the utility of something with no change in cost,
2. Retain the same utility for less cost, or
3. Combine improved utility with less cost.

Optimum value is obtained when all utility criteria are met at the lowest overall cost. Although worth and cost can be expressed in dollars, value is a dimensionless expression showing the relationship of the other two.

11.3.5 Philosophy

If something does not do what it is intended to do, no amount of cost reduction will improve its value. Any "cost reduction" action that sacrifices the need utility of something actually reduces its value to the owner. However, costs incurred to increase the functional capacity of something beyond that which is needed amounts to "gilding the lily" and provides little actual value to the owner. Therefore, anything less than the necessary functional capacity is unacceptable; anything more is unnecessary and wasteful.

11.3.6 Types of Value Engineering Recommendations

Within the Department of Defense and some other federal agencies, there are two types of recommendations that are the results of a value engineering effort:

1. **VALUE ENGINEERING PROPOSAL (VEP)**   A value engineering recommendation that originates from within the government agency itself, or one that was originated by the contractor and may be implemented by unilateral action. A VEP can only relate to changes that are within the terms of the contract and specifications, and thus would not require a change order to implement.

2. **VALUE ENGINEERING CHANGE PROPOSAL (VECP)**   A value engineering recommendation by a contractor that requires the owner's approval, and that, if accepted, requires the execution of a change order. This would apply to any proposed change that would require a change in the contract, the specifications, the scope of the work, or similar limits previously established by contract.

11.4   AREAS OF OPPORTUNITY FOR VALUE ENGINEERING

11.4.1   Value Engineering by the Architect or Engineer

Value engineering is a basic approach that takes nothing for granted and challenges everything on a project, including the necessity for the existence of a product or project, for that matter. The cost of a project is influenced by the requirements of the design and the specifications. Prior to completing the final design, the architect or engineer should carefully consider the methods and equipment that may be used to construct the project. Requirements that increase the cost without producing equivalent benefits should be eliminated. The final decisions of the architect or engineer should be based upon a reasonable knowledge of construction methods and costs.

The cost of a project may be divided into five or more items, such as:

1.   Materials
2.   Labor
3.   Equipment
4.   Overhead and supervision
5.   Profit

Although the last item is beyond the control of the architect or engineer, there is some control possible over the cost of the first four.

If the architect or engineer specifies materials that must be transported great distances, the costs may be unnecessarily high. Requirements for tests and inspections of materials may be too rigid for the purpose for which the materials will be used. Frequently, substitute materials are available nearby that are as satisfactory as other materials whose costs are considerably higher. The suggestions of the contractor can be of value here.

The specified quality of workmanship and methods of construction have considerable influence on the amount and class of labor required and upon the cost of labor. Complicated concrete structures are relatively easy to design and draw but may be exceedingly difficult to build. A high-grade concrete finish may be justified for exposed surfaces in a fine building, but the same quality of workmanship is not justified for a warehouse. The quality of workmanship should be in keeping with the type of project involved.

Architects and engineers should keep informed on the developments of new construction equipment, since this information will enable them to modify the design or construction methods to permit the use of economical equipment. The resident engineer or inspector is a vital link in the chain of information that supplies the architect and engineer with the latest developments in construction methods and equipment. The normal daily construction report contains sufficient information to keep the architect and engineer adequately informed, and upon noting new methods or equipment in the inspector's report, these leads can be followed to determine the specific capabilities and advantages of each case. For example, the use of a dual-drum concrete paving mixer instead of a single-drum mixer can increase the production of concrete materially, and for most projects will reduce the cost of pavement construction. The use of a high-capacity earth loader and large trucks may necessitate a change in the location, size, and shape of the borrow pit, but the resultant economies may easily justify the change.

The utilization of higher-capacity delivery equipment does not always result in a cost savings, however. On some recent projects in a hot, dry climate, as an example, the use of 7-cubic-yard ($5.35m^3$) transit mixers for delivering concrete to a project proved far more costly than making twice as many trips using 3-yard ($2.29m^3$) mixers. The placing requirements involved the construction of thin concrete columns and wall sections with a high concentration of reinforcing steel, with the resultant reduction in the rate of placement. Before a 7-yard ($5.35m^3$) truckload of concrete could be completely discharged under the existing conditions, the concrete mix started to set in the delivery vehicles because of the high temperature, low humidity, and three-hour time span from the addition of water to the mix to the final placement in the forms. Long delivery routes are often the cause of this, combined with slow pour conditions. The resultant frequency of rejection of portions of the 7-yard ($5.35m^3$) load (retempering was prohibited by specifications) was more costly than the increase in the number of deliveries and the smaller batch size that allowed the use of a fresh load after every 3 yards placed.

The following are some of the methods that the architect or engineer may use to reduce the cost of construction:

1. Design concrete structures with as many duplicate members as is practical to allow the reuse of forms without rebuilding.

2. Confine design elements to modular material sizes where possible.

3. Simplify the design of the structure wherever possible.

4. Design for the use of cost-saving equipment and methods.

5. Eliminate unnecessary special construction requirements.

6. Design to reduce the required labor to a minimum.

7. Specify a quality of workmanship that is consistent with the quality of the project.

8. Furnish adequate foundation information wherever possible.

9. Refrain from requiring the contractor to assume the responsibility for information that should have been furnished by the architect or engineer, or for the adequacy of the design.

10. Use local materials when they are satisfactory.

11. Write simple, straightforward specifications that state what is expected of the contractor. Define the results expected, but within reason permit the contractor to select the methods of accomplishing the results.

12. Use standardized specifications that are familiar to most contractors whenever possible.

13. Hold preconstruction conferences with contractors to eliminate any uncertainties and to reduce change orders resulting from misunderstandings.

14. Use inspectors who have sufficient judgment and experience to understand the project and have authority to make decisions.

11.4.2   Value Engineering by the Contractor

One desirable characteristic of a successful contractor from the standpoint of value engineering is a degree of dissatisfaction over the plans and methods under consideration for constructing a project (a characteristic not always appreciated by the architect or engineer). However, complacency by members of the construction industry will not develop new equipment, new methods, or new construction planning, all of which are desirable for providing continuing improvements at lower costs. A contractor who does not keep informed of new equipment and methods will soon discover that his competitors are underbidding him.

Suggestions for possible reductions in construction costs by the contractor include, but are by no means limited to, the following:

1. Study the project before bidding and determine the effect of

    (a) Topography

    (b) Geology

    (c) Climate

    (d) Sources of materials

    (e) Access to the project

    (f) Housing facilities, if required

    (g) Storage facilities for materials and equipment

    (h) Local services

2. The use of substitute construction equipment that has greater capacities, higher efficiencies, higher speeds, and lower operating costs.

3. Payment of a bonus to key personnel for production in excess of a specified rate.

4. The use of radios as a means of communications between headquarters office and key personnel on projects covering large areas.

5. The practice of holding periodic conferences with key personnel to discuss plans, procedures, and results. Such conferences should produce better morale among the staff members and result in better coordination among the various operations.

6. The adoption of realistic safety practices on a project as a means of reducing accidents and lost time.

7. Consideration of the desirability of subcontracting specialized operations to other contractors who can do the work more economically than the general contractor.

8. Consideration of the desirability of improving shop and servicing facilities for better maintenance of construction equipment.

Improvements in the methods of construction, long the domain of the contractor, can result in significant savings in the cost of the project. This type of cost saving, if implemented after award of a contract, is seldom shared with the owner. However, such cost-reducing considerations are an integral part of the competitive bidding system. Thus the owner benefits in lower bid costs. As an example, an estimator for a contracting firm prepared a bid for a project. When the bids were opened, it was discovered that his firm's bid was so low that the other members of the firm feared that a serious error had been made in preparing the bid. The estimator was called in and asked if he could actually construct the project for the estimated cost. He replied that he could if he were permitted to adopt the construction methods that he used in estimating the cost. The firm agreed; he was placed in charge of the construction of the project and he completed the work with a satisfactory profit to the contractor. At the same time, the owner benefited by receiving his project at a low cost.

11.4.3   Potential Savings

L. D. Miles, in his book, *Techniques of Value Analysis and Engineering*, defines value engineering analysis as "an organized, creative approach which has for its purpose the effective identification of unnecessary cost, i.e., costs which provide neither quality nor use nor life nor appearance nor customer features." But to whom do these savings accrue, and what are they worth?

Governmental agencies with formal construction value engineering programs will include the U.S. Army Corps of Engineers, the Navy Facilities Command, the Bureau of Reclamation, the Post Office Department, the National Aeronautics and Space Administration, the U.S.

Department of Transportation, and the Public Building Service of the General Services Administration. Possibly the Public Building Service has received the most favorable comments from its value engineering incentive program.

In 1974 the Corps of Engineers estimated that the cumulative savings through value engineering was almost $234 million. The Public Building Service indicated that the value engineering program had generated savings of $4.53 for every dollar spent in the program for a total savings to GSA of $1,800,000 in fiscal year 1973. During fiscal year 1970 the Department of Defense estimated a savings of about $4.40 from contractor sharing incentives for each dollar spent on the program. The department further estimated an additional return of four times this amount due to in-house programs during the design phase prior to contract award.

A. J. Dell'Isola, in his book, *Guide for the Application of Value Engineering to the Construction Industry*, establishes potential savings guidelines as follows: (1) on total budget, 1% to 3%; (2) on large facilities, 5% to 10%; and (3) incentive contracting, 0.5% to 1%. To realize these potential savings, an organized creative approach must be used. Generally accepted techniques include a job plan for value engineering, which will have a number of phases: (1) develop information and requirements; (2) speculate on alternatives; (3) analyze and evaluate alternatives; (4) development of the program; and (5) proposal, presentation, and selling. This plan can be implemented over the life cycle of a construction project and will have time-cost related savings potential in varying degrees depending upon the individual phases of development of the project, which will include (1) conceptual; (2) development; (3) detail design; (4) construction; and (5) start-up and use.

11.5 DEVELOPING AND APPLYING VE PROGRAM

A task that is accomplished in a planned and systematic manner is much more likely to be successful than one that is unplanned and relies upon undisciplined ingenuity. Most successful value engineering organizations follow a "scientific method" to assure a planned, purposeful approach. This procedure is called the VE Job Plan. It is set up as a group action because it is unlikely that a successful value engineering proposal will be the product of a single individual. The group plan produces benefits that the efforts of one or two individuals can seldom match. Among the principal benefits are

1. More talent is directly applied to the problem.
2. The scope and depth of the effort is increased.

3. More efficient use is made of the available time because problem areas are more readily resolved through direct communications.

4. Team participation provides productive training for those not previously exposed to formal VE training.

A. J. Dell'Isola, in his book, has designed a Value Engineering Job Plan that can be accomplished in four phases: (1) information—get facts; (2) speculative—brainstorm; (3) analytical—investigate, evaluate; and (4) proposal—sell. These phases are expanded and explained in the following sections.

11.5.1   Informative Phase

The purposes of this phase are (1) to gather and tabulate data concerning the item as presently designed; (2) to determine the item's function or functions; and (3) to evaluate the basic function or functions.

During information gathering, certain questions must be answered: (1) what is the item; (2) what does it do; (3) what is the worth of the function; (4) what does it cost; (5) what are the needed requirements; (6) what is the cost/worth ratio; and (7) what high cost or poor values areas are indicated?

O'Brien, in his book, *Value Analysis in Design and Construction*, makes the point that the question "What does it do?" should be answered by two words (a verb and a noun) for each function, that is, a water pipe transports water. Such definitions may require careful analysis. For example, a door may provide access, limit access (as in a prison), provide security, exclude or contain fire, control traffic, provide visibility, or express prestige.

Considerable effort, ingenuity, and investigation are required to answer these questions. The group must determine what criteria and constraints existed at the time of the original design, and whether they still apply at the present time. Other important questions might be: (1) How long has this design been used; (2) what alternate systems, materials, or methods were considered during the original concept; (3) what special problems were or are unique to this system; and (4) what is the total use or repetitive use of this design each year?

11.5.2   Brainstorming

The purpose is to generate numerous alternatives for providing the item's basic function or functions. By definition, a brainstorming session is a problem-solving conference wherein each participant's thinking is stimulated by others in the group. A team might consist of four to six people of different disciplines, sitting around a table and spontaneously producing ideas. Production of the maximum number of ideas is encouraged and no idea is criticized. The purpose of this brainstorming is to produce ideas related to the performance of the required function.

The Gordon Technique has also been successful. With this technique, only the group leader knows the exact nature of the problem, and he asks questions to generate ideas. This technique may stimulate freer thinking than brainstorming.

11.5.3   Analytical Phase

The purposes of the phase are (1) to evaluate, criticize, and test the alternatives generated during the speculation phase; (2) to estimate the dollar value of each alternative; and (3) to determine the alternatives that offer the greatest potential for cost savings. During this phase, also known as the evaluation and investigation phase, the group examines alternatives generated during the brainstorming and tries to develop lower cost alternate solutions. Principal tasks include evaluation, refinement, cost analysis, and formation of a possible list of alternatives in order of descending savings potential.

Aristotle has said that worth can have economic, moral, aesthetic, social, political, religious, and judicial value. This is a valuable precept for value engineering team members as well as for philosophers. O'Brien believes a Value Index such as "worth divided by cost" or "utility divided by cost" can be beneficial during this phase. Route of ideas include

1. Eliminate ideas that do not meet environmental and operating conditions.

2. Set aside for future analysis ideas with potential but beyond present capability or technology.

3. Cost analyze remaining ideas.

4. List ideas with useful savings. Include potential advantages and disadvantages.

5. Select ideas where advantages outweigh disadvantages and with the greatest cost savings (often, dollar values are not readily assignable, and they must be considered using statistical approaches).

6. Finally, weighted constraints such as aesthetics, durability, and salability must be considered and the list finalized.

11.5.4   Proposal Phase

Also called the program planning and reporting phase, this is the final portion of Dell'Isola's plan. This phase must accomplish three things: (1) a thorough review of all alternate solutions being prepared to assure that the highest value and significant savings are really being offered; (2) a sound proposal must be made to management, and (3) the group must present a plan for implementing the proposal. If the proposal will not convince management to act, no savings will result.

11.5.5   Other Value Engineering Job Plans

A better perspective of this process can be achieved by considering other job plans. The U.S. Army Corps of Engineers utilizes the job plan involving information, speculation, analysis, development, and presentation. This list differs from Dell'Isola's phase list through splitting the proposal phase into the development phase and the presentation.

1.   DEVELOPMENT PHASE   The purposes are (1) to assess the technical feasibility of each surviving alternative; (2) to obtain firm information concerning each surviving alternative; and (3) to develop written recommendations.

2.   PRESENTATION PHASE   The purposes are (1) to present a value engineering study report; (2) to present the report to the decision maker or makers; and (3) to ensure that the report recommendations are implemented. In 1968 the Department of Defense (DOD) made two changes to this list. First, a new phase identified as Orientation was added to the top of the list, with three basic purposes: (1) the selection of appropriate areas to be studied; (2) the selection of the appropriate team to accomplish the study; and (3) the determination of the policies needed to assist in the accomplishment of these studies.

Second, the last phase, Presentation, was expanded to include follow-up as shown in Figure 11.1. By 1972 the DOD job plan had again been expanded, this time by splitting the last phase, Presentation and Follow-up, into separate phases, and adding the Implementation phase in between them, as shown in Figure 11.2.

A composite list of value-engineering-job-plan categories is shown in Table 11.1. Though these plans emphasize various aspects of the process, they are basically similar in approach and sequencing. With a sound knowledge of both the purposes for each phase and route of ideas, you can select the job plan best suited to your needs or create a new one.

11.6   LIFE-CYCLE COSTING

Accurate cost measurement is one of the most important requirements of a successful value engineering program. Life-cycle costing of a facility ranges from concept and feasibility studies through design, procurement, construction, start-up, to operation and maintenance.

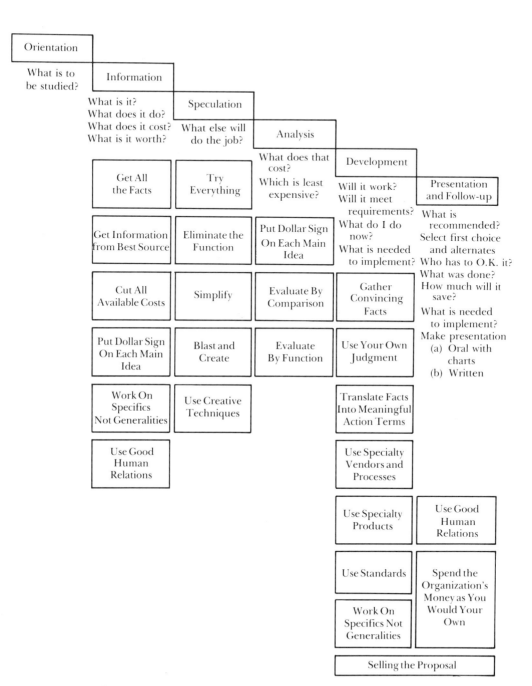

Figure 11.1. Value Engineering Job-Plan Chart. Adapted from General Services Administration, Public Building Service, Manual No. P8000.0, *Value Engineering*, Washington, D.C.

ORIENTATION

Procedure
- Submit ideas for projects
- Evaluate their potential for
  - Return on investment
  - Time to implement results
  - Select projects for planning
- Plan the specific project
  - Appoint the team
  - Allocate resources
- Set goals
- Set milestones
- Reconfirm project potential
- Establish priority
- Approve project start

1 INFORMATION

Questions
- What is it?
- What does it do?
- What must it do?
- What does it cost?
- What is it worth?

Procedure
- Use good human relations
- Get all the facts
- Get information from the best sources
- Obtain complete information
- Perform functional evaluation
  - Define functions
  - Determine cost
  - Determine worth
  - Compute value indexes

2 SPECULATION

Questions
- What else will do the job?

Techniques
- Blast — create — refine
- Functional comparison
- Simple comparison
- Scientific research

Procedure
- Free wheel
- Try everything
  - Oversimplify
  - Modify and refine
  - Eliminate

3 ANALYSIS

Questions
- What does each cost?
- Will each perform the basic function(s)?

Techniques
- Evaluate by
  - Comparison
  - Advantage vs disadvantage
  - Ranking
  - Checklist
  - Probability
  - Creative approach

Procedure
- Establish criteria
- Evaluate ideas
  - Put dollar sign on each idea
  - Use services of experts
  - Use own judgment
  - Refine ideas

4 DEVELOPMENT

Questions
- Will it work?
- Will it meet all the requirements?
- Who has to approve it?
- What are the implementation problems?
- What are the costs?
- What are the savings?

Procedure
- Use good human relations
- Gather convincing facts
- Work on specifics — not generalities
- Translate facts into meaningful actions
- Select first choice and alternatives

5 PRESENTATION

Procedure
- Make presentations
  - Written proposal
  - Oral with illustrations (brief and pertinent)
  - Present problem
  - Explain before and after
  - Explain advantages and disadvantages
  - Present facts quickly, concisely, and convincingly
  - Present implementation plans
  - Acknowledge contributors
  - Request approval

6 IMPLEMENTATION

Procedure
- Fund it!
- Translate ideas to actions
- Prevent idea compromise

Expedite
- Use VE team
- Solve problems
- Overcome roadblocks

Monitor progress
- Set deadlines
- Designate responsibilities

7 FOLLOW-UP

Procedure
- Audit actual results
- Prepare reports
  - Cost savings
  - Technical cross feed
  - Evaluate project conduct
  - Initiate new project ideas
  - Make awards

Figure 11.2. Major Phases of Job-Plan. Adapted from General Services Administration, Public Building Service, Manual No. P8000.0, *Value Engineering*, Washington, D.C.

Table 11.1. Job-Plan Category Comparison[1]

DELL'ISOLA*	GSA-PBS P 8000.1 1972	L. D. MILES† 1961	L. D. MILES‡ 1972	E. D. HELLER§ 1971	A. E. MUDGE¶ 1971	PBS VM WORKBOOK 1974
Information	Orientation	Orientation	Information	Information	Project selection	Information
Speculation	Information	Information	Analysis	Creation	Information	Function
Analysis	Speculation	Speculation	Creation	Evaluation	Function	Creative
Proposal	Analysis	Analysis	Judgment	Investigation	Creation	Judicial
	Development	Program planning	Development	Reporting	Evaluation	Development
	Presentation	Program execution		Implementation	Investigation	Presentation
	Implementation	Summary and conclusion			Recommendation	Implementation
	Follow-up					Follow-up

1. Adapted from Barrie [10:427].
* A. J. Dell'Isola, *Value Engineering in the Construction Industry*, Construction Publishing Corp., Inc., New York, 1974.
† L. D. Miles, *Techniques of Value Analysis and Engineering*, 1st ed., McGraw-Hill, New York, 1961.
‡ L. D. Miles, *Techniques of Value Analysis and Engineering*, 2d ed., McGraw-Hill, New York, 1972.
§ E. D. Heller, *Value Management, Value Engineering and Cost Reduction*, Addison-Wesley, Reading, Mass., 1971.
¶ Arthur E. Mudge, *Value Engineering*, McGraw-Hill, New York, 1971.

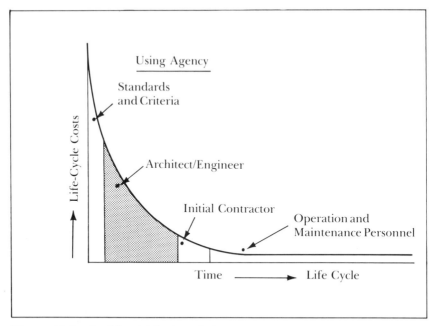

Figure 11.3. Decision Maker's Influence on Cost.

11.6.1 Maximum Potential

Figure 11.3 is a curve that shows whose decision has most influence over the expenditure of funds during the life cycle of a facility. For example:

1. The using agency prescribes the quantity of lavatories per occupancy. The A-E's influence on cost is reduced because he cannot determine quantity. He does have influence as to layout, color, and so forth.

2. The contractor's influence on cost is further restricted. He can influence the cost of materials and installation by only a few percent.

3. Maintenance and operations personnel are left with the least influence because they must live with that given them.

Figure 11.4 represents the distribution of costs as expended over the life cycle of a typical facility. The design effort represents the smallest expenditure, and all of the initial costs of a facility are less than 50% of the total costs. Combining these two figures, one can note that the smallest cost area in the life cycle of a facility is expended by the designer whose decisions make the greatest impact on total costs. Therefore, the highest return on investment can be expected when resources are allocated for VE early in the design process. Such is the opportunity provided in this text.

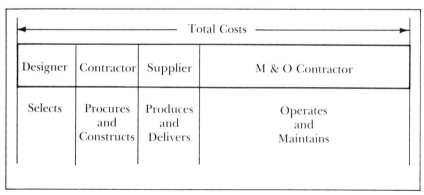

Figure 11.4. Distribution of Costs for a Facility.

11.6.2 Life-Cycle Application

Two important factors influencing the selection of the most appropriate time for applying VE are (1) the magnitude of the savings likely from the effort and (2) the ease or difficulty with which VE may be applied. Figure 11.5 illustrates the typical life-cycle phases for any given facility and portrays a common situation in which savings potential decreases as the program ages. Each phase of a program represents a known base line that

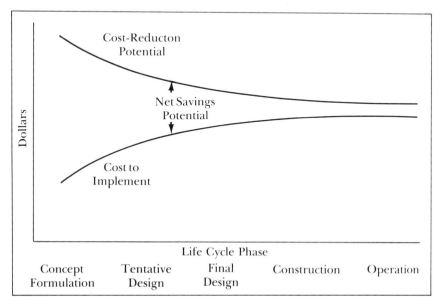

Figure 11.5. Life-Cycle Phases and Savings Potential.

starts out broad in content and becomes more and more definitive as time goes on. The heart of the VE concept is to work against a given base line in order to change or redirect the base line and arrive at an end result that will satisfy the original functions. For this reason, VE may be applied repeatedly at any point or phase in the life cycle that seems fitting.

1. CONCEPT FORMULATION   The purpose of the conceptual phase is to translate requirements and program directives into feasible concepts that will result in defining future operational and support requirements. Value improvement generated early in the life cycle produces benefits lasting through the life of the item or system; however, the savings generated in this phase are the most difficult to document. The engineering competence of VE personnel is of special importance in this phase. Decisions and appraisals must often be made before the complete picture is available. The goal of low total cost of ownership (rather than just low acquisition cost) emphasizes the need for a VE effort in related planning, design, construction, and maintenance fields. VE effort in this phase is directed toward furnishing inputs needed to ensure the most economical decisions.

2. DESIGN TENTATIVE   During this phase approved concepts are definitized, preliminary drawings and outline specifications are stated, and sufficient detailed information is developed to substantiate all quantities and costs that have been presented in the program directive. This is the opportune time to question performance characteristics. A VE study that analyzes the essential requirements, technical characteristics, and the design tasks may reveal alternatives offering improved value. Comparisons during this phase require special skills to validate the projected economic benefits. VE efforts in this phase are directed toward creating Value Indexes of function, cost, and worth of these systems as a whole, and their major subsystems. By defining value in measurable terms, VE can produce a function cost analysis to improve visibility of the costs directly related to necessary requirement.

3. WORKING DRAWINGS   It is during this phase that specific design details are formulated and schedules created. Continuity of VE effort in this phase is essential to ensure that hidden costs are not intentionally engendered in the project during the development of specifics. VE efforts in this phase are usually limited to eliminating unnecessarily restrictive detail for requirements, ensuring standardization for details, minimizing the quantities of different types, and eliminating items not necessary. Usually, redesign as a result of VE effort at this stage cannot be accomplished economically due to the implementation costs involved, unless the life-cycle savings potential is large enough to justify the expense. However, when projects are designed and placed on the shelf for a year or more, that time could well be spent in a VE effort updating requirements and improvements.

4. CONSTRUCTION   During this phase VE can be performed both internally and by the contractor. Internal VE can be accomplished by reviewing specific contract requirements and initiating change orders to save money. Another fruitful area for internal application is performing a VE review of all potential change orders tending to increase contract cost. They should be reviewed to prevent the addition of nonessential functions and to create alternate solutions that would lower the cost or eliminate the necessity for the change. The contractor program provides the owner with knowledge of costs and products that can be used in future efforts.

5. OPERATION   The total cost of ownership is affected by operation, maintenance, and other support costs. Reducing these costs (in excess of any attendant increase in procurement cost) results in lower life-cycle cost. Large potential savings often justify the investment for the VE study and subsequent implementation expenses during the operational phase. VE studies during this phase offer an opportunity to make changes not made earlier due to a lack of time or other constraints. Also, the reasons leading to the entry into the supply system of some items may no longer be valid. Therefore, they may no longer represent an optimum choice. VE studies during the operational phase have resulted in

(a)   Extension of an item's life by the application of new state-of-the-art designs, materials, and processes;

(b)   Reduced repair costs by achieving the required function in a more economical manner;

(c)   Elimination of items and work through reexamination of user needs;

(d)   Savings in energy and other operating costs;

(e)   Reduction in number of supply items in stock.

11.7   OTHER USES OF VE

11.7.1   Problem Solving

Since the VE process is basically a problem-solving technique, it can be applied to a wide variety of problem areas using the same approach. It can be used to solve problems regardless of the cost of the solution; therefore, application of the technique, in itself, does not necessarily mean that money will be saved. When VE is used for the purpose of solving

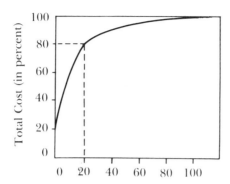

Number of Constituents (in percent)
Figure 11.6.   Pareto's Law of Distribution.

problems, management can expect that the solution will be arrived at analytically and documented with respect to its economies. Use of the program for this sole purpose should be done with great care. Such use could be counterproductive to the most effective use of VE, which is really to preempt problems before they become a concern to management.

11.7.2   Preempting Problems

VE is most effectively applied to search out areas of application where no problems exist and everything is running smoothly. The optimum application of VE on every design or procedure would result in receiving total cost control, good value for every dollar spent, no deductive bid items, no cost overruns, no design deficiencies—no problems. However worthwhile that objective seems, it remains impractical to VE everything. Like any profitable program or business, the successful value margin and manage program is based on maximum return from optimum investment. Following Pareto's Law of Distribution (see Fig. 11.6), VE attempts to identify and isolate the 20% of the elements in a single system that contribute to 80% of the cost of the system. Those with the greatest potential for impact on cost, then, become the candidates for application of VE.

11.8   RELATED CONCEPTS

11.8.1   Introduction

Many new management techniques are being accepted and used in facilities procurement, and a certain amount of confusion exists in the minds of many people as to the role and scope of these concepts and their relationship to VE. Specific questions that come up from time to time include the following:

(a) Does VE overlap or replace any of these techniques?

(b) Are the objectives of VE opposed to the objectives of these techniques?

(c) If ideas emanating from the various techniques result in conflicting recommendations, should the decision consider only the VE recommendations?

There is an interface between other techniques and VE; however, there should be no basic conflict between any two. While each has its own goals and uses, each has the overall goal of supporting planning, design, construction, and maintenance objectives. This section discusses the relationship of VE to some of these techniques.

11.8.2   Design-To-Cost

This technique requires that cost be an essential design parameter. As such, cost becomes of equal importance with performance and schedule in making decisions. The availability of clear cost targets through a design-to-cost program for a facility, coupled with increased visibility of minimum/maximum performance levels and schedule requirements, is an essential first tool for the value process. When the design-to-cost budget is divided into facility system and subsystem level of detail, and that budget is based upon worth, then good value will be easier to attain.

11.8.3   Trade-Off Analysis

Trade-offs by definition and usage involve interrelated changes. Thus, reliability, quality, or maintainability is reduced to bring costs down; floor loading or lighting levels are increased, so costs go up; delivery is expedited and costs go up. By contrast, VE makes necessary function or minimum performance levels a constant rather than a variable. In VE, these may not be reduced as a means of reducing cost. VE does not involve trade-offs if it provides the necessary function at lowest overall cost. Whereas minimum performance requirements are not traded off for lower cost in VE, the way of accomplishing this performance may be altered to reduce cost. That is, the necessary performance of components of certain products-systems may be derived from the performance of other components in the system. In this restricted sense, VE may be thought to involve exchanges to allow for use of standardized parts in the system, or to reduce the cost of integrating components into the system. But the necessary performance of the product-system itself is not changed.

11.8.4 Cost Reduction

Cost reduction is an effort to make a product, system, or facility cheaper. It means accepting things as they are to reduce cost, often through redesign or simply deleting work. VE, on the other hand, is a more fundamental approach that takes nothing for granted and questions everything about a product including the very existence of the item itself, subject to the restriction that its required function or performance must not be degraded. However, the act of cost reduction, itself, does provide a useful function in the value process. Cost reduction forces the separation of "needs" from "desires"—for example, the need for an automobile from the desire for a Mercedes, the need for an office building from the desire for a monument. VE can sacrifice desires but not needs. Cost reduction often sacrifices both.

11.8.5 Economic Analysis

Cost effectiveness and VE share a common objective. Both represent a systematic analysis of alternative ways of accomplishing given functions and of the costs associated with each alternative. Cost effectiveness studies (sometimes called present value analysis) are employed in the early planning stage to compare the overall effectiveness and associated costs of alternative concepts in broad contexts. Typically, such studies might compare the impact of (1) site location in a community, or (2) alternative ways of providing space such as to lease, construct, consolidate, or rehabilitate existing facilities. A cost effectiveness study may be complemented by VE efforts to ascertain the value levels of the proposals presented and, if suitable, propose additional alternatives. VE also may be used to achieve or even reduce the cost predicted for the selected alternative.

11.8.6 Systems Analysis

Systems analysis has been defined as "an inquiry to assist decision makers in choosing preferred further courses of action by systematically examining and re-examining the relevant objectives and quantitatively, where possible, the economic costs, effectiveness (benefits), and risks of the alternatives."[1] True systems analysis is more a research or predesign strategy than a method or technique. It may be viewed as an approach to, or way of looking at, complex problems of choice under conditions of uncertainty.

A refined level of systems analysis is used when a designer is given operational performance requirements to describe a system and is then required to use traditional cost analysis techniques to analyze competing

---

1. GSA, Public Building Service, Manual No. P8000.0, *Value Engineering*, Washington, D.C.

systems, that is, structural, mechanical, heat recovery, and fuel. During subsequent development of the selected overall system, design of a subsystem is often assigned to various design groups. A coordinating group should be assigned the task of assuring that the subsystems will work together. The combined output of these individual groups is a design reflecting the emphasis on achieving functional compatibility and required performance with limited funds and time. Integration of VE into the systems analysis effort contributes to the creation of an overall design having a total cost that is consistent with the worth of the system functions.

11.8.7 Standardization

Standardization and VE are not opposing philosophies with the former attempting to "freeze" the "status quo" and VE trying to change it. Standardization efforts include procedures to enhance effectiveness by accommodating innovations in technology and changes in the user's needs. Used where appropriate, standards can reduce total cost. In some cases, unnecessary costs occur because the standards used are obsolete or inappropriately applied. In either instance, VE provides a useful input to any standardization effort.

11.8.8 Life-Cycle Costing

Life-cycle costs include all costs pertaining to the planning, design, construction, operation, maintenance, supply, disposal, and relocation of a system or facility, calculated in terms of present value or annual owning and operating cost. It is a method used to compare and evaluate the total costs of competing proposals for identical functions based on the anticipated life of the facility or product to be acquired. This approach determines the least costly of several alternatives. However, the selected alternative may represent only the best of several poor candidates. VE may be used to develop additional worthy alternatives to consider before selecting the best choice. Whereas life-cycle costing emphasizes cost visibility, VE seeks value optimization. The two disciplines are complementary because the former is required to achieve the latter.

11.9 SUMMARY

This chapter has reviewed value engineering methods utilized by a number of government agencies and has summarized the job-plan concept. The agencies have reported significant savings achieved through the use of the formalized program, which has been claimed to be effective in the public sector but has had widespread acceptance in the private sphere as well.

However, the construction management approach offers a greater application of the potential benefits of value engineering due to the elimination of adversary relationships and to the utilization of the original engineer or architect to analyze the technical acceptability of the proposed modifications.

Experience has shown that value engineering can encourage teamwork and cooperation among team members and can result in significant savings without involving significant additional costs upon the part of either the architect-engineer, owner, or construction manager. Because of the personalities and motivations of the people involved, almost all designers resent the formal critique of a completed design by a multi-disciplinary team or by their peers. In some cases, actual financial hardship is apparent.

12

Procurement

12.1 PROCUREMENT CONCEPTS

Procurement is an important job and can make or break the profit situation on a specific contract and for the company as a whole. The best procurement manager is not a wheeler-dealer but a competent businessman who recognizes that there are more facets to his or her responsibilities than the basic establishment of purchase price. A single-minded, old-fashioned procurement group that fails to recognize this broad, comprehensive scope of responsibilities can go on buying trees and never find the right forest.

Procurement involves purchasing of equipment, materials, supplies, labor, and services required for construction and implementation of a project. It includes related activities of tracking and expediting, routing and shipment of materials and equipment, as well as handling, accountability and warehousing, final acceptance documentation, and ultimate disposal of surplus items at job end. Thus procurement involves management of purchasing, inspection, expediting, traffic, transportation and warehousing of the needed equipment, supplies, and services so that they can be obtained in the required quality, quantity, and time and at the lowest cost. Fortunately, the construction industry is now maturing to recognize the need and importance of procurement.

Procurement is normally performed at several levels. Major equipment, such as a reactor on a nuclear power plant, may be purchased by the owner long before the ground-breaking ceremony. A general contractor's home office may arrange for procurement of subcontractors and major materials and equipment to be installed by the contractor's own forces. The field office will normally procure supplies, incidental rentals, and other requirements. On a construction management project, certain long-lead items may be procured by the owner, others by the manager, and less critical items by each of the contractors involved in the program.

Procurement methods and practices differ with individual firms and projects. A general contractor may receive bids from subcontractors, material suppliers, and equipment manufacturers who can refer to completed plans and specifications before bidding. On a traditional project he will have procurement practices that differ significantly from those of a design-constructor or turn-key firm normally engaged in a phased construction program. Nevertheless, certain principles are common to each general approach to construction procurement.

Procurement is more than an act, because it constitutes a process; therefore, those engaged in procurement should have an awareness of the interlocking activities contained in process.

Procurement should not be performed without considering the design and construction schedule of a project. It is essential that procurement be considered as a grand plan involving a number of stages. The procurement process is affected by a number of different factors and hence should not be performed in isolation. The use of networks greatly facilitates the strategy for procurement. There must be flexibility in the plan, and it is often necessary to veer from the original schedule. Sound management practice involves the use of value engineering methods for the consideration of alternatives. Procurement is a science as well as an art, and decisions should be based on a logic that considers long-range as well as short-range impacts.

Sound evaluation is an important aspect of the procurement process. Some contracts such as environmental services are difficult to evaluate because most of the time the client leaves the guidelines too open-ended. It is to the client's advantage to provide the consultants with specific, definitive, and clearly stated criteria. Otherwise, there is apt to be a great variance in the bid proposals with the low bidder usually basing his/her bid on minimal services. Under such conditions, if the client accepts the low bidder's proposal, he, the client, might ultimately find himself paying more with extras to the low bidder than he would have paid to a higher bidder offering more comprehensive services.

12.2   PROCUREMENT DOCUMENTS

In addition to the internal procurement document, the procurement department requires a standard series of documents, including invitation to bid, bidder information forms, and binding contractual agreements for price and delivery. In addition, subcontractors are bound to the same project conditions as the general contractor to preclude nonliability on the part of subcontracts.

Forms should include

(a)   Requisition

(b)   Purchase order

(c)   Request for bid

(d)   Subbid form

(e)   Purchase-order commodities

(f)   Letter of intent

(g)   Subcontract form

(h)   Contract form

(i)   Agreements and leases forms

(j)   Contract-amendment forms

The basic contract includes types of items covered, length of contract, prices and discounts, delivery times, terms of payment, shipping points, method of transportation, methods for altering or revising contracts, receiving conditions, and special conditions.

Agreements and leases are forms of contract used for procurement of technical services and for rental or leasing of automobiles, construction or office equipment, or other temporary items that are not consumed or do not become part of the finished work.

The procurement manager should review the specifications prepared by the A-E and look for ambiguities in the language. It is advantageous to all concerned that the specifications describe the required material and equipment with clarity. Specified items should be available on a competitive basis. No two pieces of equipment are equal, but when items are specified that are not competitively manufactured by another vendor, complications might arise. Furthermore, dependence on a single manufacturer who knows that his equipment must be used is not conducive to getting good service.

Shop drawings should be reviewed promptly, and compatibility with the design requirements must be assessed. A log should be kept that reflects the drawings, specifications, and manufacturing status of equipment. Manufacturers' progress payment schedules must be carefully examined, and the value of the equipment should be assessed and projected before the payment schedules are approved. The procurement manager should consult with the estimating group and scrutinize a vendor's proposal.

No contract should be awarded unless it contains a defined scope and a budget. In certain instances, such as environmental impact studies, it is difficult to predict the number of interrogations that might arise from the regulatory agencies. Nonetheless, it is possible to project and describe the professional assignments in which the consultants might engage. If the technical staff's tasks are defined, progress can be measured against them. Describing the objectives of a consultant's contractual function contributes greatly to the development of insight with respect to a project's total requirements.

12.3   PURCHASING AND CONTRACTING

Normal purchasing and contracting practices and procedures differ from company to company and also from one project to another. Each firm will develop its own methods and documents; but each must be flexible enough to cope with an ever-changing construction climate, to meet special client directions, or to comply with other outside requirements. Listed in this section are purchasing and contracting procedures and practices normally found in the construction industry.

1. REQUISITIONS   Where a formal procurement department is maintained, construction managers or supervisors usually initiate purchasing and subcontracting by issuing standard-form requisitions asking the department to obtain bids for equipment, materials, work, or services as described in the requisition and the applicable plans and specifications attached or referenced.

2. PREQUALIFICATION AND BID LIST PREPARATION All procurement departments develop and maintain lists of material suppliers, specialty contractors, equipment suppliers, and other vendors. Prequalification of suppliers, manufacturers, contractors, and subcontractors is often appropriate on certain work, but may be less desirable in other situations. Where possible, prequalification to ensure that the award can always be made to the low responsive bidder can often improve jobsite performance, particularly in the emerging project delivery systems other than the traditional design-bid-construct method. On government and other selected work, use of minority contractors or subcontractors may be specified, and prequalification takes on different aspects from the usual performance and financial requirements. On certain work, requiring a payment and performance bond results in prequalification of bidders by their ability to obtain a bond from a bonding company.

Preparation of bid lists varies with the different contractual methods. General contractors on competitively bid projects often advertise in trade papers that they will accept subbids up to a stated deadline. Other general contractors will make telephone calls or send out postcards to a predetermined list. When potential subcontractors cannot be prequalified, last minute decisions regarding the qualifications of a low bidder can often become difficult just before bid time.

Design-constructors often keep card files and qualification data on a large number of potential vendors and subcontractors in different areas of the country. An area investigation will also normally turn up firms that may be more qualified in the local area than larger regional or nationwide suppliers and contractors. On the other hand, large international projects may include procurement of major engineered equipment from a pre-qualified list of firms from different countries. On one major hydroelectric project, turbines were purchased from Germany, generators from Japan, and all the coordination required to ensure compatibility was handled from the California jobsite where the equipment was ultimately erected.

Prequalification to ensure that only qualified firms are invited to bid, and restriction of the bid list to a reasonable number of the firms so that all will be interested, are extremely important in a construction management and other emerging project delivery programs.

3. REQUESTS FOR QUOTATION   Requests for quotation can range from a simple advertisement in a local trade journal requesting subbids to an elaborate bid package with plans, specifications, and other contract documents delineating all aspects of the proposed purchase. Bid packages should be kept simple and consistent with individual requirements, but they might include some or all of the following documents:

(a)   Specifications

(b)   Drawings

(c)   Scope of work

(d)   Bills of materials

(e)   Commercial documents

(f)   Notice to bidders

(g)   Proposal form

(h)   Contract form

(i)   Terms and conditions

(j)   Shipping instructions

(k)   Schedules

(l)   Insurance requirements

(m)   Special requirements

(n)   Payment and performance bond form

4. BID RECEIPT AND EVALUATION   As in other procurement actions, good practice will vary with the nature of the project. Acceptance of last minute telephone quotations on materials and subbids is common practice in many areas on competitively bid, single general contracts. Such a practice, however, would not be considered normal for an engineer-constructor who has sufficient time to accept written quotations on prepared forms.

Government agencies generally hold public bid openings, whereas many private owners open all bids privately and never divulge the comparative figures to the bidders. In the construction management method, bids are often opened at a semiprivate bid opening to which all persons submitting bids are invited. Other owners open bids in private but furnish all responsive bidders with a tabulation of actual evaluated results. Such a tabulation may show the component parts of each bid compared with the estimate (if available) and may also note any omissions, inaccuracies, or other discrepancies. An evaluation to cover such discrepancies is often made so that the evaluated bid price may be higher than the actual bid.

If negotiations are required, they should be conducted with the low bidder or others equally in contention. It is in this sensitive area that ill will and misunderstandings often develop. The construction manager should endeavor to conduct himself above even the hint of suspicion.

5. RECOMMENDATION FOR PURCHASE   Most medium-sized and large firms formalize recommendations for purchase with a document approved through various levels of management; the level of approval required normally depends on the dollar value or potential risk associated with the transaction. In the case of complicated items of engineered equipment, an engineering review is usually required as part of the preparation of the "Recommendation for Purchase." With reasonable care in the preparation of bidding documents and in the selection of bidders, awards can almost always be made to the evaluated low bidder.

6. AWARD AND PREPARATION OF DOCUMENTS   Award of purchase order, contract, or subcontract can be made verbally with completed documents to follow, or can be formalized by a "Notice of Award" advising the successful bidder that his quotation has been accepted. Purchase orders may be issued confirming a bidder's offer, and may not always require the vendor's signature. On the other hand, contracts and subcontracts are almost always formally signed by both parties. Bid bonds are often used by some owners, especially in the public sector, to ensure that the low bidder will in fact execute the contract.

7. CHANGES IN CONTRACT DOCUMENTS   Changes in purchase orders, contracts, and subcontracts should conform where possible to general principles outlined in the original procurement action. Above all, one should avoid verbal instructions, authorizations, or agreements; these may expedite initiation of the work, but cause substantial honest disputes among the contracting parties when the bill is submitted.

12.4   INSPECTION

See Chapter 16. Information provided in 16.4 equally applies here. Also see Section 12.5.3 of this chapter for more information on inspection.

12.5   EXPEDITING, SHIPPING, AND RECEIVING

12.5.1   Expediting

After material has been ordered, the procurement department must maintain contact with the vendor to ensure delivery. Many things occur in the course of the delivery cycle, particularly when there are great demands for material. Telephone expediting can be very effective, but job visits must be made periodically to the production shop. The purpose of this visit is not only to check quality and view testing but also to demonstrate contractor interest in the material itself. The expediter will continue periodic contacts with the vendor or factory by mail, telephone, telex, telegram, or personal visit to ensure maintenance of the factory schedule and deliveries as required by purchase-order terms and conditions.

The popular image of expediting is that it is a frantic, last-ditch effort to speed up the movement of materials that were not delivered when they were needed. In organizations that terminate the procurement function with the issuance of a purchase order, this is too often the case. With good project control, however, expediting involves monitoring all steps in the procurement cycle, with special focus on those involving the vendor or subcontractor, to assure reliable, economical, on-schedule delivery. The essence of expediting is in anticipating problems before they arise and in offering solutions before delays are encountered.

Expediting for major or critical items often requires periodic visits to vendors' shops and factories on a routine basis, plus frequent telephone follow-ups to check vendor progress, raw materials supplied, work load, completed product inventory, shop drawings, manuals, fabrication procedures, quality control, code certifications, and delivery status. The underlying purpose in this is to be sure the contractor retains high priority among other firms for whom the vendor may be working.

Even with the best procedures, however, problems will arise that require corrective action. Sometimes the contractor's own schedule changes require that procurement of critical items be accelerated. Other delays might arise from design, purchasing, vendor fabrication, shipping, and so forth.

It is largely the role of experienced and professional expediters to find the most effective means to keep procurement on schedule with the minimum adverse effect on cost. Alternatives may include seeking backup or secondary suppliers, switching to faster means of shipment, or merely identifying snarls in red tape. All too often, delays result because a procurement document—a requisition, purchase order, or shipping request—gets lost in some clerk's "In" file.

The expediter should be scheduled automatically or keyed semiautomatically from the CPM schedule or other project requirements, however they are stated. Electronic data processing can reduce the paper work involved in setting up a tickler file for expediting periodically, by category of material, and by furnishing prepared expediting reports. All data can be introduced into the report, leaving the expediter only to include a brief report on actual contact made. This can be returned to a procurement department data bank and will be recycled for review or introduced into appropriate management reports. Where deliveries become critical, it is sometimes possible—if project management is forewarned—to rearrange work sequences or introduce work-arounds.

12.5.2   Shipping

The procurement department also designates, in most cases, the method of shipping to the warehouse or jobsite. In certain cases, the project management team will place priorities upon certain items—requesting special shipment such as air freight. Again, in many cases, this can be precluded by preplanning, utilizing scheduling such as CPM. The procurement department must do cost evaluations between kinds of shipment and storage charges such as rail demurrage. In certain cases, it is advantageous to hold rail cars at the jobsite rather than transfer to a more expensive warehousing situation.

The procurement department must also be cognizant of varying rates or different types of freight—less than carload (LCL) versus carloads lots, and other such factors. In a large procurement department, often there is a transportation department specializing in this type of information.

The procurement department should build a data bank, either cardfile or computerized, which combines its own experience with basic information regarding delivery methods and rates.

12.5.3   Receiving

Receiving reports can be generated in the same manner and are important to maintenance of a useful materials file. The receiving report should also trigger the beginning of the project inventory-information file and reporting system. Receiving responsibilities should also be a procurement department function, and the basic receiving report should indicate condition as well as quantity. Quality inspection should be cursory, as long as the items specified can be identified properly. In bulk materials, test samples should be taken as required by the job specifications. Where any missing items or damage is noted, the receiving report should be structured so that the information is recycled into the project-scheduling flow—again to bring the proper management attention to any problem areas.

12.6   INVENTORY AND AVAILABILITY

Inventory and availability of major items (equipment, materials) is normally maintained at the central headquarters procurement department. The control records will be kept either manually in the department or, more often at larger companies, in the electronic data processing section. The inventory will include, in addition to make, type, year, cost, and sources of the items, such information as date and cost of purchase.

A more complete description of each item is kept on individual record cards, giving such information as the purchase order number under which it was acquired; modifications or additions, if any, to the item(s) and dates of such changes; serial numbers of all major components; and jobs or locations to which assigned by indicating dates from acquisition to the present.

The item is allocated to the contractor's various operating divisions according to their individual needs. Each division controls and is responsible for the item assigned to it, within the contractor's established policies for usage rates, depreciation, overhaul and repairs, and time used. The procurement manager, with consent of the divisional manager to whom the item is assigned and when authorized by management, transfers the item from one division to another as needed.

13

Marketing

13.1 INTRODUCTION

The industries engaged in construction in America can be proud of their accomplishments. They have created a supply of houses, commercial and industrial facilities, highways and other transportation facilities, civil engineering structures, and other economic assets for the United States that are the envy of the world. In conjunction with the architectural and engineering professions and the procedures of construction materials, equipment, and supplies, this industry has developed advanced construction technology sufficient to meet the needs of our economy and to satisfy the goals of thousands of firms in the industry that have capitalized on the opportunities offered by an expanding economy. However, the economic and demand conditions that prevailed up to the 1970s, and that

This chapter is based on references by Bessom (18:647–659) and Murray (99:665–678).

offered these opportunities, are changing dramatically. Thus production technology will no longer be enough for firms in this industry. The market is changing, the industry's capacity to supply construction services is becoming greater than the demand for them, competition is increasing, and the firms that survive and prosper will need to develop marketing expertise to find and hold profitable markets for their construction services. Modern marketing methods can also help individual firms to cope more effectively with the problems created by the cyclic nature of the market for construction.

This chapter first discusses the need for marketing. It next discusses marketing concepts. The rest of the chapter explores marketing methodology, marketing systems planning, and adaptive marketing strategies.

13.2   NEED FOR MARKETING

Marketing is the planning and implementation of all customer-impinging activities of the firm to create customers by causing them to perceive and realize greater satisfactions from consumption of the firm's product than could be realized from any competitive product.

In the construction industry—as in any other—the importance of a firm's marketing efforts, relative to the other basic business functions of production and finance, is a function of the relationship between supply and demand and the intensity of competition in the market. When the demand for an industry output is strong relative to industry supply, an individual firm capable of producing a product or service that satisfies market needs can afford to concentrate on production, buyers being plentiful and easy to find. There is likely to be more competition among buyers seeking a source of supply than among sellers seeking markets (as during the acute housing shortage in the years following World War II), and buyers often accept products or services less than satisfactory to their needs. When supply catches up with demand as a result of the entry of new suppliers into the industry, or there is a reduction of demand because of economic reasons, or a combination of both, buyers become more discriminating about their choice of products, services, and suppliers. Consequently, competition among sellers increases. Usually, some or many firms in the industry drop out and those remaining exert greater sales efforts to maintain their sales volumes. But this is not enough; selling must be integrated into a more comprehensive marketing effort.

The construction industry now faces this kind of situation. As a result of inflation, shortages, and the resultant increases in the costs of materials, equipment, and construction labor, combined with uncertainty about the health and future of the entire economy, demand for construction services has been significantly reduced. On the supply side, the industry is highly fragmented and composed of thousands of firms attracted to it during the properous years since World War II. Related to both the supply and the demand side is the fact that many customers find time an important element; they are dissatisfied with the traditional process of hiring the architect-engineer, designing the structure, taking and evaluating bids, awarding a construction contract, and finally they are dissatisfied with construction itself amid continual changes in an adversary environment between the architect-engineer and the contractor. Each competitive firm faces a need for new 'survival' strategies.

Many contractors are adopting one or both of the following strategies to maintain their viability under the current and more competitive conditions: (1) improvement of their construction management techniques to incorporate modern cost estimating and accounting methods, modern management concepts, and such techniques as "fast tracking" and "construction management" to compress the time period for construction and reduce the impact of inflation on the costs incurred by customers or "owners" during construction; and (2) increased personal selling and promotional efforts to obtain contracts for the services the firm has developed and for which it believes there should be a market. Most firms, however, remain essentially "production oriented" and need to become "marketing oriented" to ensure their survival in an ever-changing environment.

13.3   MARKETING CONCEPTS

13.3.1   Market Segments

Market segments arise from the fact that each buyer is interested in, and therefore tends to focus on, a small set of attributes considered to be most important. Even when buying a simple product—a kitchen chair—we know that some buyers evaluate competitive chairs by comparing their strength. Other buyers focus upon the most pleasing design, and still others on the color or type of finish. Some buyers even consider the price of the chair to be of overriding importance!

When considering the entire marketplace, individual buyers can be, by and large, conceptually grouped by similarity of interests. These conceptual groups are called market segments. Within each market segment are buyers who focus on a relatively small set of product or service attributes that they consider important. Knowledge of the existence of market segments is important because, in general, no one firm can successfully sell to all segments. This is true for two major reasons. First, the image of the firm must remain clear in the marketplace. Potential customers must be able to distinguish the firm from the rest of the field. Firms that attempt to serve widely disparate market segments often create a "fuzzy" image that confuses buyers. The second reason that firms tend to specialize in serving market segments is that the people employed by the firms become attached to these same attributes, and they are not interested in producing a product or service having very different attributes. On the surface such specialization might appear to be a temporary phenomenon—one due to technical and production limitations. The addition of new facilities with different technology and tolerances; the hiring of a new sales force to open different distribution patterns; and the development of new service packages would seem to be feasible in many situations.

However, such an approach overlooks the strong human and interpersonal elements in such decisions. Many top executives feel comfortable when doing what they know best, and do not want the personal and business risks associated with entering new markets. It is the rare executive team that can successfully manage the production and sales diversity, as well as maintain a clear market image, which would be required to serve such widely different market segments.

13.3.2   Target Markets

A target market consists of the market segment, or segments, that the firm selects for its marketing efforts. Often, of course, the target market is not consciously selected but occurs through the haphazard choices made during the history of the firm. However, it is a rare industry that does not have enough dynamic change in its markets to require conscious choice of target markets on a continual basis. Technological change, the acts of competitors, and changing demands all combine to require constant marketing decisions and adjustments in the target markets.

13.3.3   The Majority Fallacy

All too often, firms will attempt to target only those segments having the majority of buyers, believing that in this way they can become large and profitable. As such, they are committing what in marketing is called "The Majority Fallacy."

If a firm discovers and enters an entirely new market, it is appropriate to consider the largest segments as target markets. However, in many, if not most, markets, one or two strong competitors are already serving the largest segments. Attempting to sell such segments is both expensive and most likely doomed to failure. An alternative marketing strategy is to target smaller market segments that are not well served by the strong competitors. Such an approach not only avoids the possible disaster associated with committing the majority fallacy, but can result in a profitable and relatively secure market target.

13.4   METHODOLOGY

In any attempt to discern market segments, the analysis of customer preferences must eventually focus on the most basic question, "Will this particular customer buy?" Until very recently such a question could not be evaluated properly with the statistical methods available. In 1977 an appropriate statistic—the Del, ∇—was discovered. A few comments on this methodology are in order.

13.4.1   Ordinal Data

Marketing analysis frequently requires the use of ordinal data—a type of data that may not be encountered often by engineers or contractors. Ordinal data reflects only the ordering of choices: "A is preferred to B." It lacks the precision of interval or ratio data. Such precision is desirable when possible, not only because it allows the relative comparison of interpoint distances, but because it allows for the calculation of means, variances, and the use of sophisticated statistical methods such as regression and correlation.

However, in marketing research the limits of respondents' abilities to discriminate are often reached when simply asking which of two complex proposals are preferred, and why. Perhaps an example will make the use of ordinal data clearer. Suppose you are deciding upon which subcontractor to use for a particular job. Three subcontractors have the following attributes:

1. "A" made the lowest bid, but tends to run late on jobs and has trouble working with other subcontractors;

2. "B" nearly always completes jobs on time, has trouble working with other subcontractors, and bids a little higher; and

3. "C" works well with other subcontractors but bids high.

You are forced to make a choice, but no one firm is perfect from your viewpoint. There are trade-offs that you must evaluate. You may be able to state your ranking of preferences among these subcontractors, but would probably be unable to say precisely just how much stronger your preference of A to B is in comparison to your preference of B to C, and so forth.

13.4.2   The Del Statistic

The Del Statistic is the latest and sharpest addition to the methodologies available for the analysis of this type of preference ranking. It is

Table 13.1.   Ranking of Cost and the Construction Manager by Clients
When Evaluating a Construction Proposal

		COST IS RANKED FIRST, SECOND, OR THIRD MOST IMPORTANT	COST IS RANKED FOURTH OR LOWER IN IMPORTANCE
CM		x_1	x_2
Construction manager is ranked first, second, or third most important	Y_1	4	7
Construction manager is ranked fourth or lower in importance	Y_2	5	1

Adapted from Murray (99:669).

distinguished from previous methodologies, such as Chi Square, by two important differences. First, the Del Statistic requires the careful use of a prediction logic. That is, a prediction about the expected state of a dependent variable, given the independent state, must be stated clearly and unambiguously. Second, the Del compares the actually observed errors in prediction to those that would occur had the dependent states occurred randomly. For those familiar with much of the literature of the social sciences, this is a significant step forward.

Table 13.1 illustrates the nature of the necessary prediction logic and the use of the Del Statistic. Here are shown the actual results from one question of the client survey, in a standard cross-tabulation form, which asked for a ranking of ten factors when considering the award of a construction contract. In the left-hand column are those firms that ranked cost as first, second, or third most important to them when considering a list of attributes for evaluating a construction contract. The number of clients who also ranked the construction manager as important are in the top row, while those ranking the construction manager from fourth to tenth in importance are in the bottom row. The right-hand column contains clients who ranked cost from fourth to tenth in importance, placed in the appropriate rows. Let us predict that clients tend to make a trade-off between the importance of cost and the importance of the CM to the award of bid. This is the type of prediction commonly found in the industry, and it usually is accepted without comment. With the prediction logic required by the Del Statistic, however, such a statement can be seen as misleading at best, and fatuous at worse.

Below Table 13.1, three predictions are shown. Each of these predictions is consistent with our previous trade-off example.

1. **Prediction 1,** ∇P_1, says that clients who consider cost to be important will tend to consider the CM as unimportant. For this prediction, the only error that can occur is event x_1, y_1, when the construction manager is also ranked as important by the firm. This prediction contains no statement about firms that rank cost as being less important.

2. **Prediction 2,** ∇P_2, is also consistent, but makes prediction only for those firms that do not consider cost as one of their top three priorities. Therefore, the only error that can be made with this prediction is x_2, y_2, when a client ranks both cost and the CM as less important. While on the surface this may appear to be a twisting of logic, a little reflection should result in accepting the argument that, in fact, we are not often in a symmetric situation and therefore cannot reasonably expect, automatically, to find perfect symmetry in the behavior of people, or of clients. For these reasons, both predictions 1 and 2 are wholly compatible with the original statement of the trade-offs.

3. **Prediction 3,** ∇P_3, the strongest of the three because it is symmetrical, predicts that firms giving high importance to cost will give low importance to CM, and also predicts what clients giving low importance to cost will give high importance to the construction manager. For this prediction, there are two errors that can occur: x_1, y_1, and x_2, y_2.

The Del Statistic measures a proportionate reduction in error (PRE), using the probability of expected error as that which would occur from random chance:

$$\nabla = \frac{\text{expected errors} - \text{observed errors}}{\text{expected errors}}$$

The upper limit for the Del is $+1.0$, where prediction is perfect and there are no observed errors. When Del $= 0$ the prediction is no different from that of pure random chance. As Del becomes negative, it indicates that the prediction is worse than random chance. The Del has no lower limit.

In illustrating these three prediction logics, each of which is consistent with the statement that there is a trade-off in importance between cost and the CM, the Dels are:

for ∇P_1, Del = .313; for ∇P_2, Del = .651; and for ∇P_3, Del = .421

The managerial interpretation of ∇P_1 is that this prediction resulted in committing 31.3% fewer errors than pure random chance. ∇P_2 makes 65.1% fewer errors, and ∇P_3 makes 42.1% fewer errors.

It is important to stress that the comparison of these three predictions is for illustration only. It is highly improper to calculate a series of Del Statistics and then to choose the best one. Such research methodology is erroneous because it is a virtual certainty that by scrutinizing a set of data, even random data, Dels will be found that show important prediction power—but without true logic. The point at which a prediction is deemed "successful" is one that must be determined by each firm. For the purposes of this text, predictions that result in a Del of 0.400 or larger are said to be important. Thus, had we been reporting Table 13.1, this chapter would have mentioned only predictability of ∇P_2 and ∇P_3.

13.5   MARKETING SYSTEMS PLANNING

13.5.1   Marketing Systems Planning for Construction Firms

To understand what must be done by a construction firm to market effectively and profitably, a systems approach is helpful. Construction managers are accustomed to viewing their operations as a system. The product concept for the project to be undertaken is usually developed jointly by the contractor, the customer or "owner," and an architect-engineer; the architect-engineer then refines the product concept into a design and ultimately working drawings and specifications; competitive bids are taken or negotiation for the job is completed; and the various phases of actual construction are completed by the contractor's organization or subcontractors, or both. The organizational units that perform parts of the total construction process, and the functions they perform, are interrelated and interconnected and constitute a system that must be managed and directed to achieve the construction goals specified in the design.

The system of operations will not be performed, however, unless a contract is obtained. And most construction firms do not seek all kinds of contracts but only those best suited to the specific types of construction services they are able to offer, and those that contribute to the optimization of their profits and the reputation they need to assist in securing future contracts. The construction firm is also a part of a marketing system, a system of interrelated organizational units and marketing functions that connect the firm with its market. The firm's management of the system can secure contracts of the right kind, provide the means of adapting the total firm to changing market conditions, and contribute to the achievement of the firm's goals of profit, growth, and survival.

1. CONSTRUCTION FIRM AS MARKETING SYSTEM   A system's model is a simplification of reality that omits detail for the purpose of showing the fundamental parts of the system and their relationships. Figure 13.1 is such a model of a construction firm as a marketing system composed of two kinds of parts. The first kind are organizational units (the construction firm, the architect-engineer, customers, and competitive contractors). The second kind of parts are the contractor's marketing mix of service capabilities, market selection, promotion, and pricing; the architect-engineer's functions of design services and pricing; the customer's functions of problem solving and purchasing; and competitors' efforts to serve the same customers through their marketing efforts. The system also includes objectives and resources of the contractor and the changing environmental factors that affect customers' needs and purchasing behaviors. All parts of the system should operate together to accomplish the dual goal of satisfying customers and achieving the objectives of organizations in the system.

The concern herein is with the planning and control of the system by the construction firm. First, however, it must be observed that the following parts of the system are wholly or partially beyond the control of the construction firm:

(a)   Environmental factors such as economic conditions and the social and cultural factors that influence buyers' needs

(b)   The behavior of architect-engineers, although the firm may occasionally choose from among architect-engineers available or perform design work itself. (In practice, it is usually the "owner" or customer who selects the architect-engineer. However, construction firms with stronger market orientations and more aggressive marketing strategies could change this tradition.)

(c)   The competitive efforts of other contractors who attempt to serve the same market

A primary purpose of marketing, as a management function, is to develop dynamic competitive marketing strategies to adapt the firm's operations to these changing customer needs and competitive and environmental conditions.

The parts of the system that are controllable by the firm include its marketing strategy variables of objectives, resources, intelligence, and its own particular mix of marketing activities, shown as the contractor's marketing mix in Figure 13.1. Formulating or planning an effective marketing strategy for the construction firm is a process of integrated

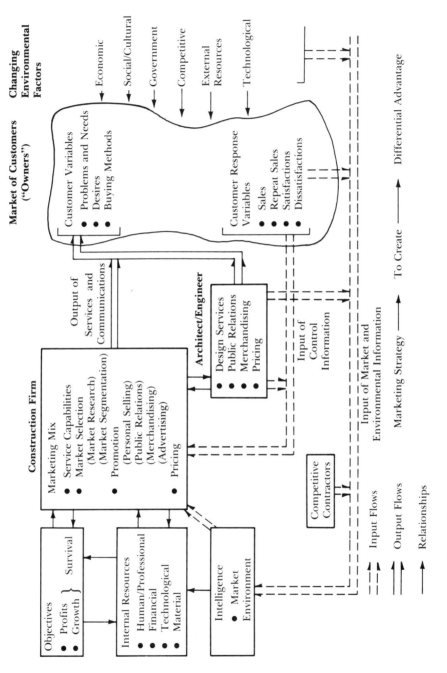

Figure 13.1. Construction Firm as Marketing System. Adapted from Bessom (18:650).

decision making and action with respect to all of these variables. The marketing system shown in Figure 13.1 is an input-output system. The first input into the firm is information about the market and the changing environmental forces that affect both the market and the firm. When analyzed and interpreted in light of the firm's goals and resources, this information becomes intelligence that is then used to develop marketing policies, shown in Figure 13.1 as the marketing mix: service capabilities; market selection of customers whose business will be sought; personal selling or sales force plans; public relations to build a favorable image of the firm in the potential market; merchandising; advertising when appropriate; and pricing policies.

The mix of marketing policies, when implemented, results in the firm's output of professional construction services and of communications about them to the chosen market of customers. No customer can be expected to contract for services to be rendered without full information of those services and the firm's ability to perform them as well or better than other contractors.

The firm's second input is information from the market about customers' responses to the services rendered during and after construction, essentially information about satisfactions, as well as dissatisfactions that require remedial action by the contractor to maintain good relationships and lay the foundations for future contracts. Just as it is the job of the contractor to manage his construction or production system, so is it his job to manage the marketing system both to obtain the jobs best suited to the firm's professional expertise and to maintain a flow of contracts that will satisfy clients and achieve the firm's objectives.

2. MARKETING STRATEGY FOR CONTRACTORS   Construction firms are service businesses. Although the performance of their services results in tangible products such as houses, commercial engineering, or industrial structures, their principal output is a service—a service that adds value to tangible products. For example, a good contractor can manage the construction of a bank and add greater value for the bank owner than can a poor contractor using the same operational inputs of materials and labor. He does this by practicing his expertise so that the job is completed with greater efficiency to result in better quality construction (in terms of the banker's needs) or a lower cost, or both. The contractor's principal output is construction management—a professional service.

A. SERVICE CAPABILITIES AND MARKET SELECTION The first step in marketing strategy design is dichotomous. It involves both the objective appraisal or inventory of the firm's service capabilities and intelligence about the kinds of construction service needs that exist or are developing in the market. At any given time a firm will possess certain resources in the form of material, technological, and financial assets; but more importantly, it will possess certain human/professional skills in the form of people; people who, as a result of the firm's past experience, training, and hiring practices have the expertise to manage certain kinds of jobs, but not others.

In the construction industry, most firms specialize: some in residential construction, others in hospital or shopping centers, others in various kinds of industrial structures, and others on a functional or location basis. A firm should carefully inventory its service capabilities and determine those in which it has a competitive advantage and those in which it has a competitive disadvantage vis-à-vis the firms with which it may compete in the markets it chooses to serve. Because it is natural and understandable for management to overestimate a firm's capabilities, an objective inventory of its resources and capabilities as well as those of competitors is a prerequisite for the planning of promotions the firm will undertake to obtain the work it can perform best.

At the same time, the firm should engage in market selection, which involves the marketing techniques of market research and market segmentation. Because the services a customer purchases from a contractor are inseparable from the contractor, that is, they must be performed on the construction site, contractors tend to serve local markets (a city, state, or regional market). Larger construction firms can of course serve larger market areas—national or even multi-national markets—by opening branches staffed with construction managers, each of which, however, serves the local market in which it is located. Improved transportation facilities also permit some firms to serve more distant markets by having staff members travel to the distant jobsite to render their services. In any case, having determined the geographical parameters of the market to be served, the contractor needs to identify and list the market segments (groups of customers or specific customers in various construction classifications) that he wants to serve and that he will be able to serve competitively.

Market research can then be employed to obtain data on each potential market segment. Such data as growth indicators, income trends, industrial growth or decline of specific segments, economic and other environmental trends, and competitive conditions can be obtained from secondary sources such as *Dodge Reports*, government statistics and publications, and trade association reports. For example, *Dodge Reports*, published by McGraw-Hill Information System Company, contain current information on prospective construction jobs and ones available for bidding. The reports are published on a regular basis for each major metropolitan area in the United States. *Construction Review* and *Commerce Business Daily*, both published by the United States Department of Commerce, Domestic and International Business Administration and Domestic Commerce, are available from the Superintendent of Documents, United States Government Printing Office, Washington, D.C. More specific information can be gathered from primary sources such as interviews with banks, industry leaders, and even surveys by marketing research firms. Analyses of such data can reveal those potential customers or groups of customers that the firm is capable of serving and that can be served most profitably. These customers or groups then become the market targets for the firm, and service capabilities and sales and promotional activities can be planned for their specific needs.

An example of this application of market segmentation and market research is in order here. A firm, serving essentially one state, has service capabilities in the fields of hospital, commercial, and industrial construction for private and government customers, capabilities it has acquired through experience on jobs it obtained through the competitive bidding process. Recently, however, the firm suffered declining profits because of intense competition in several of the market segments it served and employed a marketing manager to help it seek more profitable markets for its services. Market research data revealed steadily declining profits for government contracts and market saturation for hospital work, but a high growth rate in industrial construction. The state offers a growing market, good labor availability and low-cost real estate, as well as government-sponsored incentives for industrial growth in this area. As a result, industry is moving into the area, and the firm selected this market as its prime target. It seeks out industrial firms with plans to move into the state, sells its capabilities to them, negotiates contracts, and performs work tailored to the clients' needs. This firm now has control of its marketing system, selecting its market to a large client rather than being selected by the market through the competitive bidding process, adapting its service capabilities to specific market needs, and building an excellent reputation in its new specialty while enjoying higher profits.

B. MARKETING AND CONSTRUCTION MANAGEMENT

The relationship between the business functions of marketing and construction management is shown in Figure 13.2, which modifies Figure 13.1 to show the marketing process of a construction firm and the interface of marketing functions and construction management functions. In the marketing process, the firm's marketing management first includes intelligence about the market (customer's needs and problems that can be satisfied and solved by construction services). Then it selects markets to serve in accordance with its service capabilities and develops service policies. It is at this point in the process that the greatest cooperation between marketing management and construction management occurs. Service policies must match market needs with construction management capabilities, and this matching is a "two-way street." Marketing management

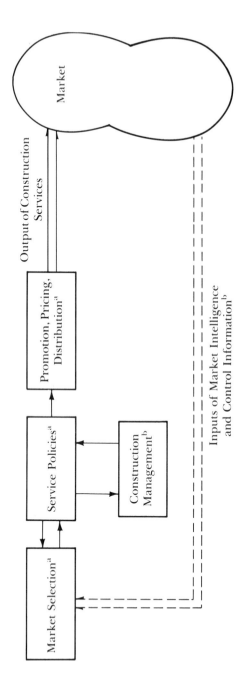

Figure 13.2. Marketing Process and Construction Management. Adapted from Bessom (18:650).

[a]Marketing Functions

[b]Construction Management "Production" Functions of Design, Purchase of Materials and Equipment, Supervision of Construction, and Technology Such As "Fast-Tracking", "Design-Build" Operations, and Time and Work Management.

may adopt service policies in accordance with the needs of selected market targets and the service capabilities already possessed by construction management, or it may ask construction management to develop new service capabilities needed by the market. Conversely, construction management may develop new service capabilities, for example, new technology, and ask marketing management to find a market for the service it can perform.

The construction management functions of a construction firm are analogous to those of a production department in a firm producing and marketing physical products. Construction management "produces" a service capability that marketing management must match with market needs. Then, as shown in Figure 13.2, the marketing process continues with the development of promotion, pricing, and distribution (making the services available at the right time and places) strategies to result in an output of construction services to the market that will satisfy customers and achieve the firm's profit goals.

C. FOCUS ON CUSTOMER AND HIS PROBLEM   According to Drucker, an outstanding authority on management, the most important function of management is to create customers. Once the construction firm has selected market targets that both match its service capabilities and offer means of achieving its profit and growth objectives, it must plan its promotion and pricing methods; it must create customers in its selected market targets. But first, it must understand the buying behavior of those who need to purchase construction management services.

Most construction firms today are production oriented. Having developed a staff of construction managers and personnel who from experience and education possess production skills of certain kinds, the firm's management accepts jobs that will keep the personnel employed and make profits for the firm. By bidding and sometimes negotiating for contracts, often of a broad variety, the personnel seek to obtain business for the firm. Often called "shotgunning," the kind of interaction with the market may involve selling, but it is not marketing. It focuses on the need of the seller to dispose of what he has to sell. Marketing focuses on the needs of the customer and adapts the capabilities of the seller to solve the customer's problems as a means to the end of profit. The marketing-oriented firm will develop a thorough understanding of the customer's problems that can be solved by construction and, within the limits of the firm's professional and other resources, develop a service to solve those problems.

The first requirement for marketing orientation is to perceive the construction need from the customer's point of view. The potential customer has a problem all or part of which can be solved by the construction of some physical facility. Since construction technology is probably outside his field of expertise, he is uncertain about the construction solution to his problem, that is, whether the facility can be built in a way that will solve his problem and at a cost and in a time period in line with the value he places on the satisfaction of his need. Also, he is uncertain about his ability to select the contractor who will satisfy his expectations.

A purchaser of a product makes his commitment after the product is completed and has a tangible object to consider; a purchaser of a service makes his commitment before production and has only intangible promises of the seller about performance to consider, a much more difficult purchasing decision. Thus the marketing task of the contractor consists of (1) understanding the customer's total problem and the role that construction may play in solving that problem; (2) reducing the customer's uncertainty about the construction solution to the problem; and (3) helping the customer identify the proper professional contractor to undertake the job.

A supermarket chain will serve as an example for the foregoing points made. The chain's management sees a market opportunity for a new outlet in a growing suburb of a city. The construction of the new outlet involves many problems related to the retail food business, competition, and the environment. The new store must satisfy the owner's merchandising requirements such as aisle widths, location of check-out stations, proper display facilities, and parking needs. It must be attractive to patrons vis-à-vis competitive stores, satisfy government building codes, satisfy cultural-social values in its aesthetics, accommodate the latest merchandising equipment technology, and be built for a cost within the chain's budget constraints.

The would-be contractor, and the architect-engineer involved, must understand these problems and be able to plan and manage the construction of the store in a way that solves the construction problem, as well as supplements and enhances the solution to the other related problems for the customer. The contractor must also reduce the uncertainty in the customer's mind by demonstrating a record of past performance on similar jobs, providing evidence of the use of an effective construction system, as well as assurance or guarantees of ability to keep construction costs within a prescribed budget. And he must demonstrate his professionalism by convincing evidence of his high standards of performance. Based on this customer orientation, the firm then must market: (1) its performance; (2) its methods; and (3) the competency of its professional personnel.

D.   MARKETING SERVICES IS MARKETING PEOPLE

When a customer signs a construction contract, he is buying a service to be performed. In the end, he will be the owner of a tangible structure, but the quality and cost, as well as the suitability of that structure as a solution to his problem depend largely on the services rendered by the contractor. The buyer's best evidence of the quality and competitive superiority of the service he will buy is the impression he gets of the professional capabilities of the manager and staff of the contractor. Therefore, the selling and creation of satisfaction for the buyer before, during, and after construction is the responsibility of the construction firm's personnel who interact with the customer and who are assigned to the project.

Too often a construction contract is "sold" by the contractor's manager or salespeople and carried out by other supervisory personnel who feel too little responsibility for satisfying the customer throughout the construction process. The personnel who will both supervise the construction and work with the customer should be known to and evaluated by the customer from the time of the contract negotiation or awarding of contract, and they should have the responsibility of providing feedback to management during construction so that corrective action can be taken or negotiated should performance fall short of the customer's expectations.

E. PROMOTION AND PRICING   Effective promotion has not been widely practiced in the construction industry. The reasons for this may seem obscure, but note that architects and engineers have long considered promotion unethical, and perhaps as construction management has become increasingly professional, contractors (many of whom are registered engineers) have been inclined to emulate the conduct of architect-engineers with whom they are so closely associated. Also, the contract bidding process, used by most contractors to obtain business, decreases the need for promotion. According to the theory of bidding, all licensed contractors are presumed equally capable of performing the contract, and the buyer need only select the lowest bid to obtain maximum value for dollars expended. The prevalence of securing bids for construction supports the contention that those who need to purchase construction services suffer great uncertainty. Their main concern is cost, and bidding is supposed to keep cost down. But buyers have to assume that all contractors, whose bids are considered, are capable of the same quality of performance—which, of course, they are not, and which is a source of even greater uncertainty for the astute buyer. However, as many contractors and their customers know, the theory is not always supported by practice. Presumably, the only promotion needed by a contractor who is getting business on a competitive bid basis is the effort required to get on the customer's list of bidders.

But contractors are business firms with something of value to market and profit goals to achieve. With the market needs for construction changing in response to dynamic environmental factors (as suggested on the far right of Figure 13.1), and with competition increasing, no construction firm can afford to take a passive role in the valuation of its services. It needs to communicate and explain the time value of its service to selected customers whose business it seeks and to obtain fair prices relative to the real value of services performed—it needs promotion.

For contractors, the available tools of promotion in order of importance are personal selling, public relations, merchandising, and advertising. While mass-produced and mass-consumed products and some industrial products can be best promoted by advertising and sales promotions, construction services are sold to a limited number of customers and must be explained and sold in a personalized problem-solving manner, which is best done by personal selling. The salespeople should be construction managers themselves, capable of solving the customers' problems by application of the firm's unique set of service capabilities.

Public relations, construed as a process of two-way communication between the firm and all publics that affects the long-run viability of the firm—customers, the community, government, employees, and others— can be used to supplement and support sales activities. A good reputation, or image of the firm, is a prerequisite for effective sales efforts, and the firm can take an active part in building this reputation. Managers of the firm and its salespeople can develop contacts with potential customers, land sales companies, bank development companies, utility companies, architects, and engineers. Such public relations activities can result in preselling by communicating the strengths and capabilities of the firms, and can provide feedback to the firm of any negative attitudes or opinions. If such negative attitudes are based on misinformation, corrective communication can be disseminated; if they are based on aspects of the firm's behavior that are damaging its reputation in its market, corrective action by the firm can be planned.

For small firms, advertising in mass media or even direct mail is likely to be less effective than the person-to-person instant-feedback type of communication previously suggested. For large firms with large regional, national, or international markets, institutional advertising helps build a favorable image of the company; as a door-opener for salespeople, it can be an economical and effective substitute for more personal contact.

Merchandising by contractors usually takes the form of point-of-sale activities such as brochures, displays, and signs; advertising specialties; special events such as company birthdays, ground breakings, or dedications; and sponsorships of clubs or conferences. Such activities should be viewed as part of the firm's public relations or advertising efforts and coordinated with those programs. At best, their true value is uncertain, and they should be considered only as supplements to the firm's more important personal selling activities.

The prices charged by construction firms, along with other elements of their marketing outputs, should be considered from the customer's perspective. For the customer, the price must be less than or equal to the monetary equivalent of the values he expects to receive from the contractor.

The prices paid for the largest elements of cost for construction—materials, labor, and equipment—are beyond the control of contractors and customers, and can therefore be considered as constants in competitive bidding or negotiations situations. The variable under the control of the contractor, and part of his marketing mix, is the price charged for his management of the services he offers during the construction process and the efficiency of the construction methods he employs. It is for this reason that competitive bidding for contracts offers the poorest opportunity for creative and innovative marketing by construction firms. A bidding firm has little or no opportunity to explain and demonstrate the real value of its services to the customer, which in many cases can justify a higher price because greater value would be created.

Good competitive marketing strategy is designed to optimize the values received by the customer as the best means of optimizing the goals of the firm. From a marketing point of view, negotiated contracts offer greater marketing opportunities for the benefit of both the contractor and his customer. With the open channels of communication that negotiation entails, the contractor can reduce the customer's uncertainty in connection with the project, fully comprehend the problems involved, and effectively demonstrate his professionalism. In return, the customer can understand more fully the values he will receive, and a price can be agreed upon that accurately reflects those values, which should cover the costs of rendering the services and a fair profit for the contractor. Many successful contractors are employing this kind of modern marketing and pricing through negotiation.

Based upon thorough market intelligence, such contractors seek out target customers and communicate both their service capabilities and problem-solving abilities through negotiation. They often charge a fixed fee for their services (which is calculated to obtain a desired return on investment in those resources needed to render construction management services) plus the actual costs of materials, construction labor, and equipment based upon prevailing prices in the area of construction. The customer can verify these latter "constant" costs and compare the value and price of services offered with those of competitive contractors.

Such contractors can compete successfully because they offer the customer a differential advantage of their management technology—but they also market their services instead of waiting for invitations to bid. Three examples of the many current management technologies that construction firms can market are "fast tracking," which shortens the time and costs of construction; "design-build" operations, which incorporate architectural-engineering design functions into the construction firm for better coordination, increased efficiency, and resultant lower costs and usually improved quality; and "construction management," which offers the expertise of the contractor through design phases and during construction to effect savings in both time and costs.

13.5.2 Marketing Systems Planning for Architectural and Engineering Firms

This section includes the evaluation of the relative importance of factors that clients consider important in the marketing of design, construction, and design-build services. The overall rankings of the clients' average responses to the top four factors for each type of proposal are shown in able 13.2. This table provides an overview of clients' perceptions of their own needs. Thus all generalizations must eventually be evaluated in the light of the specific needs of each market segment.

On an overall basis, the client evaluations of a Design-Only or a Design-Build proposal rank the scope of work statement as most important, followed in order of importance by the proposed construction manager, the time-cost completion schedule, and the fixed-cost budget. In terms of the ten attributes used, clients tend to evaluate the design-build proposal and the design-only proposal in almost the same manner. For projects requiring only construction services, the client's estimate of the perceived quality of the proposed CM staff is the most important criterion for acceptance. Estimated costs, statements detailing how the project will be administered by the firm, and construction supervision follow in order of importance.

Overall, firms are awarded contracts on the basis of an assessment of perceived quality, with proposed costs seen as one of several other factors considered. The assessment of quality appears to be embodied in the CM, prior project-specific experience, and the scope of work statement. The "ideal" firm, from the client's perspective, costs not withstanding, is the firm that proposes a CM who has done this type of work before, and that presents a detailed understanding of the task complexities and ordering necessary for the project under bid. Only in the case of construction

Table 13.2. Why Process Engineering and Design Clients Accept or Reject Proposals

DESIGN ONLY AND DESIGN BUILD	CONSTRUCTION ONLY
1. Scope of work	1. Construction management staff
2. Construction management staff	2. Fixed-cost budget
3. Time-cost schedule	3. Project administration
4. Fixed-cost budget	4. Construction supervision

Adapted from Murray (99:671).

service contracts are two of these "quality assessment" parameters partially outweighed by the importance of costs.

Since market segments exist because some clients have acceptance criteria that differ from other clients, the Del Statistic can be used to analyze a survey data. That is, predictions about the perceptions of sets of clients who tend to accept or reject professional service proposals on similar criteria, which are separate and distinct from the criteria employed by other sets of clients, can be made. High predictability implies that a specified market segment actually exists.

1. LUMP-SUM PREFERENCES   An important feature in client preferences is the type of contract award. While most clients prefer to use a lump-sum contract award for construction services and variations of the cost-plus award for design services, not all clients have such preferences. Some prefer to use the lump-sum for both types of services, while others regularly use, and prefer, cost-plus contracts.

An examination of clients regularly using lump-sum awards resulted in the following two significant predictions:

(a)   Clients who use lump-sum contracts, and who are seeking a bid on design-only contract, will tend to consider the CM as more important than the costs.

(b)   Clients who use lump-sum contracts, and who are seeking a bid on either a construction-only or a design-build contract, will tend to consider the fixed-cost budget to be more important than the CM.

These two predictions indicate the presence of three different market segments, with a different market strategy indicated for each: (1) faced with a lump-sum requirement by the client, a firm should strive to be the low-cost bidder on construction-only projects. Efforts to convince the client that a superior quality CM will be assigned is less important; (2) for lump-sum design-only projects, the client can be expected to weigh the importance of the proposed CM more heavily, with costs of secondary importance; and (3) a lump-sum design-build contract will be considered in a manner similar to that of lump-sum contracts for construction-only services.

Predictions of market segments seem to be appropriate given the contract award criteria. A lump-sum contract is an upper limit on cost, with the client stating a preference for strict adherence to this parameter. However, the degree of adherence is relative. Construction-only and design-build contracts require the greatest degree of sensitivity to the cost parameter, while design services are different. A client's perceived quality of the proposed CM outweighs the strict adherence to the cost standard, thereby permitting the design firm more flexibility in marketing its services.

2. COST-PLUS PREFERENCES   For clients specifying cost-plus award in the RFP, the importance of the CM in a firm's marketing efforts is paramount. Whether for design-only, construction-only, or design-build contracts, clients rate the CM as more important than costs.

It is important to note the strength of these predictions. Clients who prefer the cost-plus award tend to evaluate both the design-only and design-build contracts in a similar manner, with the CM being much more important to the contract award than are costs. The importance of the CM, as compared to costs, for construction-only contracts is not as significant.

Again, the logic of these predictions is apparent, given the basic intent of the cost-plus award. A typical client prefers to use the cost-plus award for projects that are more difficult and complex than is the average project. As such, the client anticipates the project's complexities and searches for a firm that can be expected to "do the job." Upon picking the most outstanding candidate, the client awards cost-plus renumeration in recognition of the unknowns contained within the project. The key to the client's perception of the ability of the firm to deal with these complexities is the CM.

3. CONSTRUCTION MANAGER PREFERENCES   Another element of market segmentation is the client's perception of the importance of the CM. Overall, most clients prefer that the proposed CM visit with the client before the contract award is made.

As discussed previously, when a client feels strongly about the importance of the CM, costs tend to be of less importance. Similarly, the more important the role of the CM in the client's evaluation criteria, the less important the firm's scope of work statement. As the CM is considered to be less important by the client, both costs and the scope of work statement are considered to be more important.

Thus, when a firm can determine the importance a client will place on the CM before the proposal is prepared, the firm may be able to adjust its proposal format accordingly. While it is important that the firm not diminish the importance of the CM under any circumstances, a heavier emphasis can be given to the scope of work statement and, if possible, to lower cost estimates. Even the answer to a simple question may provide a clue to the client's preference early in the negotiation state. "Do you want to visit with our CM before we submit our bid?" In any event, some before-the-proposal knowledge should be considered as useful for the development of a marketing strategy.

4. ACCEPT/REJECT CRITERIA   Many clients prequalify firms. RFPs are therefore sent to firms that, in the client's mind, can be expected to do the work. Especially for design work the client's acceptance criteria are heavily weighted by quality assessment, e.g., the CM, scope of work, and past project-specific experience. Costs are of secondary importance.

However, proposals are largely rejected on the basis of two equally weighted criteria. Costs that are too high and the perceived lack of service quality are the key elements of the typical client's rejection criteria.

The importance of costs in the reject criteria is the basis that rejections are due to lower-cost bidders. While firms may have been actually told this by clients, the primary reason for accepting the winning firm's bid is not low cost. High-quality services tend to be much more important in deciding upon the winning proposal.

13.6   ADAPTIVE MARKETING STRATEGIES

A final and key point to be made herein is also shown in Figure 13.1. The marketing strategies employed by marketing-oriented contractors are not static one-time plans but dynamic ones, subject to constant revision. The needs and problems in the market that can be satisfied and solved by construction are in a state of flux in response to changing environmental forces. Some environmental changes occurring today that affect construction (Figure 13.1) include inflation (economic), new types of residential and commercial structures (social/solidus cultural), new laws and ordinances (governmental), mergers and larger, more competitive construction firms (competitive), new materials and shortages of others (external resources), and increasing prefabrication and more efficient equipment (technology).

The sole purpose of the construction firm is to satisfy market needs, although its motivation for doing so is profit. Because the market is changing, the firm must adapt to those changes to remain viable. It can accomplish this by proper management of the controllable elements of its marketing system. The intelligence system, like a military intelligence system, detects or anticipates the market changes. Then management adjusts its internal resources, its marketing mix of service offerings, market target selections, promotion and pricing strategies to provide a better match between the new market needs (or the needs of new markets) and its service offerings. Management may also have to develop different working relationships with architects and engineers, and it must always monitor the activities of competitors so that it develops the capability of matching or bettering their service offerings.

And finally, while strategies are being implemented, the firm seeks information about customer responses to its services as inputs for additional adaptations of the firm's marketing behavior. Selling is persuading customers to buy the services offered. Marketing is a systematic adaptation of the service capabilities and communication about them, to the real and changing needs of customers. Effective selling is always required, but the development of an adaptive marketing system to tailor the service offerings to the needs of selected target markets can replace aggressive selling with more consultative, problem-solving relationships with customers. An effective marketing system can greatly improve the firm's ability to engage in progressive construction management for the benefit of both the contractor and his customers.

13.7   SUMMARY

Modern marketing practices by business firms have developed in recognition of the fact that consumption is the sole purpose of production. In a free society where products and services are produced and offered to the market by competitive enterprises, the buyer can choose from competitors' various offerings for the satisfaction of his particular product and service needs and desires. Thus any firm producing a product or a service should (or must, if competition is effective) engage in marketing to increase its probability of being selected by buyers as their supplier.

Marketing activities include product or service design, in accordance with customer needs, distribution (or making the offering available where and when the consumer wants it), promotion (to ensure knowledge of the offerings and its relative advantages), and pricing (to conform with the real value of the product or service for the customer).

Decisions in these areas should be made in advance of production to ensure that what is offered to the consumer will be in accordance with his needs—needs that must also be known and understood in advance by the marketer. The careful advance planning of marketing activities is a firm's best insurance against making mistakes that could result in lost sales—after the cost of production and marketing have been incurred.

The perceived quality of a firm's services and estimated costs are two ingredients in the evaluation criteria of the typical client. Quality measurement is a mix of the client's estimate of the quality of the proposed construction manager, the scope of work statement, and past project-specific work. Quality tends to outweigh costs in importance.

14

Safety in Construction

14.1 INTRODUCTION

There is a justifiable demand for construction safety throughout the world. The laws place the responsibility on us all to act in a manner that does not endanger the life or property of others. Although an accident is defined as an unintentional or unexpected happening, the law assumes that, except in the case of acts of God, accidents are caused by negligence— which is the failure to exercise such care as would normally be expected of a reasonable man or woman.

A contractor must be safety-conscious because of humanitarian concern, economic benefits, legal requirements, and the desire for improving his company's public image. Humanitarian objectives boil down to reducing the human pain and suffering resulting from accidents and illnesses. Economic incentives include not only reducing insurance premiums, but minimizing the staggering indirect costs as well.

Effective implementation programs should focus on both the physical and behavioral sides of safety and health. A balance between the different components of safety and health is therefore essential.

On the behavioral side, recent research has produced practical and workable guidelines aimed at the attitudes and actions of top management, project managers and superintendents, foremen, and workers. The physical side of safety involves

1. Education and training;

2. Proper utilization and maintenance of correct tools and equipment;

3. Equipment for personal protection;

4. Good housekeeping;

5. Frequent inspections by knowledgeable and objective professionals;

6. Integrating safety and health into preplanning for field operations.

Also, it is not necessary to trade productivity and efficiency for safety. In fact, it has been found that safer workers, foremen, and superintendents are usually also more productive.

This chapter first examines the importance of construction safety and the benefits of safety. It next discusses construction safety problems. The chapter then attempts to explore safety organizations. It finally examines the approaches to improve safety performance.

14.2 IMPORTANCE OF CONSTRUCTION SAFETY

The construction industry, employing an average of 5% of the total labor force in this country, has accounted for about 11% of all occupational injuries and 20% of all deaths resulting from occupational accidents. The cost of accidents is expensive; the accident-related costs to the construction industry are estimated to run up to $10 billion per year. However, economic cost is not the only reason why a contractor should be conscious of construction safety. The reasons for considering safety include

1. **HUMANITARIAN CONCERN**   When an accident happens, the resultant suffering the injured workers and their families have to bear is difficult to quantify in economic terms. The contractor should never ignore this, even if he has insured against the accidents.

2. **ECONOMIC REASONS**   Even if a contractor has insurance, he still will find out that the cost of accidents comes out of his own pocket

through the increase of future insurance premiums. In addition, there are indirect costs that will result from the accidents. The direct and indirect costs of accidents can be

(a) *Direct Cost:*
- **(i)** Medical care expenses for injured
- **(ii)** Workers' compensation costs
- **(iii)** Insurance premium increase
- **(iv)** Replacement costs of equipment and material damaged in accidents
- **(v)** Facility repair and cleanup
- **(vi)** Fees for legal counsel

(b) *Indirect Cost:*
- **(i)** Slowdown in operations
- **(ii)** Decrease in morale, which affects productivity
- **(iii)** Productive time lost from injured worker and fellow workers
- **(iv)** Administrative work associated with accident
- **(v)** Loss of client confidence
- **(vi)** Overtime necessitated by work slowdown

3. LAWS AND REGULATIONS   The Occupational Safety and Health Act of 1970 (OSHA) requires that "each employer furnish to each of his employees, employment, and a place of employment which is free from recognized hazards that are causing or are likely to cause death or serious physical harm to his employees." Violation of this law will be subject to federal penalty.

4. ORGANIZATION IMAGE   A good safety record can produce higher morale and productivity and stronger employee loyalty. Also, it will improve the company's public image and, therefore, make it easier to acquire negotiated jobs.

14.3   SAFETY BENEFITS TO EMPLOYERS, EMPLOYEES, AND CUSTOMERS

14.3.1   Safety Benefits to Employers

Because safety and profit have an integral relationship, the discussion of safety itself would become a moot question if construction companies were not making a profit. There is no lack of humanitarian concern if we view safety from a profit standpoint, providing we recognize that it is profitable not only to the employer, but to the worker as well. The construction worker who is injured suffers a financial loss as well as pain and discomfort. The construction employer who disregards safety suffers an indirect cost that could ultimately affect his survival. With at least half of the construction cost consisting of labor, any constructive type of safety program will result in economies and be of great importance to the worker, to the contractor, and to the public as a whole.

It is not sufficient to merely say that an adequate safety or accident prevention program is an important way to reduce labor costs. It is not difficult to see that accidents and losses involving both people and equipment result in a waste of time and money. What is not so evident, however, is the extent of those losses. All too often an employer believes that as long as he has insurance to protect himself against direct losses resulting from accidents, he has no longer any concern as to profit and loss once he has paid that premium. This attitude can lead to disastrous results, and a simple evaluation of the relationship between insured costs and uninsured costs will reflect the importance of this relationship.

The most immediate and obvious financial benefit is the savings realized because of accidents that do not happen. Mention has already been made of the indirect costs of accidents that are not covered by insurance and that can constitute serious financial loss.

Construction workers appreciate and value job safety even though they are sometimes careless in their work habits. Safety is one of the potent forces that makes workers proud of the company they work for, proud of the manner in which they perform their jobs, and proud of their record in preventing accidents. The fruits of good worker morale are higher production and better workmanship, two economic benefits to the employers. Another important financial benefit to the employer is the reduction in the cost of insurance as a result of fewer or no accidents. Safety is also an important public relations tool, a great potential for building goodwill. Good public relations have important financial and business implications for the employer.

14.3.2 Safety Benefits to the Employees

When a worker covered by Workmen's Compensation is injured on the job, he can expect compensation for wages lost and payment of medical expenses, unless in some jurisdictions he has been found guilty of intoxication, deliberate infliction of injury upon himself, violation of safety rules, violation of a law or an order, deviation from his work to attend to personal affairs, or other actions that can be described as intentional or willful misconduct. The amount of benefits vary by state, but rarely does the benefit exceed two-thirds of his wages. The maximum weekly benefits hardly compare with those wages normally earned by a construction worker. The loss in wages alone creates a burden for the injured worker. If you couple that burden with the pain and anguish the worker and his family experience, the loss is truly noncompensable.

When a dismemberment occurs, usually that employee can no longer apply his craftsmanship in the construction industry. The worker is normally forced to accept less skilled and lower-paid labor than was his previous occupation. Even after time has healed the physical wounds, mental discomfort may remain. A worker in such a physical industry as construction usually develops pride in his physical capabilities. If he attempts to return to work in the construction industry with a permanent partial disability, he often resents the special concern other workers afford him. Whether or not it is true physically, often the injured worker considers himself a cripple.

Special care must be afforded the injured worker in both physical and mental rehabilitation. Due to necessity or desire, rehabilitation frequently requires retaining for employment in another industry. The worker's life-style may be completely changed. He may be forced to relocate to find employment in his new vocation. In any event, no injury can be considered anything but an unfortunate occurrence. Every aspect is normally negative. If an accident prevention program prevented such an occurrence, that in itself would justify its existence; but safety pays in less obvious ways.

The worker who has learned to do his work efficiently and safely is a better employee. Employers continually seek out this type of employee; therefore, the employee increases his chances of steadier employment and higher lifetime earnings. His actions indicate that he can analyze the work to be performed and select the most efficient and safest methods. One could even generalize further to say that normally he could be expected to work well with other employees, for in the construction industry, teamwork prevents accidents. A safe, efficient employee is then an asset to himself and the industry.

14.3.3   Safety Benefits to the Customer

Because the expenses of industrial accidents are to be considered a cost of operation and as such are to be transferred from the worker and employer to the consumer, eventually the customer will bear the cost of poor accident prevention programs. It is very possible that the immediate cost will not affect the customer, particularly in the case of fixed-bid contract construction, but the effect that losses due to injury create within the cost of providing Workmen's Compensation Insurance will eventually be felt.

The cost of a project as viewed by the customer not only includes the price for construction but also the cost of nonproductive capital. High interest rates make it mandatory that money be used in the most productive manner possible. Accidents create time losses: the time a project is delayed while another piece of equipment is brought in to replace one damaged accidentally, the time spent replacing an injured worker, and time spent training the injured worker to bring him to full production. Serious accidents can create delays that may never be overcome. When that occurs, the on-line projection of the customer must be revised and all moving plans must be revamped. Often, customers have new equipment in transit to be installed after construction is completed, and delay in completion of construction can create a chain reaction effect, causing real hardship to the customer. If an employee can do his work efficiently and safely, everyone benefits, particularly the customer.

14.3.4   Insured versus Uninsured Costs[1]

It can be surmised from the foregoing that uninsured costs are approximately nine times greater than insured costs. Thus for every dollar in direct loss or cost of an accident, nine additional dollars are spent indirectly. Those nine dollars show up eventually on the profit and loss statement and are as real a drain on company profits as any other whole dollar loss.
   Insured costs include

INJURIES	PROPERTY DAMAGE
1. Compensation for lost earnings	Insurance premiums or charges for
2. Medical and hospital cost	(a) Fire
3. Awards for permanent disabilities	(b) Loss and damage
4. Rehabilitation costs	(c) Use and occupancy
5. Funeral charges	(d) Public liability
6. Pensions for dependents	

Uninsured costs that result in indirect losses are as follows:

INJURIES	ASSOCIATED COSTS
1. First-aid expenses	1. Difference between actual losses and amount recovered

---

1. This subsection is adapted from Lee E. Knack, "Safety Procedures and Practices," in *Handbook of Construction Management and Organization*, Joseph J. Frein (Editor), Van Nostrand Reinhold Co., New York, 1980, pp. 601.

INJURIES	ASSOCIATED COSTS
2. Transportation costs	2. Rental of equipment to replace damaged equipment
3. Cost of investigations	3. Surplus workers for replacement of injured workmen
4. Cost of processing reports	4. Wages or other benefits paid to disabled workers
	5. Overhead costs while production is stopped
	6. Loss of bonus or payment of forfeiture for delays

WAGE LOSSES	OFF THE JOB ACCIDENTS
1. Idle time of workers whose work is interrupted	1. Cost of medical services
2. Man-hours spent in cleaning up accident area	2. Time spent on injured workers' welfare
3. Time spent repairing damaged equipment	3. Loss of skill and experience
4. Time lost by workers receiving first aid	4. Training replacement worker
	5. Decreased production of replacement
	6. Benefits paid to injured worker or dependents

PRODUCTION LOSSES	INTANGIBLES
1. Product spoiled by accident	1. Lowered employee morale
2. Loss of skill and experience	2. Increased labor conflict
3. Lowered production of worker replacement	3. Unfavorable public relations
4. Idle machine time	

14.4   CONSTRUCTION SAFETY PROBLEMS

There are numerous problems associated with construction site hazards, which result in injury and even death. These problems can range from negligence to even construction equipment accidents. A few of these problems are listed here so the nonprofessional reader can grasp an idea of the situation.

1. Cohesive crews will have fewer accidents.

2. The company with more humane attitudes will have better safety records.

3. Less congested work sites.

4. Proper shore and reshoring.

5. Individual social statistics of workers.

6. The foreman with a more considerate attitude has a better accident record in his crew.

7. Pressure tends to increase the accident occurrence rate.

8. Competition among workers will tend to increase the accident occurrence.

9. Fatigue will increase accident occurrence.

10. The worker's attitude can have an impact on accident occurrence.

11. Workers who fear for their job security tend to have more accidents.

12. The jobs that have more essential hazards contribute to more accidents.

13. Participative management can improve the safety performance of the company.

14. Speedy jobs are more accident-prone.

15. The workers who are loyal to the company are safe workers.

16. Workers who are not satisfied and are worried are inclined to accidents.

17. New workers at the site are liable to have accidents.

18. Workers that are not taught safety rules and regulations pertaining to the job are accident-inclined.

19. Long working hours—lack of rest can cause tiredness that results in accidents.

20. Unsafe working tools and equipment can cause serious accidents.

21. Unsupervised jobs can result in accidents.

22. Attitudes, as expressed through worker turnover and grievances, have been linked with an increase in injuries.

23. Adequate construction safety apparel is neglected. (Safety equipment)

24. Potential hazards by nature of work.

14.4.1   Poor Safety on Construction Sites

The previously mentioned items are but a few of many safety hazards that cause accidents on construction sites. It has long been recognized that many types of construction operations present serious hazards. Only recently, however, have occupational health problems in construction received much attention.

Safety hazards are those that pose imminent danger of causing injury or death to workers or damage to materials, equipment, or structures. They result not only from obvious physical dangers, but also from human factors, such as lack of training, poor supervision, attitudes, poor planning, or even from workers who are so familiar with the work that they become oblivious to it.

Until recently it was popularly assumed that construction provides rugged, out-in-the-fresh-air work and ideal summer training for athletes, and is healthy for anyone who can stand its pace. Although hard hats had gained some legitimacy as a safety device, health protectors such as earplugs, respirators, and shock absorbers were considered to be for "sissies" and not "real men." Too many workers, unfortunately, are dead for lack of using them, and others are handicapped for life. Health hazards in construction include, among others, heat, radiation, noise, dust, shocks and vibrations, and toxic chemicals. Increasingly, it is being recognized that occupational diseases have indeed been a serious problem in construction. There are substantial direct costs for medical treatment and disability claims, and indirect costs through the premature loss of skilled workers. Many of the hazards have been not only identified but eliminated. Asbestos is but one of many recent examples. It is vitally important that all organizations involved in construction stay up to date with developments in occupational health and implement methods proven to reduce health hazards. If humanitarian concerns are not really sufficient, then the liability implication should be more than enough reason.

14.4.2   Adverse Effect of Poor Safety

There are numerous adverse effects on all parties concerned due to poor safety practices, especially when serious accidents occur. A few of these adverse effects caused by poor safety are

1. Waste of labor resources

2. Hardships encountered by both the construction worker and his family

3. Strain and stress encountered by both the owner and the builder caused by poor safety resulting in accidents

4. High-premium rates on insurance

5. Delay of the project

6. Training new workers to replace the injured

7. Effect on other workers, which shows in their performance on the job

8. Delayed time for investigations, meetings, high cost of project

9. Cost to Workers' Compensation

10. Loss of productivity

11. Disrupted schedules

12. Wages paid for time not worked

13. Adverse publicity that embarasses the construction company and may hurt its future in the acquiring of jobs

14. Cleanup and repair

15. Third-party liability claims against the owner

16. Equipment damage

14.5 SAFETY ORGANIZATIONS

Recognizing that employers have more control over work areas and methods than employees do, the states have prescribed accident prevention regulations that make employers responsible for accidents to employees regardless of the cause. The federal government has also established safety and health regulations, the latest of which is the Williams-Steiger's Occupational Safety and Health Act (OSHA). This regulation states that "each employer shall protect the employment and places of employment of each of his employees, by complying with the appropriate standards prescribed."

The construction industry has long recognized that construction is a high-risk activity and that active safety measures are needed. The accident frequency and severity rates in this industry are naturally well above the averages of all other industries. Of the four million workers in the industry, some 2,700 die and 240,000 are injured each year. In 1972, the General Building Contractor's Association of America published its first edition of a *Manual of Accident Prevention* in an endeavor to persuade construction executives to take more interest in safety. Besides OSHA, there is the National Institute for Occupational Safety and Health (NIOSH), which is a part of the Department of Health and Human Services (HHS). In Canada, there are quite a few safety organizations, one of which is the Construction Safety Association of Ontario. It produces several safety manuals on cranes, rigging, equipment, and so forth.

14.5.1 Employer and Employee Safety Responsibility

During the process of construction, there is often a risk of loss or damage to employer's own material or equipment if safe construction methods are not followed. OSHA has specified that every employer is responsible, so far as possible, to provide safe and healthful working conditions for each of his employees. OSHA issued minimum regulations that must be adhered to in order to be in compliance. In addition to this responsibility for the safety and health of employees, each employer is, according to the law, responsible for property damage to third parties caused by actions due to negligence. The contractor then has a three-part safety responsibility, which requires planning, estimating, and administering adequate, safe, and economical methods of construction.

The contractor's management should establish a general safety policy and designate an executive as an overall safety officer to oversee all projects. Because conditions on each project differ, it is the superintendent's responsibility to plan and implement a program for his job. In order for his plan to be successful, the plan must have the cooperation of everyone in the construction program. The contractor should furnish tools and materials that are as safe as possible and should educate the men on the proper methods of use, if deemed necessary.

When the contractor prepares his price for the work, he should allocate a sum for accident prevention. The superintendent then has the responsibility for providing an adequate safety program within this budget. He also should assign part of these responsibilities to the subcontractors and see to it that the program is implemented. It is very important that the superintendent establish who has control of the actual work performed. If an electrician is in charge of work being done, he is responsible. However, the contractor, by contract agreements, is responsible for the supervision of the electrician to the extent that his supervision is not negligent.

Owners can take measures to achieve better safety performance by

1. Providing safety and health guidelines that the contractor must follow.

2. Requiring the use of permit systems for potentially hazardous activities.

3. Requiring the contractor to designate a responsible supervisor to coordinate safety on the site.

4. Discussing safety at owner-contractor meetings.

5. Conducting safety audits during construction.

6. Requiring prompt reporting and full investigation of accidents.

14.5.2 Allocation of Responsibility

There is a responsibility shared by the owner, architect, and the contractor in creating a facility or producing a project that complies with safety standards for the protection of people and property. The idea is to minimize the hazards to the public and its property, the occupier's property and personnel, and the contractor's workmen and property. The workmen also have the responsibility of performing their work in accordance with recognized safety standards.

There is the responsibility on the team's part—the owner's responsibility, the architect-engineer's responsibility, the contractor's responsibility, and the workmen's responsibility. All add up to produce the environment that would eliminate hazards on the jobsite and therefore create a safe construction environment.

14.5.3   Professional Responsibility

In the construction manager approach for the overall management of a project, the three-member team comprised of the owner, the architect-engineer, and the construction manager function in their individual roles to provide the overall direction and management of the project. Actual construction work is performed by individual contractors, usually under contract to the owner.

The organization serving as the construction manager, in addition to having certain responsibilities in the preconstruction phase, is overall manager at the jobsite during the construction of the facility, subject to the general direction and control of the owner. As such, the CM is generally regarded as the owner's agent or representative at the jobsite. With respect to the construction work, the CM is responsible to direct, coordinate, and assist the contractors in achieving a finished product that conforms to the technical specifications in the construction contract documents and meets the schedule objectives of the owner. The CM does not, however, supervise or direct the means, methods, or techniques used by the construction contractors.

For safety, the role of the CM is not generally understood. It should be noted that on some sites the CM may provide general support services, such as providing construction utilities, operating major cranes, and performing maintenance and site cleanup, by the direct hire and supervision of craftsmen. When this occurs, the CM clearly has the role of a construction employer with respect to the safety of his own employees. Notwithstanding, this section explores the safety issues relating to the CM in the role of manager, not as an employer of construction workers. There are several types of exposure that a CM could have with respect to liability in the construction safety area.

1.   OSHA CITATION   The CM could receive a citation from OSHA for violation if he is deemed to be "engaged in construction" or "in control of the construction."

2.   PRIVATE LITIGATION   Litigation may possibly be brought by injured parties, their representatives, or insurers against the CM in a civil court.

3. LIABILITY TO CLIENTS   A suit from clients, alleging the CM's failure to comply with his contractual obligation to the clients.

4. CONSTRUCTION MANAGER EMPLOYEE EXPOSURE There could be an increase in workers' compensation rates and other costs.

5. CRIMINAL NEGLIGENCE   There is the potential for prosecution by law-enforcement agencies for criminal negligence.

6. VIOLATION OF LOCAL STATUTES   The possibility for citation by local officials alleging the violation of a local ordinance or statute.

7. CONTRACTOR LITIGATION   A suit from site construction contractor claiming interference by the CM, with a resultant economic impact on the contractor's activities.

The CM could use several alternate safety approaches regarding safety at the construction site. These are

1. SAFETY TRAINING   The CM assists the contractor in coordinating site safety meetings, distribution of safety literature and posters, maintaining a central safety library, providing professional safety training.

2. THE CM's DIRECTION   The owner-CM contract provides specific language for the CM to direct a site-wide safety program for the benefit of all contractors and employees.

3. OWNER REPRESENTATIVE   The owner employs a safety professional on site separate from the CM, either to direct a safety program or to function in a supporting role.

4. SAFETY CONSULTANT   The owner employs a separate safety consulting organization to provide safety management services.

5. SAFETY CORPORATION   Project participants: the owner, the contractor, the construction manager, and the employees.

6. OWNER WRAP-UP INSURANCE   The owner secures overall insurance coverage on the site to include workers' compensation, general liability, auto, or other coverage for all other project participants.

Construction contractors in general should have a vital interest in performing their work in the manner that provides a safe working environment for their employees. They usually should have an economic interest in their workers' compensation rates and in the general efficiency and productivity of the work. They should have the humanitarian interest that exists for all employers to be concerned with the welfare of their employees. The owner has a natural interest in ensuring that a project associated with his name is a safe project. The CM, therefore, should desire to manage the site in a professional and efficient manner and to please the owner.

14.5.4   Safety as a Function of Job Control

Accidents receive particular attention from contractors since injuries have a direct effect on insurance premiums. In addition to the physical discomforts associated with injuries, accidents interfere with job productivity and increase the direct costs of construction. Hence the direct costs associated with injuries represent only a small portion of the eventual overall costs.

The key element is a complete understanding of accidents and the prevention of injury on the job. It is rather difficult to narrow down the definition of job control. It may be regarded as a combination of management's knowledge of field conditions and its ability to react quickly to any special needs that should arise. There are various means of establishing and maintaining good job control. Job control may be achieved

1. By having capable field supervisors on each project.

2. Through frequent job visits by company managers.

3. Through close communication between the field and company management by radio or telephone contact.

4. By any of these combinations.

It is theorized that closer job control by company management would be associated with fewer job inquiries. It is further hypothesized that field problems are minimized where job control is good; a smooth-running job is a safe job. Therefore, with the ready knowledge and awareness of field problems, company managers can quickly exert their efforts to solve the problems immediately. Hence job control eases the pressure on the field personnel and enables them to work with less frequent interruptions. Such interruptions can affect job safety, particularly if the problems are such that the field personnel do not know how to deal with them. Consequently, the interruptions could make the workers more vulnerable to accidents.

Proper job training is the answer to improved accident prevention. Knowledge of the equipment and materials with which the construction crew work is one of the most important factors in accident prevention. Each piece of equipment and material should be designed and developed to serve a specific purpose, and knowledge of what it can do and cannot do, not only improves efficiency but also eliminates hazards.

14.6   APPROACHES TO IMPROVE CONSTRUCTION SAFETY

There have been many rules and recommendations laid down through research by societies, organizations, institutions, and engineering organizations on how to improve construction safety. The OSHA and other pertinent groups should rally together at least twice a year to produce one national document set as guidelines to the construction industry, to be put into effect as a safety program to be taught and implemented by each construction contractor. Incentives or bonuses should be a policy adopted by all construction throughout the United States. This idea would create an environment within the construction industry so valuable that it would really reduce the percentage of accidents to almost nil. Safety education should be a must by all construction firms and contractors. This program must be mandatory and minutes taken to be forwarded to OSHA or some organization set up by the Federal Safety Organization.

All of the construction problems should be taken into consideration and avoided by means of learning and planning to work to eliminate them. All research and findings should be compiled by a central safety committee and made available to the construction industry for a minimal fee.

Regular safety meetings should be held at all levels within the construction industry, and the awareness should be stressed by management along with the incentives for workers on the line of safety.

Recognizing the importance of improving safety performance, a contractor can approach the problem from four different ways: Organizational approach, physical approach, behavioral approach, and economic incentives.

14.6.1   Organizational Approach

A safety program cannot be successful without an appropriate organizational setup. A company safety program should be a part of the contractor's business just as scheduling and cost accounting are. Several guidelines can be drawn up:

1. SAFETY DEPARTMENT   A formal safety department is essential in a company. This department should be in charge of hiring safety staff and jobsite representatives, recording and analyzing safety information of each project, and preparing safety orientations and other accident prevention programs. The safety representative on each site should not be hired by the project management, since this may result in compromising on safety issues later. The safety personnel should report to both the project manager and the safety director in the home office. He reports to the project manager so that timely corrections can be taken. But he must also report to his own boss to prevent being ignored by the project manager. The safety director must have enough authority to carry out his policies. Also, he must be able to have access to top management.

2. COMMITTEE   A safety committee should be set up to guide the operation of safety programs. The members of the committee should include all levels of workers and management to reflect their opinions on safety. It also will have to review the company's safety programs periodically. This committee should be chaired by a vice-president or the executive vice-president.

3. FIELD PROCEDURES   A system must be designed to process safety suggestions from workers. Workers are persons who carry out daily construction processes; they are in the best position to detect any possible accidents. They should be reminded and encouraged to bring out any unsafe procedure detected in daily routine. Timely responses and proper corrections should be made according to the suggestions. The Building and Construction Trades Department of the AFL-CIO has set up a standard procedure for its members to file safety complaints. The procedure is

(a)   Hazard observed by craftsman, solve himself or bring it to craft foreman;

(b)   If not solved, bring it to the craft steward, who should correct the problem with the job superintendent;

(c)   If not solved, bring it to the business agent, who will resolve the issue with the project manager;

(d)   If still not corrected, bring it to the local building trades council;

(e)   If still not changed, file formal complaint with OSHA office;

(f)   If still not resolved, bring the case before the Secretary of Labor through the appropriate area, regional, or national union office.

A construction company itself must have a similar process for its workers to make suggestions. And the process must be clearly understood by all its employees.

4. INCENTIVES   Field management and supervisors should be evaluated for promotions and salary increases in terms of safety record as well as productivity and cost. This will give them more incentive to carry out safety policies set up by the company.

5. SAFETY COST   The cost accounting system should be adjusted to encourage safety by allocating safety costs to a company account and accident costs to a project account. Conventionally, project safety costs are treated as project indirect costs, while the main office keeps a special account to take care of all costs resulting from accidents. This approach can make the project management reluctant to spend money in safety programs in order to keep the project within budget. If this new system is adopted, the project manager will be more conscious of accident prevention, since if any accident occurs, the cost will be charged to his project, thus making his performance a poor one. This strategy, when used with the evaluation method described in (4), will have tremendous influence on the middle-level management's attitude toward safety.

14.6.2 Physical Approach

In physical aspects, a contractor can improve his company's safety performance according to the following guidelines:

1. New workers should be given a safety orientation. Studies have shown that new workers usually cause more accidents, especially in their first few months on a new jobsite. If given an orientation, the accident rate can be reduced.

2. The contractor must study in advance for every project the possible accidents that the proposed construction methods, procedures, and equipment may create. Then, an accident prevention plan should be devised to take care of those potential accidents. Table 14.1 is an example of analyzing possible accidents. The results of the analysis should be explained to workers, especially in orientations for new workers.

3. The contractor should enforce the use of approved equipment for personal protection: hard hats, seat belts, gloves, and so forth, as required by specific operations.

4. The contractor should integrate safety programs with other programs, such as scheduling and budgeting, during preplanning procedures. This will help to identify possible accidents inherent in the work to be done, to suggest remedial training if necessary, to assure that proper tools and equipment will be available for the work, and to verify that the methods selected are safe, according to required standards.

5. Periodical checking of tools and equipment is necessary to make sure that they are well maintained.

6. Conducting periodical safety meetings, such as tool box meetings, to provide safety education on the job. The craft foremen play the most important roles in this process. They can advise workers, according to their acts in the past few days, on what kinds of accidents are inherent in their acts.

7. Seek and obtain full cooperation from all subcontractors on the project. Many accidents occur just because of lack of coordination. This type of accident can be avoided easily by some administrative efforts.

Table 14.1.   Processing Hazards

Operational Step	Equipment and Materials	Potential Hazardous Condition	Potential Human Error	Potential Accident	Accident Probability Estimate			Effect	Haz. Class.	Applicable Standard
					1	2	3			
1. Erection of engineered shoring system	Crawler Crane app. 65 ton w/150' of boom and rigging	Failure of rig or equipment (slings, cable, belts, brakes, etc.)	Not properly maintained or inspected slings, cable, belts, etc. improper/lack of signals Unqualified operator	Dropping load on adjacent ground or people		x		Death, injury, property damage	IV	1926.550(a) and (b) 1926.51 and Tables H-1 through H-20
		Unstable placement of rig	Lack of mats	Shift of load or entire rig	x			Death, injury, property damage	III	1926.550(b) (2)
			Improper placement of crane on base capable of support	Losing load and possible fall	x			Death, injury, property damage	III	None
			Working too close to excavations, trenches, tunnels, non-compacted areas	Overturning rig	x			Death, injury, property damage	IV	1926.651(q) and (S)
		Swing radius of rotating superstructure	No physical barrier or observer provided for protection to rear end of crane	Crushing individual between superstructure and cats.			x	Death, injury	III	1926.550(a) (9)
	Crawler Crane	Operating close to overhead power lines or other existing lines, equipment structures	Miscalculation of proper working area Malfunction of operator signalman or equipment Improper positioning of crane	Shock hazard, fire			x	Death, injury, damage to equipment or structures from boom, cable, load contact with energy source	III	1926.550(a) (15)

Operational Step	Equipment and Materials	Potential Hazardous Condition	Potential Human Error	Potential Accident	Accident Probability Estimate			Effect	Haz. Class	Applicable Standard
					1	2	3			
		Overload and stressing crane beyond working limits	Improper calculation of load weight or use of damaged or insufficient rigging	Losing load and having it fall on adjacent ground or people	x			Death, injury, property damage	IV	1926.550(a) 1 through (f) (16) (b) 1926.251 and Table H-1 H-20
	Tubular frame shoring (joists, deck, etc.	Using incorrect size shieve/cable arrangement	Not inspecting crane before lifting load	Shieve failure— cable failure			x	Death, injury, damage to crane, structure, etc.	IV	
		improper erection or foundation contact	Not following design or specifications	Failure of system, possible collapse under load	x			Death, injury, property damage	IV	1926.700(e)
		damaged equipment or material	Not inspecting equipment or material before use	Failure of system, possible collapse under load	x			Death, injury, property damage	II	1926.700(e)
		material falling off deck	Lack of protective screening	Material falling on individuals below			x	Death, injury	II	1926.451(a)(6)
		erection fall hazard	individual not secured	Fall of individual doing erection			x	Death, injury	III	None
		working deck on open side	Lack of perimeter guarding	Fall of workmen on deck			x	Death, injury	III	1926.500(d) and (b), 1926.451(a) (4) and (5)
		tripping hazards on deck	Tools and material not properly stored or secured	Tripping and falling of workmen on deck or to level below			x	Death, injury	III	None
		Protruding rebar below	Not protecting workmen or eliminating hazard	Impalement			x	Death, injury	III	None
	Stairways (metal erected)	Damaged equipment, improper erection or support	Faulty erection, equipment or material	Failure or collapse of stairway	x			Death, injury	IV	1926.501

Table 14.1. *(continued)*

Operational Step	Equipment and Materials	Potential Hazardous Condition	Potential Human Error	Potential Accident	Accident Probability Estimate			Effect	Haz. Class.	Applicable Standard
					1	2	3			
2. Erection of formwork		Debris, materials, tripping hazards	Tools, materials, leads, etc., not properly secured or stored	Tripping and possible fall of workmen			x	Death, injury	II	1926.501(c)(d)(e)
	Crane (see previous notes)	Material conveyance								
	Formwork	Damaged equipment or material—improper erection	Lack of inspection or disposal of damaged material	Failure of system at high elevaton; fall hazard	x			Death, injury, property damage	III	1926.700(a) 1926.701
		Workmen performing erection above deck	Not tying off when securing forms	Fall hazard			x	Death, injury	III	None
	Tie rods	Protruding rods from formwork	Not providing protective guards or cutting rods off short	Workers tripping and falling on rods			x	Injury, death remote	II	None
	Curing Compounds (spray on forms)	Compounds highly combustible	Application of material in presence of source of ignition	Spray atomizes—highly flammable			x	Injury, fire	II	None
3. Set reinforcing steel (including misc. metals, dowels, etc.	Crane (see previous notes)	Material conveyance								
	Reinforcing Steel	Walking hazard created by grid and tools and equipment on grid	Improper or unstable working surface	Worker falling onto or through grid			x	Death, injury	III	1926.700(b)(2)
	Welding or cutting of misc. metals	Briefly: ventilation, eye protection, fire prevention, grounding, etc.	Lack of inspection, improper or damaged equipment, use by unqualified personnel, etc.	Fire, flash, eye damage, explosion, etc.			x	Death, injury, property damage	III	1926.350 through .354

14.6.3   Behavioral Approach

Studies conducted by insurance companies disclosed that more than 80% of all accidents are results of workers' unsafe acts, only about 10% are results from failure of equipment or improper procedures. Apparently, this is the most potential aspect in improving safety performance. Also, the behavior of managers from every level has significant influence on workers' safety performance. Guidelines, drawn for all levels of construction personnel, to follow are

1.   The top management, while visiting jobsite or meeting in the main office, should talk about safety in the same way as they talk about schedules and costs. This will make their subordinates understand that safety is as important to them as costs and schedules. Also, the top management should give workers timely appraisal for good safety performance. Studies have shown that the more the management show their concern for workers, the better safety performance can be expected.

2.   The project manager and the superintendent should not place unnecessary pressure on foremen, such as overemphasizing the importance of meeting the estimated budget and schedule. Usually, this will make the foremen choose unacceptable methods that often lead to higher possibility of accidents. If the workers' performances are not satisfactory, the project manager should analyze the problem with the foremen rather than just telling them to work harder. The competition between crews should not be encouraged.

3.   Craft foremen are the key persons in behavioral approaches to better safety, because they are the persons who have daily contact with workers. They are also the persons in the best position to detect workers' abnormal behavior. Since people tend to act differently if they are psychologically unbalanced, these observations provide excellent information for accident prevention. People with some of the following characteristics are more likely to be involved in accidents and should be given special attention:

(a)   Persons with abnormal absenteeism.

(b)   Persons with problems in family or involvement in legal processes.

(c)   Persons who require unusually more supervision to produce normally.

(d)   Persons whose personal appearance or acts change.

(e)   Persons working in isolated areas.

(f)   Persons making lots of complaints about situations.

(g)   Persons who act strangely to attract attention.

4. The foremen, along with project managers and superintendents, should try to create and maintain good relationships between members of craft crews. If workers have pleasant relationships with each other, they tend to be more concerned about their co-workers' safety. Also, the good relationships will help reduce labor turnover so that the higher accident rate associated with new labor can be avoided.

14.6.4 Economic Incentives

Owners as well as contractors should bear in mind and take into consideration the economic incentives benefited by them due to safety at the work site. If a complete estimate could be taken into account for the cost of their "safety program" as a percentage of direct field labor costs, their estimates would result in some positive return for perceived dollars spent on safety programs.

The most obvious financial benefit is the savings realized because of accidents that do not happen at the jobsite; that is, the reduced cost of insurance due to the lack of accidents at the jobsite. Lower insurance premiums means lower bids, which is one key economic incentive to the contractor.

The contractor should also have some financial incentive for his workers due to their safety performances. This creates an air of perseverance on their part to learn, know, practice, and strive toward a very good safety practice at the jobsite. This would result in a better working relationship with the contractor and his workers, and over the years, the contractor would gain recognition for his company's safety policy and thereby profit from the positive returns for accidents that do not happen at his jobsites.

15

Labor Productivity

15.1 INTRODUCTION

Productivity is theoretically defined as a ratio between outputs and inputs. According to the Bureau of Labor Statistics, a measure of productivity is more specifically an expression of the physical or real volume of goods and services (outputs), related to the physical or real quantities of inputs (labor, capital, energy). In the context of the construction industry, the output is the structure or facility that is built or some component thereof. The major inputs into the construction process include manpower, materials, equipment, management, energy, and capital.

The emerging role for the construction manager is that of productivity improvement expert. It is not enough to just get the job done. Today's large, complex construction projects must be done efficiently. The key to improvement is to understand what factors affect productivity, identify opportunities for improvement, and then take effective action. Opportunities for improvement may be due to deficiencies on a particular project or new techniques that are now available and applicable to the project. The manager establishes the environment for good labor productivity. He needs to consider how improvements in one area, such as information availability, may influence other areas.

The basic equation for determining labor cost is established as

$$\text{Labor cost} = \frac{(\text{Quantity of work})}{(\text{Productivity})} \times (\text{Cost per unit of time})$$

Both the quantity of work to be performed and the crew cost per hour can be established with considerable accuracy. The real variable in the equation is productivity. Thus an understanding of the labor costing process is an understanding of productivity.

This chapter focuses on productivity factors and their measurements as well as productivity improvement in general.

15.2 PRODUCTIVITY FACTORS[1]

The manager who chooses to lead in the area of productivity finds himself confronted with many different subjects. There are many factors that affect performance. Productivity factors include a wide range of subjects, such as hours worked per day, open shop labor, and new earth-moving equipment. It should be helpful to identify and then categorize the various factors. This categorization is done in such a way that the manager can use the list in analyzing his own opportunities. The list may serve as a reminder of subjects to consider when asked, "What are the factors that affect productivity?"

Labor productivity factors can be divided into three groups. The worker must "want to" do a good job, "know how to" do the job, and be "allowed to" do a good job. Management controls most of the constraints on all three categories. The "want to" factors are goals, which include job content, interpersonal atmosphere, compensation, working conditions, physical capability, and society. The "know how to" factors are education and training. The "allow to" factors are organization, raw materials, tools, information, and time to act. Figure 15.1 shows a listing of these labor productivity factors.

Improvements of the "allow to" factors are a fruitful area for management attention. Information availability has an especially important impact on a worker's productivity. A crew of highly motivated, well-trained, well-supplied men can remain completely idle without information.

---

1. This section is based on Lynn D. Dorsey in Kern (71:225–231).

Figure 15.1. Labor Productivity Factors.

WANT TO	KNOW HOW TO	ALLOW TO
Goals	Education	Organization
Job content	Training	Raw materials
Interpersonal atmosphere		Tools
Compensation		Information
Working conditions		Time to act
Physical capability		
Society		

Adapted from Lynn D. Dorsey in Kern (71:226).

The crew must know what to do before they can even get started. Manpower needs to be allocated properly to project tasks to be most effective. The task should be well defined, which implies good design information being available. Other associated tasks should not constrain the task at hand.

Figure 15.2 identifies many of the causes of low productivity. It can be seen that many of these detracting factors are of a type that good management can eliminate or ameliorate. Obviously, all nonproductive time could never be eliminated. So, what is the practical limit of direct work time that can be achieved? There is no exact answer, of course, but research has suggested that it can approach 55%. If true, there is ample room for productivity improvement among most labor crews.

What are some of the actions that management can take? Time lost to workers while instructions are being given or while they are waiting are prime targets for management improvement actions. If a company develops and maintains a manual of construction procedures that are standard throughout the firm, the necessity for new and detailed instructions for each work item can be greatly reduced. Such standard operating procedures would outline the actual methods for accomplishing all common tasks, whether it be warehousing of materials or the pouring of concrete in a slab. Waiting time can be reduced by better scheduling of work to ensure that the labor, materials, and equipment are available simultaneously and one element is not waiting on the other. Efficient site layout is important. The area for check-in and check-out (brass alley) of employees should be located to minimize travel time to and from work locations. Laydown areas for construction materials should be as close as possible to place of use to prevent costly movement time or double handling. Construction water, air, gas, and other service lines should be

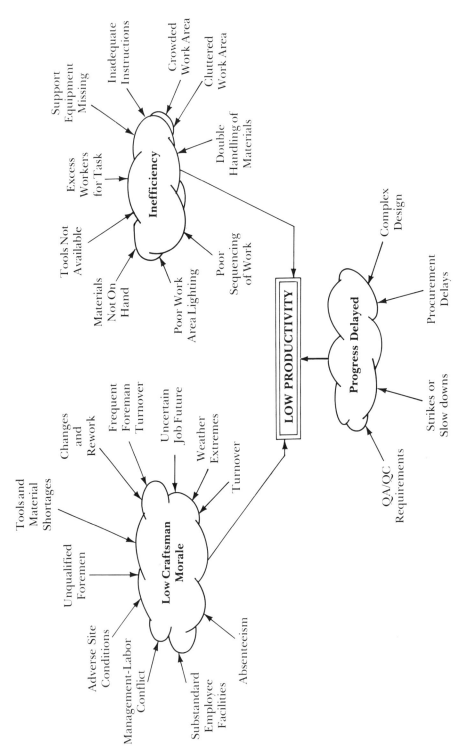

Figure 15.2. Low Productivity Problem. Adapted from Neil (101:124).

located for quick and easy access. These are but a few of the many management actions possible.

15.3 PRODUCTIVITY MEASUREMENT IN THE CONSTRUCTION INDUSTRY

Construction productivity can be measured in different ways. The particular form adopted depends on the type of information desired. Measuring construction productivity is not an easy task. Because of tremendous diversities in type, size, and quality of construction products as well as variations in the resources utilized in their production, it is difficult to find a homogenous measure for the outputs. The different inputs are also measured in different ways and expressed in different units. Their quantities vary according to the type, size, quality, and geographical location of the structure. In order to limit the potential problems created by the heterogeneity of the outputs, productivity statistics for the construction industry are generally categorized by similarities of project characteristics, essentially, construction type, labor and material requirements, geographical location, total costs and factor costs. Most of the methods that have been used to measure construction productivity are based on labor productivity, cost or price data, profits, or models. Suffice to say that neither of these systems has provided a satisfactory and reliable analysis of construction productivity.

1. LABOR PRODUCTIVITY   Labor productivity is the most available data because labor productivity is the easiest to measure. It is normally expressed in man-hours. It is calculated as man-hours per unit of production, and the total man-hours expended in production. The latter includes direct and indirect man-hours. Direct man-hours are defined by the Bureau of Labor Statistics as including all man-hours involved in actual production and included in the accounts procedure as direct labor costs. Indirect man-hours are also defined as other man-hours involved in production except general administration, office engineering, and sales.

The major shortcoming of labor productivity is its inability to indicate the performance of other factors. The impact of other inputs, such as equipment, work methods, and management on output as well as on labor performance itself, is obscured. Thus labor productivity does not accurately measure labor contribution in the production process and offer a satisfactory assessment of changes in productivity. Changes in productivity are caused by a variety of factors and not only labor. For labor productivity to be representative of the total input, it would be necessary for the labor time involved in production to be so large, in relation to the other inputs, that changes in labor input would be the only means of appreciably influencing the level of output.

2. COST AND PRICE DATA   Financial measures are also commonly used to evaluate total productivity. Some of the most discussed methods of measurement are based on the use of cost and price data. These methods include price per unit of output, total costs per unit of output, prime costs per unit of output, and labor costs per unit of output. The major reason for using construction costs for measuring productivity is because the total costs of construction products can be integrated in spite of differences in their complexity, size, type, and other components.

The shortcomings of cost and price data include the inappropriateness of aggregating the costs of different structures irrespective of differences in their nature. Cost data does not put into consideration the variations in total production costs due to differences in type, size, construction method, location, labor productivity, and so forth. For example, labor productivity varies with type of construction, geographical location, and construction methods. The differences are reflected in the total project costs. Material and equipment costs are also influenced by many factors. Cost data obscures individual impact of the input and the effects of changes in the utilization of inputs on the level of total costs. Costs data, therefore, do not provide reliable guides to the true effectiveness with which resources are used.

Another limitation of costs data is that they are based on the costs of both the products and the factors of production. However, their values fluctuate individually with the economy. Price movements do influence resource utilization. Costs per unit of output are poor measures of intertemporal changes in resources utilization.

3. PROFITABILITY   Profit is another financial measure of productivity. It is defined as total profits or profits per unit of output. The major problem with this approach is the difficulty in defining the relationship between changes in the level of profits of an organization and its productivity. Variations both in costs of inputs and the price of products cause distortions in the relationship between profits and productivity. Except in a competitive tender in which the winning tender price is assumed as the absolute value of construction, it is difficult to determine accurately the profit realized by the contractor. Under little or no competition, the tender price may be higher. This will cause an increase in profits even though there has not been any increase in productivity. In fact, it is possible that productivity has decreased. Fierce bidding competition may force a decrease in profits even though productivity might have increased. Such inconsistencies in the relationships between profits and productivity make it imperative to investigate the causes for the changes in profits, which might be or not be due to better utilization of resources.

4. HIERARCHY MODEL OF CONSTRUCTION PRODUCTIVITY

Different institutions and individuals have presented other productivity models to measure construction industry productivity. Unfortunately, none have adequately addressed all the factors associated with measuring total factor productivity for the construction industry. Most of the models have concentrated mainly on on-site construction operations. The hierarchy model of construction productivity developed by Kellogg et al., in the article "Hierarchy Models of Construction Productivity," proposed a wholistic model that could be the basis of a cognitive plan to solve the problems of pulling together all the elements of the construction industry and permit the "total study" of productivity in the industry.

The hierarchy model addresses the productivity of the construction industry at five industry levels: (1) policy formation, (2) program management, (3) planning and design, (4) project management and administration, and (5) on-site construction. These levels are defined as macro-macro, macro, macro-micro, micro, and micro-micro levels, respectively. The quantities and impacts of decisions and actions are greatest at the macro-macro level.

The macro-macro level deals with policy definition issues that are primarily considerations at the federal government or other national forums. At the macro level, policy interpretation takes place as specific programs and criteria are developed and the scope of projects is defined. At the macro-micro level, professionals interpret the project in terms of specifics and determine, to a significant extent, the cost of physical construction through the choice of materials, dates of commencement and completion, selection of construction details, and so forth. At the micro level, the range of choices is narrowed by the project implementation team who makes choices of suppliers and contractors, performs detailed scheduling and planning of labor and equipment, and other decisions. Finally, at the micro-micro level, only effective employment of labor and equipment offers any hope of improving productivity as the project is executed.

By defining the primary components at each level, their impacts on total factor productivity can be evaluated, measured, and controlled. This will facilitate systematic productivity improvement and cost effectiveness of the project and also measurement of total productivity of the industry. Reduction of the construction end product into its basic component makes it possible that productivity factors can be identified and analyzed under basic generic headings for all of the major construction end products. By identifying common elements, similar operations can be compared from one construction product area to another. That is, the cost per square foot of the concrete forms for bridges, hydropower, houses, commercial buildings, institutional buildings, and so forth, can be compared with one another.

The major contribution of the hierarchy model is that it can be used to define and measure all the elements and factors that influence total productivity at each level of the construction process. The effects of the external elements impinging on construction productivity can also be assessed.

The major shortcoming of the model is that it failed to develop alternative measurement parameters for construction productivity. More research and study is necessary to generate reliable measurement methods that would eliminate the deficiencies of the existing methods that are based on traditional methods.

15.4   JOB PRODUCTIVITY ADJUSTMENT FACTORS

This section discusses a number of conditions that affect labor productivity. Each discussion also presents a procedure for determining an adjustment factor for that condition. Ultimately, these adjustment factors will be tabulated and totaled for each project being analyzed and then used in the following equation:

$$\text{Productivity multiplier} = \frac{\text{Area Productivity Index}}{1 + \sum \text{Adjustment factors}}$$

The adjustment factors suggested in these paragraphs cannot be considered as rules. They are "ball park" factors only and must be adjusted by each contractor as he or she gains experience. Additional conditions, not discussed in this text, may be foreseen that could affect productivity. It is the estimator's job to identify these conditions and assign an adjustment using his or her best judgment. The adjustment factors discussed in this section include factors relating to (a) project type (e.g., project complexity, quality assurance/quality control), (b) project location (e.g., weather, labor availability, jobsite congestion), and (c) projection organization (e.g., overtime, management organization, project schedule, and schedule control).

1. PROJECT COMPLEXITY   It is relatively easy to draw a straight line or a perfect circle as compared to a complex curve. Similarly, with construction work it is much easier to handle the commonplace construction tasks as compared to those associated with exotic construction. Estimators normally have considerable data on the ability of their company's crews to form a standard straight foundation wall. But if this wall is of unusual configuration, that productivity data is completely misleading since much more time must be spent per square foot in building an alignment of unique forms. There also may be features of the project that involve construction operations never performed by the estimator's

Table 15.1.   Design Complexity Adjustment Factors

PROJECT TYPE	ADJUSTMENT
Standard type project for firm	0.00
Project design complex. Unique work packages.	0.1–0.50

Adapted from Neil (101:131).

company. A new or one-of-a-kind operation on a construction project will be done with a lower average productivity rate than if done for the second, fifth, or fiftieth time. It is all a matter of the learning curve, which is based upon the well-known fact that a person's ability to do a given job improves with each repetition and that the time required for each repetition decreases with the number of repetitions.

Much of the information in the estimating group's data base reflects repeated experience. The time spent on the first effort in each case is certainly more than that for the last, and the overall average productivity would exceed that of the first effort. On the other hand, some of the information in the data base could be that for unique operations, those that were executed once and not repeated again. It should not be too difficult for an estimating group with experience in a firm to know which applies.

In considering the productivity of a crew that will repeat an operation many times in a project, no productivity adjustment would be applied if the data base reflects experience crews. In other words, for a standard job for the construction firm, there is no adjustment. However, if a new project is extremely complex in comparison to the firm's past experience, or contains largely one-of-a-kind work packages, an adjustment factor should be applied. The amount of adjustment should be weighted to reflect the percentage of the project that contains the unusual work packages. The range is given in Table 15.1.

If a type of structure is repeated one or more times on a project and the structures are built in succession rather than concurrently, a contractor can expect greater overall productivity on the second and later structures. As a rule-of-thumb, the effort on the first structure, in terms of employee hours per unit, will be about 10% higher than on following structures.

2. QUALITY ASSURANCE/QUALITY CONTROL   If the project is subject to quality assurance control (as with nuclear safety-related construction), all affected work is subject to more frequent and stringent inspection and testing. This causes the workers to be more deliberate or frustrated in their work so their productivity is lowered. In addition, the time lost for quality control actions and preparation of QA/

QC documentation contributes to more nonproductive time for the workers. An adjustment factor of from 0.10 to 0.20 is appropriate if QA/AC control applies.

3. WEATHER FACTORS   The effect of extreme weather conditions on productivity is easy to visualize. On a hot, humid summer day, a worker will be taking frequent breaks to wipe his or her brow or get a cool drink of water, and sweat-drenched clothing will cling to his or her body. Under extreme cold conditions, the worker must have heavy gloves and more layers of clothing, all of which will tend to impede efficiency, and he or she frequently will be seeking the shelter of a warming house or bonfire. Actually, a human being can work without degradation of efficiency over a broad range of temperature and humidity conditions. However, once extremes are encountered, rapid degradation can be expected. Figure 15.3 shows a series of curves that represent adjustment factors to be applied to compensate for efficiency degradation due to temperature and humidity. Note that one enters the chart with the temperature (or chill factor, in case of colder temperatures) and the relative humidity, and then, by interpolation, reads the appropriate adjustment factor.

The factors shown in this figure are applicable to workers performing manual labor without particular exertion (such as electrical installation). The factors should be increased by up to 30% if great exertion (lifting heavy materials) or strong mental concentration (arc welding) is required.

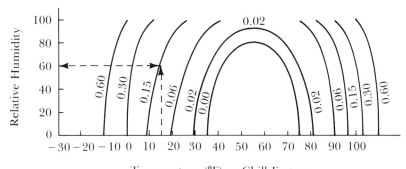

Example

Temperature = 15°F
Relative Humidity = 60%
Adjustment Factor = 0.14

Figure 15.3.   Temperature/Humidity Adjustment Factors. Adapted from Neil (101:132).

Since most projects of any size will involve a number of months or even years to complete, it is important that an estimator apply an adjustment factor for temperature and humidity using a weighted average.

If conditions outside the normal (0.0) range are seldom encountered, it would be appropriate to ignore any adjustment. Another cautionary note is in order. The conditions considered are those that will be encountered in the area where work is actually performed. Thus if a large building under construction is enclosed during the winter in plastic film, and space heaters are employed to protect workers inside, there would be no degradation of performance even though outside conditions are extremely cold.

4. LABOR AVAILABILITY   If labor is plentiful in an area, a contractor will have a better chance of hiring the more skilled individuals in each craft since competition for work will be high. Also, the workers will tend to be more productive on the job since they know they can be replaced. The overall productivity will tend to decrease as the size of the work force enlarges on a job, or more jobs in the area become available to absorb all available labor. These conditions particularly apply to the large contractors with work forces that exceed several hundred. The small contractor would probably experience less productivity fluctuation during the life of his or her projects, but the overall productivity of the small contractor's crews can suffer if he or she is competing for labor with large contractors on nearby projects. The large contractor often will offer a higher wage, some extra benefits, or job continuity that the small contractor cannot provide. Construction labor loyalty is transitory; therefore, such attraction may cause a movement of labor to the larger contractor. Thus the small contractor may be left with lower quality workers and frequent worker movement, both conditions lowering overall crew productivity. To develop an adjustment factor for labor availability, a ratio is first established between size of qualified labor force available and labor force required. Once this ratio is calculated, and adjustment factor can be obtained from the curve in Figure 15.4.

5. JOBSITE CONGESTION   It is no surprise that it is easier to build a building in an open field on the edge of town than it is to sandwich it between two existing buildings on Main Street. In other words, jobsite congestion has a considerable effect on productivity, since people, machines, and material are competing for use of the same space. This problem can apply to total jobs or to parts of a job. In the case of an industrial plant being built in a rural area, adequate perimeter space is generally available for all administrative and construction activities. But some structures of the project are complex networks of piping and electrical lines that stagger the imagination. An estimator cannot assume that a welder, pipe fitter, or electrician can perform a given task in a confined

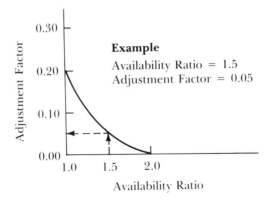

Example

Normal productivity of a crew under excellent conditions of labor availability is 100 units/day. What productivity should be expected if the Availability Ratio is 1.5?

Answer

$$\frac{1}{1 + 0.05} \times (100 \text{ units/day}) = 45 \text{ units/day}$$

Figure 15.4.   Labor Availability Factor. Adapted from Neil (101:133).

space at the same rate the task could be done in an open space. The adjustment factors for various degrees of congestion are given in Table 15.2.

6.   OVERTIME   An employee who knows he or she is going to work overtime will reduce his productivity throughout both the normal period of work and the overtime period. This is a psychological effect but nonetheless very real in its effect. A normal work day is eight hours and

Table 15.2.   Work Space Adjustment Factors

CONDITION	ADJUSTMENT FACTOR
Adequate crew work space	0.00
Crowded. Approximately one-half space desired.	0.15
Very congested. Approximately one-third space desired.	0.30

Adapted from Neil (101:134).

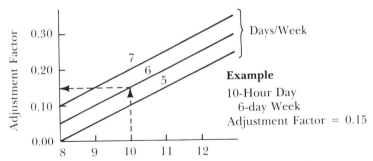

Figure 15.5. Overtime Adjustment Factors. Adapted from Neil (101:135).

a normal work week is five days. Thus work beyond these normal periods will cause an overall reduction of productivity. The adjustment factor to account for this loss of productivity is found by reference to Figure 15.5.

An estimator should adjust the average productivity figures for overtime only if that overtime is used heavily. On some projects, the nature of the work being performed calls for considerable scheduled overtime. This is particularly true on projects that are weather-sensitive (such as earth moving), on projects in areas of the world with short construction seasons (such as Arctic regions), or on any project with no-later-than completion dates. There are also those projects on which the overtime is only casual (or spot); for example, overtime would be used to ensure that a freshly placed concrete slab is finished before it sets. When overtime is casual, the productivity is not adjusted, but any adjustment will be made to the hourly cost of the employee or a lump sum will be added to the estimate to reflect the anticipated added cost of casual overtime. Estimators should not necessarily make productivity adjustments in proportion to the anticipated amount of premium pay for the project, since, on some projects, premium pay is based upon the time of day or week and not upon whether such time represents working time in excess of eight hours per day or forty hours per week. In other words, a worker on a late shift or whose five-day work week includes Saturday may receive premium pay, but the worker is not actually working overtime and the productivity should be considered normal.

7. PROJECT/CONSTRUCTION MANAGEMENT ORGANIZA-TION   The ability of management to control the project can vary, even within the same firm. Another factor that can affect productivity is the organizational structure employed by the client to administer the overall project. If the various management responsibilities are split, overlapping, and poorly defined among the client, the design element, and the construction element, there are bound to be conflicts, omissions, and delays in construction. These are much less likely with an organizational structure in which responsibility and authority are clearly defined and allocated.

Evaluation of a potential project/construction management structure is difficult. Those construction firms that have been in business a number of years will have served a number of clients and will have built from designs provided by different architect-engineering firms. They will have found that each client and each A-E firm has its own personality, the character of which can affect job progress. Contractors may have had such unfavorable experiences with some clients and A-E firms that their work will no longer be considered. But, this past experience will give the contractor a feel for the general effect of management form of project productivity so that unfavorable situations can be flagged in advance and appropriate adjustments made.

The following are some specific management organization features that should be closely examined and evaluated for their effects on productivity.

a) ACCESSIBILITY OF DESIGNERS   It must be assumed that there will be change orders during the course of a project due to errors, deletions, or additions. If the responsible design agency maintains a staff at the project site or nearby with change authority, responsiveness will be greater than would be the case if all authority were located in a distant city. Any lack of responsiveness on the part of the design group can cause project delays with attendant impact on productivity.

b) FIRST-TIME EXPERIENCE FOR PROJECT/CONSTRUC-TION MANAGEMENT GROUP   As discussed under project complexity, there is a learning curve that applies to all repeat operations. The learning curve also applies to management. If this is a first-time experience on this type of project for a management group, they will do a lot of expensive learning. The added expense will come about through the lowered productivity of a confused and frustrated work force that is subjected to poor decisions or indecisions. An experienced group will have fully developed procedures that have been refined through experience. In fact, the larger firms will have all such procedures stated in writing.

Table 15.3 gives suggested adjustment factors to be used based upon the project/construction management situation.

8. CONTROL OF PROJECT SCHEDULE   It is assumed that any contractor, large or small, will use planning and scheduling procedures available and appropriate to the level of operation to assure the most efficient integration of labor, equipment, and materials. Such planning is definitely possible if the project has been fully defined, adequate labor and equipment are available, and material and installed equipment deliv-

Table 15.3.   Management Experience Adjustment Factors

SITUATION	ADJUSTMENT FACTOR
Well-coordinated, experienced management team including client, A-E, and contractor	0.00
Possibility of difficulty among client, A-E, and contractor	0.05–0.20
First-time experience for client or A-E project management elements or construction management team	0.20–0.50

Adapted from Neil (101:136).

eries can be assured when needed. For many projects, one or more of these conditions is not assured at the start of construction. On turn-key projects, engineering may find it hard to keep up with construction. This causes designs to become rushed with attendant errors, change orders, and rework. Rework is extremely demoralizing to crews, and crew productivity suffers accordingly. Procurement difficulties are another problem. Very often, key items of construction or installed equipment or construction materials will not have off-the-shelf availability or firm delivery dates. Delays of any of these items can delay an entire work force. The problem becomes compounded if a contractor is working against an established completion date because he or she can be forced into overtime conditions, or the addition of crews to the job cause congestion and subsequent loss of productivity.

A number of scheduling problems can be expected in any project. In fact, the base data used by the estimating group is for average performance during normal conditions, and average performance implies that some problems were encountered since better performances have been registered. Thus a productivity adjustment factor to reflect lack of project scheduling control should be introduced only when unusual circumstances are expected that can throw the scheduling off more than that of the average project. The adjustment factor selected is even more judgmental than some of the previous factors. Ranges are given in Table 15.4.

9.   OTHER ADJUSTMENTS   The conditions and suggested adjustment factors described thus far are among the more common possibilities. Additional conditions affecting labor productivity may certainly exist. Determination of an appropriate adjustment factor can be done using the guidelines of Table 15.5.

Table 15.4.   Scheduling Uncertainty Adjustment Factors

SCHEDULING CONDITIONS	ADJUSTMENT FACTOR
Average project, average problems scheduling constraints reasonably predictable	0.00
Some possibility of problems due to poorly defined work, materials shortages, labor strikes, deadlines, or procurement lead times	0.01–0.50

Adapted from Neil (101:137).

Table 15.5.   Adjustment Factor Rules-of-Thumb

CONDITION	ADJUSTMENT FACTOR
The condition, by itself, would tend to cut productivity in half	1.0
The condition, by itself, would tend to cut productivity by 25%	0.3
The condition, by itself, would tend to cut productivity by 10%	0.1

Adapted from Neil (101:138).

15.4.1   Establishing the Productivity Multiplier

Area Productivity Index for based area = 1.00. Area Productivity Index for new area is a function of section of nation or world and union or open shop.

$$\text{Productivity multiplier} = \frac{\text{Area Productivity Index}}{1 + \Sigma \text{ Adjustment factors}}$$

Adjustment factors include

1. Overtime
2. Labor availability
3. Jobsite congestion
4. Control of project schedule
5. Project complexity

6. Project/construction management organization
7. Average climatic conditions
8. Quality assurance/quality control and
9. All other factors

SAMPLE PROBLEM:

An industrial contractor based in Houston normally can expect his crews to produce one hundred units per day under normal forty-hour work weeks and other conditions. He is preparing a bid on a new process plant in the same area of the Gulf Coast as another large plant under construction by a competitor. Unfortunately, the area is relatively remote from Houston and the competition for quality labor is extremely high. The personnel department estimates that it will be necessary to hire two out of every three applicants to staff the job, under these conditions, and assuming the crew will work ten hours a day and six days a week, what productivity can be expected on the new job?

SOLUTION:

Availability = 1.5
From Figure 15.4 Adjustment factor = 0.05
From Figure 15.5 Adjustment factor for ten hours
a day, six days a week = 0.15

$$\text{Productivity multiplier} = \frac{1}{1 + (.05 + .15)}$$

$$= 1/1.2$$

$$= .83$$

$$\text{Productivity per day} = \frac{(.83 \times 100)}{8} \times 10 = 103.7 \text{ units}$$

15.5 PRODUCTIVITY IMPROVEMENT OPPORTUNITIES

15.5.1 Improvement Opportunities

What can be done to improve productivity? The answer to this question may take two forms. One is that a problem may be identified and then corrective action taken. A second answer is that improved techniques or tools may be identified and applied to the project. The emerging role of the construction manager is to be more than a problem solver. He must also maintain an awareness of the state of the art of the many productivity improvement techniques and be an advocate for their use where appropriate.

One of the rapidly changing aspects of construction management is in the area of information processing. Computer processing of large amounts of data makes it practical to manage projects on a more detailed level. In reviewing the labor productivity factor list, this opportunity can improve productivity in two categories. Improved information "allows" the worker to perform more efficiently. He is not constrained by lack of data on what to do or how he is performing. The effective use of an information data base to establish goals and feedback of performance also helps motivation or "want to" factors. Also, the problem of starting a task and then stopping part way through due to lack of information is minimized.

15.5.2   Tracking Improvement Opportunity

Construction tracking can be done at several levels of detail. Management summaries are needed to show overall progress in terms of cost and schedule. Computer systems providing information at this level are often based on critical path method (CPM) schedules and large blocks of work identified as construction cost codes. A computer with a large computational capability may be needed to handle the many calculations needed. These management systems are updated by a quantity surveyor gathering data on progress, summarizing it, and then putting this data in the computer. One of his problems in supplying data is to determine percent complete. This same problem occurs in reporting construction costs. A typical cost code is a collection of labor and material costs for a group of items. Again, the quantity surveyor must determine how much quantity has been earned during the reporting period.

In both the cost and schedule example, the accuracy of the percent of complete determination is the key to measuring project productivity. Performance factors, calculated as earned divided by actual man-hours or dollars, will be unrealistic if the "earned" quantity is not correct. What is needed for effective construction tracking is a method to collect and manipulate data on a detail level and make the percent complete calculation more accurate. This calculated quantity could then be fed into either the project CPM schedule or the project cost report for preparation of the necessary management reports.

15.5.3   Measuring Percent Complete

What type of system is needed for measurement of percent complete? Ideally, the system would be easy to use and would eliminate the need for a judgmental determination of progress. One needs a system capable of listing the detailed activities that make up a cost code or a CPM network activity and then collecting status information at the detail level. These lists are available as a normal product of the engineering design effort. Examples on an industrial project are the equipment list, piping line list, electrical and instrument cable schedule, and instrument index. What is

Figure 15.6. Pipe Spool Activities and Earned Percent Complete.

ACTIVITY	PERCENT EARNED
Spool received	0
Hanger installed	10
Spool in place	35
Weld out	35
Trim out	10
Test and flush	10
TOTAL	100

Adapted from Lynn D. Dorsey in Kern (71:229).

needed is to match the items on the list with the appropriate cost of activity codes, assign man-hours to each item, and develop a data gathering procedure so the completed item can "earn" its appropriate number of man-hours.

The task of assigning man-hours to each item can be simplified by taking advantage of the computer's ability to read a matrix of man-hours per unit. In the case of piping, this can be done in two steps. First, identify each spool by specification, diameter, and length, and then set up a matrix of bogey man-hour rates for each diameter and specification of spool and assign an earned percentage complete for each. Figure 15.6 shows a list of pipe spool activities and earned percent complete.

15.5.4   Status Reporting

Once the computer data base has been established, the main problem is to collect status information. In order to maximize productivity, the goal is to have each person on the project team contribute to the completion of the project. The overhead staff can be kept smaller by having the quantity surveyor's data collection task performed by the line supervision actually responsible for the work. The status of each item on a list can be updated. Figure 15.7 shows a typical data collection form for piping status. A list of the activities to be done for each spool can be printed by the computer. This computer printout can be given to the field each week with the instructions to circle the "X" for items completed. The form can then be used for data entry to the computer by typing the data for each activity. The updated printout for the next week will show the date of items completed previously, the calculated percent complete for the spool, and a matrix of "X"'s ready for status circles.

The same type of programs and procedures as described for piping can be used for the other disciplines. An example of the activities to be

Figure 15.7. Piping Status (Example).

SPEC & LINE #	SPOOL	DIAM	LENGTH	REC'D	HGR 10%	IN PLC 35%	WELD OUT 35%	TRIM OUT 10%	TEST 10%	PERCENT CMPL'T
AM-3110-2	A	2.5	11.5	2-15	X	X	X	X	X	
	B	2.5	11.5		X	X	X	X	X	
	C	2.5	11.5		X	X	X	X	X	
WWC-3007-1	A	16.0	9.0	3-18	4-15	4-20	X	X	X	45
	B	8.0	15.0	3-18	X	X	X	X	X	

Adapted from Lynn D. Dorsey in Kern (71:229).

Figure 15.8.   Activities to Be Tracked.

Instruments—List by Loop Number

1.	Instrument description	5.	Cable terminated at instrument
2.	Pneumatic tube installed	6.	Cable terminated at source
3.	Conduit installed	7.	Check-out
4.	Cable pulled		

Mechanical—List by Equipment Number

1.	Set baseplates and equipment	5.	Final align motor
2.	Align motor	6.	Final align reducer
3.	Align gear reducer	7.	Attach belts, couplings, accessories
4.	Grout equipment base		

Electrical—List by Cable Number

1.	Install tray or conduit	4.	Terminate "to" location
2.	Cable pulled	5.	Check-out
3.	Terminate "from" location		

Adapted from Lynn D. Dorsey in Kern (71:229).

tracked for instruments, mechanical equipment, and electrical cables are shown in Figure 15.8.

15.6   PRODUCTIVITY IMPROVEMENT

Improving the accuracy of reporting percent complete does not necessarily improve productivity. This information must be summarized to a cost code level, combined with time-card information on man-hours expended, and then used to calculate a performance factor (PF). A PF of 1 means the work is progressing at the estimated rate. A PF of less than 1 means that the work is progressing slower than estimated and may be an indication of labor productivity. A low PF should be used as a signal for management to analyze the situation and take appropriate action. The chart showing the factors that affect labor productivity may give the manager some ideas on improvement options. A flow chart showing the productivity measurement cycle is shown in Figure 15.9.

The advantage of tracking installation status at the detail level becomes evident as the project nears completion. Prior to start-up, each piece of equipment, pipe, cable, and instrument must be checked and noted as complete. The term "punch list" is used to describe the list of items that must be completed as an area nears start-up. The tracking system used for gathering percent complete information is, in effect, a giant punch list. To make the list more usable for commissioning, it is useful to identify the items that can be grouped together to make up a process system. The

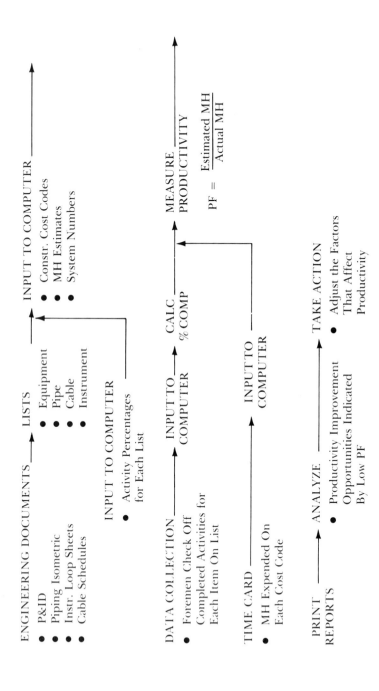

Figure 15.9. Productivity Measurement Flow Chart. Adapted from Lynn D. Dorsey in Kern (71:230).

Piping and Instrument Diagrams (P&IDs) can delineate each of these process systems. The system number can then be matched with each piece of equipment, each cable, each instrument, and each pipeline. The tracking reports now can be sorted by process system and a percent complete calculated by the system. When matched with the system's scheduled completion date, this can prove to be a useful planning tool. Resources can be allocated to the various systems in the quantity needed for meeting completion dates. More efficient manpower allocation will, in turn, help to reduce costs and improve the performance factors.

15.7   SUMMARY

The construction manager of the future will play a major role in improving project productivity. His actions determine how efficiently a project uses its allocation of resources to accomplish cost and schedule goals. The manager sets the climate for good productivity. To carry out this role, the various factors that affect productivity must be recognized. These factors can be grouped into three classes: A worker must "want to" do a good job, "know how to" do a good job, and be "allowed to do" a good job. A major "allow to" factor is information availability, especially information that tells the worker what to do. Most of the methods used to measure productivity include (1) labor productivity, (2) cost and price data, and (3) profits. These methods, however, do not provide satisfactory and reliable analysis of construction productivity. Getting the crew to work on activities in the proper sequence, and where the design information is the most complete, is a proven benefit of project scheduling. Improved information can improve scheduling and thus allow more efficient allocation of manpower. The state of the art of useful techniques to improve each productivity factor is constantly changing. One of the more rapid areas of change is in information processing. The ability to collect, analyze, and feed back construction progress data is greatly enhanced by the use of a computer. This information improves the "allowed to" productivity factor by ensuring that the worker is not constrained by lack of direction. Information tracking at a detailed level, for example, each pipe spool, can be used to support CPM networks, construction cost reports, and commissioning punch lists. It is hoped that the reader will find the tracking techniques useful additions to the set of tools available to him. These techniques are designed to improve just one factor of the many that affect productivity. The emerging role of the construction manager as a productivity improvement expert requires an awareness and sensitivity to the spectrum of productivity factors.

16

Quality Assurance and Quality Control (QA/QC) Practice

16.1 THE NEED FOR QA/QC PROGRAM

The importance of quality control has long been recognized. Professional liability and accountability for construction quality date from the time of Hammurabi, circa 1700 BC. The need for a systematic control of quality in the construction process is eminent. Apart from nuclear power plant construction, organized, formal, quality control efforts embracing the entire construction process are generally lacking. This has hindered opportunity to integrate quality control efforts at all levels of design, manufacture, application, and fabrication. The interrelationship of all construction activities negates isolated quality control at each stage. A process by which causes of construction faults can be traced will help identify places where intensified quality control is needed. In other words, there is increased concern for construction quality. This concern stems from the fact that the quality standards obtained from today's construction products have not improved commensurate with developments in technology and management in the construction industry. The industry incessantly experiences problems of failure and defects in design, manufacture, and construction. Recurrences of faulty designs and construction have caused untold number of damages and loss of life and property. The economic and legal implications of construction failures are nothing compared to the human lives that are lost and the permanent or temporary physical, mental, and psychological sufferings.

A major cause of controversies in quality control is delegation of responsibilities and authorities pertaining to quality assurance. Traditionally, designers, as the agents of the owner, are responsible for ensuring compliance to design specifications. The responsibility of the supervising contractor's performance can be delegated to the designer's field staff— the clerk of works. The roles and functions of the clerk of works are generally indeterminate. He is responsible for seeing that the work is performed according to specifications, but he has no power to enforce compliance. Conflicts do occur among the project team as to responsibility for inspection and acceptance of work performed. To alleviate the problems of responsibility and authority in quality control, a linear responsibility chart (LRC), which describes all the persons within the quality control program, their responsibilities, authorities, and interrelationships relative to quality control tasks, is proposed. The LRC is facilitated by the quality control matrix, which clearly defines the quality control requirements and the quality control methods. These two charts form the basis for developing the quality control organization as well as procedures for a quality control program. A well-defined quality control program should be established for each project, and the organizational structure of the program should be very explicit.

For an efficient quality control system, it is essential to develop and encourage cooperation among the participants in order to minimize the adversary relationships the traditional contract methods sometimes generate. The designers should be able to work together with the contractors to meet the project quality objectives. Situations in which the designers "police" contractors' performances alienate them from the contractors. Quality control should be the responsibility of the entire project team, including the owner. Quality control inspections should be done with the motive of encouraging and ensuring good workmanship, rather than catching the culprits. Specifications to be realistic must consider natural variations in workmanship.

More public legislation and regulations have been enacted in recent years to ensure the health, safety, and welfare of the public, by assuring better construction quality. For instance, quality assurance and quality control (QA/QC) programs are mandatory in nuclear power plant construction. The reasons for this are obvious. Professional liability and responsibility of the project team—the project owner, designers, contractors, manufacturers, and others—have increased. Judicial problems that have resulted from construction failures have generated more concern for better quality control from the project team, and have also caused some changes in contract agreements. Irrespective of these changes, construction failures have become the proverbial bad coin that keeps turning up.

In spite of the diverse factors influencing construction quality control, it is still possible to attain good quality in construction. The process entails a system approach that will make all participants in the construction process work as a team. Many of the elements identified in the design and construction phases are within human control. By taking more care and employing some incentives for good workmanship, quality construction can be attained.

This chapter examines quality assurance and quality control methods in the construction process. The approach adopted is to evolve a systematic evaluation of the subject by answering six key questions—What, Why, When, Where, How, and Who—pertaining to quality in construction. In view of the interrelationships between the elements in the construction process, the final quality obtained is determined by the quality of decisions and actions taken at all stages of the construction cycle. The systems approach provides practical and efficient methods to integrate and coordinate control of construction quality.

16.2   DEFINITIONS AND OBJECTIVES OF QA/QC

16.2.1   What Is QA/QC?

There is not much difference in the definitions of QA/QC that have been presented by various organizations and individuals. However, some people confuse quality assurance with quality control, and misconstrue quality control as being synonymous with inspection. The greatest emphasis on QA/QC is in nuclear power plant construction. In fact, the recent increased concern for QA/QC in the construction industry can be linked to the advent of nuclear power plant construction. It is appropriate, therefore, to use definitions presented by institutions related to nuclear construction as a basis for any other definitions.

As defined by the Nuclear Regulatory Commission (NRC),

> Quality assurance comprises all the planned and systematic actions necessary to provide adequate confidence that a structure or system will perform satisfactorily in service. Quality assurance includes "quality control" which comprises those quality assurance actions related to the physical characteristics

of a material, structure, component or system which provide a means to control the quality of the material, structure, component, or system to predetermined requirements.

This is very similar to the definition presented by the American National Standards Institute.

It should be noted that quality control is an element of the quality assurance program. It entails performing inspections, testings, measurements, and documentations that are necessary to ensure conformance with the contract specifications on the quality of construction materials and methods. According to Ward, quality control programs consist of

1. A definition of a standard of quality.

2. A defined procedure for the measurement of attainment of that standard.

3. The execution of that procedure to determine probable attainment or nonattainment of the standard.

4. The power to enforce and maintain the defined standard as measured according to the defined procedure.

Quality control is basically the responsibility of the production personnel. It is administered by the contractors or by special consultants—consulting engineers, testing laboratories.

Quality assurance activities include administrative and surveillance functions initiated by the project owner or regulatory agents to enforce, and certify with adequate confidence, compliance with established project quality standards to ensure that the completed structure or its components fulfill desired purposes efficiently, effectively, and economically. Quality assurance programs encompass the following:

1. Establishing the procedure for defining, developing, and determining high-level standards in design, construction, and sometimes the operational stages of the structure or its components.

2. Establishing the procedures to be used to monitor, test, inspect, measure, document, and review activities to assure compliance with established quality standards in regard to construction materials, methods, and personnel.

3. Defining the administrative procedures and requirements, organizational relationships and responsibilities, communications and information patterns, as well as other management activities required to execute, document, and assure attainment of the established quality standards.

16.2.2   Objectives of QA/QC

The primary objectives of quality control have been established as being essentially to produce a safe, reliable, and durable structure so that the owner gets the best value for his involvement. As the complexity, cost, and importance of a structure increase, more efficient quality assurance measures will be initiated to ensure compliance to contract specifications. The objectives and advantages of QA/QC programs to other members of the project team, and others interested in construction processes, are described by Parsons in his article "Systems for Control of Construction Quality" as

1. REGULATORY AGENCY-ORIENTED OBJECTIVES

(a) Assure that the construction and construction materials will meet the minimum requirements, as defined in applicable codes that are necessary to protect the public health and safety.

(b) Provide a basis for inspection and control of those construction activities that have the potential for creating irreparable damage to plant and animal habitats.

2. OWNER-ORIENTED OBJECTIVES

(a) Provide adequate confidence that the constructed product will perform satisfactorily in terms of reliability, safety, durability, function, and appearance.

(b) Provide documentation to regulating agencies and customers that is adequate to provide compliance with codes and licensing requirements.

(c) Provide data upon which in-service inspections, failure investigations, and performance studies can be based.

(d) Provide a system for surveillance of contractor and enforcement of contract provisions. This protects the owner's investment and ensures that the specified quality is obtained or documents the level obtained so that management action can be taken.

3. DESIGNER-ORIENTED OBJECTIVES

(a) Contribute to better design by serving as a source of feedback upon which to base future project designs.

(b) Permit use of less stringent design standards and reduction of safety factors with resultant savings in cost in those areas where quality can be assured.

(c) Provide tight quality control of area using new material and techniques, thereby encouraging use of new design and construction methods that result in a savings in cost.

4. CONSTRUCTOR-ORIENTED OBJECTIVES

(a) Reduce rework due to rejected or unacceptable material by developing and following procedures having a maximum probability of success.

(b) Ensure that the quality level of the constructed product does not greatly exceed that required by the plans, specifications, and contract documents.

Another factor that has generated emphasis on quality control is the increase in litigation and claims on facility failures and defects. Changes in the judicial system and processes, as well as more public awareness and accessibility to the judiciary, have increased claims against the design professional, contractors, manufacturers, owners, and others for damages resulting from facility failure. Most design professionals do not carry adequate liability insurance to meet litigation expenses or pay court judgments. Efforts by the designers to reduce their accountability to project failures has caused changes in contract agreements and responsibility during construction. Consequently, the project owner increases focus on quality assurance, demanding more quality control in design and construction.

16.3   FACTORS INFLUENCING CONSTRUCTION QUALITY

Construction defects develop as a result of some undetected faults in the construction process cycle. Faults could result in errors or omissions in design, manufacturing, application, or installation stages or cumulative effects in all stages. Faults can be categorized according to the degree of danger that could result from them. Three categories identified by Newlove are

1. *Critical faults:*—These could create hazardous conditions or could lead to dangerous conditions when the facility is in use.

2. *Major faults:*—They seriously reduce the utility of a facility or could lead to disintegration or failure of some kind.

3. *Minor faults:*—Although undesirable, minor defects will not appreciably affect the use of a facility unless they appear in sufficient numbers to produce a major fault.

The quality of a structure can be described in terms of the quality of design and the degree of conformance to specified quality standards by the contractors. The quality of design is determined by the architects and engineers on behalf of the project owner. The quality level desired is defined by the quality of design, and it is described and influenced by the drawings, specifications, and other contract documents proceedings. The quality attained is determined by the degree of conformance to the contract documents by the manufacturers and constructors. In this section, the effects of some technical and nontechnical factors on construction quality will be reviewed; *when* and *where* some of these factors occur will also be discussed.

16.3.1   Design

It is in the design stage that the required quality of the structure is determined. The design should satisfy the functional and aesthetic requirements of the structure as well as assure that the structure will be safe, durable, efficient, and economic to maintain. The design process entails enormous skills to arrive at optimum decisions in terms of cost, time, material, and method of construction. The best quality is desired at the minimum cost; care is also taken to avoid overdesign. As the quality of design increases, both the cost and value of attaining the quality characteristics of the structure also increase. An optimum design stage is reached in which it becomes too costly to specify higher quality standards. Beyond this level, the additional quality costs no more than it is really worth for functional objectives of the project.

Construction materials and methods specified must be carefully considered before selection. Their quality must meet the minimum quality standards specified in the relevant codes and regulations, and also satisfy the design criteria. Factors such as costs, availability, workability, maintainability, durability, labor skills, and construction practices influence selection. Design errors arise as a result of misjudgment, misunderstanding, and lack of adequate care. It is the responsibility of the designer to find adequate and reliable information necessary to evaluate the suitability of materials and methods specified.

Many poor project performances can be attributed to the inadequacies of the new materials and methods specified. The design professionals have little or no experience with a number of these products. Actually, in-depth, systematic performance evaluation of some of these products lags behind the rate at which new products are developed or marketed. The designers have limited information assuring that the products specified will perform satisfactorily to meet the desired requirements.

Systems approach offers reliable and efficient means to reach optimal design decisions. Many designers have successfully utilized this process. It enables objective evaluation of all the elements of a system by integrating facts, data, experience, faith, intuition, and bias to make an optimum decision or a selection from a number of alternatives. Various alternatives are judged by some clearly defined performance criteria, and that which best satisfies required performance standards is selected.

The efficacy of systems approach depends on the availability of adequate information from which optimal decisions can be made. Designers should not rely on only the information gleaned from catalogs, manufacturers' brochures, testing, and research laboratory reports. Some of this information is inadequate because it is based often on short-term laboratory tests that are not the best indications of the actual field conditions these materials may be subjected to. Designers should develop a process of properly investigating actual performances of these products. Field feedback systems should be developed to monitor, document, and disseminate information on actual field performances of construction products.

16.3.2   Drawings

Designers normally communicate design through a set of drawings, specifications, and other related contract documents. Drawings illustrate the physical aspects of the design—that is, materials, arrangements, details, dimensions, and other pertinent information. With other contract documents, they form the basis of determining project cost estimates for competitive bidding and negotiation. Since they describe the nature and quality of the job to be done by the contractors, they also form the basis of measuring the degree of conformance to quality level and settlement of claims.

Though a few standardized drawings are available for a few standard engineering details, most drawings are individually prepared for every project. They must be complete, intelligible, accurate, detailed, and well correlated for the contractors to be able to interpret the intentions of the designers. Drawing errors result in shoddy jobs, delays, many change orders and extra work orders, as well as other situations that inhibit good quality. Most problems arising from drawings can be minimized by checking and correcting errors prior to bid letting. Drawings should be detailed adequately for constructability. Time-saving drafting of measures that may reduce clarity and easy comprehensive quality must be avoided. Drafting standards must be consistent throughout a set of drawings to minimize probability of errors in the field. Some errors may not be discovered until it is impossible to rectify them.

16.3.3   Specifications

Specifications are written instructions describing how the project will be constructed and what results are expected. Also described are quality standards expected for materials, workmanship, and other technical characteristics of the project. Specifications inform the owner of the quality he should expect, establishing the criteria for acceptance or rejection.

Specifications serve not only as technical documents, but also as legal documents, incorporating other information about contract terms and provisions.

The impact of specifications on quality control cannot be overemphasized. Despite its importance, the manner in which some specifications are written or compiled for each project is questionable. The uniqueness of each project is ignored if standard specifications are used. Some of these specifications are copied from previous projects or from specification manuals. Standard specifications are not tailored to meet a particular project requirement. Thus if they are not modified, they cause standard or overspecified works.

Many contract disputes arise from misunderstanding and misinterpretation of quality standards prescribed in the specifications. Such problems could arise if multiple specifications are used for the same item. For example, by using prescriptive and performance specifications for the same item, it will be difficult to enforce a particular standard. While performance specifications stipulate the quality standard expected, prescriptive specifications provide a detailed description of the required product and the method that should be employed for fabrication and installation. For efficient quality control, specifications must be void of all ambiguities.

Specifications are generally written in an idealistic manner. This precludes tolerances for variations normally experienced in actual construction. The fact that specification requirements are not attuned to nature's variability affects quality; where one tries to enforce specifications that do not fit nature's laws, one is asking for the impossible, or has to close his eyes and accept something different from what is specified. Specifications must therefore be objective if they will be appropriate for quality control.

Specifications should be written in such a way that requirements can be understood easily by an average craftsman who has to interpret project requirements. Language used must be precise and with minimal technical complications. By this, the contractor will be able to perform and direct fieldwork with less dependence on the engineers to interpret project requirements. The contractor will therefore be more accountable for the quality of work done and will perform more efficiently.

16.3.4 Bid Preparation

The importance of realistic bid estimates to quality control can be understood if the possible consequences of poor estimates are analyzed. Failure on the part of the contractor to make proper evaluation of all requirements in the contract documents will result in underbidding. If such errors are not detected early, the contractor may not be able to preplan his works carefully to offset the underestimates. This may result in contract disputes or shoddy works, which have negative effects on quality.

Poor bid estimates may be caused by ambiguities in contract documents as well as negligence on the part of the contractors. Some works might have been constructed before the mistakes were realized, and it may be too late to remedy, or unreasonable to tear down. Such situations cause substandard works that may endanger the lives of the users and the public. Careful bid preparation enables the contractor to spot errors in drawings and specifications. It is recommended that the engineer hold prebid meetings with the contractors to clarify ambiguities and make necessary corrections, or explain construction requirements that may not be familiar.

16.3.5   Construction

Construction quality is focused mainly on the site where most fabrication takes place. The contractor is solely responsible for the quality of work performed, while the project owner and his agent—architect-engineer— are to inspect and check for compliance to contract requirements. Apart from the impact of design errors, level of quality attained is determined by the quality of workmanship, inspection, constructability of design, adequacy and competency of supervision by the designers, and application of materials.

The quality of workmanship exercised by the construction workers determines achievable construction standards. They are the ones actually translating the design into reality. The quality of work attained is determined to a large extent by the capabilities of the construction workers. There is little that management's quality control measures could do if the workers did not possess the skills and experience necessary to perform as required. The attitude of the workers also influences output. If workers do not take pride in good workmanship, substandard work will often be produced. Training programs can help improve workers' competence as well as help develop better work attitudes.

Few contractors have formal quality control arrangements to monitor and enforce quality standards. Field inspection is also done by the project superintendent, who is often saddled with other project responsibilities. As a result, inspection is casual and inadequate. Defective work may not be noticed until it is too late to be removed, or until the owner or the architect, or their agents, formally condemn the job. It is recommended that the contractor have a formal quality group charged with the responsibility of planning and making routine checks to assure compliance to contract requirements. Checklists will be helpful to reduce the probability of missing out on works that need to be inspected. The control group should be responsible directly to management and independent of the production staff control. Friendly relationships must, however, be established between the control group and the production team in order to minimize conflicts that will inhibit cooperation necessary to attain the objectives of the control group.

In an attempt to be innovative, many novel and complex designs are created by design professionals. Unusual designs that are beyond the normal experience and skills of workers and the supervisory staff often suffer drawbacks in quality. Many designers are so removed from the construction process that they are unaware of the problems their designs create on site. There is the need for designers to get more acquainted with site conditions and be more practical in their novelty. A forum where the designers and the trades foremen could meet regularly to discuss construction problems should be developed. This will encourage better communication and understanding of practical problems on site and help improve constructability.

An increase in liability claims against the designers for project failures and defects has caused changes in contract agreements and the responsibilities of designers during construction. Prior to 1961, architects were responsible for general supervision of works. Some changes have evolved since then, in response, to offset accountability to construction defects. Now the architect observes rather than supervises, makes periodic visits rather than exhaustive on-site inspections, and does his or her best, but he or she is not responsible for deficiencies or construction methods of the contractor. This has shifted the responsibility of quality control solely on the contractors, who are in a better position to control the performance of their workers and the quality of materials used. Although it is mandatory for the contractors to meet specified contract quality, regular surveillance by designers, or their competent representatives, will help to enforce good quality control, particularly at critical stages of construction.

Another factor that reduces the quality of construction is poor application of materials. This may not be the fault of the designers. Defects in materials during manufacture, transportation, handling, and storage will also reduce quality. Quality inspections are required to assure that materials are correctly applied, as directed by the manufacturers and construction specifications. Materials should be checked prior to use to assure that they are free from defects, and that they meet contract specifications.

16.3.6   Social and Environmental Factors

Some nontechnical factors affecting construction quality can be identified. Public legislations have great impact on construction quality. Codes and other regulations are intended to protect the life and property of the public. Legislatures, sensitive to public needs regarding safety of construction, as well as other political situations, influence the nature and effects of legislation on construction quality. Nuclear power plant construction has received adequate attention. Federal law requires that a comprehensive quality assurance and quality control program be established to assure that construction meets the requirements set forth by the Nuclear Regulatory Commission. More concern should be given to other constructions to assure better safety of the users and the public.

The impact of economy on construction quality is obvious. The quality level desired is generally determined by the availability of sufficient funds to finance such standards. The owner wants maximum quality with minimum expense. While overdesign should be avoided, it is important to emphasize that designs must have adequate built-in factors of safety to allow for normal variations between design and construction workmanship, as well as contingencies in use of the structure.

The cost of quality control is a major consideration to project owners. It is estimated that the cost of actual quality control varies from 4% for small jobs to about $1\frac{1}{2}\%$ for large projects. Potential savings in quality control costs may not be true savings in the long run. According to Johnson in his article "Proper Quality Control," owners can realize savings of up to 12% of original costs when proper quality control is implemented. Johnson provided the following illustration to prove this point:

Assume a construction costing "X" dollars. Assume that no quality control is provided and that, after 15 years of service, repair is required in the amount of 10% of the worth of the structure at the time of repair. Extending the current inflationary trend of about 3% per annum, the cost of repair is now 56% of the original cost of construction. Assume now, that quality control was provided and that said control 1) cost 3% of the original cost of the work, and 2) defers the need for repair by 10 years. Assuming a 6% value of money, at the end of 25 years of service, the balance appears as follows:

Cost without Quality Control	Cost with Quality Control
$0.56X (1 + 0.6)^{10}$	$0.56X (1 + .03)^{10} + .03X (1 + .06)^{25}$
$0.56X (1.79) = 1.00X$	$= 0.56X (1.35) + 0.3X (4.3)$
	$= 0.75X = .13X$
	$= 0.88X$
	Net Savings $= .12X = 12\%$ of original cost of construction

Many owners have incurred avoidable expenses on reworks, litigation, and maintenance because they tried to save a few dollars on quality control. As discussed previously, poor quality in construction constitutes a probable cause of immense danger to the users and the public. The advantages of quality control greatly outweigh the few savings in dollars. The higher the cost, complexity, and importance of a structure, the greater the need of quality control programs.

The speed at which a structure is erected determines the degree of care that could be taken during design and construction. Most errors in design and contract documents can be avoided if they are critically reviewed prior to bid preparations. However, this is often not the case when there is pressure to finish design as soon as possible. Likewise, construction craftsmen are more susceptible to frequent mistakes when under pressure. Invariably, substandard design and construction are created resulting in poor quality jobs.

Some acts of God, like earthquakes, floods, tornadoes, are beyond human control, yet they have great impacts on quality. Poor construction work can result due to damage caused by rain, snow, adverse temperatures, dust, floods, and other environmental agents. Careful preplanning can reduce the effects of some of these environmental factors by scheduling activities at a favorable time.

16.3.7   When and Where to Control Quality

After enumerating some major elements influencing construction quality, it is easy to discuss when and where these elements can be controlled. Quality can be controlled only before the job is done, and by those who perform the work. Quality problems associated with design processes can be controlled at the design phase by the designers and design personnel. Drawings and specifications must be developed by competent persons. They should be thoroughly checked to eliminate errors and omissions and to clarify ambiguities. Designers should develop and incorporate quality control plans to check their works.

Contractors and manufacturers are responsible to ensure that the materials used in construction are properly checked and certified free of defects and damages prior to use. A certificate of conformance may be requested from manufacturers, and inspection checks are to be made at delivery, transportation, and storage stages to track damaged materials. If the quality desired is not there, the material should be rejected.

However, it should be emphasized that quality control in construction is an integrated system rather than separate activities. A systems approach offers an integrative coordination of the construction process, to develop a system to trace the sources of construction faults, develop a program of control, and assure the owner that he is getting the best value for his money.

16.4   QUALITY ASSURING TECHNIQUES

The construction industry does not possess a formal quality control program as in construction-related industries. Quality control on some projects could be haphazard and inconsistent. Because of heterogeneity, it is impossible to employ a uniform approach to check quality standards of construction works. Three major quality control methods are commonly used on construction projects: (1) inspection, (2) testing, (3) sampling. The techniques used vary from subjective evaluation to objective assessment of quality attained. The type adopted depends on the characteristics of the construction activity or system being examined, and the degree of certainty desired. While all the methods may be feasible on a particular activity, only one may be applicable in some others. The methods to be used should be defined in the contract documents to eliminate probable confusion.

Because of the nature of construction works, absolute compliance to specifications is impractical. The objective of quality assurance examinations is to determine the degree of compliance to contract quality standards. A realistic approach is to first establish a minimum quality standard, which will be the basis of acceptance or rejection. Appropriate quality control methods can thereafter be used to judge if variations are within acceptable tolerances. The best result is attained if quality control is consistent and the techniques used are appropriate.

16.4.1   Inspection

Inspection usually entails checking the physical dimensions and appearance of an item. It is generally nondestructive qualitative observation. In some cases, gauges or machines may be required to do some simple measurements or examinations. Inspection is used to check conformance to descriptive specifications, judgment may be subjective. Three levels of inspection are identified by Ayers in his book *Specifications for Architecture, Engineering and Construction*:

1. *Receiving Inspection:*—It involves examining the raw materials, parts, assemblies, or other purchased items after delivery.

2. *In-process Inspection:*—It is any inspection during the process of the work prior to final acceptance.

3. *Final Inspection:*—This is the last inspection prior to acceptance.

By preparing a checklist of characteristics of the product from the drawings and specifications, easy comparison can be made to verify compliance.

16.4.2   Testing

Testing involves examining a product to check conformance to specified performance standards. Testing can be destructive or nondestructive. It can take place on site or in special laboratories. In destructive testing, the item or its elements are tested intentionally to fail.

Testing procedures entail taking representative parts of the whole product. Statistical approach is used to determine the reliability of the product and the degree of variation from some measured attributes. The statistical approach is based on the premises that the actual measurable quality attributes of a product vary in any given situation. A good example of this is the compressive strength of concrete. Actual concrete strength obtainable is normally different from the design strength specified. By studying the pattern of variations of the same mix design strength, for example; 3,000 psi at twenty-eight days, adequate data can be compiled to compute the normal distribution curves, standard deviations, mean values, and other data necessary to establish the norms for quality standards.

Tests performed will be to determine if quality obtained is within acceptable tolerances. Test samples should be taken in a strictly random pattern to reflect the variations in production. Acceptance limits are established in the specifications and are based on the number of samples tested. A typical statistical quality control specification for concrete may be in one of the following forms:

1.   No more than 10% of samples tested may fall below the specified strength.

2.   No more than 20% of samples tested may fall below the specified strength.

It should be emphasized that statistical quality control standards are based on laws of probability and are not sacred. Some experience and intuition are necessary to make objective judgments, particularly when statistical approach results are doubtful. An instance was reported in which over $5 million worth of concrete construction could have been demolished if statistical results were followed. Not more than 10% of the several hundred cylinders tested attained the required strength of 3,000 psi in twenty-eight days. However, at the end of fifty days, virtually all of the cylinders broke at over 3,000 psi, while 4,000 psi were attained by almost all cylinders tested on the one hundredth day.

16.4.3   Sampling

Sampling is the process of determining the quality of a large group by examining a part of the lot that will be statistically representative of the whole. Reliability of information obtained increases with the size of sample used. Reducing the size of sample, though, reduces the cost of inspection, but reduces reliability. Reduction might result in acceptance of works that are substandard and unsatisfactory. A good trade-off must be made between cost of inspection and reliability.

Reliability is expressed in percentages and could be determined by the equation

$$\text{Reliability} = 100 - \left(\frac{\text{Number of defective units}}{\text{Number of units tested}} \times 100 \right)$$

One hundred percent reliability requires inspection of all parts. The desired reliability may not be the same for all operations. The reliability of each characteristic should be determined prior to specifications writing. Also, the method to be used to process the data collected should be decided at the time the sampling program is developed and the population of the lot is being determined.

16.5   RESPONSIBILITY AND AUTHORITY IN QA/QC

The architect-engineer is solely responsible for the quality of design, while it is the responsibility of the contractors that construction conform to the standards inherent in the contract documents. However, several parties can perform and administer quality assurances and quality control programs. Four common approaches can be identified.

1.   The architect-engineer may develop and administer the program inclusively with project design.

2.   Contractors may be required to establish and administer QA/QC programs as part of the contract agreement.

3.   Independent special consultants unrelated to the project designer, for example, construction management firms, testing laboratories, may be responsible for all or part of QA/QC programs.

4.   Project owner may utilize his own work force (force account) to administer QA/QC programs.

16.5.1   Project Designer

Increase in liability claims against design professionals, particularly architects, has caused redefinitions of designers' responsibilities during construction. The current American Institute of Architects (AIA) standard form of agreement between architect and the owner indicates that the architect is expected to make only periodic on-site observations, and he is not expected to make exhaustive on-site inspections to check the quantity or quality of work unless otherwise agreed. Situations are beneficial in which the designer is capable and agrees to develop and administer QA/QC programs with design, particularly if the design is technically complex or requires frequent interpretation of design intentions during construction.

1. ADVANTAGES

(a) The field staff who will implement the QA/QC program can participate in the development of design and QA/QC program. This eliminates the initial problems of understanding design standards and QA/QC procedures, which external participants will encounter.

(b) Field staff familiarization with the design firm facilitates efficient project communications and coordination of construction processes by the designers as well as prompt resolution of design problems and others concerning quality requirements.

(c) Concentration of design and QA/QC services in one agent minimizes management costs and liability costs to both the project owner and designer.

(d) It enables the designer to develop efficient feedback systems on design standards and construction practices.

2. DISADVANTAGES

(a) Many design firms are not adequately staffed with well-trained personnel competent and experienced enough to implement QA/QC services efficiently. It is not unusual to find young inexperienced graduates supervising intricate projects.

(b) The probability of conflict of interests cannot be ignored. Problems such as incomplete or erroneous design documents, contractor bias when resolving errors, and manipulation of project finances can be cited.

The designer's field staff performs necessary testing and inspections, administrative and surveillance services, and coordinates specialized consultants who may engage in performing some of the field and laboratory testing and inspections.

16.5.2 Contractor QA/QC

The reasons for requesting the contractor to be responsible for both quality assurance and quality control as practiced in some military institutions' construction contracts are

1. The contractor has contractual obligations to produce the quality specified in the contract documents and should therefore be responsible for the quality of his work.

2. The owner cannot afford the costs or provide enough manpower to oversee the entire construction operation. The owner may incur financial and legal responsibilities for errors overlooked, which may be regarded as tacit approval by the contractors.

The contractor is responsible for performing testing and inspection necessary to control the quality of his work. He can utilize his own manpower or subcontract all or part of the testing, inspections, and engineering functions to testing laboratories and consulting engineers. He is required to submit QA/QC program plans indicating testing and inspection procedures, types, and qualifications of personnel involved. The owner surveys contractors' activities to ensure compliance to QA/QC programs. He also performs acceptance inspection and testing to verify conformance to quality standards and ascertain testing and inspection documentation.

1. ADVANTAGES

(a) It reduces project inspection costs expended by the owner.

(b) Construction quality control responsibilities are shifted to the contractor. In some instances, extended warranty may be required for the work performed.

(c) The contractor will have more freedom to control his work. Delays caused by waiting for inspection and approval by owner or his agents will be minimal.

(d) Contractor will be more responsive to quality control to prevent errors or correct them early in order to avoid reworks and reduce replacement costs.

2. DISADVANTAGES

(a) Documentation and inspection requirements may be elaborate and cumbersome. This may increase the costs of implementing QA/QC programs.

(b) It may be difficult to monitor effectively compliance to QA/QC requirements. Increased monitoring will be required if contractor is substantially deficient in implementing QA/QC requirements. This will cause increases in inspection cost to the owner.

(c) The QA/QC program's effectiveness depends on the contractor's capability to organize and manage his staff to meet QA/QC objectives.

Availability of a well-qualified staff is also vital to the success of the program.

(d) Potential internal skirmishes between the production team and the QA/QC personnel will inhibit good relationships essential in executing a QA/QC program. To avoid this, some contractors engage external special consultants to develop and implement their QA/QC programs.

16.5.3   Special Consultants

Independent special consultants that are unrelated to the project designer may be contracted by the owner to undertake all or part of the QA/QC functions. Such consultants include construction management firms, special testing laboratories, and specialized consulting engineers. They can be involved in developing contract requirements and documents for QA/QC programs at preconstruction stages, and perform or supervise QA/QC functions during construction.

1. ADVANTAGES

(a) It reduces potential conflict of interest and collusion. Since the consultant does not have a contractual relationship with either the designer or contractors, his loyalty will be directed to the project owner who contracted him.

(b) It enables the project owner opportunity to select field personnel that will competently monitor field operations on his behalf. Most special consultants are more competent and better equipped and staffed to handle QA/QC programs than most designers.

(c) Use of special consultants reduces fees accrued by designers for contract supervision and construction inspection, which they generally have not been doing efficiently. It also minimizes the owner's need for an in-house project control staff, particularly in situations where the owner does not have frequent construction needs to justify a full-time staff.

2. DISADVANTAGES

(a) The special consultants' late involvement in design process reduces their early familarity with design criteria and quality requirements. This will inhibit their ability to develop and implement efficient and appropriate QA/QC programs. This problem can be minimized if consultants are involved in establishing project specifications early in design.

(b) Problems often arise concerning responsibility and authority regarding some contract administration functions. This could generate adversary relationships between the designer and the special consultants, thus inhibiting project communications. The situation can be arrested if the responsibilities and functions of the various participants in the construction process are explicitly defined in the contract agreements.

16.5.4   Force Account

Government agencies, corporate and institutional owners who are continually in the construction market may find it necessary to have an in-house project management staff whose responsibilities will include administering QA/QC programs. The effectiveness of such force account programs depends on the availability of well-qualified field personnel to monitor and administer QA/QC programs efficiently. Governmental institutions could also be restrained by some legislation regarding project procedures and staffing. However, many of these organizations may still require some services of specialized laboratories to perform sophisticated testing and inspections.

1.   ADVANTAGES

(a)   Field personnel are trained and indoctrinated in the organization's QA/QC procedures. This reduces time and cost for familiarization with individual project QA/QC programs, since, in most cases, standard procedures are established and followed.

(b)   By using his own staff, the owner has better control of field supervision and direct control of quality control. This also facilitates establishment of a feedback system to evaluate construction performances and quality requirements.

2.   DISADVANTAGES

(a)   Unless the owner has frequent construction activities to justify engaging a full-time staff, force account may be uneconomical.

(b)   Organizations with force account generally have established quality standards and quality assurance procedures in which their staffs are trained. This greatly limits flexibility and receptivity to changes in construction methods, materials, quality requirements, and test procedures. However, this can be minimized by organizing continuing education programs for the staffs and also updating QA/QC procedures to meet current developments in the industry. Adequate supervision of field staff is necessary to ensure compliance to new techniques.

17

Management Methods

17.1 BASIC CONCEPTS AND DEFINITIONS OF MANAGEMENT METHODS

17.1.1 Human Interactions in Organizations

Early management theory was somewhat mechanistic in its view of human interaction. The goals of the members of an organization were assumed to be consistent with the organization goals (or at least sublimated to the organization goals). Employees were assumed to respond positively to authority and to be motivated by monetary rewards. The human relations movement, which began with the famous Hawthorne studies between 1927 and 1932, established the concept of the organization as a social system. Motivation was found to be based on more than economic reward. Work groups, co-workers, and so forth, were found to be important. Leadership styles or management methods were suggested that would increase the satisfaction of workers with the organization. The behavioral

Table 17.1.   Maslow's Hierarchical Needs

LEVEL	NEED	EXPLANATION
Lowest	Physiological	The physical needs such as satisfaction of hunger or thirst, and activity need
	Safety	Protection against danger, threat, deprivation
	Love	Satisfactory associations with others, belonging to groups, giving and receiving friendship and affection
	Esteem	Self-respect and respect of others
Highest	Self-actualization	Self-fulfillment; achieving one's potential; creativity; self-development; self-expression.

research results have not led to a single set of proved principles, but the main thrust of the research suggests the need to consider human needs in designing organizations.

Motivation is the reason for a person to carry out certain activities. This is usually explained in terms of the person's drives or needs. The needs of a person are not fixed; they change over time with the stage of his career, and as certain needs receive more satisfaction. A useful classification of general human needs is a hierarchy developed by Abraham Maslow. It cites five basic needs, but the higher needs become activated only to the extent that lower needs have been somewhat satisfied. See Table 17.1 for Maslow's Hierarchical Needs.

The Maslow hierarchy is useful because it points up an important dimension of human need. A starving man concentrates on physiological needs, but when his hunger is satisfied, he becomes concerned about safety and perhaps love and esteem. As needs for safety, love, and esteem are met, the need for self-actualization becomes important. This suggests that organizations cannot depend only on satisfactory pay and safe working conditions to motivate personnel.

Whereas the Maslow hierarchy is of general applicability, a classification more directly related to work situations was developed by Frederick Hertzberg. Two clusters of factors relate to job satisfaction. One group comprises environmental factors (called hygiene factors), which do not motivate satisfaction, but their absence will cause dissatisfaction. These are company policy and administration, supervision, salary, interpersonal relations, and working conditions. The other group of factors are termed "motivators" because they are determinants of job satisfaction (which is assumed to lead to superior performance). These are achievement, recognition, interesting and challenging work, responsibility, and advancement.

It should be noted that there is controversy over the validity of the two-factor theory of Hertzberg and to a lesser extent to the need theory of Maslow. Although there may be oversimplifications, they do provide useful descriptive categories and insight into the motivations of organizational personnel.

17.1.2 Group Dynamics

Within an organization, an individual normally belongs to one or more small groups. They may be formal organizational groups, such as production work teams or they may be based on common interests, such as ethnic background, profession, recreational pursuits (the bowling club), or car pools. Much evidence suggests that small groups are important factors influencing the relations between the individual and the organization.

17.1.3 Characteristics of Most People

Most people exhibit the following characteristics:

(a) Like to agree with those they like;

(b) Resent domination;

(c) Enjoy a good scrap;

(d) Want to know what is going on;

(e) Want to overcome obstacles;

(f) Want to feel important; and

(g) Are all different.

17.1.4 Management Goals

In this text, increased productivity and worker motivation are assumed to be the primary goals of management of individual firms. From a national standpoint, various writers have advocated various goals. Many have stressed the necessity for increased productivity, forecasting that the labor force will increase much slower than the need for goods and services. Other writers maintain that we must judge the efficiency of firms in terms of human costs of happiness and health. For example, Likert emphasizes the importance, in measuring organizational performance, of including measurement of human assets. Georgopoulos and Tannenbaum in their article "Measuring Organizational Performance"—*Harvard Business Review* 36, no. 2 (1958)—feel that "organizational effectiveness" is based on the "extent to which an organization, as a social system, fulfills its objectives without incapacitating its means and resources and without placing undue strain on its members." As criteria of effectiveness, they use not only organizational productivity, but also organizational flexibility and absence of intraorganizational strain or tension.

Some write of "higher profits" as the goal of the management of the business. This is normally the financial goal of a business, and productivity and motivation of the workers play a major role in the determination of profit. Other factors, however, notably prices or market conditions, affect profit. A firm in a monopoly or unusually favorable market position could increase profits without increasing productivity or even while productivity decreases.

17.1.5   Behavioral Science

Behavioral science is not easy to define. The term came into vogue a few years ago as a catchall for studies that were not clearly identified with any of the traditional "applied" disciplines, such as industrial engineering or industrial psychology, but that were broadly concerned with human factors that affected productivity. Thus behavioral science is an applied science and its study is for the purpose of finding application in industry.

Behavioral science aims at changing human behavior in a predetermined direction. It is based upon the belief that needs and motivations of people are of prime concern to a firm or an organization. Behavioral science, thus, emphasizes the utilization of man's potential to reach organizational goals. It is oriented toward the total working environment. It also emphasizes the effective use of group effort and interaction. Other concepts and objectives of behavioral science include the following:

1. Seeks commitment and involvement of each individual in the attainment of an organization's objectives

2. Aims to develop interpersonal relationships among individuals and between an individual and groups

3. Treats an organization like a living system or being with a personality, motivations, objectives, and so forth

4. Assumes that organizations are dynamic systems within which change is inevitable

17.2   TYPICAL MANAGEMENT METHODS

Management methods are referred to as "leadership styles" by some authors. Management or leadership is interpersonal influence that persuades or motivates a group toward the attainment of a specified goal or goals. This section describes theories about leadership styles or management methods.

The way a manager views his or her task may be conditioned by the manager's view of man. McGregor has characterized the two extremes as "Theory X" and "Theory Y." Rensis Likert and the others come in between these two extremes.

17.2.1 McGregor's Theory "X"

1. ASSUMPTIONS

(a) The average human being has an inherent dislike of work and will avoid it if he can.

(b) Because of a human's dislike for work, he or she must be coerced, controlled, directed, or threatened with punishment to get that individual to put forth adequate effort toward the achievement of organizational objectives.

(c) The average person prefers to be directed, wishes to avoid responsibility, has relatively little ambition, and wants security above all.

2. MANAGEMENT APPROACHES

(a) Hard—Uses coercion and threat of punishment to obtain desired behavior from people.

(b) Soft—Is permissive, tries to satisfy workers' demands, and otherwise tries to maintain harmony in the organization.

3. RESULTS EXPECTED

(a) Hard Line—Restricted production output, antagonism, militant unionism, subtle undermining of management.

(b) Soft Line—Abdication of management's responsibilities, harmonious but infective employees, a work force that expects more and more but gives less and less.

17.2.2 McGregor's Theory "Y"

1. ASSUMPTIONS

(a) The expenditure of physical and mental effort in work is as natural as play or rest.

(b) External control and the threat of punishment are not the only means of getting humans to work toward the organization's objectives.

People will exercise self-direction and self-control toward achieving objectives to which they are committed.

(c) Commitment to objectives is a function of the rewards associated with their achievement (i.e., esteem and self-actualization).

(d) Average individuals learn, under proper conditions, not only to accept but to seek responsibility.

(e) Most people are capable of a relatively high degree of imagination, ingenuity, and creativity in solving organizational problems.

(f) Under the conditions of contemporary industrial life, the average person's intellectual potentialities are being utilized only partially.

2. MANAGEMENT APPROACHES

(a) Limited—Management uses participative management only on noncritical matters such as fund drives and car pool committees.

(b) Balanced—Management seeks employee interaction on organizational matters but retains final decision-making authority.

(c) Consensus—Management treats employees like a committee and makes decisions based on consensus of employee group.

3. RESULTS

(a) Under Limited Approach—Employees feel no real involvement in organization and their commitment is lowered.

(b) Under Balanced Approach—Employees become committed to organization's objectives and are involved in their attainment.

(c) Under Consensus Approach—Abdication of management responsibilities; organization suffers from all the ills of rule by committee.

17.2.3   Rensis Likert's System Four

Organizational behavior based on Theory X is widespread and is clearly operational. However, those who prefer the assumptions of Theory Y claim that Theory X has a human cost in the frustration and lack of human development from its application. The trend in behavioral research suggests benefits from organization and management based on Theory Y assumptions. One such approach is termed "System Four" by Likert in his book entitled *Human Organization*, published by McGraw-Hill Book Company. Likert's four approaches are authoritative, benevolent authoritative, consultative and participative group. System Four is characterized by a supportive relation by the manager and by group decision making and supervision. See Table 17.2 for the comparative analysis of these four systems.

Table 17.2. Organizational and Performance Characteristics of Different Management Systems Based on a Comparative Analysis

Organizational Variable	System of Organization			
	Authoritative		Consultative System 3	Participative
	Exploitative Authoritative System 1	Benevolent Authoritative System 2		Participative Group System 4

1. Leadership Processes Used

Organizational Variable	Exploitative Authoritative System 1	Benevolent Authoritative System 2	Consultative System 3	Participative Group System 4
• Extent to which superiors have confidence and trust in subordinates	Have no confidence and trust in subordinates	Have condescending confidence and trust, such as master has to servant	Substantial but not complete confidence and trust; still wishes to keep control of decisions	Complete confidence and trust in all matters
• Extent to which superiors behave so that subordinates feel free to discuss important things about their jobs with their immediate superior	Subordinates do not feel at all free to discuss things about the job with their superior	Subordinates do not feel very free to discuss things about the job with their superior	Subordinates feel rather free to discuss things about the job with their superior	Subordinates feel completely free to discuss things about the job with their superior
• Extent to which immediate superior in solving job problems generally tries to get subordinate's ideas and opinions and make constructive use of them	Seldom gets ideas and opinions of subordinates in solving job problems	Sometimes gets ideas and opinions of subordinates in solving job problems	Usually gets ideas and opinions and usually tries to make constructive use of them	Always gets ideas and opinions and always tries to make constructive use of them

347

Table 17.2 (continued)

| Organizational Variable | System of Organization | | | |
| | Authoritative | | Participative | |
	Exploitative Authoritative System 1	Benevolent Authoritative System 2	Consultative System 3	Participative Group System 4
2. Character of Motivational Forces				
• Manner in which motives are used	Fear, threats, punishment, and occasional rewards	Rewards and some actual or potential punishment	Rewards, occasional punishment, and some involvement	Economic rewards based on compensation system developed through participation; group participation and involvement in setting goals, improving methods, appraising progress toward goals, etc.
• Amount of responsibility felt by each member of organization for achieving organization's goals	High levels of management feel responsibility; lower levels feel less; rank and file feel little and often welcome opportunity to behave in ways to defeat organization's goals	Managerial personnel usually feel responsibility; rank and file usually feel relatively little responsibility for achieving organization's goals	Substantial proportion of personnel, especially at high levels, feel responsibility and generally behave in ways to achieve the organization's goals	Personnel at all levels feel real responsibility for organization's goals and behave in ways to implement them

348

| | System of Organization | | | |
| Organizational Variable | Authoritative | | Participative | |
	Exploitative Authoritative System 1	Benevolent Authoritative System 2	Consultative System 3	Participative Group System 4
3. Character of Communication Process				
• Amount of interaction and communication aimed at achieving organization's objectives	Very little	Little	Quite a bit	Much with both individuals and groups
• Direction of information flow	Downward	Mostly downward	Down and up	Down, up, and with peers
• Extent to which downward communications are accepted by subordinates	Viewed with great suspicion	May or may not be viewed with suspicion	Often accepted but at times viewed with suspicion; may or may not be openly questioned	Generally accepted, but if not, openly and candidly questioned
• Accuracy of upward communication via line	Tends to be inaccurate	Information that boss wants to hear flows; other information is restricted and filtered	Information that boss wants to hear flows; other information may be limited or cautiously given	Accurate

349

Table 17.2 (continued)

| Organizational Variable | System of Organization | | | |
| | Authoritative | | Participative | |
	Exploitative Authoritative System 1	Benevolent Authoritative System 2	Consultative System 3	Participative Group System 4
• Psychological closeness of superiors to subordinates (i.e., How well does superior know and understand problems faced by subordinates?)	Has no knowledge or understanding of problems of subordinates	Has some knowledge and understanding of problems of subordinates	Knows and understands problems of subordinates quite well	Knows and understands problems of subordinates very well
4. Character of Interaction-Influence Process				
• Amount and character of interaction	Little interaction and always with fear and distrust	Little interaction and usually with some condescension by superiors; fear and caution by subordinates	Moderate interaction, often with fair amount of confidence and trust	Extensive, friendly interaction with high degree of confidence and trust
• Amount of cooperative teamwork present	None	Relatively little	A moderate amount	Very substantial amount throughout the organization

Organizational Variable	System of Organization			
	Authoritative		Participative	
	Exploitative Authoritative System 1	Benevolent Authoritative System 2	Consultative System 3	Participative Group System 4
5. Character of Decision-Making Process				
• At what level in organization are decisions formally made?	Bulk of decisions at top of organization	Policy at top, many decisions within prescribed framework made at lower levels	Broad policy and general decisions at top, more specific decisions at lower levels	Decision making widely done throughout organization, although well integrated through linking process provided by overlapping groups
• To what extent are decision makers aware of problems, particularly those at lower levels in the organization?	Often are unaware or only partially aware	Aware of some, unaware of others	Moderately aware of problems	Generally quite well aware of problems
• Extent to which technical and professional knowledge is used in decision making	Used only if possessed at higher levels	Much of what is available in higher and middle levels is used	Much of what is available in higher, middle, and lower levels is used	Most of what is available anywhere within the organization is used
• To what extent are subordinates involved in decisions related to their work?	Not at all	Never involved in decisions; occasionally consulted	Usually are consulted but ordinarily not involved in the decision making	Are involved fully in all decisions related to their work

Table 17.2 *(continued)*

Organizational Variable	*System of Organization*			
	Authoritative		*Participative*	
	Exploitative Authoritative System 1	*Benevolent Authoritative* System 2	*Consultative* System 3	*Participative Group* System 4
• Are decisions made at the best level in the organization so far as the motivational consequences? (i.e., Does the decision-making process help to create the necessary motivations in those persons who have to carry out the decisions?)	Decision making contributes little or nothing to the motivation to implement the decision, usually yields adverse motivation	Decision making contributes relatively little motivation	Some contribution by decision making to motivation to implement	Substantial contribution by decision-making processes to motivation to implement
6. Character of Goal Setting or Ordering				
• Manner in which usually done	Orders issued	Orders issued, opportunity to comment may or may not exist	Goals are set or orders issued after discussion with subordinate(s) of problems and planned action	Except in emergencies, goals are usually established by means of group participation
• Are there forces to accept, resist, or reject goals?	Goals are overtly accepted but are covertly resisted strongly	Goals are overtly accepted but often covertly resisted to at least a moderate degree	Goals are overtly accepted but at times with some covert resistance	Goals are fully accepted both overtly and covertly

	System of Organization			
	Authoritative		Participative	
Organizational Variable	Exploitative Authoritative System 1	Benevolent Authoritative System 2	Consultative System 3	Participative Group System 4

7. Character of Control Processes

- Extent to which the review and control functions are concentrated

| Highly concentrated in top management | Relatively highly concentrated, with some control delegated to middle and lower levels | Moderate downward delegation of review and control processes; lower as well as higher levels feel responsible | Quite widespread responsibility for review and control, with lower units at times imposing more rigorous reviews and tighter controls than top management |

- Extent to which there is an informal organization present and supporting or opposing goals of formal organization

| Informal organization present and opposing goals of formal organization | Informal organization usually present and partially resisting goals | Informal organization may be present and may either support or partially resist goals of formal organization | Informal and formal organization are one and the same; hence all social forces support efforts to achieve organization's goals |

- Extent to which control data (e.g., accounting, productivity, cost, etc.) are used for self-guidance or group problem solving by managers and nonsupervisory employees; or used by superiors in a punitive, policing manner

| Used for policing and in punitive manner | Used for policing coupled with reward and punishment, sometimes punitively; used somewhat for guidance but in accord with orders | Largely used for policing with emphasis usually on reward but with some punishment; used for guidance in accord with orders; some use also for self-guidance | Used for self-guidance and for coordinated problem solving and guidance; not used punitively |

353

The underlying principles and objectives of Likert's management approach are summarized as follows:

1. Likert feels that most business organizations tap very little resources and potentialities of their people.

2. He emphasizes a group-type structure in which key relationships are not person to person, but person to group.

3. He utilizes linking pin description to show how a person can be simultaneously a member of two groups—one in which he is the superior, the other a subordinate.

4. For groups to be effective, he advocates

   (a) Open communication

   (b) Mutual trust

   (c) Group participation in decision making

   (d) Use of group goals

   (e) Defined roles

   (f) Respect for manager

5. As to management authority, Likert emphasizes that

   (a) Formal authority is hierarchical and flows downward.

   (b) Real authority flows upward—What the subordinates will "allow" manager to exert.

   (c) Subordinates evaluate a superior's effectiveness on the ability of that superior to influence his superior or his peers. From this evaluation he is "allowed" more or less authority.

6. Likert classifies business organizations as

   (a) Exploitive-Authoritative

   (b) Benevolent-Authoritative

   (c) Consultative

   (d) Participative-Group

17.2.4   Situational Theory

Behavioral researchers have identified several types of management methods or leadership styles. The two most important are autocratic and supportive. See Table 17.3 for the explanations of these management methods. Other styles are laissez-faire, in which the leader provides little direction or regulation, and bureaucratic, in which leadership or management is based on a set of rules or procedures (a form of autocracy). Some

Table 17.3.   Autocratic and Supportive Management Methods

TYPE	EXPLANATION
Autocratic	The leader determines policy and directs the activities required to carry it out. He or she seldom gives reasons for orders. The leader's commands are enforced by the power to reward or punish.
Supportive	This type is called participative, consultative, or democratic leadership. The leader solicits suggestions and consults with his subordinates about decisions affecting them or decisions they will have to carry out. Supervision is general, and subordinates are encouraged to use initiative.

researchers have suggested that the most effective style of management is dependent on the personality of the manager; the task to be performed; the attitude, needs, and expectations of the subordinates; and the organizational and physical environment. This is termed "situational theory."

The evidence to date suggests that a supportive management method or leadership style leads to higher satisfaction, but not necessarily to higher production. One important consideration is the extent to which the manager carries out the management functions (planning, organizing, and so forth). Carrying out these functions (also termed "instrumental leadership" or "management behavior") provides the structure that is important to productivity. When highly supportive management is combined with effective instrumental management or leadership behavior, the results have indicated both high satisfaction and high productivity.

An autocratic, nonparticipative management method is apparently most effective (especially if benevolent) when decisions are routine, there are standard procedures and rules, and subordinates do not feel a need to participate. Supportive, participative management is apparently most effective when decisions are not routine, information and rules for decision making are not standardized, there is sufficient time to involve subordinates, and subordinates feel the need for independence and that their participation is legitimate.

17.2.5   The Grid Theory

The Grid Theory was developed by Dr. Robert Blake and Dr. Jane Mouton. This theory considers concerns for people and for production. Table 17.4 summarizes the philosophies underlying the Grid Theory.

Table 17.4.   The Grid (Developed by Dr. Robert R. Blake and Dr. Jane S. Mouton)

1, 9
Thoughtful Attention to Needs of People for Satisfying Relationships Leads to a Comfortable Organization Atmosphere and Work Tempo

9, 9
Work Accomplishment Is from Committed People; Interdependence through a "Common Stake" In Organization Purpose Leads to Relationships of Trust and Respect

5, 5
Adequate Organization Performance Is Possible through Balancing the Necessity to Get Out Work While Maintaining Morale of People at a Satisfactory Level

1, 1
Exertion of Minimum Effort to Get Required Work Done Is Appropriate to Sustain Organization Membership

9, 1
Efficiency In Operation Results from Arranging Conditions of Work In Such a Way That Human Elements Interfere to a Minimum Degree

Concern for People — High 9, 8, 7, 6, 5, 4, 3, 2, Low 1

Concern for Production — Low 1, 2, 3, 4, 5, 6, 7, 8, 9 High

17.3   RECOMMENDED GUIDELINES FOR DEVELOPING A WORKABLE MANAGEMENT METHOD

Managers, in general, are frequently guilty of mechanistic views of human beings and their interactions in organizations. In most cases, human beings are viewed to perform and act like machines when considering productivity or productions. Considerations such as human needs, job enrichment, job environment, and human relations are often ignored.

Table 17.5.   Autocratic Nonparticipative Management Factors

PROBLEM	COMMENTS
Not all managers have the same leadership style	This may mean that a project or job designed for a nonparticipative manager will not suit a participative management method or leadership style.
Computerizing some activities may reduce task variety and make a job less interesting	Computers do not need variety; humans do. Computers make possible assembly-line-style pacing for many clerical and managerial activities, but if the job is reduced in variety, it may cause boredom.
Not all work groups have the same need for participation	For example, where decisions must be made quickly, there will be little demand for participation. But where the technical ability of subordinates is equal to or even greater than the leader/manager (such as in a research group), participation is likely to be important.

If an autocratic, nonparticipative method of management and a mechanistic, economic motivation are assumed, the job or project is clearly less complicated. Functions can be allocated on the basis of relative efficiency. Computer-based decision rules provide instant decisions with little management participation. However, the following factors (as seen in Table 17.5) suggest difficulties in pursuing this view for all projects or jobs.

The importance of the structuring activities of the manager suggests that management should not overlook the use of the style or method as a tool for helping the manager initiate structure by planning, organizing, and so forth. For example, planning forms assist the manager to do the planning activities. In much the same way, man/machine routines can aid the manager's instrumental behavior.

The manager may find the area of organization interaction difficult because the rules and principles are not well defined, most of the time. However, there are some central tendencies that can be relied upon. Man is clearly adaptable and operates successfully in a wide range of conditions or jobs. Therefore, a manager need not only strive for meeting goals or objectives but should not overlook the behavioral implications of alternatives and the people under him or her.

The following thoughts are provided to guide each manager in developing his or her management method or leadership style:

1. You can make more friends in two months by becoming interested in other people than you can in two years by trying to get other people interested in you.

2. Whenever you are in an angry mood, stop and find out why; then figure out something constructive to do about it. Never stay angry—people who do are digging their own graves.

3. It is very easy for a busy person to fall into the habit of telling people to do things without further explanation. It seems like the quickest and easiest way to get things done. However, it is rarely the best way. When you ask a subordinate to do something, take time to explain why. Explaining why you want something done automatically removes the curse of "bossiness"—that is, the bad taste that comes from "ordering people around."

4. To get better results from his or her people, a manager should let them know they have his or her full backing and support. Then make good on the promise.

5. I have yet to find a person, however exalted his or her station, who did not do better work and put forth greater effort under a spirit of approval than under a spirit of criticism.

17.4   SUMMARY

It is vital that managers and supervisors understand organization and management theory because their jobs or projects affect both the organization and its management.

The management functions of planning, organizing, and others involve structuring activities, decision making, and human interactions. The structuring activities consist of formulating the problems to be solved, putting priorities on various activities, defining the limits for solutions to be worked on, and so forth. Both manual and computer-based procedures can assist the manager to provide structure by suggesting possible structures.

The organizing function involves formulating an organization structure and assignment of responsibility and authority. There are a few "principles" that traditionally have been used to decide on the organizational form. However, the organization best suited for a task depends on many factors, one of the most important being the requirement placed on the organization for communication and information processing (by individuals, not computers).

Human interaction is a vital ingredient in an organization. The production effect of different patterns of management or leadership seems to depend on several factors, but the satisfaction of employees is generally higher with participative, supportive management. Goal setting is an important element of management. One theory is that such goals are a result of bargaining among the individuals in the group, each one having his or her individual goals. Planning is carried on at all levels of an organization. Control is exercised through a feedback mechanism and requires elements such as a standard of performance against which to measure actual performance. A basic understanding of individuals and groups of people is the main requirement of the behavioral scientist. A project group should have team spirit, which can assist productivity. The most fascinating works in behavioral science to which only brief reference can be made here are

1. Mayo—the human relations approach, which is founded on the thought that work is a group activity.

2. Hawthorne experiments—studied the effect of illumination on the workers and their work.

3. McGregor—Theory "X", which assumes work is distasteful, versus Theory "Y", which assumes people want to contribute to meaningful goals and that work is as natural as play or rest.

4. Likert—identified four main types of management style, for example, authoritative, authoritative-benevolent, consultative, and participative. He stated that the participative system is ideal for profit-oriented- and human-concerned organizations.

5. Blake and Mouton—This work is based on the use of the "Blake" grid, which considers concern for the task and concern for people.

6. Maslow—Hierarchy of human needs, which considers a scale of basic needs as follows:

    (a) physiological needs, hunger, thirst;

    (b) security, shelter, warmth;

    (c) to belong;

    (d) for self-expression;

    (e) self-fulfillment.

The highly motivated individual has the ambition to get the desired results, but there are others who are content with security.

7. Hertzberg—Motivation and hygiene theory and his thoughts are based on reaction to the environment. He identifies certain factors in the work situation as hygienic factors. These have to be watched to keep the place 'clean.' On the other hand, he identifies motivational factors. Hygiene is set out as salary, security, conditions of work, supervision, interpersonal relationships, fringe benefits. Motivation is set out as participation, recognition, achievement, advancement, type of work, responsibility for increased tasks.

18

Labor Relations
and Construction Management

18.1 REVOLUTION OF LABOR-MANAGEMENT RELATIONS IN THE UNITED STATES

Unionism in the United States is as old as the nation itself. The first signs of industrial organization were employee guilds based on the English pattern—joint associations of employers and craftspeople. As one example, in 1648 the Boston coopers and shoemakers formed a joint employer-employee guild to enforce manufacturing standards as a means of protecting jobs and checking competition from newly arrived immigrants. In addition to the guilds, in New York and Philadelphia there were a number of licensed trades—occupations regarded as essential to public welfare—whose members were licensed by the city corporations. The trades, like the guilds, sought to benefit employer and employee alike. They hoped to reduce outside employer alike, as well as outside competition, which, they felt, produced inferior goods.

The first unions of employees were only local. They were formed in the last decades of the eighteenth century by craftsmen in carpentry, shoemaking, and printing. The first strike was called in 1768 by printers in Philadelphia trying to maintain their existing wages. The employers won, and the union was dissolved. Generally, employee-oriented strikes were unknown before 1820, since only two industries, shoemaking and printing, were engaged in collective bargaining. The Philadelphia cordwainers strike, to be discussed later, was an important exception.

In the 1820s the first labor movement on a scale larger than that of the local craft union appeared in the form of city-wide federations. These federations aided each other in strikes and organizing efforts, and in promoting the sale of union-made goods. They (1) represented the labor movement in its dealings with city authorities and the general public; (2) created local labor parties and elected a few candidates to office; (3) advocated the ten-hour day, free public education, abolition of imprisonment for debt, regulation of child labor, and the legality of mechanics' liens; and (4) attempted to counter the practices of the many employers who were using prisoners or other cheap labor then in response to the current economic recession.

In 1834 an effort was made to form a national trade union organization by federating a number of the local central labor bodies. The National Trades' union achieved very little before it was wiped out with most of the existing labor movement during the depression that followed the Panic of 1837. Between 1850 and 1869 there were two occurrences that would have a lasting impact on organized labor. The first was the Civil War, which brought mass production and, in turn, reduced the need for skilled craftspeople and brought semiskilled and unskilled employees under one factory roof. Out of this grew increased employee concern for working conditions. This type of situation held attraction for organized labor. The second occurrence was employers' use of "scapegoating," or blaming violent incidents on outside, possibly foreign, labor agitators. For example, the Irish immigrants, known as the Molly McGuires, engaged in violence against railroad and coal mining owners. Other employers and the media blamed them for other crimes not of their doing. Scapegoating identified organized labor with violent anti-American values and actions, and employers learned to use it to bring the media, and sometimes government troops, to their aid in quelling employee unrest. During this period, aided by new and improved means of communication, national unions were formed in some industries. The National Labor union, established in 1866, sought to unite the growing labor movement. It campaigned for the eight-hour day, for producers' cooperatives, and for political action by labor. It survived until the 1872 elections, when the candidates it backed were not elected.

As a continuous, more or less unified movement, unionism in the United States began between 1880 and the beginning of World War I. The Knights of Labor, organized in secret in 1869 so that its members would not be fired from their jobs, emerged in 1880. The Knights were followed by the American Federation of Labor in 1886, and by the Industrial Workers of the World in 1905. The experience of each of these groups during this time offers lessons still heeded by organized labor.

The 1880s were one of the most dramatic decades in the history of U.S. labor. At the beginning of the decade, the Knights of Labor (KOL) was barely known. By 1886, the Knights, under the leadership of Terrence Powderly, had nearly a million members, and their influence transcended their size. The KOL's fade from power, though, was as swift as its rise. The Knights were popular partially because they were identified with the campaign to shorten the work day from ten to eight hours. They were also successful in their strike against Jay Gould's railroads in 1885. The KOL was based on the concept of "one big union." Everyone was welcome, including employers. Only those judged to be morally unfit were excluded. These included owners of gold, bankers, stockbrokers, lawyers, gamblers, and anyone dealing in the sale or manufacture of liquor. The real power of the Knights was concentrated at the top—with Powderly. The KOL had two goals. First, it wanted to change the existing industrial and societal system. Powderly particularly disliked the currency and banking system. He believed that bankers and owners of gold were villains who coerced Congress to pass legislation beneficial to their interests. He further believed that mass production was dehumanizing, reducing employees' pride and feelings of accomplishment. Changing the system, Powderly hoped, would help accomplish the KOL's second goal—that of moral improvement and increased dignity for its members. The Knights had several strategies for bringing these goals to pass. They engaged in political action; they lobbied but never tried to form an independent party. They also encouraged producer and consumer cooperatives; however, they did not give financial aid to the cooperatives, and most failed quickly. Powderly shunned the use of strikes. Instead, he preferred to educate members to the evils of the existing industrial system. The KOL's rapid demise was partially due to the lack of protective labor legislation then. However, the Knights were also predicated on some faulty assumptions. They believed technology could be halted. They believed that all those in "one big union" would share common interests. This approach was complicated not only by the inclusion of employers, but also by the many immigrant members who differed in race, language, and religion. The main reason, though, was Powderly's belief in moral improvement as a goal, rather than the short-term interests of the members. He could not identify with members' needs.

The Chicago Haymarket Riot of 1886 signaled the end of the KOL and the rise of the American Federation of Labor (AFL). Three thousand workers came to Haymarket Square to call out a nationwide strike for the eight-hour day. After a peaceful beginning, a bomb was thrown into a group of police who responded by opening fire on the crowd. Several people were killed and over 200 wounded. The event and subsequent trial received wide, inflammatory press coverage. Nearly 340,000 employees across the country then struck for the eight-hour day. Public opinion blamed the Knights for the riot and the strikes, though the newspapers never said so. At the same time, the KOL members thought their group had not participated enough. This paradox ended the power of the Knights.

The AFL came into being in 1886 after some KOL members, mainly the cigar makers led by Samuel Gompers, were expelled for leading a strike in defiance of Powderly's wishes. Gompers became the dominant force in the AFL and remained so until his death in 1924. His philosophies, which varied greatly from those of the Knights, are still the basis of current thinking of organized labor. There has been relatively little change in orientations, strategy, and organization since then. Gompers shunned the KOL goal of moral improvement and its strong centralized leadership. He believed the issues should originate from the members' needs, and flow from the "bottom up." He believed in "pure and simple unionism" with two major objectives. First was the economic improvement of union members. Second was the enhancement of the capitalistic system, a system he endorsed. He believed that when the system flourished, the union member would be better off economically. Gompers believed in the strike and the boycott as major tactics. He also endorsed political involvement—not by forming a separate party, but by "defeating labor's enemies and rewarding its friends." The AFL structure, under Gompers' guidance, was based on "exclusive jurisdiction" and decentralized authority. There was no "one big union," but separate unions for each craft. The real authority in the AFL rested with the various national unions and their member locals. Two events occurred in the 1890s that enhanced the position of the AFL, though the events were defeats for the labor unions involved. They were the Homestead Incident and the Pullman Strike.

The Homestead Incident occurred in 1892 at the Carnegie Steel Works in Homestead, Pennsylvania. Members of the AFL affiliate, the Amalgamated Association of Iron, Steel, and Tin Workers, were locked out of the plant over a wage dispute. Six thousand employees, gathered around the plant, were stormed by company-hired Pinkerton detectives. Shooting occurred for twelve hours, and 8,700 National Guardsmen were called in to secure the town. Five months later the steel workers decided to return to work. Homestead was the Waterloo of unions in the steel industry until the 1930s. Carnegie's profits rose during the strike, and other employers were encouraged to take a similar stance. However, since Gompers had helped to defray the workers' legal expenses after the incident, other union members felt increased loyalty to the AFL. Also, the newspaper accounts were somewhat sympathetic to the unions.

The 1894 Pullman Strike became a nationwide strike in one industry (railroads), and came close to involving all industries. The American Railway Union (ARU), headed by Eugene Debs, was an independent union; it accepted any railway worker and competed with the AFL brotherhoods. The ARU waged a two-month strike against the Pullman Company. The company responded by putting federal mail on all their trains, and then convinced President Cleveland to dispatch 16,000 federal troops to operate the trains and protect strikebreakers. Later, the strikers burned 700 railcars in the Chicago yards. Debs turned to Gompers to call a nationwide strike and was refused. Gompers said he did not have such authority. The strike failed, Debs was convicted under the Sherman Anti-Trust Act, and the ARU folded. Many of the disenchanted members joined the AFL.

In 1905 the Industrial Workers of the World (IWW), headed by "Big Bill" Haywood, was formed. The goal of the IWW was to overthrow the existing capitalistic system by any means, and to remove any group that supported capitalism, including the AFL. However, the organization was short-lived. Its leaders never could agree on how to organize. Furthermore, there were four major reasons for the IWW's demise. First, IWW lacked a permanent membership and financial base; members (many of them transient workers) were asked to contribute, guided by "inner conviction" rather than a set dues schedule. Also, IWW did not appeal to members' basic interests; instead, it emphasized revolution. The IWW became identified with sabotage and violence. And, finally, the IWW alienated the news and government officials—often intentionally.

By the start of World War I, the AFL was the dominant labor force in the country, despite the fact that it represented mainly skilled labor, and not the larger proportion of labor—the unskilled industrial employees. (There were some large independent unions then, too—e.g., certain railroad brotherhoods and the Amalgamated Clothing Workers.) During the war the AFL pledged cooperation, and the government, seeing the necessity of uninterrupted production, attempted to help labor. It elevated labor to a more important position and placed labor representatives in many government agencies. Congress legislated against the immigrant influx, which had reached 1,285,000 newcomers in 1907. In response, AFL membership rose from 2,370,000 to 3,260,000 between 1917 and 1919.

It was different, though, after the war. The "Golden Twenties" was a dreary decade for labor. The cost of living rose and brought on a number of strikes. And labor's increased militancy brought on counteractions by employers. These were mainly in two forms—aggressive opposition to unions, and formation of alternatives to unions. Employers hired industrial spies to infiltrate unions, and often discharged and blacklisted union members. Companies began paternalistic practices, offering free lunches, baseball fields, vacations, and began to form company unions called Employee Representation Plans (ERPs). In 1928, 1,548,000 workers were in ERPs. In these company unions, employers would influence the election of employee members to the labor-management committees and could veto any decision by the committee not of their liking.

Because it could not overcome antiunion sentiment, organized labor was unable to grow during the 1920s. Times were good and who needed a union then? Also, many believed that labor was corrupt and harbored Communists and other political radicals. Labor's concern with this problem detracted from its organizing efforts, particularly among the large ranks of unskilled and semiskilled workers.

The AFL's inattention to these employees led to the formation and split of the CIO from AFL ranks in the 1930s. The AFL convention delegates in 1935 voted to reject the concept of industrial unionism—that is, organizing employees by industry rather than by craft. This decision ignored the fact that craft employees no longer dominated the scene. At Ford Motor Company in 1926, for example, 85% of the hourly employees required less than two weeks of training. After the convention, though, a Committee of Industrial Organizations was formed in the AFL without knowledge of AFL leaders. Early in 1936 the committee requested granting industrial charters to the rubber workers and the auto workers. The committee also pressed for organizing the steel industry. John L. Lewis of the United Mine Workers provoked a confrontation, and when AFL leaders refused to agree to the committee demands, a million members left the AFL and formed the Congress of Industrial Organizations (CIO). Within one year's time, the CIO had organized 75% of the steel industry, 70% of the auto workers, 65% of the rubber workers, and 33% of the textile and maritime industries.

The CIO grew rapidly for several reasons. It had aggressive leaders—John L. Lewis, Sidney Hillman, and David Dubinsky. Although it was "one big union" like the ill-fated KOL and IWW, it worked on realistic short-run goals. It pioneered the effective use of sit-down strikes; the 1936 strike at General Motors in Flint, Michigan, was successful, and this drew new members to the CIO before the Supreme Court ruled the tactic illegal. The CIO was also aided by favorable legislation, the Wagner Act of 1935. And, finally, the depression made workers see the need for unions mainly for help with job security. The AFL, despite membership defection, continued to grow, too. The Wagner Act and the depression brought members to them, and employers now promoted the AFL because they preferred to deal with labor's more conservative group rather than the CIO.

By the beginning of World War II, organized labor membership was almost nine million. There had been great union growth during the preceding decade, and there was intense rivalry between the AFL and the CIO. During the war, labor again pledged its cooperation to the war effort. But the cooperative spirit was not total. Cost of living increases were greater than wage increases permitted by the government. The United Mine Workers struck and got a compromise wage settlement from the government, and strong negative sentiment from the public.

At the war's end, labor remembered how employers after World War I had tried to restrict union gains. Now, labor wanted full employment and further wage increases, and they backed these desires with a flurry of strikes after VJ Day—4,600 strikes within one year! This undoubtedly contributed to more restrictive legislation, such as the Taft-Hartley Act of 1947. In the postwar period, the unions have tried to organize both white-collar workers and public employees with mixed success. They have directed their efforts to guaranteeing job security in the face of technological advance, to cushioning worker displacements, and to gaining compensation when jobs have to be given up. They have negotiated cost of living increases into their contracts, which now generally span several years. In fact, the modern labor agreement no longer covers only wages and hours, but virtually all aspects of employment. Often, in collective bargaining, a "pattern" agreement is worked out, where a settlement for one company or industry influences subsequent bargaining tactics at another location.

The most dramatic development of this period has been the AFL-CIO merger. The early rivalry did not change, but other factors did. The earlier presidents of the rival unions, who had each gone on record saying, "No merger!," were succeeded by new men. Union raiding between the two groups used time and energy that could be better spent organizing nonunion employees. The organizations, operating separately, were ineffective politically. Senator Robert Taft, coauthor of the Taft-Hartley Act, was not defeated, and presidential candidate Adlai Stevenson, a friend of labor, was not elected, despite the fact that most union members have voted Democratic since the 1930s. The AFL-CIO merger was accomplished in 1955. It united 15,550,000 members, thus making the organization the largest trade union in the world.

Organized labor has not changed much since the end of World War II. It remains a minority movement in the United States though it is still influential. Since 1945, union membership has never exceeded 28% of the civilian work force. In 1974, there were 21,643,000 union members representing almost 22% of the work force.

Labor continues to have minimal effectiveness in the political community, possibly because of negative public opinion and the difficulty of mobilizing younger union members. Labor's goal of pursuing short-range material goals has not changed, nor have its basic tactics.

Robotics and a sagging economy are major concerns today. Some unions are currently agreeing to wage cuts in exchange for job security.

18.2   SOME LEGAL MILESTONES IN LABOR RELATIONS

18.2.1   The Philadelphia Cordwainers Strike of 1806

The Philadelphia cordwainers (journeymen shoemakers) banded together to try to raise their wages, refusing to work with outsiders or at a wage rate less than they demanded. They were indicted, convicted, and fined $8 each for forming an illegal criminal conspiracy. This was the first labor relations case in United States legal history.

This application of the criminal conspiracy doctrine to attempts by employees to organize unions aroused much public protest, not only from employees, but also from factory owners who feared their factories would be closed if employee sentiment ran too high.

18.2.2   The Commonwealth of Massachusetts v. Hunt—1842

Seven members of the Journeymen Bootmakers Society refused to work in shops where nonmembers were employed at less than their scheduled rate of $2 per boot. They were convicted of criminal conspiracy. Massachusetts Supreme Court Justice Shaw set aside the conviction and cut the heart from the criminal conspiracy doctrine. He insisted that to determine the legality of a particular labor union, an investigation must be made of its objectives and of the means used to achieve them. He stated that an association of workers might be for useful and honorable purposes, rather than always for purposes of oppression and injustice. The decision virtually ended the use of the criminal conspiracy doctrine in labor relations.

18.2.3   Vegelahn v. Guntner

A Massachusetts court issued an injunction against a union that was picketing for higher wages and shorter hours. The court agreed that the union's purposes were legitimate, but decreed that picketing and refusing to work would lead to more serious trouble. Thus injunctive relief was warranted.

This established the use of a civil conspiracy doctrine, which replaced the criminal conspiracy doctrine. Courts generally favored the employer and issued injunctions against unions for many years, since there was no legislative act to deal with these situations.

18.2.4 "Yellow Dog Contract" Injunctions

A "yellow dog contract" was an agreement stating that an employee would neither join nor assist in organizing a union. Signing such a contract was required by many employers before hiring jobs applicants. The contract was a condition of continued employment; violating it allowed the company to discharge the employee. If union organizers tried to solicit those who had signed such contracts, they would be interfering with a contract between the employers and their employees. The employees could be sued for breach of contract, and the employers could get an injunction against the union organizer.

18.2.5 Sherman Anti-Trust Act of 1890 and Loewe v. Lawlor (The Danbury Hatters' Case)—1908

The Sherman Anti-Trust Act stated that "every contract, combination in the form of trust or otherwise, or conspiracy, in restraint of trade or commerce among the several states . . . is hereby declared to be illegal." The wording made it debatable whether Congress intended unions to be covered.

The Danbury Hatters' Case tested this in the Supreme Court. The United Hatters of America had tried to organize a hatters' union in Loewe and Company. When the company resisted, the union struck; strikers were replaced and operations continued. The United Hatters then organized a nationwide boycott, assisted by the AFL, and directed it against retailers, wholesalers, and customers of the company. The boycott was successful. The company lost $85,000 in one year. Loewe and Company carried their case against the union to the Supreme Court. The Court said the unions were covered by the Sherman Anti-Trust Act, and it levied damages ($252,000) against the union.

Organized labor responded by pressing for changes in the Sherman Act. The campaign led to the Clayton Act of 1914.

18.2.6 Clayton Act of 1914

The Clayton Act said that

> The labor of a human being is not a commodity. Nothing contained in the anti-trust laws shall be construed to forbid the existence and operations of labor unions . . . nor shall they be construed to be illegal combinations or conspiracies in restraint of trade. No restraining order or injunction shall be granted for a dispute concerning terms or conditions of employment, unless to prevent injury to property. No restraining order shall prohibit any person (from striking).

At first, Samuel Gompers called it "U.S. labor's Magna Charta." However, Supreme Court decisions in the 1920s rendered it otherwise. Under the act, an injunction was easier to obtain. Previously, only a U.S. district attorney could seek an injunction; now an employer could. It was also ruled that only employees of a company could boycott it. If other sympathetic union members joined in the boycott, they could be restrained by a legal injunction. And finally, the Court defined "peaceful picketing" as a single person at a plant entrance with a sign—a one-person picket line. Anything more could bring an injunction.

18.2.7   Norris-LaGuardia Act of 1932 (Federal Anti-Injunction Act)

In the early 1930s, with the beginning of the country's most severe economic depression, political pressure on Congress mounted, reflecting the general dissatisfaction with judicial restrictions in labor relations. Passing the Norris-LaGuardia Act marked a change in philosophy in labor relations.

The act gave employees full freedom of association and of negotiation, with freedom from employer coercion. There could be no injunctions unless an employer could prove that there had been unlawful acts committed, injury would follow, there was no legal remedy, the employer had no adequate protection, and he had made an all-out effort to reach agreement. The act also outlawed the "yellow dog contract." However, there was no enforcing agency.

18.2.8   The Wagner Act (National Labor Relations Act)—1935

The Wagner Act guaranteed certain employee rights, detailed employer unfair labor practices, and created the National Labor Relations Board to enforce its provisions. The board would judge unfair labor practices and conduct representation elections. The act specified that an employer cannot restrain an employee from forming a union, joining or not joining a union, from collective bargaining, striking, picketing, or boycotting. In addition, an employer cannot dominate a union (no company unions, no sweetheart agreements). Employers cannot discriminate, by hiring or firing, to encourage employees to agree with them. An employer cannot discriminate against an employee who has filed charges against the employer. The employer must bargain in good faith.

Employers sought to have the act declared unconstitutional, but the Supreme Court upheld it in NRLB v. Jones & Laughlin Steel Corporation in 1937. Union membership rose drastically.

18.2.9   The Taft-Hartley Act (Labor-Management Relations Act)—1947

Labor lost its advantageous position with the passage of this act. The main purpose of the act was to insure that public interest was protected in the conduct of labor affairs.

The act said that the union or the employees cannot restrain or coerce employees in their individual rights. The union cannot force the company to discriminate against any employee. The union must bargain in good faith. The union may not force "hot cargo" agreements, secondary boycotts, discriminatory work agreements. The union cannot levy discriminatory or excessive dues. There will be no featherbedding. The act also established the Federal Mediation and Conciliation Services and gave the President of the United States powers to act in the case of a labor dispute that imperiled national health or safety.

Union membership stabilized after this act, and then began a slow decline.

18.2.10   The Landrum-Griffin Act (Labor-Management Reporting and Disclosure Act)—1959

This act was passed after publication of abuses of power and corruption of union leaders. The act targeted on internal union affairs to safeguard the rights of individual union members, ensure fair union elections, and prevent corruption and racketeering.

The act specifies that members have equal participation in the union. Officers must give financial disclosures. The union trusteeships will be regulated. Union elections must be fair. There can be no criminals or Communists in union offices. Certain officers must be bonded, and fiduciary responsibilities of officers outlined.

18.2.11   The Civil Rights Act—1964

The Civil Rights Act of 1964 was passed by Congress. This act confirmed and established individual rights pertaining to (a) voting; (b) access to public accommodations, public facilities, and public education; (c) participation in federally assisted programs; (d) and opportunities for employment. It also prohibits discrimination in employment or union membership. It is unlawful for an employer (a) to refuse to hire or to discharge any individual or otherwise discriminate against him or her regarding conditions of employment because of his or her race, color, religon, sex, or national origin, or (b) to limit, segregate, or classify employees in any way that would deprive the individual of employment opportunity or adversely affect his or her status as an employee because of race, color, religion, sex, or national origin.

18.2.12   The Equal Employment Opportunity Act—1972

This act amended the Civil Rights Act of 1964 in several respects. It also expanded the Civil Rights Act's coverage substantially. This act made the Equal Employment Opportunity Commission (EEOC) responsible for the administration and enforcement of the Civil Rights Act. EEO Act authorized the EEOC to go directly to court for temporary restraining orders and for permanent injunctions against unlawful discrimination.

18.3 SOME POSITIVE ACCOMPLISHMENTS OF THE UNION MOVEMENT

1. Union have given dignity to the working person.

2. Unions have ensured that the working person draws a saving pay.

3. Unions have provided skill training to millions of workers.

4. Unions serve as a source of trained workers.

5. By increasing the buying power of the working person, unions have contributed to the expansion of the American economy.

6. The workers have been given a voice that must be heard by management.

18.4 PREHIRE AGREEMENTS

Section 8(f) of the National Labor Relations Act allows an employer engaged primarily in the building and construction industry to sign a union-shop agreement with a union that has not been elected as the representative of his employees. The agreement can be made before the contractor has hired any employees and will apply to them when they are hired. This proviso is called the "prehire" provision of the act. Contractors frequently make prehire agreements with construction unions at the outset of large projects as a means of trying to stabilize labor costs and securing a source of skilled manpower.

The union's right to maintain and enforce such a labor contract can be challenged at any time, however. The law provides that the employer can test by a representation vote the majority status of the union. Until the union can show it has the support of the majority of the employees, the contractor is free to ignore the prehire bargaining agreement or unilaterally change the terms and conditions of employment. The courts have ruled that prehire agreements are not mandatory subjects of bargaining, and unions cannot strike or picket to obtain them. In addition, the law does not give the union any right to enforce such an agreement, either by picketing or in the courts, unless the union can demonstrate that it represents the majority of the company's employees at the company's various jobsites. Hence no enforceable agreement exists prior to a representation election.

18.5   THE CONTRACTOR AND EMPLOYEE RELATIONS

The value of qualified workmen is understood by all contractors, but contractors often pay too little attention to relations with their employees and the representatives of their employees.

Unanticipated labor problems that often arise on a job can easily cut down the profit on a project. Both legal requirements and collective-bargaining agreements have become increasingly complex in recent years. Further, federal and state regulations regarding equal employment opportunities have recently become a very difficult and legally treacherous area for contractors, despite the desire of most employers to conform to both the letter and the spirit of the law.

In such an environment, the contractor and his supervisory personnel are well advised to acquire both a working knowledge of what the law requires of them in relationships with their employees and access to competent legal advice regarding these matters. In many areas a contractors' association renders the services. A contractor of sufficient size may find it useful to hire a staff member to handle personnel policy exclusively. At the least, any contractor, however small, should assign himself or some staff person responsibility for personnel matters. Failure to exercise caution in labor and other personnel relations will eliminate the gains from careful estimating and performance of a job.

18.6   MANAGEMENT RELATIONS

The project manager should create a working relationship with the management of the contractors on the project. It is important to know who makes the decisions that guide the work of the various contractors. This is sometimes difficult. If the contractor is a large corporation, the major decision maker may be far removed from the project and often is not given an evaluation of the problem that is fair to the owner. This is an area where the construction manager is valuable to the project, since he can contact the top management of the contractors on an equal footing. Similarly, the owner is often acquainted with the contractor's management and can discuss the problem with them.

In dealing with management of small contractors, the construction manager may be so involved in many projects that he does not become sufficiently involved in your project. Sometimes he may even be unavailable. The solution to this problem is unrelenting pressure.

The construction manager should insist that the trade contractor's managers or their deputies visit the project before each trade starts work to arrange delivery and storage space, hoisting facilities, and mutually plan the manpower to be assigned and the scheduled progress. Periodic meetings to discuss progress should be held throughout the construction phase.

18.7   SUMMARY

This chapter is designed to acquaint the contractor with the fundamental aspects of employee relations by describing the structure of industrial relations and other aspects of the employment process in the construction industry. Specific problems may require more knowledge than may be available from trade-association representatives or legal counselors.

References

1. Abdun-Nur, E. A., "Inspection and Product Control," *Proceedings of the Sixth Annual Conference*, Utah State University, Utah, March, 1964, pp. 1–17.

2. Abdun-Nur, E. A., "Product Control and Incentives," *Journal of the Construction Division*, ASCE, Vol. 92, No. CO3, Sept., 1966, pp. 25–40.

3. Abdun-Nur, Edward A., "Control of Quality—A System," *Journal of the Construction Division*, ASCE, Vol. 96, No. CO2, Oct., 1970, pp. 119–136.

4. Adrian, James J., and Boyer, LeRoy T., "Modeling Method Productivity," *Journal of the Construction Division*, ASCE, Vol. 102, No. CO1, March 1976, pp. 157–168.

5. AGC, *Construction Management (CM) Delivery Systems for Hospital Facilities—Proceeding from Symposium*, Associated General Contractors of America, 1983.

6. Ahuja, N. N. Martin, and Handa, V. K., "Construction Cost Control System," *American Association of Cost Engineers Bulletin*, Vol. 15, No. CO3, June, 1973, pp. 81–89.

7. Allen, C. R., "Construction Management Concept," *American Association of Cost Engineers Bulletin*, Vol. 15, No. 6, December 1973, pp. 169–173.

8. Aras, R. M., and Surkis, Julius, "PERT and CPM Techniques in Project Management," *Journal of the Construction Division*, ASCE, Vol. 90, No. CO1, March, 1964, pp. 1–26.

9. Barrie, Donald S., and Paulson, Boyd C., Jr., "Professional Construction Management," *Journal of the Construction Division*, ASCE, Vol. 102, No. CO3, Sept., 1976, pp. 425–436.

10. Barrie, Donald S., and Mulch, Gordon L., "The Professional Construction Manager Discovers Value Engineering," *Journal of the Construction Division*, ASCE, Vol. 103, No. CO3, Sept., 1977, pp. 423–436.

11. Barrie, D. S., "The Trade Contractor's View of Construction Management," *Journal of the Construction Division*, ASCE, Vol. 105, No. CO4, Dec., 1979, pp. 381–387.

12. Barrie, D.S., "Guidelines for Successful Construction Management," *Journal of the Construction Division*, ASCE, Vol. 106, No. CO3, No. 6, Sept., 1980, pp. 237–245.

13. Barrie, D.S., *Directions in Managing Construction*, John Wiley & Sons, Inc., New York, N.Y., 1981.

14. Barrie, D.S., "Alternate Management Approaches to Construction Project," in *Engineering and Construction Projects: The Emerging Management Roles*, D.R. Kern, ed., American Society of Civil Engineers, 1982, pp. 198–212.

15. Barrie, D.S., and Paulson, B.C., Jr., *Professional Construction Management*, McGraw-Hill Book Co., Inc., New York, N.Y., 1978.

16. Bartram, Peter, "Construction Computer," *Data Systems (Great Britain)*, Vol. 4, No. 3, March, 1971, pp. 12–16.

17. Benjamin, Neal B.H., and Young, Arthur W., "Comparison of Construction Labor Agreements," *Journal of the Construction Division*, ASCE, Vol. 101, No. CO1, March, 1975, pp. 182–200.

18. Bessom, Richard M., "Marketing's Role in Construction Firms," *Journal of the Construction Division*, ASCE, Vol. 101, No. CO3, Sept., 1975, pp. 647–659.

19. Bhandari, Narindar, "Computer Applications in Construction Management," *Journal of the Construction Division*, ASCE, Vol. 103, No. CO3, Sept., 1977, pp. 343–356.

20. Bhandari, Narindar, "Interaction of Information Flow with Construction Management System," *Journal of Construction Division*, ASCE, Vol. 104, No. CO3, Sept., 1978, pp. 261–268.

21. Borcherding, John D., and Oglesby, Charles H., "Construction Productivity and Job Satisfaction," *Journal of the Construction Division*, ASCE, Vol. 100, No. CO3, Sept. 1974, pp. 413–432.

22. Borcherding, John D., and Oglesby, Charles H., "Job Dissatisfaction in Construction Work," *Journal of the Construction Division*, ASCE, Vol. 101, No. CO2, June 1975, pp. 415–434.

23. Borcherding, John D., "Improving Productivity in Industrial Construction," *Journal of the Construction Division*, Vol. 102, No. CO4, Dec., 1976, pp. 599–614.

24. Borg, R. F., "The General Contractor and the Professional Construction Manager," in *Engineering and Construction Projects: The Emerging Management Roles*, D.R. Kern, ed., American Society of Civil Engineers, 1982, pp. 121–139.

25. Breeze, J. E., "Coming Changes in Construction Management," *Engineering Journal (Canada)*, Vol. 56, No. 3, March, 1973, pp. 38–40.

26. Bush, Vincent G., *Construction Management—A Handbook for Contractors, Architects and Students*, Reston, Virginia, Prentice-Hall Co., 1973.

27. Choromoskos, James, Jr., and McKee, Keith E., "Construction Productivity Improvement," *Journal of the Construction Division*, ASCE, Vol. 107. No. CO1, March, 1981, pp. 35–48.

28. Christensen, Kai, "Renewal of the Building Process," *Build International*, Vol. 5, No. 5, Nov./Dec., 1972, pp. 237–332.

29. Christensen, R.J., and Tatum, C. B., "Labor Relations Considerations on PCM Projects," *Journal of the Construction Division*, ASCE, Vol. 106, No. CO4, Dec., 1980, pp. 535–549.

30. ——, "The Civil Engineer's Role in Productivity in the Construction Industry" presented at the August 23–24, 1976, ASCE National Conference, held at New York, N.Y., 1977.

31. Clough, R.H., and Sears, G.A., *Construction Project Management*, 2nd ed., John Wiley & Sons, Inc., New York, N.Y., 1979.

32. Clough, R. H., *Construction Contracting*, 4th ed., John Wiley & Sons, Inc., New York, N.Y., 1980.

33. ——, "Construction Economy Through Contract Administration, Progress Report of the Special Committee of the Construction Division of the San Francisco Section," *Journal of the Construction Division*, ASCE, Vol. 88, No. CO1, Jan., 1962, pp. 1–12.

34. ——, "Construction Cost Estimating and Control, Progress Report of the Committee on Estimating and Cost Control of the Construction Division," *Journal of the Construction Division*, ASCE, Vol. 88, No. CO2, Sept., 1962, pp. 83–88.

35. Davis, Edward W., and White, Lindsay, "How to Avoid Construction Headaches," *Harvard Business Review*, Vol. 51, No. 2, March/April, 1973, pp. 87–93.

36. Davis, Edward W., "CPM Use in Top 400 Construction Firms," *Journal of the Construction Division*, ASCE, Vol. 100, No. CO1, March, 1974, pp. 39–50.

37. Dean, Joseph, C., et al., "Contractor Quality Control," *Journal of the Construction Division*, ASCE, Vol. 102, No. CO3, Sept., 1976, pp. 535–546.

38. Dressler, J., "Construction Management in West Germany," *Journal of the Construction Division*, ASCE, Vol. 106, No. CO4, Dec., 1980, pp. 477–487.

39. Elvers, Douglas A., "Planning Monitoring Frequencies for CPM Projects," *Journal of the Construction Division*, Vol. 97, No. CO2, Nov. 1971, pp. 211–226.

40. Fenves, Steven F., "Computer in Building Design and Construction," *Building Research*, Vol. 3, No. 2, March/April, 1966, pp. 9–12.

41. Fisk, E. R., *Construction Project Administration*, John Wiley & Sons, Inc., New York, N.Y., 1978.

42. Fondahl, John W., *Some Problem Areas in Current Network Planning Practice and Related Comments on Legal Applications*, Construction Institute, Dept. of Civil Engineering, Stanford University, Cal., TR 193, April, 1975.

43. Foxall, W. B., *Professional Construction Management and Project Administration*, Architectural Record and The American Institute of Architects, New York, N.Y., 1972.

44. Freedman, Arthur R., "Construction Management: An Overview," Paper presented to the Advanced Management Research Seminar, 1970, pp. AF1–AF38.

45. Galbreath, Robert V., "Computer Program for Levelling Resource Usage," *Journal of the Construction Division*, ASCE, Vol. 91, No. CO1, May, 1965, pp. 107–124.

46. Galloway, Patricia, and Nielsen, Kris, "Schedule Control for PCM Projects," *Journal of the Construction Division*, ASCE, Vol. 107, No. CO2, June, 1981, pp. 323–336.

47. Galloway, P. D., "Scheduling the Superprojects," *Engineering and Construction Projects: The Emerging Management Roles*, D. R. Kern, ed., American Society of Civil Engineers, 1982, pp. 140–151.

48. Gan, George M., Jr., "The Construction Manager and Safety," *Journal of the Construction Division*, ASCE, Vol. 107, No. CO2, June 1981, pp. 219–226.

49. Gates, Marvin, et al., "Construction Economy Through Contract Administration, Report of Special Committee of the Construction Division of the San Francisco Section," *Journal of the Construction Division*, ASCE, Vol. 88, No. CO2, Sept., 1962, pp. 93–103.

50. Goldhaber, S., Jha, C. K., and Macedo, M. C., Jr., *Construction Management: Principles and Practices*, John Wiley & Sons, Inc., New York, N.Y., 1977.

51. Gosliner, Leo S., "Champion of Construction Management," *Daily Pacific Builder*, April 27, 1972.

52. GSA Report, *Construction Contracting Systems—A Report on the System used by PBS and Other Organizations*, GSA's Public Building Service, Washington, D.C., March, 1970.

53. Guevara, Jose M., and Boyer, LeRoy T., "Communication Problems within Construction," *Journal of the Construction Division*, ASCE, Vol. 107, No. CO4, Dec., 1981, pp. 551–558.

54. Halpin, Daniel W., and Tutos, Nicolai, "Construction Information Systems in Romania," *Journal of the Construction Division*, ASCE, Vol. 102, No. CO2, June, 1976, pp. 335–346.

55. Halpin, D. W., and Woodhead, R. W., *Construction Management, A Systems Approach*, John Wiley & Sons, Inc., New York, N.Y., 1977.

56. Hannan, Roger J., "Construction's Changing Professionals—Probing the Future," *Engineering News Record*, Vol. 192, No. 13, March, 1974, pp. 271–278.

57. Hazeltine, Craig, "Motivation of Construction Workers," *Journal of the Construction Division*, ASCE, Vol. 102, No. CO3, Sept., 1976, pp. 497–510.

58. Health, Education and Welfare Dept. (HEW), *Technical Handbook for Project Applicants; Construction Management Services*, Washington, D.C., HEW, 1972.

59. Heery, George T., "Let's Define Construction Management," *Architectural Record*, Vol. 155, No. 3, March, 1974, pp. 69–71.

60. Heery, George T., *Time, Cost and Architecture*, McGraw-Hill Book Co., New York, 1975.

61. Hinze, Jimmie, and Parker, Henry W., "Safety, Productivity and Job Pressures," *Journal of the Construction Division*, ASCE, Vol. 104, No. CO1, March, 1978, pp. 27–34.

62. Hinze, Jimmie, and Pannullo, John, "Safety: Function of Job Control," *Journal of Construction Division*, ASCE, Vol. 104, No. CO2, June 1978, pp. 241–249.

63. Hinze, Jimmie, "Turnover, New Workers, and Safety," *Journal of the Construction Division*, ASCE, Vol. 104, No. CO4, Dec. 1978, pp. 409–418.

64. Hinze, Jimmie, "Human Aspects of Construction Safety," *Journal of the Construction Division*, ASCE, Vol. 107, No. CO1, March, 1981, pp. 61–72.

65. Hinze, Jimmie, and Harrison, Charles," Safety Programs in Large Construction Firms," *Journal of the Construction Division*, ASCE, Vol. 107, No. CO3, Sept., 1981, pp. 454–468.

66. Hunt, Hal, et al., "Contract Award Practices," *Journal of the Construction Division*, ASCE, Vol. 92, No. CO1, Jan., 1966, pp.1-16.

67. Jordan, Mark H., and Carr, Robert I., "Education for the Professional Construction Manager," *Journal of the Construction Division*, ASCE, Vol. 102, No. CO3, Sept., 1976, pp. 510–520.

68. Justin, J. Karl, "Architect's Rates on Construction Management," *Architectural Record*, Vol. 155, No. 1, Jan., 1974, pp. 75–77.

69. Kaiser Engineers, "Project Control, Schedule, Progress and Cost," Brochure, Oakland, California, undated.

70. Kawal, Donald E., "Information Utilization in Project Planning," *Journal of the Construction Division*, ASCE. Vol. 97, No. CO2, Nov. 1971, pp. 227–240.

71. Kern, D.R., ed., *Engineering and Construction Projects, The Emerging Management Roles*, American Society of Civil Engineers, 1982.

72. Kern, D.R., "Relationships and Responsibilities of Project Parties Under the Construction Management Approach," *Engineering and Construction Projects: The Emerging Management Roles*, D.R. Kern, ed., American Society of Civil Engineers, 1982, pp. 88–106.

73. Kellog, Joseph C., et al., "Hierarchy Model of Construction Productivity," *Journal of the Construction Division*, ASCE, Vol. 107, No. CO1, March 1981, 137–152.

74. Kettle, Kenath, "Project Delivery Systems for Construction Projects," *Journal of the Construction Division*, ASCE, Vol. 102, No. CO4, Dec., 1976, pp. 575–586.

75. Kittides, Christopher P., "Construction Management: State of the Art in 1974," *Professional Engineer*, Vol. 44, No. 6, June, 1974, pp. 22–26.

76. Knab, Lawrence I., "Numerical Aid to Reduce Construction Injury Losses," *Journal of the Construction Division*, ASCE, Vol. 104, No. CO4, Dec., 1978, pp. 437–446.

77. Kosro, Jerry, "Construction Management Works at Federal Hospital," *Civil Engineering*, Vol. 44, No. 1, Jan. 1974, pp. 40–43.

78. Kouskoulas, Vasily, and Grazioli, M., "Integrated Management System for Construction Projects," *Journal of the Construction Division*, ASCE, Vol. 103, No. CO1, March, 1977, pp. 101–112.

79. Langberg, John, "Purchasing, Expediting, Traffic and Transportation," in *Handbook of Construction Management and Organization*, Frein, Joseph J. (Editor), Van Nostrand Reinhold Co., New York, 1980, pp. 178–194.

80. Langford, D., "Cost Control on CM Projects," *Engineering and Construction Projects: The Emerging Management Roles*. D. R. Kern, ed., American Society of Civil Engineers, 1982, pp. 152–162.

81. Larkin, Franklin J., and Wood, Stuart, Jr., "Past and Future of Construction Equipment—Part 1," *Journal of the Construction Division*, ASCE, Vol. 101, No. CO2, June, 1975, pp. 309–316.

82. Laufer, Alexander, and Borcherding, John D., "Financial Incentives to Raise Productivity," *Journal of the Construction Division*, Vol. 107, No. CO4. Dec., 1981, pp. 745–756.

83. Lee, D. M., "The Professional Managers Dilemma—Leadership vs Liability," *Engineering and Construction Projects: The Emerging Management Roles*, D. R. Kern, ed., American Society of Civil Engineers, 1982, pp. 43–55.

84. Levitt, R., Richard, "New Methods in Construction System," *Journal of the Construction Division*, ASCE, Vol. 100, No. CO3, Sept., 1974, pp. 211–222.

85. Levitt, Raymond R., and Parker, Henry W., "Reducing Construction Accidents—Top Management Role," *Journal of the Construction Division*, ASCE, Vol. 102, No. CO3, Sept., 1976, pp. 465–478.

86. Logcher, Robert D., and Collins, Williams W., "Management Impact on Labor Productivity," *Journal of the Construction Division*, ASCE, Vol. 104, No. CO4, Dec., 1978, pp. 447–462.

87. Lorsch, J. W., and Lawrence, P. R., *Organization and Environment*, Homewood, Illinois, Richard D. Irwin, 1969, 280 pp.

88. Maevis, Alfred C., "Pros and Cons of Construction Management," *Journal of the Construction Division*, ASCE, Vol. 103, No. CO2, June 1977, pp. 169–178.

89. Maher, Richard P., "Complex Problems with Separate Contract System," *Journal of the Construction Division*, ASCE, Vol. 105, No. CO2, June 1979, pp.129–138.

90. Maloney, William F., "Productivity Bargaining in Construction," *Journal of the Construction Division*, ASCE, Vol. 104, No. CO4, Dec. 1978, pp. 369–384.

91. McKee, Jr., Gerald, "Development and Trends in Construction Management," *Construction Specifier*, Vol. 25, No. 5, May, 1972, pp. 93–98.

92. McNally, Harold E., and Havers, John A., "Labor Productivity in Construction Industry," *Journal of the Construction Division*, ASCE, Vol. 93, No. CO2, Sept., 1967, pp. 1–12.

93. Melchers, Robert E., "Influence of Organization on Project Implementation," *Journal of the Construction Division*, ASCE, Vol. 103, No. CO4, Dec., 1977, pp. 611–626.

94. Miller, E.J., and Rice, A.K. *Systems of Organizations*, London, Tavistock Publications, 1967.

95. Monsey, Arthur, "Construction Expediting," *Journal of the Construction Division*, ASCE, Vol. 96, No. CO1, June, 1970, pp. 19–28.

96. Morris, David, "Economic Analysis of Accelerated Construction," *Journal of the Construction Division*, ASCE, Vol. 103, No. CO2, June 1977, pp. 273–288.

97. Morris, P.W.G., "An Organizational Analysis of Project Management in the Building Industry," *Build International*, Vol. 6, No. 6, December 1973.

98. Muller, F., "Definition of Construction Management," in *Engineering and Construction Projects: The Emerging Management Roles*, D.R.Kern. ed., American Society of Civil Engineers, 1982, pp. 19–28.

99. Murray, William L., et al., "Marketing Construction Management Services," *Journal of the Construction Division*, ASCE, Vol. 107, No. CO4, Dec. 1981, pp. 665–678.

100. Nave, Henry J., Jr., "Construction Personnel Management," *Journal of the Construction Division*, ASCE, Vol. 94, No. CO1, Jan., 1968, pp. 95–105.

101. Neil, James M, *Construction Cost Estimating for Project Control*, Prentice-Hall, Inc., Englewood Cliffs, N.J., 1982.

102. Nielsen, K.R., and Nielsen, M.J., "Legal Implications of Professional Project Management," *Engineering and Construction Projects: The Emerging Management Roles*, D.R. Kern, ed., American Society of Civil Engineers, 1982, pp. 56–76.

103. O'Brien, James J., and Zilly, Robert G., *Contractor's Management Handbook*, McGraw-Hill Book Co., New York, 1971.

104. O'Brien, James J., et al., *Construction Management: A Professional Approach*, McGraw-Hill Book Co., New York, 1978, pp. 1–17.

105. Panagiotakopoulos, Demetrios, "Cost-Time Model for Large CPM Project Networks," *Journal of the Construction Division*, ASCE, Vol. 103, No. CO2, June, 1977, pp. 201–212.

106. Park, William R., "Pre-Design Estimates in Civil Engineering Projects," *Journal of the Construction Division*, ASCE, Vol. 89, No. CO2, Sept., 1963, pp. 11–23.

107. Paulson, Boyd, Jr., "Project Planning and Scheduling: Unified Approach," *Journal of the Construction Division*, ASCE, Vol. 99, No. CO1, July 1973, pp. 45–58.

108. Paulson, Boyd C., Jr., "Estimation and Control of Labor Costs," *Journal of the Construction Division*, ASCE, Vol. 101, No. CO3, Sept., 1975, pp. 623–634.

109. Paulson, Boyd C., Jr., "Concept of Project Planning and Control," *Journal of the Construction Division*, ASCE, Vol. 102, No. CO1, March 1976, pp. 67–80.

110. Paulson, B.C., Jr., and Tsuneo, A., "Construction Management in Japan," *Journal of the Construction Division*, ASCE, Vol. 106, No. CO3, Sept., 1980, pp. 281–296.

111. Peer, Shlomo, "Network Analysis and Construction Planning," *Journal of the Construction Division*, Vol. 100, No. CO3, Sept., 1974, pp. 203–210.

112. Peurifoy, Robert L., "Fifty Years of Construction Cost-Reducing Analyses," *Journal of the Construction Division*, ASCE, Vol. 101, No. CO2, June, 1975, pp. 299–308.

113. ——, "Planning, Engineering and Constructing the Superprojects," presented at the ASCE Engineering Foundation Research Conference held at New York, N.Y., April 30–May 5, 1978.

114. Post, Dian, et al. (Editors), *CM for the General Contractor—A Guide Manual for Construction Management*, AGC Inc., 1974.

115. ——, "Professional Construction Management Services, by Subcommittee on Construction Organization and Evaluation of the Committee on Professional Construction Management of the Construction Division," *Journal of the Construction Division*, ASCE, Vol. 105, No. CO2, June, 1979, pp. 139–156.

116. Rad, Parviz F., and Miller, Marion C., "Trends in Use of Construction Management," *Journal of the Construction Division*, ASCE, Vol. 104, No. CO4. Dec. 1978, pp. 515–524.

117. Reiner, L.E., *Handbook of Construction Management*, Prentice-Hall, Inc., Englewood Cliffs, N.J., 1972.

118. Roe, Raymond L., Jr., "Construction Management: Beware of Undertows in the Wave of the Future," *Professional Engineer*, Vol. 44, No. 12, Dec., 1974, pp. 23–24.

119. Rossow, Jannet Ann Koch, and Moavenzadeh, Fred, "Management Issues in the U.S. Construction Industry," *Journal of the Construction Division*, ASCE, Vol. 102, June, 1976, pp. 277–294.

120. Ruvkin, S., "Construction Experience in Latin America," *Journal of the Construction Division*, ASCE, Vol. 107, No. CO2, June, 1981, pp. 313–322.

121. Scarola, J. A., and Tatum, C. B., "Definition of Project Management," *Engineering and Construction Projects: The Emerging Management Roles*, D.R. Kern, ed., American Society of Civil Engineers, 1982, pp. 318–325.

122. Schlick, Haim, "Project Integrated Management System (PRIM)," *Journal of the Construction Division*, ASCE, Vol. 107, No. CO2, June, 1981, pp. 361–372.

123. Schlick, Haim, "Schedule and Resources of Fast Track Renovation Work," *Journal of the Construction Division*, ASCE, Vol. 107, No. CO4, Dec., 1981, pp. 559–574.

124. Scott, Donald F., "Effective Contract Administrative in Construction Management," *Journal of Construction Division*, ASCE, Vol. 100, No. CO2, June, 1974, pp. 117–132.

125. Scott, Donald, and Sheikh, Naveed Athar, "Use of Alternative Construction Methods," *Journal of the Construction Division*, ASCE, Vol. 104, No. CO2, June, 1978, pp. 141–152.

126. Sears, Glenn A., "CPM/Cost: An Integrated Approach," *Journal of the Construction Division*, ASCE, Vol. 107, No. CO2, June, 1981, pp. 227–238.

127. Smith, S. E., et al., "Contractual Relationships in Construction," *Journal of the Construction Division*, ASCE, Vol. 101, No. CO4, Dec., 1975, pp. 907–921.

128. Smith, G. A., and Harrison, S. B., "Legal Implications of Professional Management," *Engineering and Construction Projects: The Emerging Management Roles*, D.R. Kern, ed., American Society of Civil Engineers, 1982, pp. 107–120.

129. Special Report, "Special Report on Construction Management," Reprints from *Construction Methods & Equipment*, March/April, 1972.

130. Stanley, Richard H., et al., *Report of CEC Study Committee on Construction Management*, Consulting Engineers Council–USA, Washington, D.C., Jan., 1972.

131. Tatum, C. B., "Evaluating PCM Firm Potential and Performance," *Journal of the Construction Division*, ASCE, Vol. 106, No. CO2, June, 1980, pp. 141–153.

132. Teicholz, Paul, "Requirements of a Construction Company Cost System," *Journal of the Construction Division*, ASCE, Vol. 100, No. CO3, Sept., 1974, pp. 255–263.

133. Teicholz, Paul, "Labor Cost Control," *Journal of the Construction Division*, ASCE, Vol. 100, No. CO4, Dec., 1974, pp. 561–570.

134. Tenah, K. A., *Integrated Planning, Design and Construction of Building Works in Developing Countries Including the Role of Computers*, Engineers Degree Thesis, Stanford University, Stanford, California, 1975.

135. Tenah, K. A., *Construction Management Information Control Systems* (*CMICS*), thesis presented to Texas A&M University in partial fulfillment of the requirements for the degree of Doctor of Philosophy, College Station, Tex., 1979.

136. Tenah, K. A., "Management Information Organization and Flow in the Construction Organization," *Conference Proceedings*, Canadian Society of Civil Engineering, New Brunswick, Canada, May, 1981.

137. Tenah, K. A., "Construction Management Information Control Systems (CMICS)," *Proceedings of the ASCE Specialty Conference On Construction Equipment Techniques for the Eighties*, Purdue University, West Lafayette, Ind., Mar., 1982, pp. 370–380.

138. Tenah, K. A., "Management Information Organization and Routing," *Journal of the Construction Engineering and Management*, Vol. 110, No. 1, Mar., 1984, pp. 101–118.

139. Thomsen, Charles B., "Selecting a Construction Manager and the Construction Management: Overview," Brochure of CM Associates in Houston, Texas, undated.

140. Thomsen, C. B., *CM: Developing, Marketing and Delivering Construction Management Services*, McGraw-Hill Book Co., Inc., New York, N.Y., 1982.

141. Walker, Nathan, et al., *Legal Pitfalls in Architecture, Engineering, and Building Construction*, McGraw-Hill Book Co., New York, 1979.

142. Warszawski, Abraham, "Integrated Contracting System," *Journal of the Construction Division*, ASCE, Vol. 101, No. CO1, March, 1975, pp. 213–221.

143. Wilkening, R. M., "The Use of CM on a 1500 Student High School," *Engineering and Construction Projects: The Emerging Management Roles*, D.R. Kern. ed., American Society of Civil Engineers, 1982, pp. 297–317.

144. Wilson, Woodrow, W., "Past and Future Contract Administration," *Journal of the Construction Division*, ASCE, Vol. 101, No. CO3, 1975, pp. 559–564.

145. Wong, A. K., "Program Management: Intent, Tools, Practice," *Engineering and Construction Projects: The Emerging Management Roles*, D.R. Kern, ed., American Society of Civil Engineers, 1972, pp. 29–42.

146. Yates, M.K., and Tatum, C. B., "Definition of Engineering Management," *Engineering and Construction Projects: The Emerging Management Roles*, D.R. Kern, ed., American Society of Civil Engineers, 1982, pp. 1–18.

147. Zink, D.A., "Practical Cost Control System for Force Account Construction Project," *American Association of Cost Engineers Transactions*, 1973, pp. 172–182.

Index